hip
waist
chest
head
hand
arm
hair
forearm
foot
thigh
leg
calf
a
a

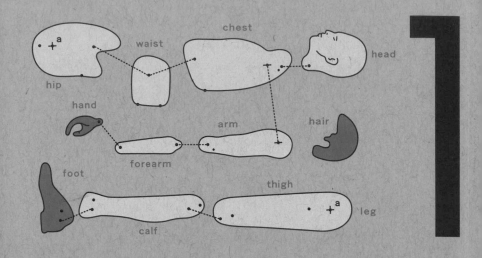

1

the KUROSAGI corpse delivery service

黒鷺死体宅配便

eiji otsuka 大塚英志 housui yamazaki 山崎峰水

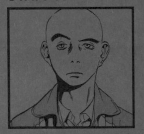

STAFF A

Psychic
[イタコ]：死体との対話

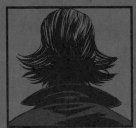

STAFF B

Dowsing
[ダウジング]：死体の捜索

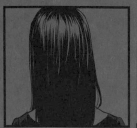

STAFF C

Hacking
[ハッキング]：情報の収集

YOUR BODY IS THEIR BUSINESS!

黒鷺死体宅配便
the KUROSAGI corpse delivery service

1

story
EIJI OTSUKA

art
HOUSUI YAMAZAKI

original cover design
BUNPEI YORIFUJI

translation
TOSHIFUMI YOSHIDA

editor and english adaptation
CARL GUSTAV HORN

lettering and touch-up
IHL

contents

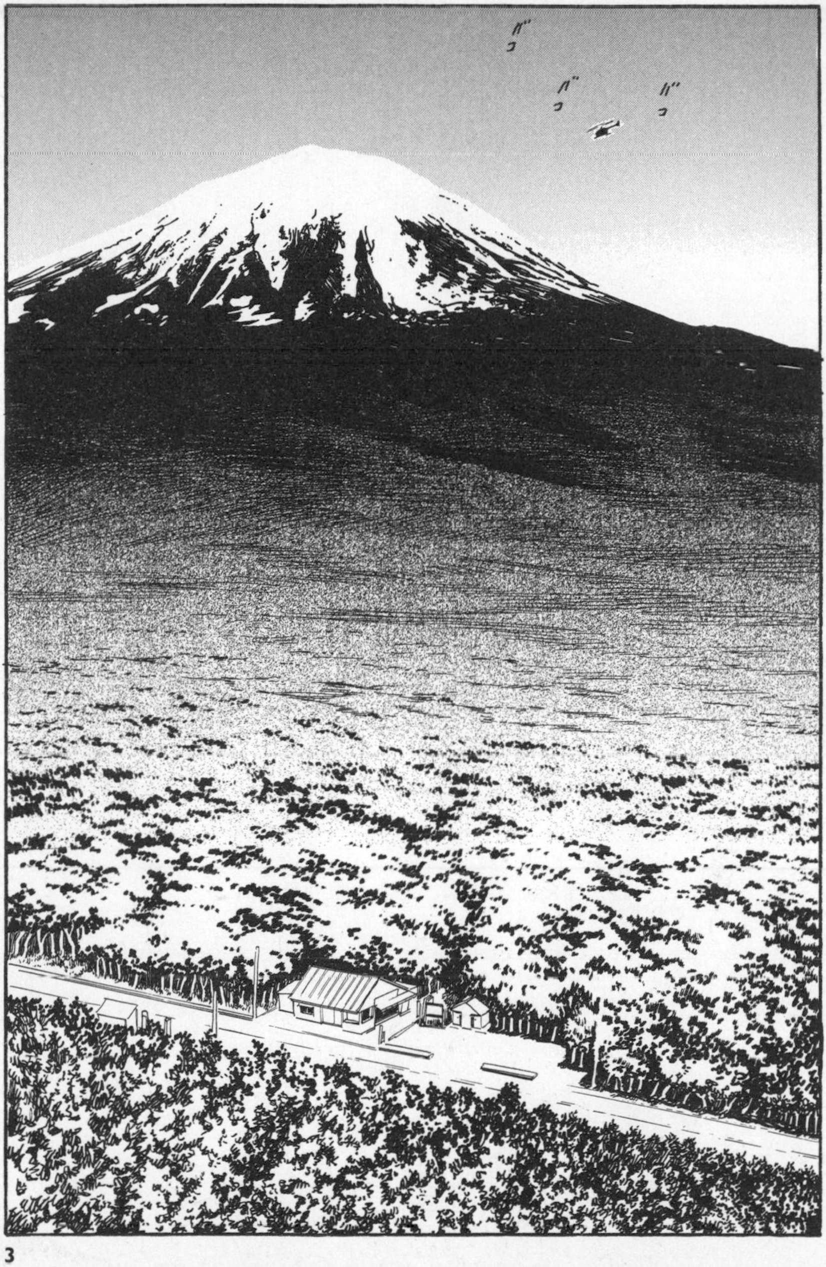
バコ
バコ
バコ

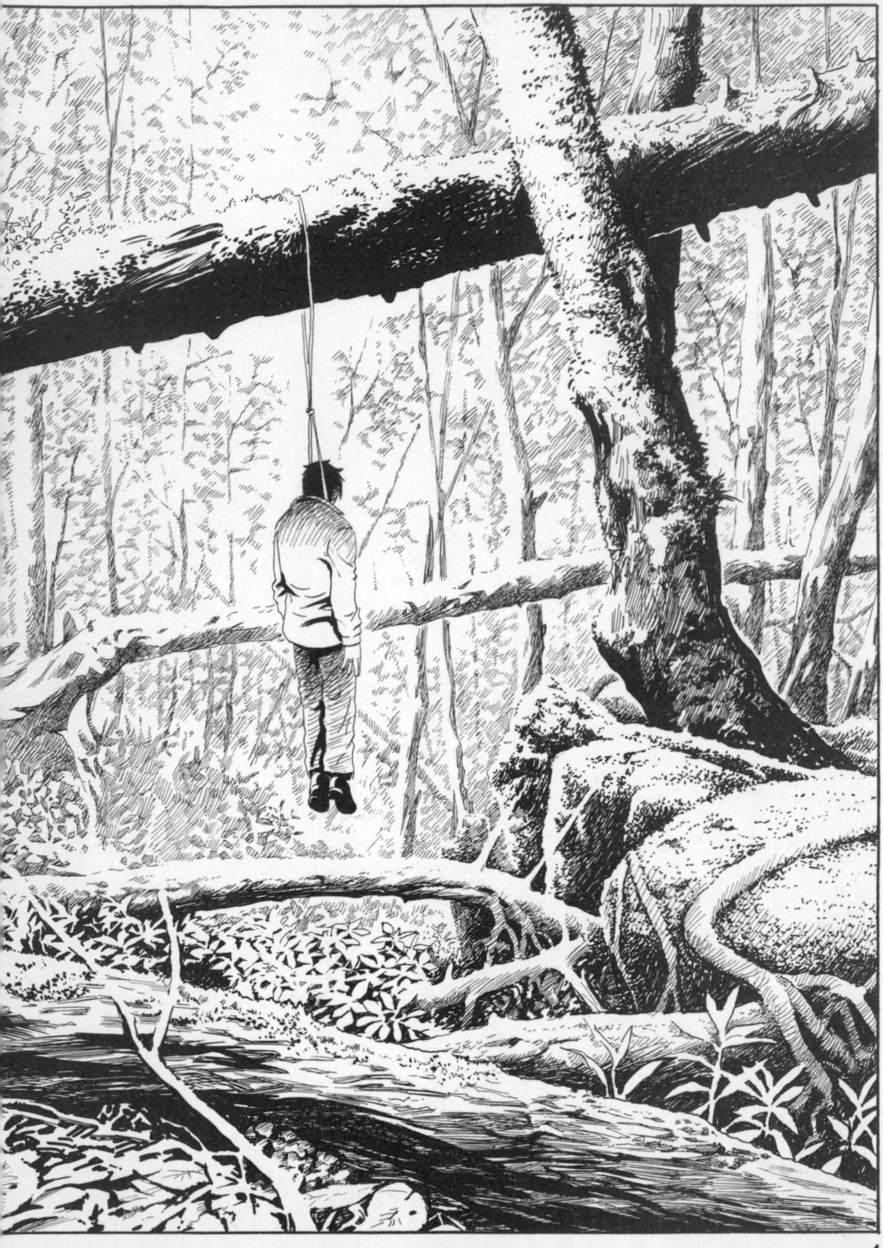

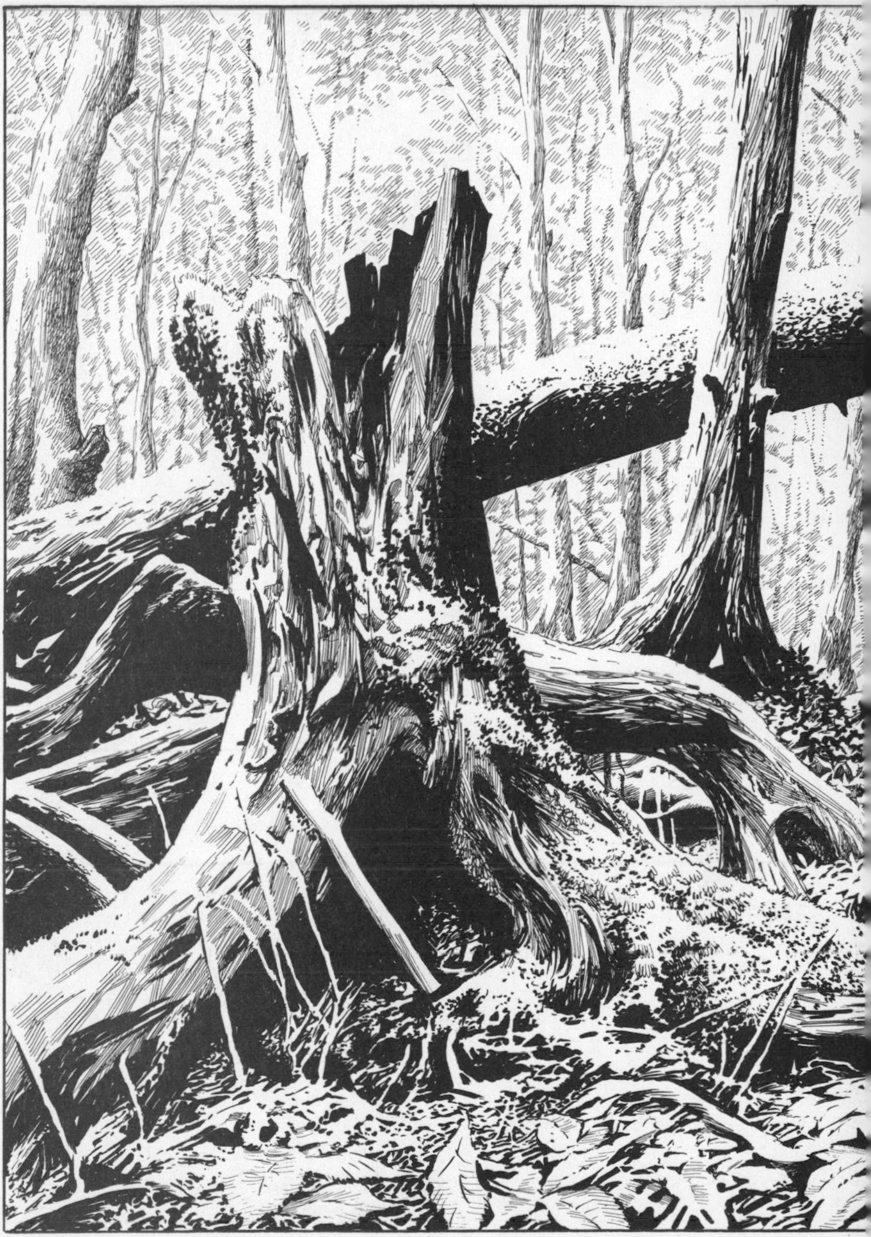

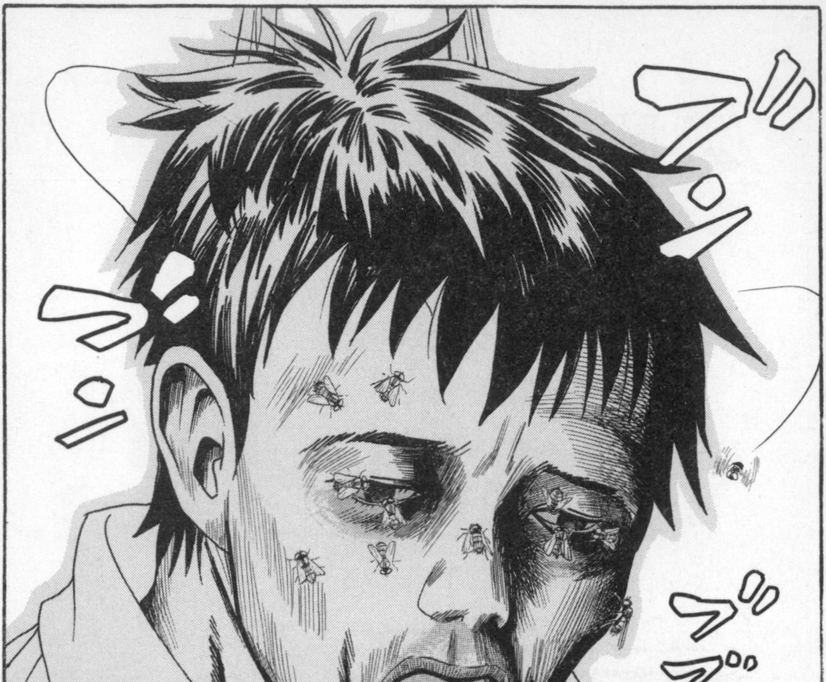

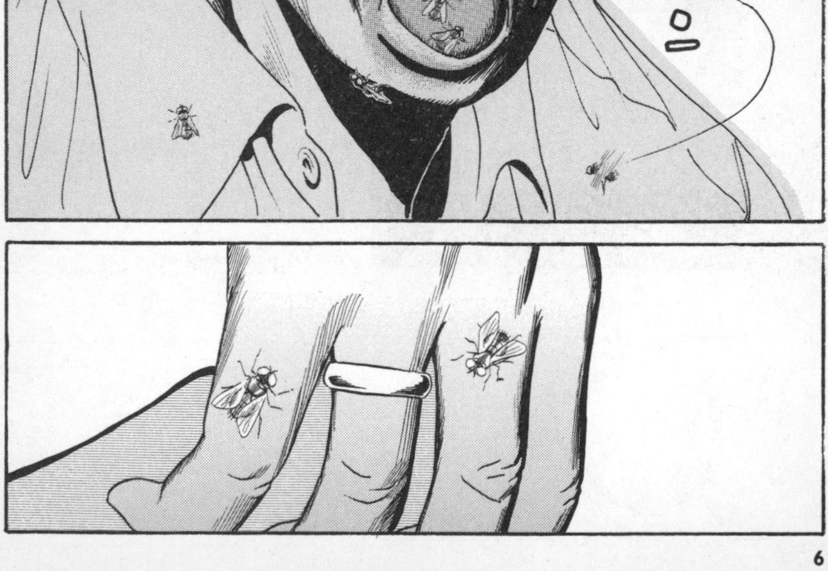

ビクッ
ビク
ビクン
ビクン
ブチ
ドサッ
ず
ずる
ンッチ
ズン
ンッチ
チャカ
ズズ
チャカ

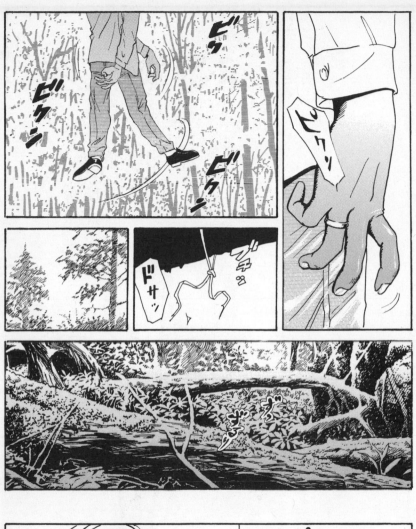

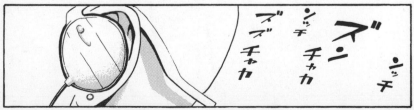

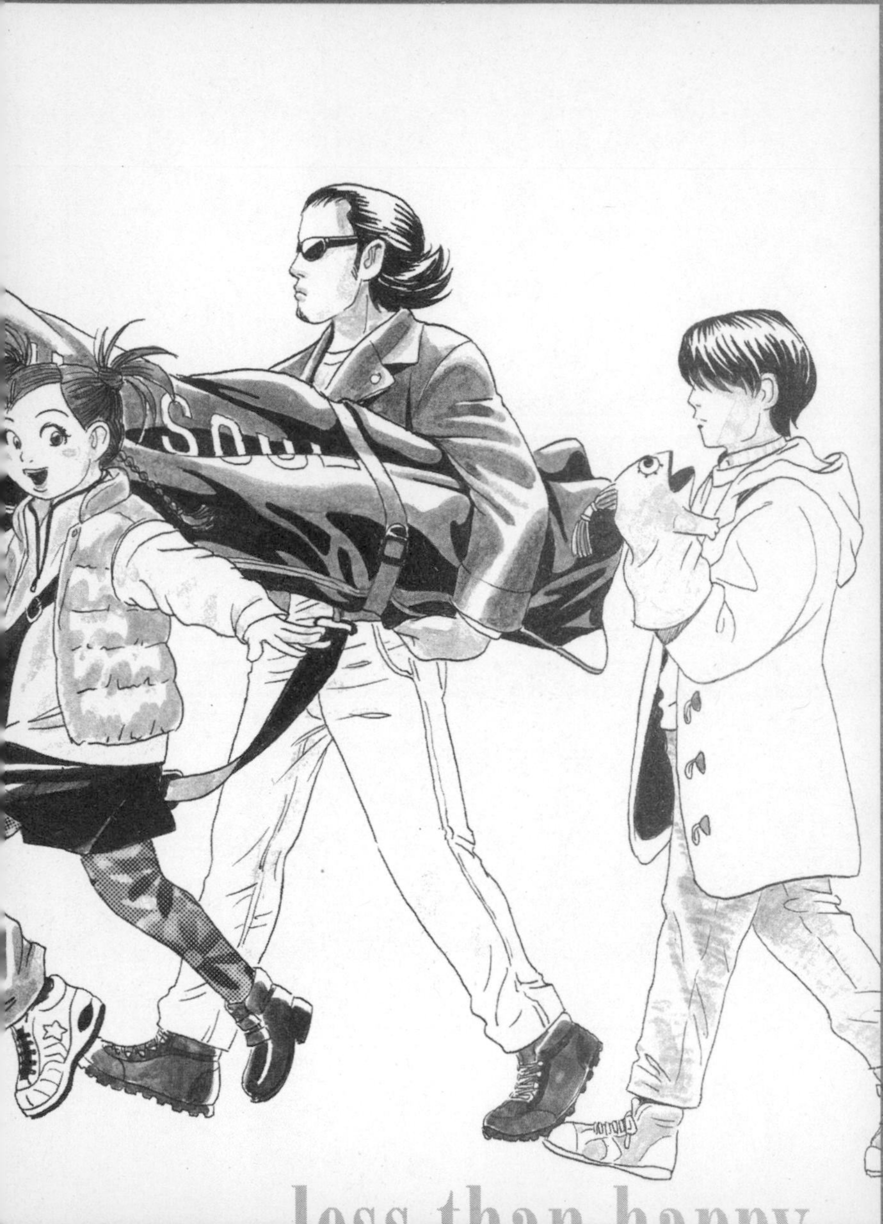

less than happy

1st delivery
しあわせ未満

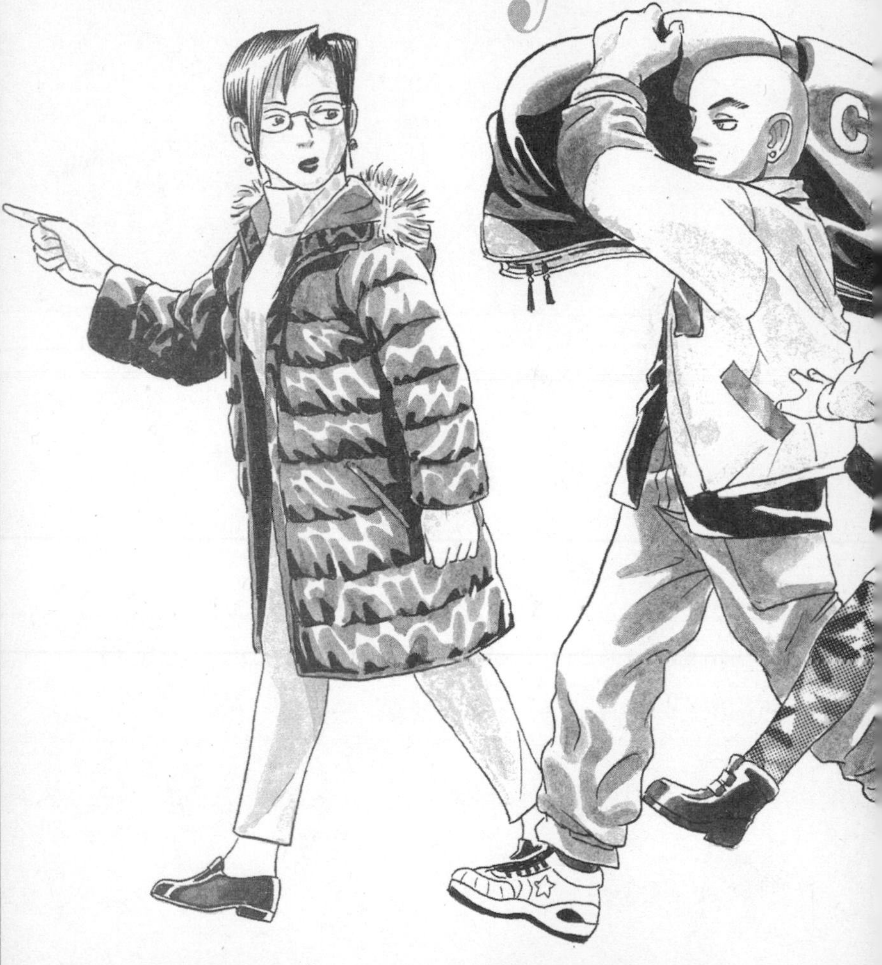

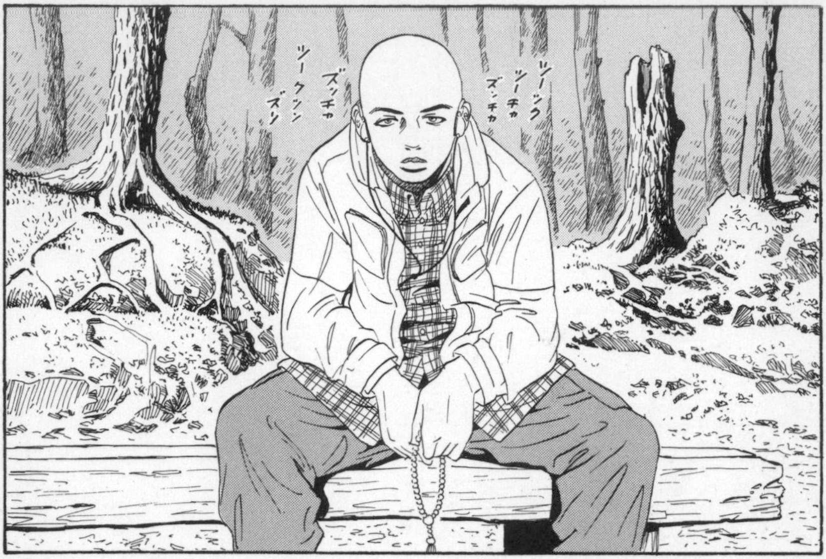
ツーック
ツーチャ
ズンチャカ
ズンチャ
ツークッン
ズン

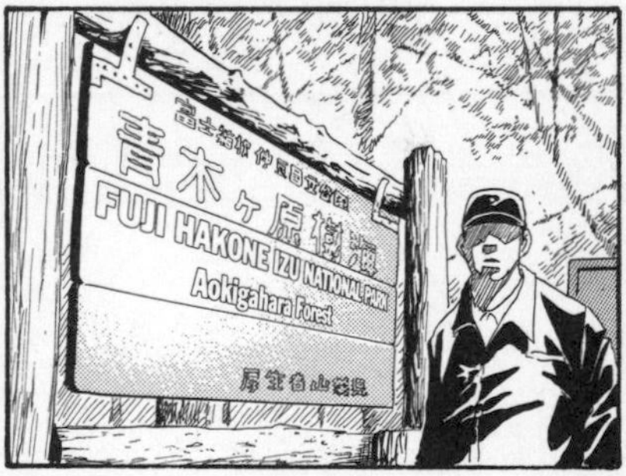
青木ヶ原樹海
FUJI HAKONE IZU NATIONAL PARK
Aokigahara Forest

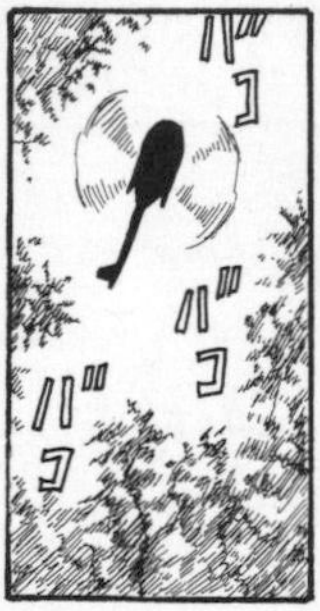
バコ
バコ
バコ

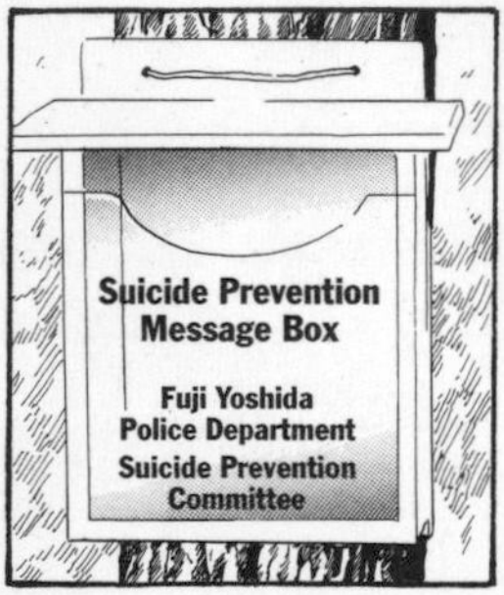
Suicide Prevention
Message Box
Fuji Yoshida
Police Department
Suicide Prevention
Committee

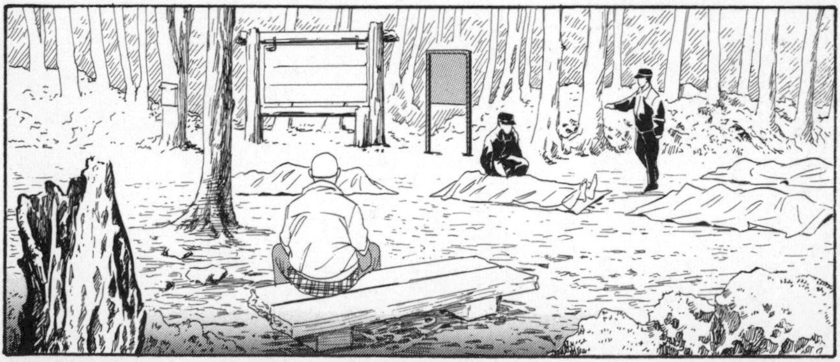

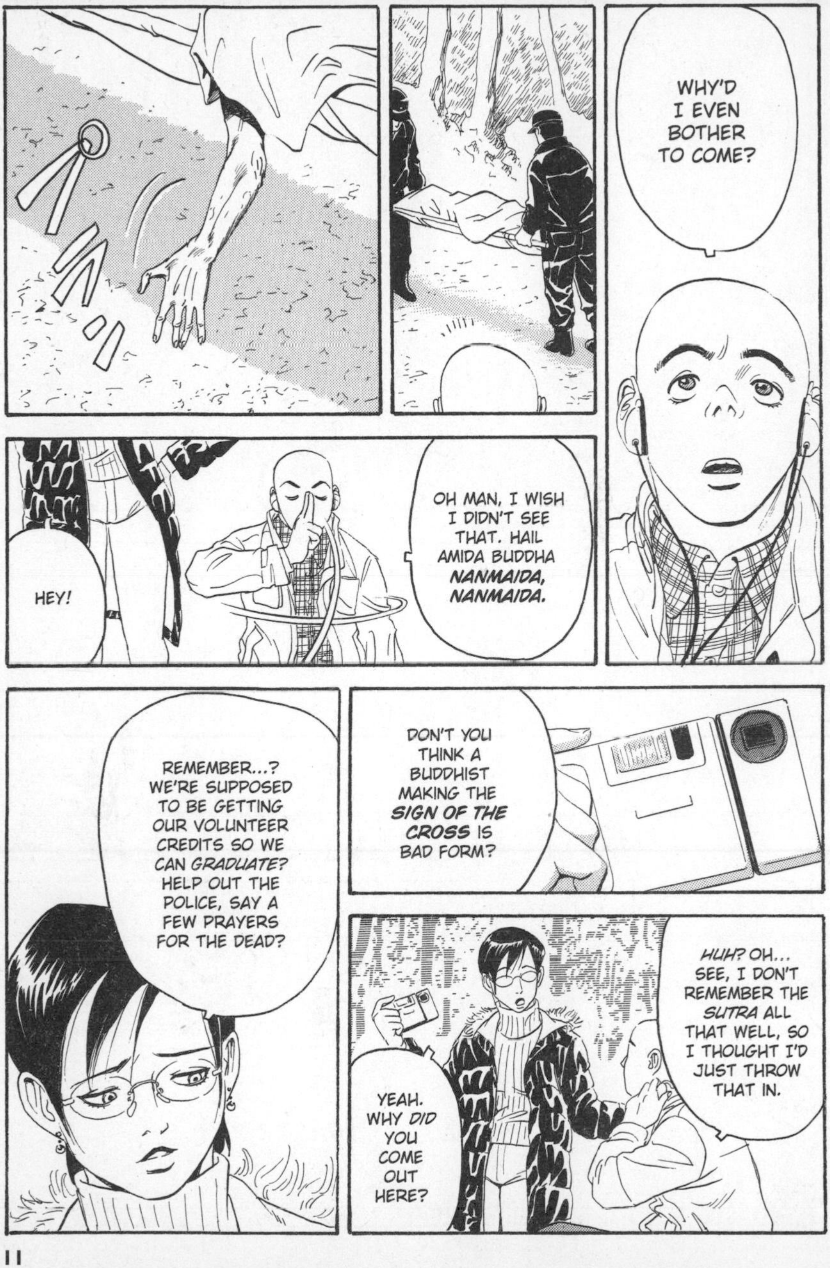
WHY'D I EVEN BOTHER TO COME?
OH MAN, I WISH I DIDN'T SEE THAT. HAIL AMIDA BUDDHA ***NANMAIDA, NANMAIDA.***
HEY!
DON'T YOU THINK A BUDDHIST MAKING THE ***SIGN OF THE CROSS*** IS BAD FORM?
HUH? OH... SEE, I DON'T REMEMBER THE *SUTRA* ALL THAT WELL, SO I THOUGHT I'D JUST THROW THAT IN.
YEAH. WHY *DID* YOU COME OUT HERE?
REMEMBER...? WE'RE SUPPOSED TO BE GETTING OUR VOLUNTEER CREDITS SO WE CAN *GRADUATE?* HELP OUT THE POLICE, SAY A FEW PRAYERS FOR THE DEAD?

OH...
YEAH.

MY
NAME'S
KURO
KARATSU.

A
FOURTH-
YEAR
STUDENT
IN AN
AVERAGE
BUDDHIST
UNIVERSITY.

AND
THERE'S
NOTHING
SO COLD
AS
WINTER
BREAK,
YOUR
SENIOR
YEAR...

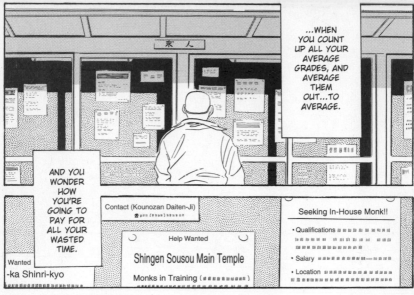

...WHEN YOU COUNT UP ALL YOUR AVERAGE GRADES, AND AVERAGE THEM OUT...TO AVERAGE.
求人
AND YOU WONDER HOW YOU'RE GOING TO PAY FOR ALL YOUR WASTED TIME.
Seeking In-House Monk!!
• Qualifications
• Salary
• Location
Help Wanted
Shingen Sousou Main Temple
Monks in Training
Contact (Kounozan Daiten-Ji)
Wanted
-ka Shinri-kyo
DOESN'T ANYONE WANT, LIKE, AN OFFICE ASSISTANT? A FILE CLERK?
MAN, IT SUCKS BEING AN ENTRY-LEVEL BUDDHIST.
!
CHANT SUTRAS IN AOKIGAHARA FOREST!
BE A VOLUNTEER!
let's go see some dead people!
NAMU!
DATE: 21ST DON'T FORGET YOUR BEADS!
HEH, EVEN THE VOLUNTEER JOBS ARE LIKE THIS.
ヌッ
I could use some volunteer help...

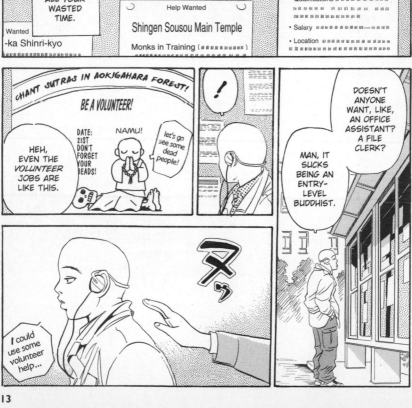

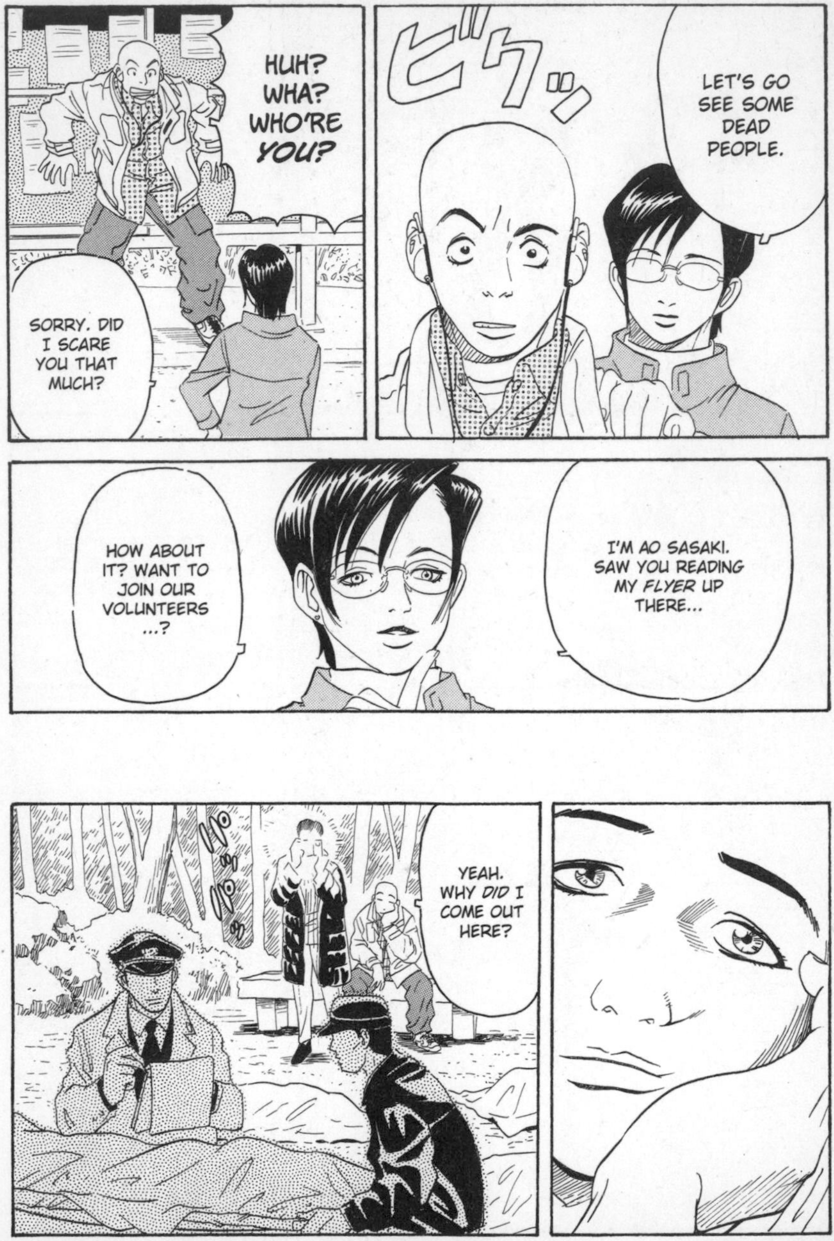
ビクッ
LET'S GO SEE SOME DEAD PEOPLE.
HUH? WHA? WHO'RE *YOU?*
SORRY. DID I SCARE YOU THAT MUCH?
I'M AO SASAKI. SAW YOU READING MY *FLYER* UP THERE...
HOW ABOUT IT? WANT TO JOIN OUR VOLUNTEERS ...?
YEAH. WHY *DID* I COME OUT HERE?

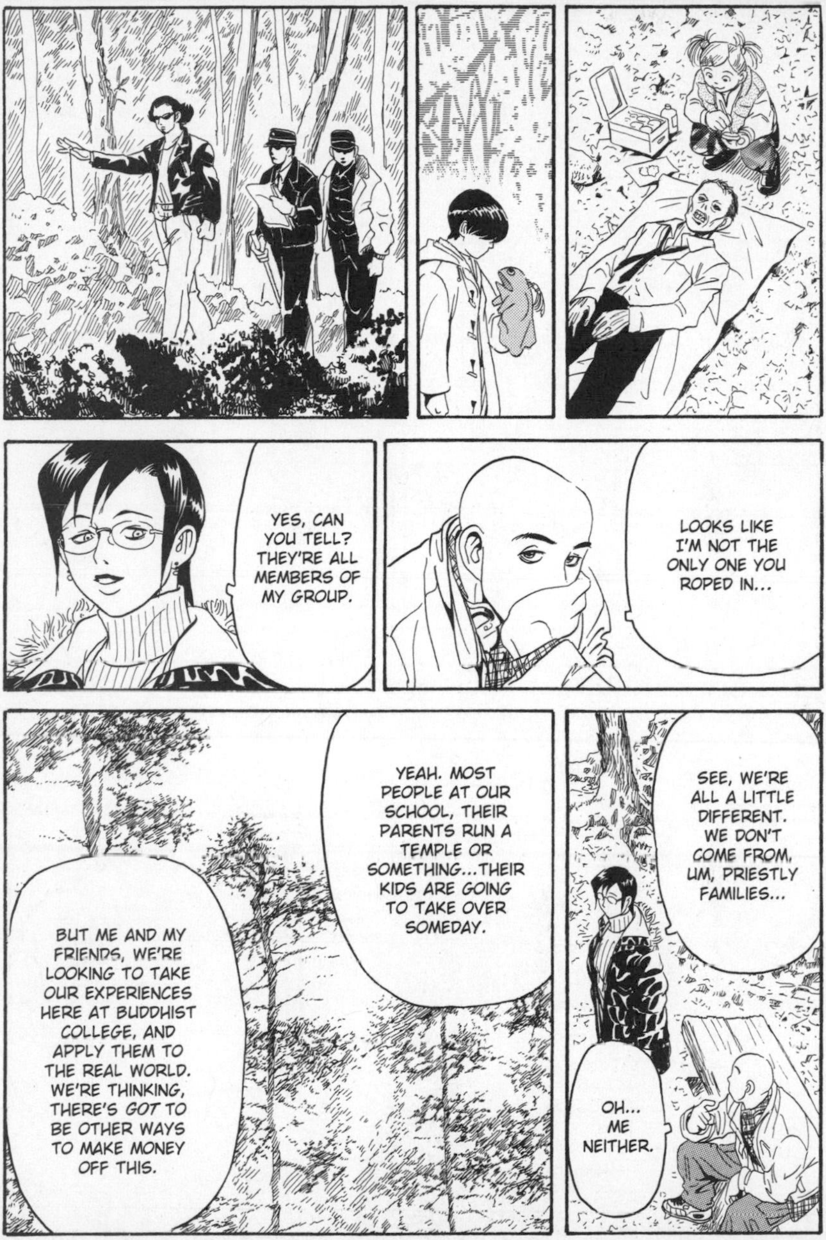
LOOKS LIKE I'M NOT THE ONLY ONE YOU ROPED IN...
YES, CAN YOU TELL? THEY'RE ALL MEMBERS OF MY GROUP.
SEE, WE'RE ALL A LITTLE DIFFERENT. WE DON'T COME FROM, UM, PRIESTLY FAMILIES...
OH... ME NEITHER.
YEAH. MOST PEOPLE AT OUR SCHOOL, THEIR PARENTS RUN A TEMPLE OR SOMETHING...THEIR KIDS ARE GOING TO TAKE OVER SOMEDAY.
BUT ME AND MY FRIENDS, WE'RE LOOKING TO TAKE OUR EXPERIENCES HERE AT BUDDHIST COLLEGE, AND APPLY THEM TO THE REAL WORLD. WE'RE THINKING, THERE'S GOT TO BE OTHER WAYS TO MAKE MONEY OFF THIS.

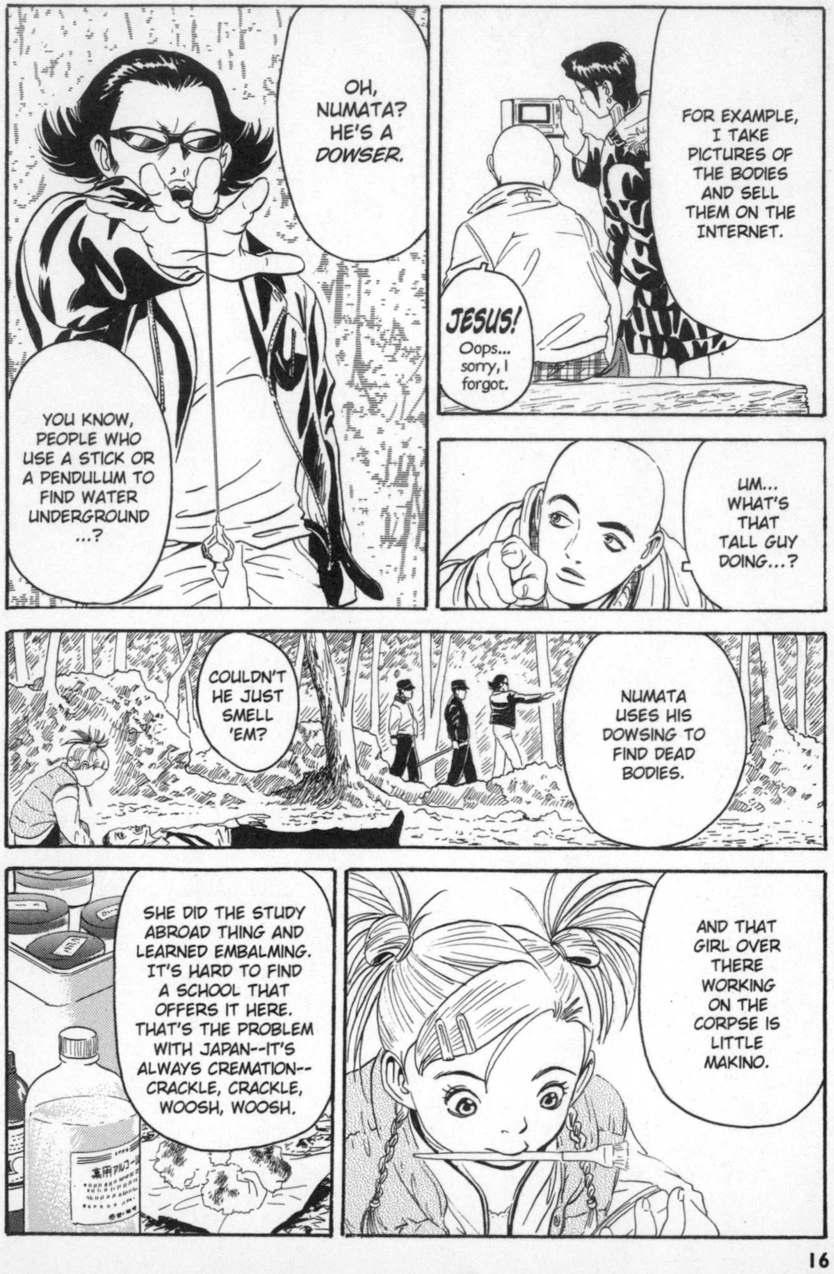
FOR EXAMPLE, I TAKE PICTURES OF THE BODIES AND SELL THEM ON THE INTERNET.
JESUS!
Oops... sorry, I forgot.
UM... WHAT'S THAT TALL GUY DOING...?
OH, NUMATA? HE'S A *DOWSER.*
YOU KNOW, PEOPLE WHO USE A STICK OR A PENDULUM TO FIND WATER UNDERGROUND ...?
NUMATA USES HIS DOWSING TO FIND DEAD BODIES.
COULDN'T HE JUST SMELL 'EM?
AND THAT GIRL OVER THERE WORKING ON THE CORPSE IS LITTLE MAKINO.
SHE DID THE STUDY ABROAD THING AND LEARNED EMBALMING. IT'S HARD TO FIND A SCHOOL THAT OFFERS IT HERE. THAT'S THE PROBLEM WITH JAPAN--IT'S ALWAYS CREMATION-- CRACKLE, CRACKLE, WOOSH, WOOSH.

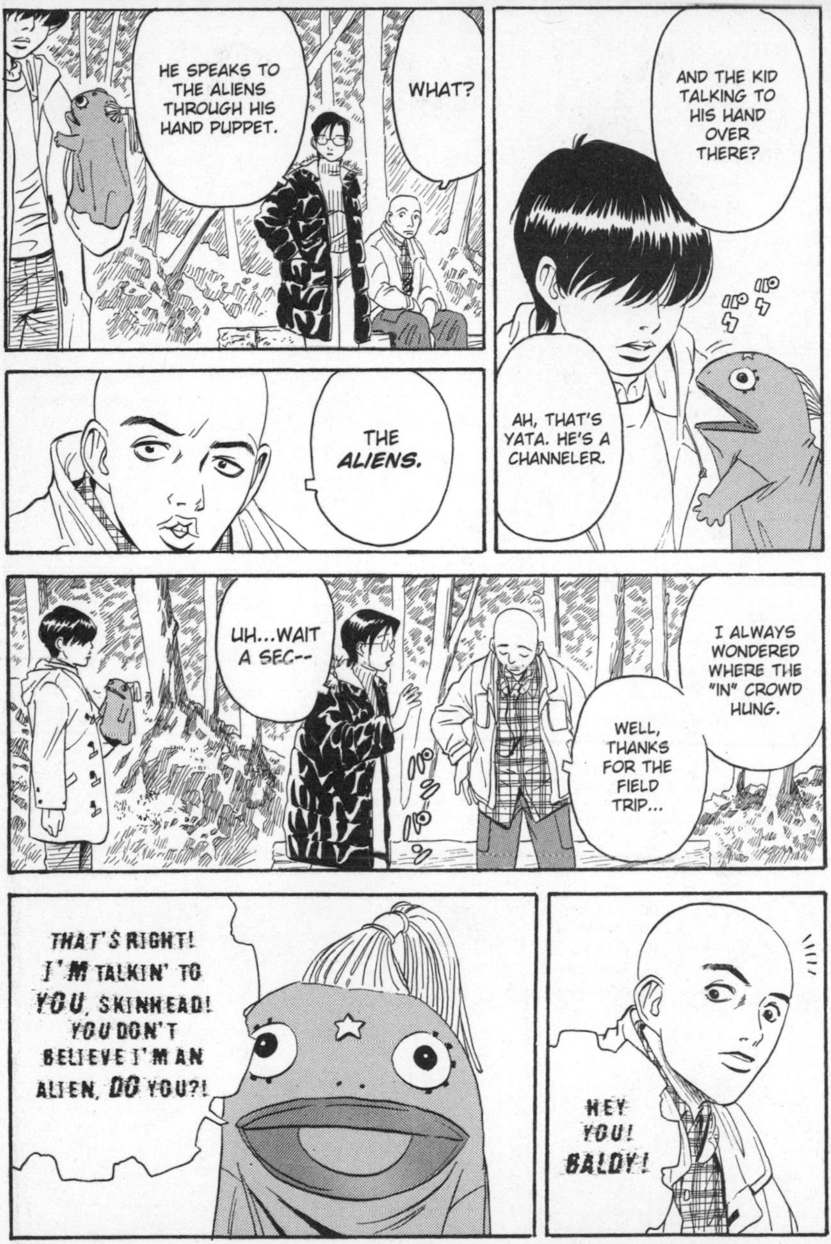
AND THE KID TALKING TO HIS HAND OVER THERE?
AH, THAT'S YATA. HE'S A CHANNELER.
WHAT?
HE SPEAKS TO THE ALIENS THROUGH HIS HAND PUPPET.
THE ALIENS.
I ALWAYS WONDERED WHERE THE "IN" CROWD HUNG.
WELL, THANKS FOR THE FIELD TRIP...
UH...WAIT A SEC--
HEY YOU! BALDY!
THAT'S RIGHT! I'M TALKIN' TO YOU, SKINHEAD! YOU DON'T BELIEVE I'M AN ALIEN, DO YOU?!

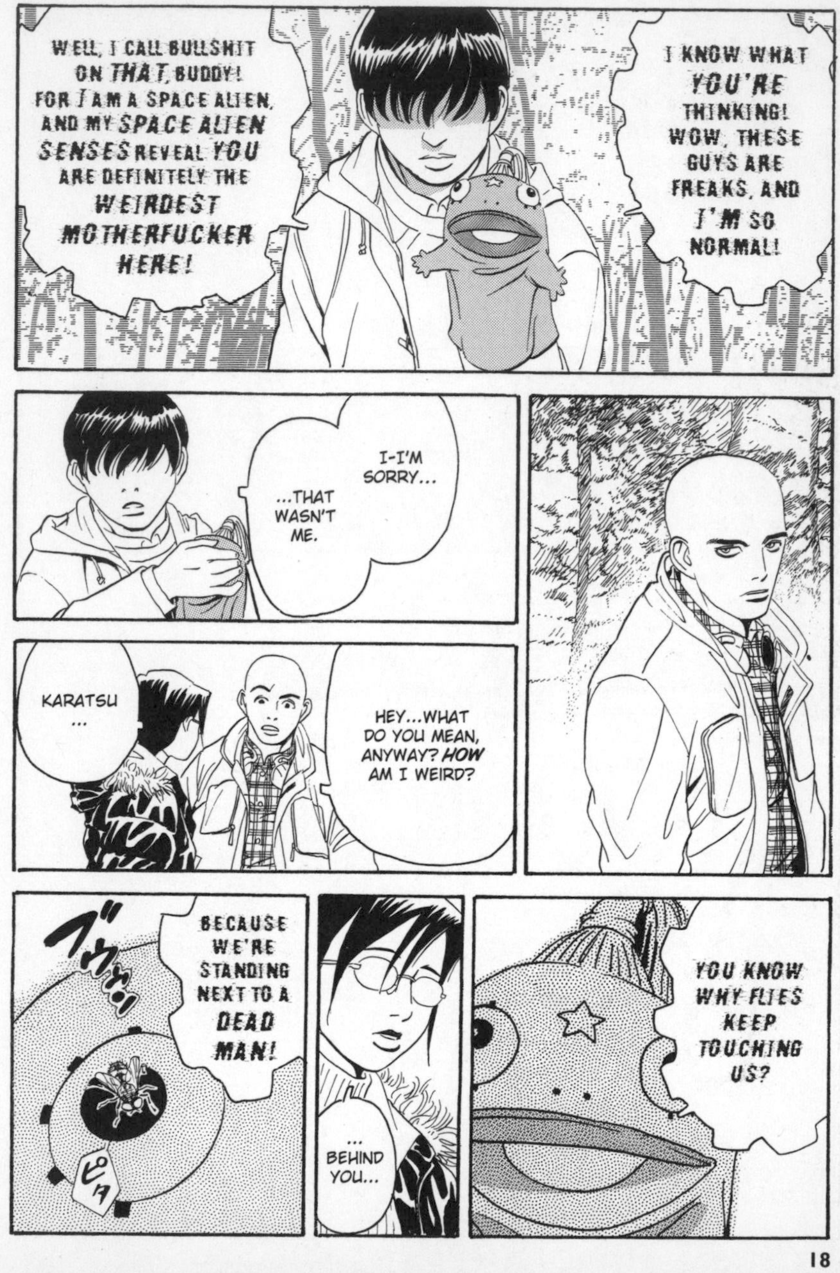
I KNOW WHAT YOU'RE THINKING! WOW, THESE GUYS ARE FREAKS, AND I'M SO NORMAL!
WELL, I CALL BULLSHIT ON THAT, BUDDY! FOR I AM A SPACE ALIEN, AND MY SPACE ALIEN SENSES REVEAL YOU ARE DEFINITELY THE WEIRDEST MOTHERFUCKER HERE!
I-I'M SORRY...
...THAT WASN'T ME.
HEY...WHAT DO YOU MEAN, ANYWAY? HOW AM I WEIRD?
KARATSU ...
YOU KNOW WHY FLIES KEEP TOUCHING US?
... BEHIND YOU...
BECAUSE WE'RE STANDING NEXT TO A DEAD MAN!

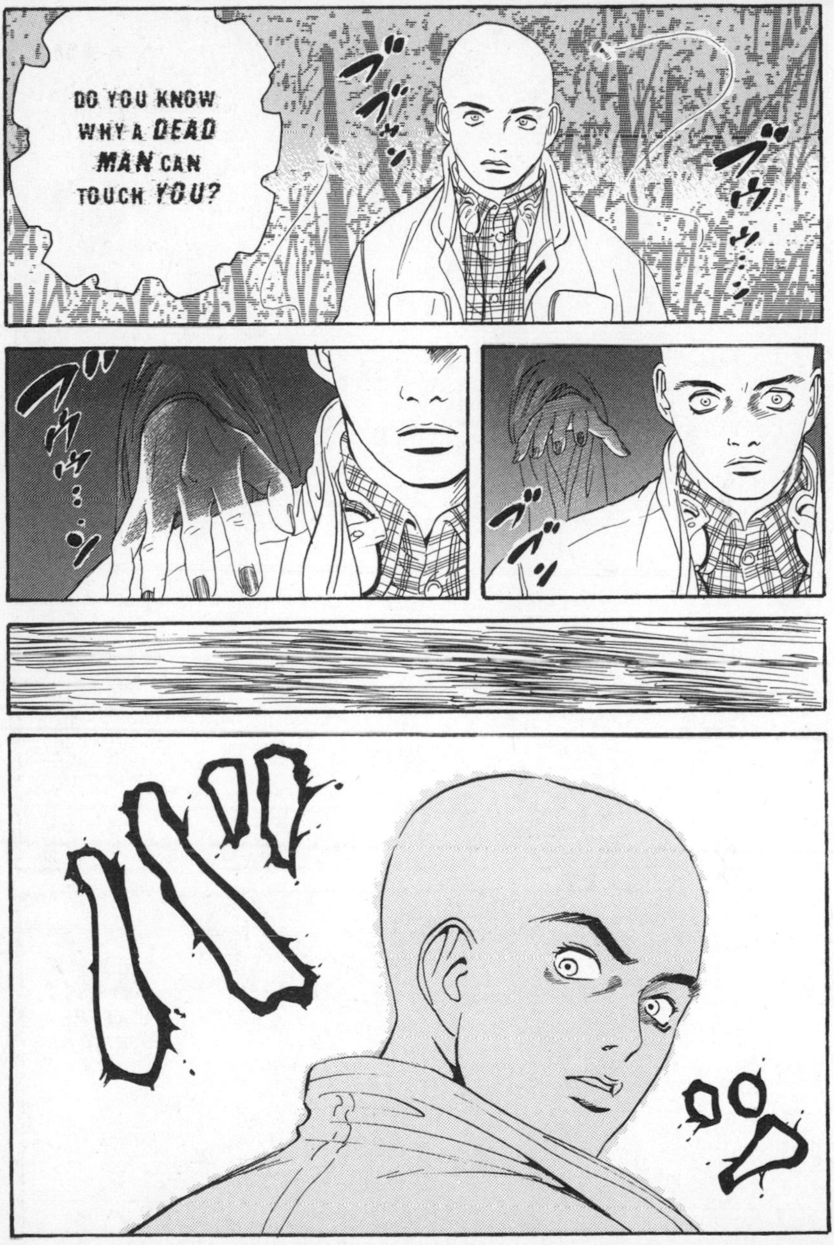
DO YOU KNOW WHY A DEAD MAN CAN TOUCH YOU?

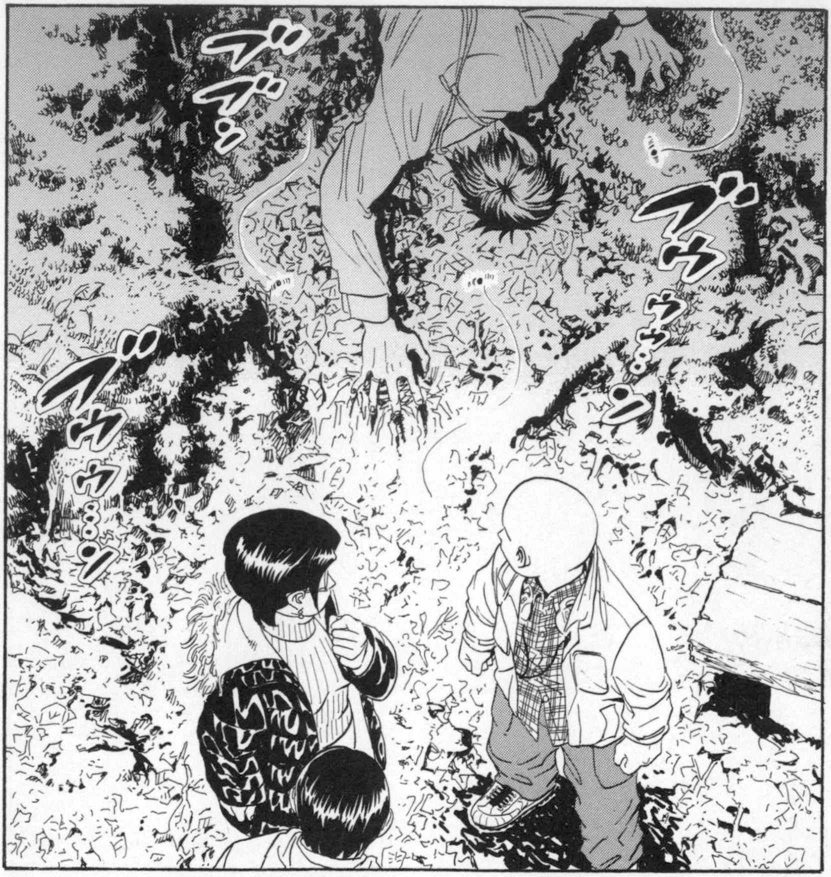
ブウゥ…ン
ブブブ…
ブウウ…ン
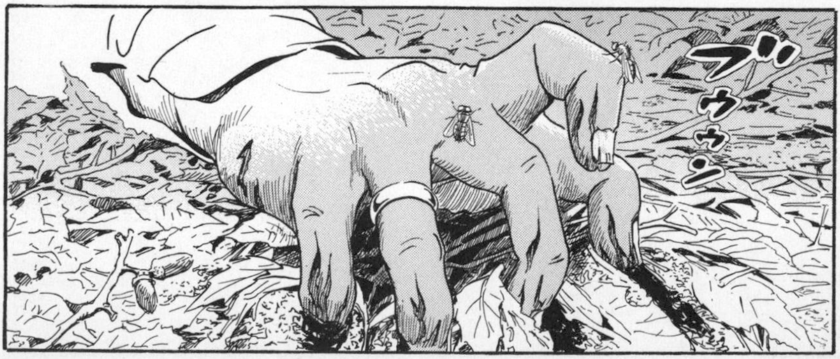
ブウゥン

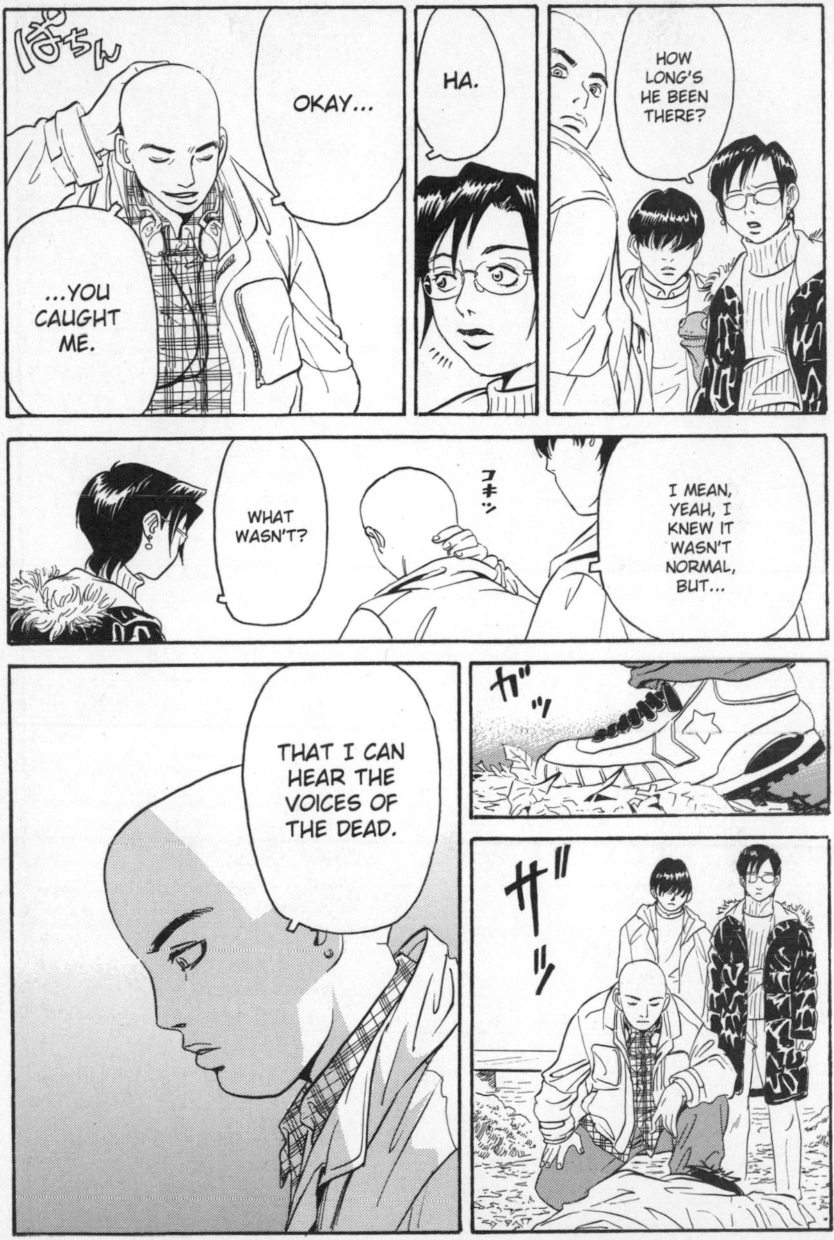
HOW LONG'S HE BEEN THERE?
HA.
OKAY...
ぱちん
...YOU CAUGHT ME.
I MEAN, YEAH, I KNEW IT WASN'T NORMAL, BUT...
コキッ
WHAT WASN'T?
ガッ
ザッ
THAT I CAN HEAR THE VOICES OF THE DEAD.

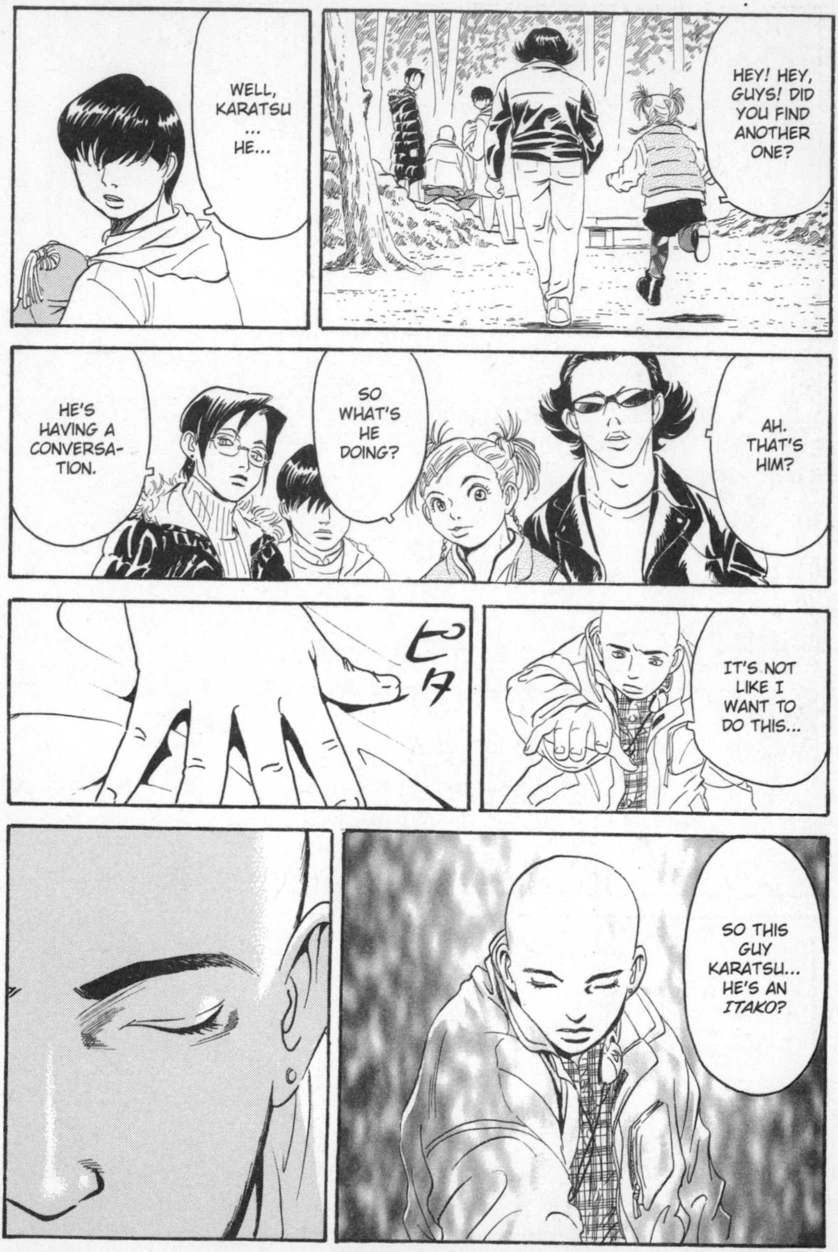
HEY! HEY, GUYS! DID YOU FIND ANOTHER ONE?
WELL, KARATSU ... HE...
AH. THAT'S HIM?
SO WHAT'S HE DOING?
HE'S HAVING A CONVERSA-TION.
IT'S NOT LIKE I WANT TO DO THIS...
ピタ
SO THIS GUY KARATSU... HE'S AN *ITAKO*?

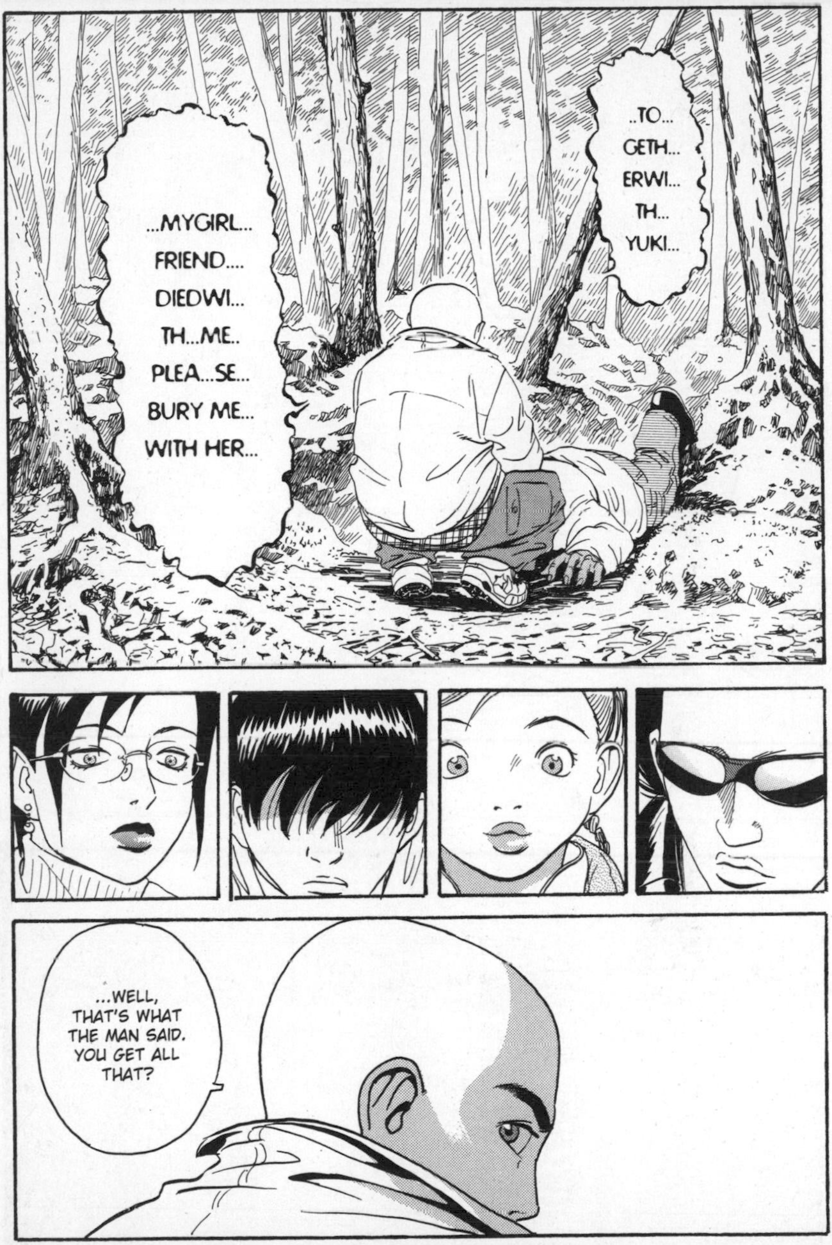
..TO... GETH... ERWI... TH... YUKI...
...MYGIRL... FRIEND.... DIEDWI... TH...ME.. PLEA...SE... BURY ME... WITH HER...
...WELL, THAT'S WHAT THE MAN SAID. YOU GET ALL THAT?

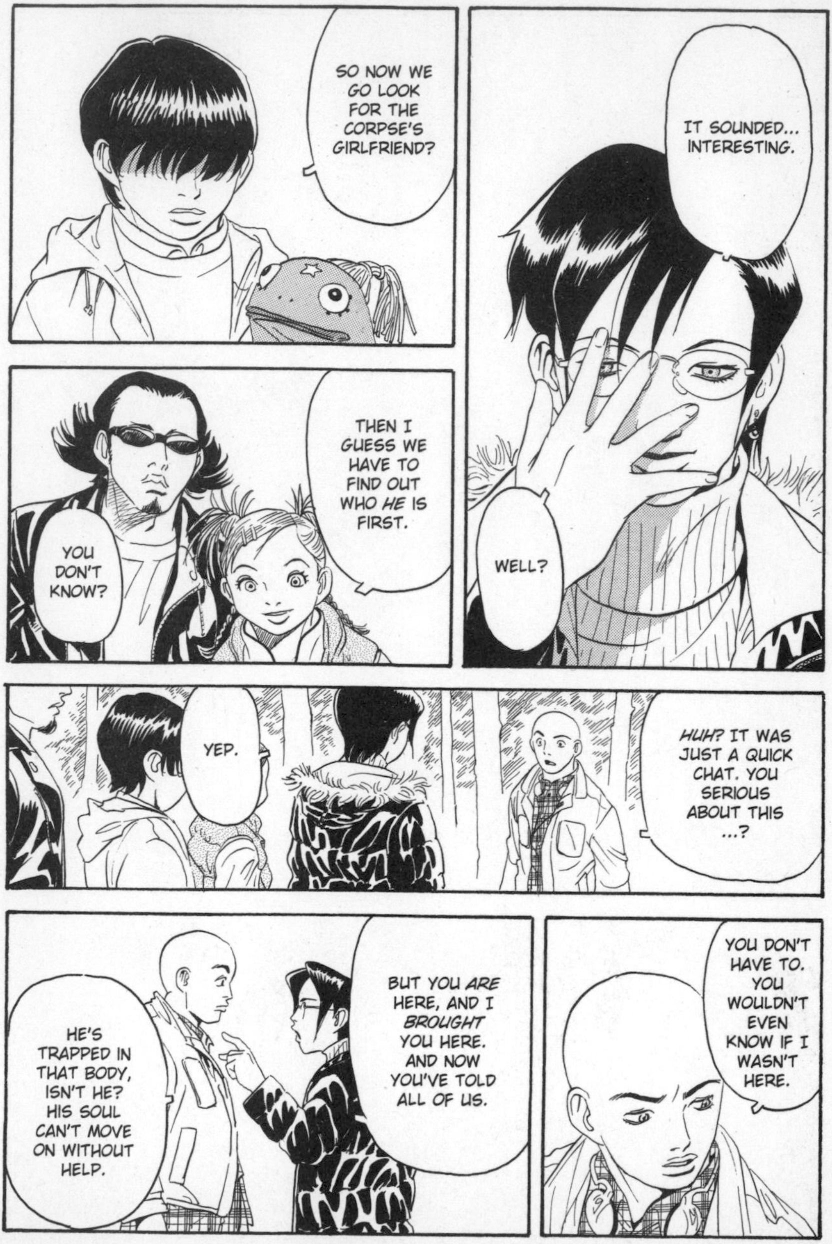
IT SOUNDED... INTERESTING.
WELL?
SO NOW WE GO LOOK FOR THE CORPSE'S GIRLFRIEND?
THEN I GUESS WE HAVE TO FIND OUT WHO *HE* IS FIRST.
YOU DON'T KNOW?
YEP.
HUH? IT WAS JUST A QUICK CHAT. YOU SERIOUS ABOUT THIS ...?
YOU DON'T HAVE TO. YOU WOULDN'T EVEN KNOW IF I WASN'T HERE.
BUT YOU *ARE* HERE, AND I *BROUGHT* YOU HERE. AND NOW YOU'VE TOLD ALL OF US.
HE'S TRAPPED IN THAT BODY, ISN'T HE? HIS SOUL CAN'T MOVE ON WITHOUT HELP.

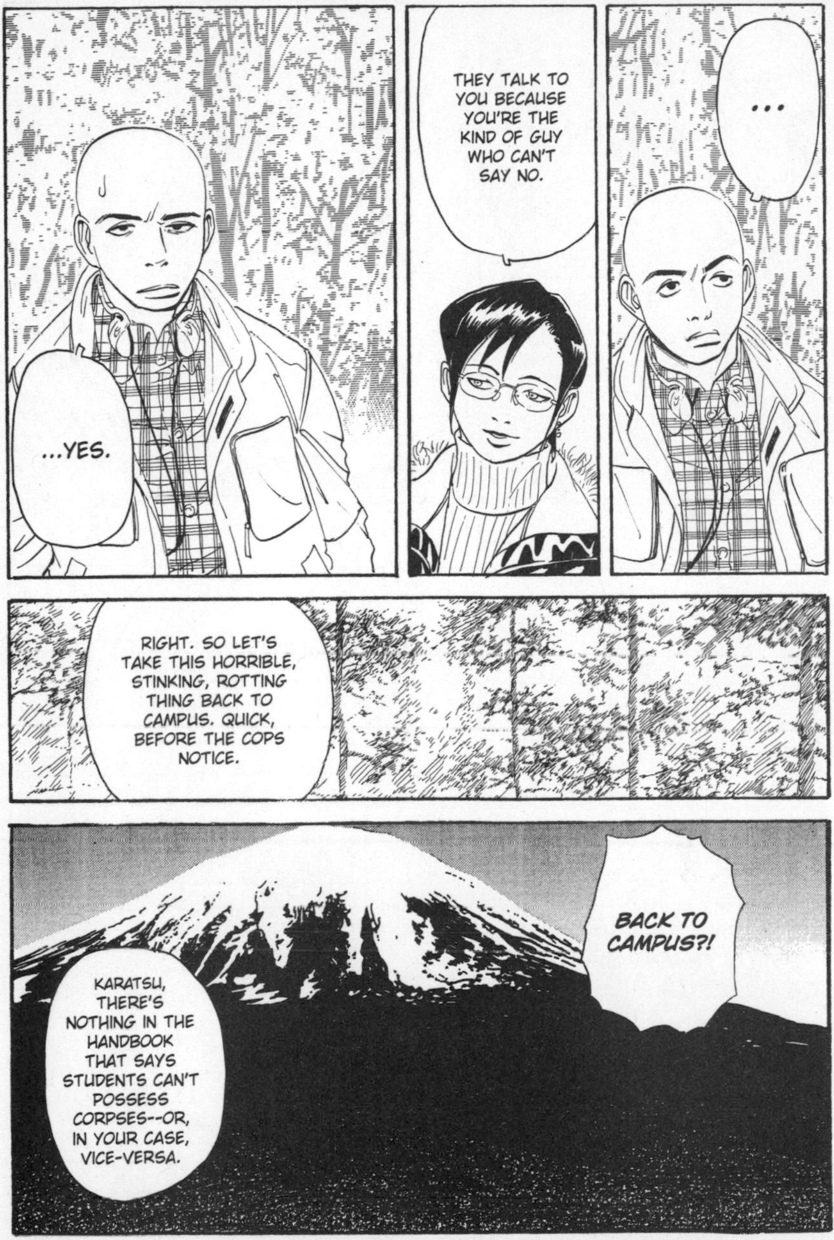
...
THEY TALK TO YOU BECAUSE YOU'RE THE KIND OF GUY WHO CAN'T SAY NO.
...YES.
RIGHT. SO LET'S TAKE THIS HORRIBLE, STINKING, ROTTING THING BACK TO CAMPUS. QUICK, BEFORE THE COPS NOTICE.
BACK TO CAMPUS?!
KARATSU, THERE'S NOTHING IN THE HANDBOOK THAT SAYS STUDENTS CAN'T POSSESS CORPSES--OR, IN YOUR CASE, VICE-VERSA.

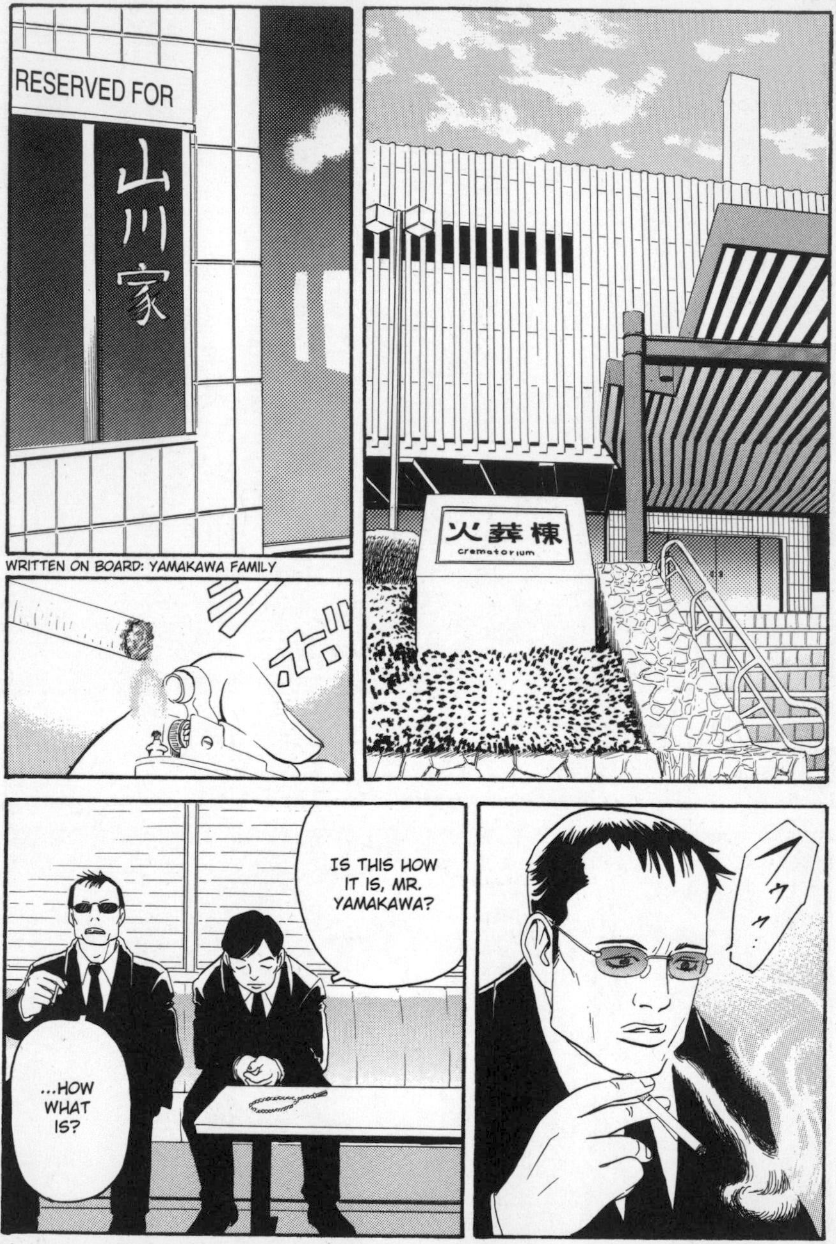
火葬棟
crematorium
RESERVED FOR
山川家
WRITTEN ON BOARD: YAMAKAWA FAMILY
IS THIS HOW IT IS, MR. YAMAKAWA?
...HOW WHAT IS?

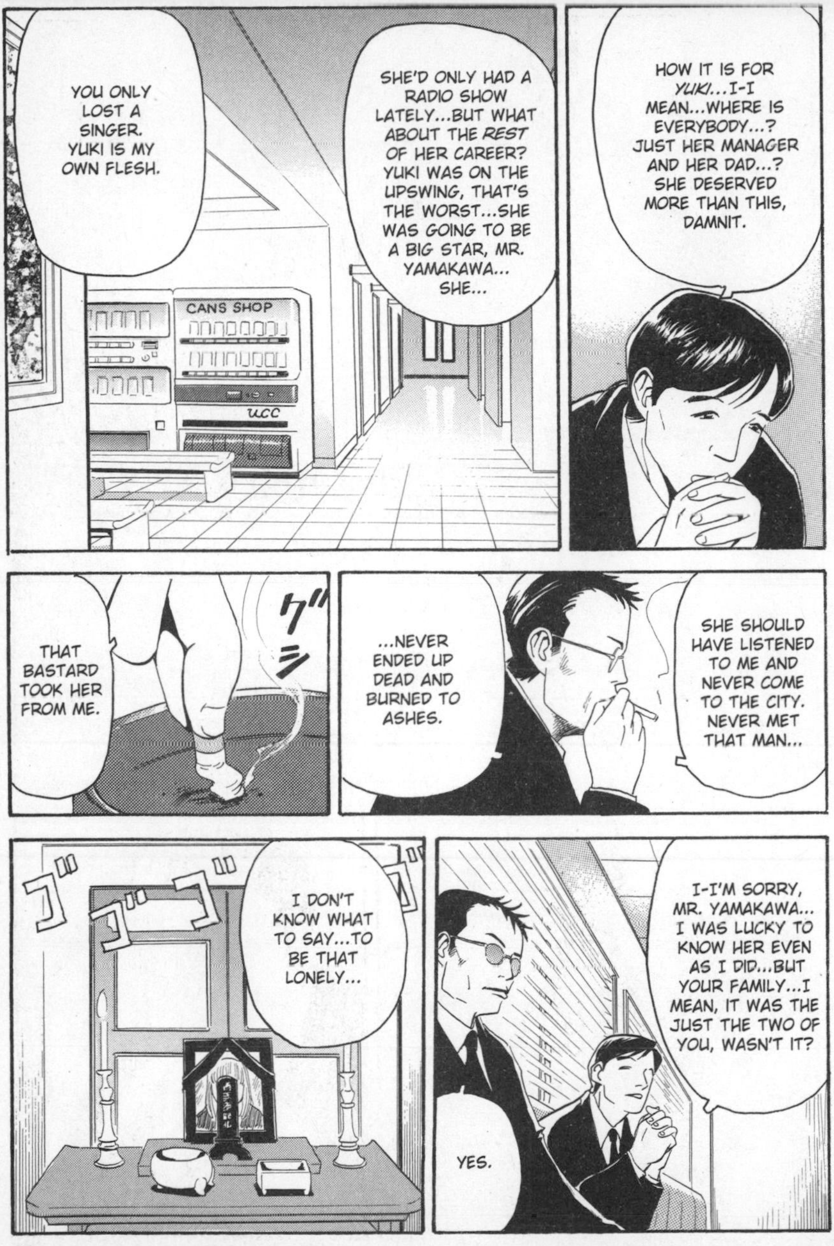
HOW IT IS FOR *YUKI*... I-I MEAN...WHERE IS EVERYBODY...? JUST HER MANAGER AND HER DAD...? SHE DESERVED MORE THAN THIS, DAMNIT.
SHE'D ONLY HAD A RADIO SHOW LATELY...BUT WHAT ABOUT THE *REST* OF HER CAREER? YUKI WAS ON THE UPSWING, THAT'S THE WORST...SHE WAS GOING TO BE A BIG STAR, MR. YAMAKAWA... SHE...
YOU ONLY LOST A SINGER. YUKI IS MY OWN FLESH.
CANS SHOP
UCC
SHE SHOULD HAVE LISTENED TO ME AND NEVER COME TO THE CITY. NEVER MET THAT MAN...
...NEVER ENDED UP DEAD AND BURNED TO ASHES.
THAT BASTARD TOOK HER FROM ME.
I-I'M SORRY, MR. YAMAKAWA... I WAS LUCKY TO KNOW HER EVEN AS I DID...BUT YOUR FAMILY...I MEAN, IT WAS THE JUST THE TWO OF YOU, WASN'T IT?
YES.
I DON'T KNOW WHAT TO SAY...TO BE THAT LONELY...

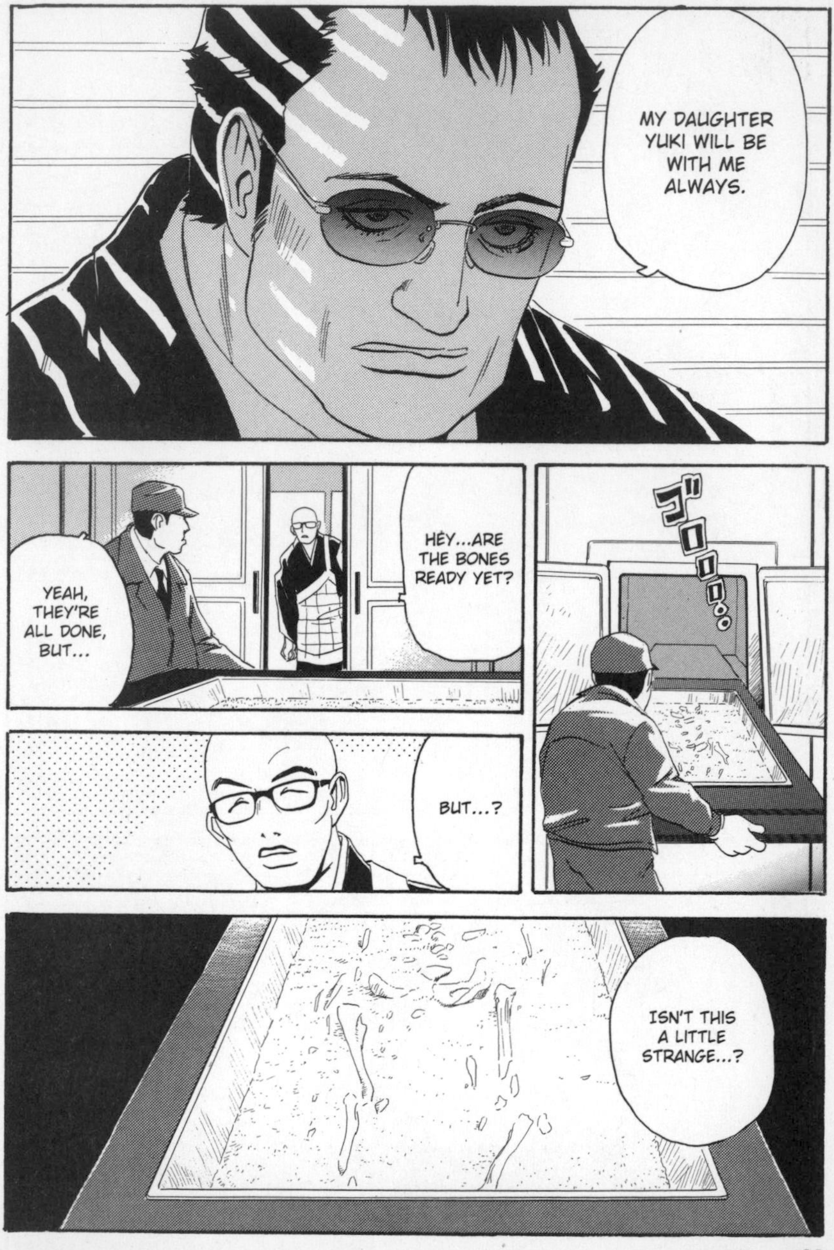
MY DAUGHTER YUKI WILL BE WITH ME ALWAYS.
ゴロロロロ
HEY...ARE THE BONES READY YET?
YEAH, THEY'RE ALL DONE, BUT...
BUT...?
ISN'T THIS A LITTLE STRANGE...?

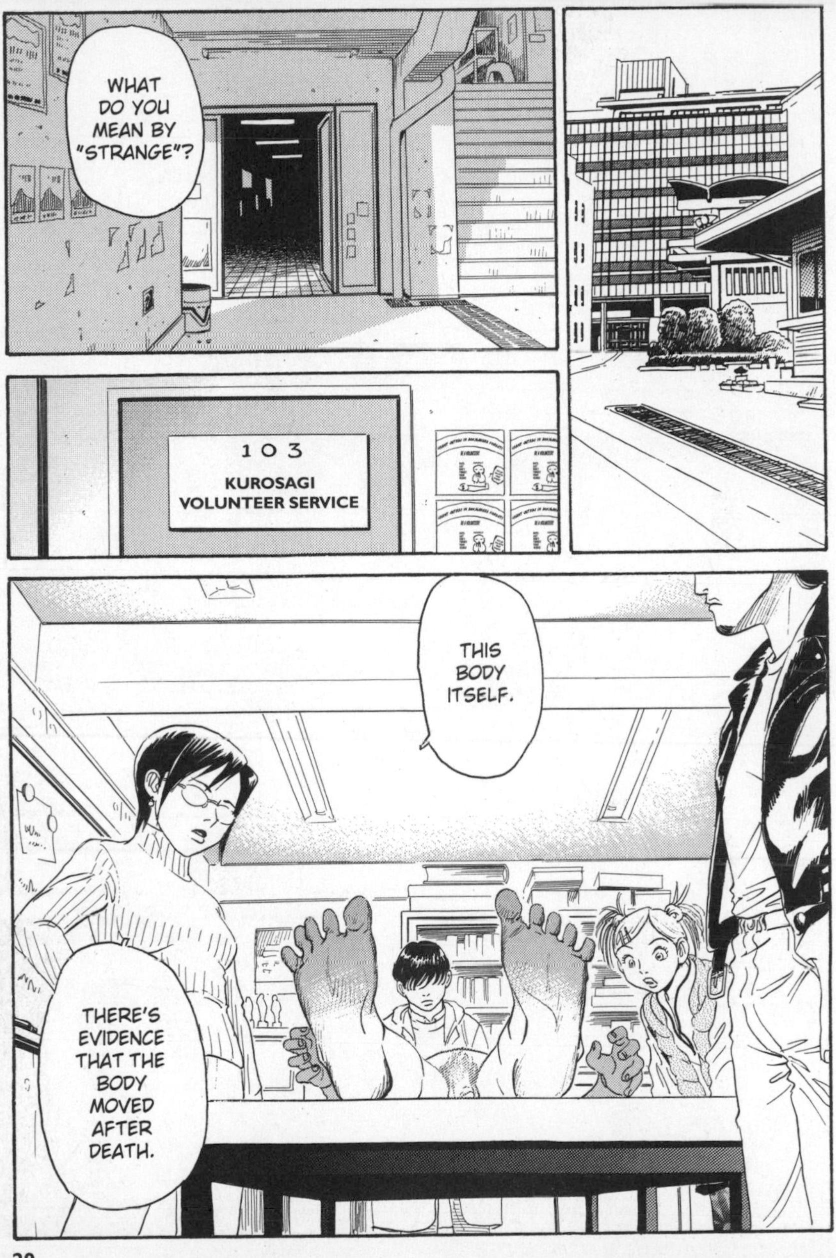
WHAT DO YOU MEAN BY "STRANGE"?
103
KUROSAGI VOLUNTEER SERVICE
THIS BODY ITSELF.
THERE'S EVIDENCE THAT THE BODY MOVED AFTER DEATH.

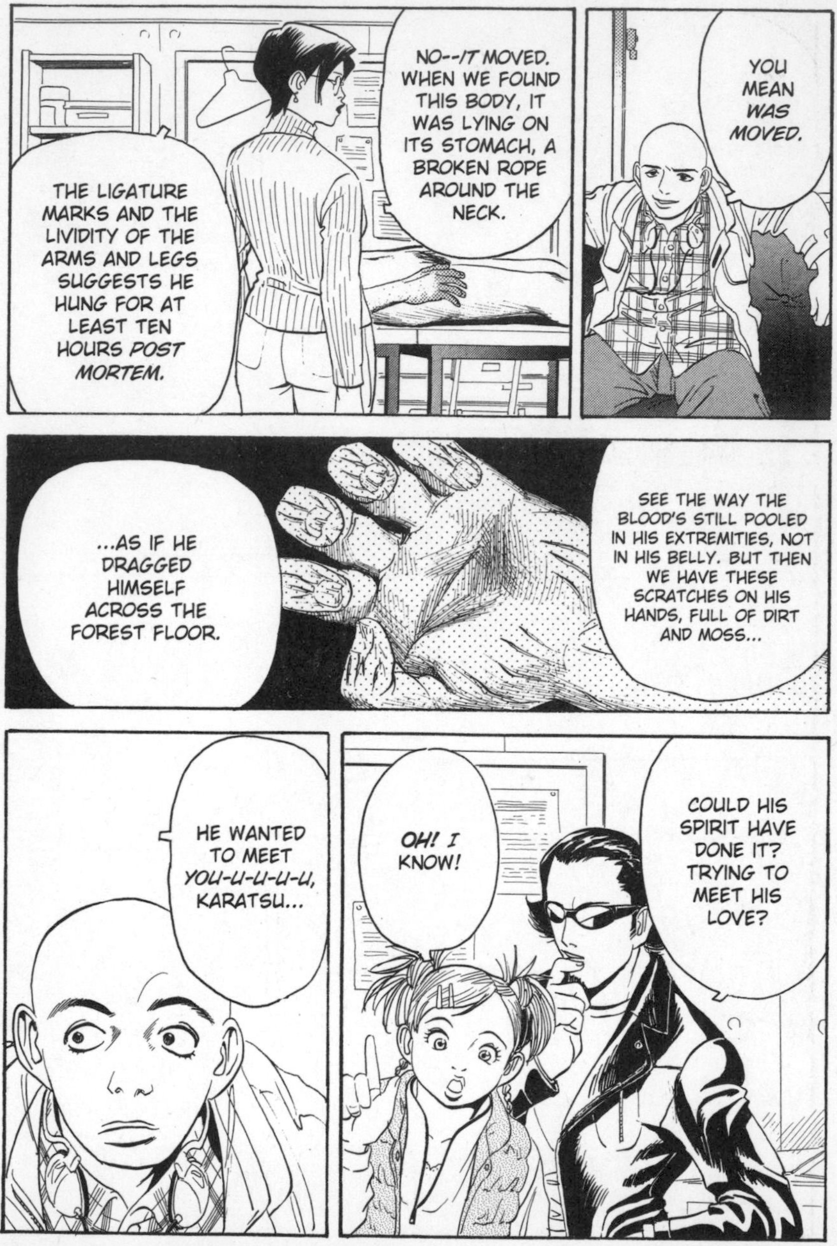
YOU MEAN *WAS MOVED.*
NO--*IT* MOVED. WHEN WE FOUND THIS BODY, IT WAS LYING ON ITS STOMACH, A BROKEN ROPE AROUND THE NECK.
THE LIGATURE MARKS AND THE LIVIDITY OF THE ARMS AND LEGS SUGGESTS HE HUNG FOR AT LEAST TEN HOURS *POST MORTEM.*
SEE THE WAY THE BLOOD'S STILL POOLED IN HIS EXTREMITIES, NOT IN HIS BELLY. BUT THEN WE HAVE THESE SCRATCHES ON HIS HANDS, FULL OF DIRT AND MOSS...
...AS IF HE DRAGGED HIMSELF ACROSS THE FOREST FLOOR.
COULD HIS SPIRIT HAVE DONE IT? TRYING TO MEET HIS LOVE?
OH! I KNOW!
HE WANTED TO MEET *YOU-U-U-U-U,* KARATSU...

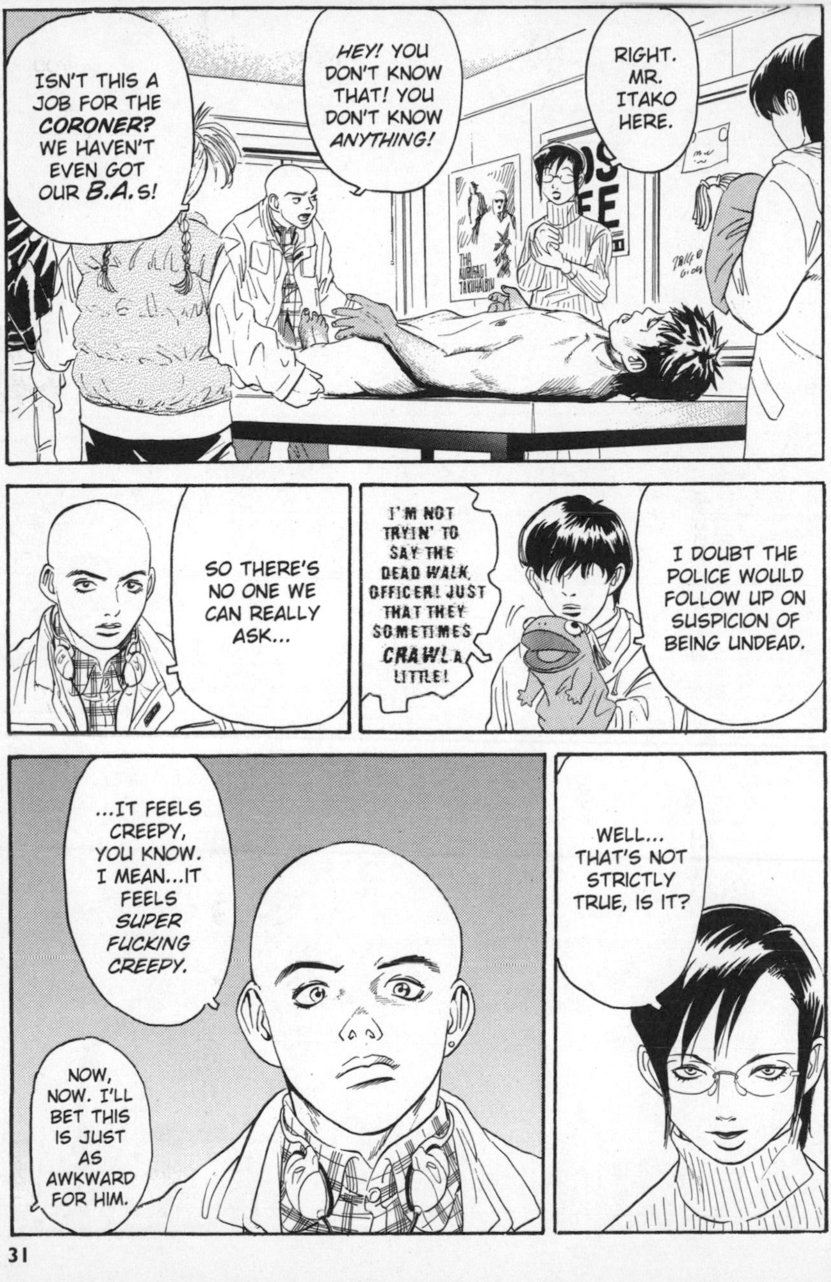
RIGHT. MR. ITAKO HERE.
HEY! YOU DON'T KNOW THAT! YOU DON'T KNOW ANYTHING!
ISN'T THIS A JOB FOR THE CORONER? WE HAVEN'T EVEN GOT OUR B.A.s!
I DOUBT THE POLICE WOULD FOLLOW UP ON SUSPICION OF BEING UNDEAD.
I'M NOT TRYIN' TO SAY THE DEAD WALK, OFFICER! JUST THAT THEY SOMETIMES CRAWL A LITTLE!
SO THERE'S NO ONE WE CAN REALLY ASK...
WELL... THAT'S NOT STRICTLY TRUE, IS IT?
...IT FEELS CREEPY, YOU KNOW. I MEAN...IT FEELS SUPER FUCKING CREEPY.
NOW, NOW. I'LL BET THIS IS JUST AS AWKWARD FOR HIM.

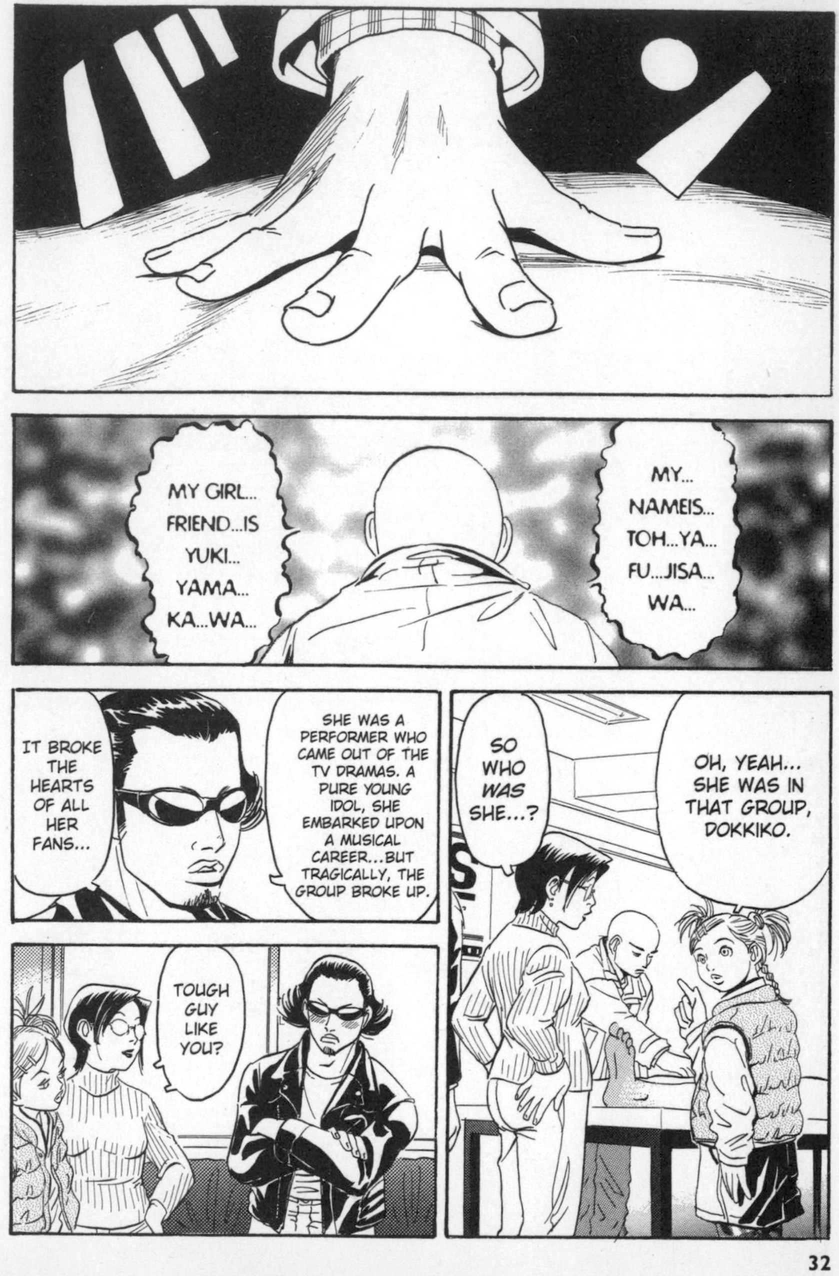
MY... NAMEIS... TOH...YA... FU...JISA... WA...
MY GIRL... FRIEND...IS YUKI... YAMA... KA...WA...
SO WHO *WAS* SHE...?
OH, YEAH... SHE WAS IN THAT GROUP, DOKKIKO.
SHE WAS A PERFORMER WHO CAME OUT OF THE TV DRAMAS. A PURE YOUNG IDOL, SHE EMBARKED UPON A MUSICAL CAREER...BUT TRAGICALLY, THE GROUP BROKE UP.
IT BROKE THE HEARTS OF ALL HER FANS...
TOUGH GUY LIKE YOU?

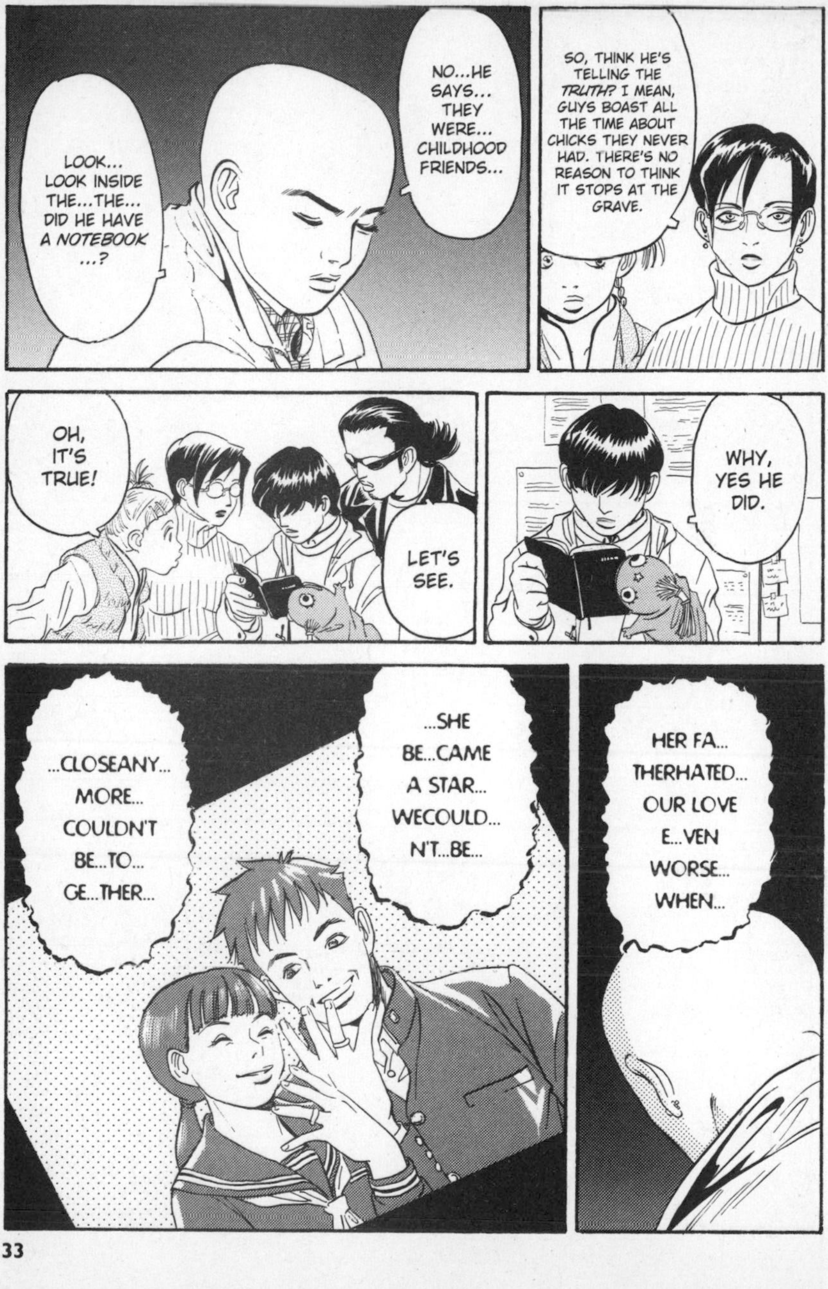
SO, THINK HE'S TELLING THE *TRUTH?* I MEAN, GUYS BOAST ALL THE TIME ABOUT CHICKS THEY NEVER HAD. THERE'S NO REASON TO THINK IT STOPS AT THE GRAVE.
NO...HE SAYS... THEY WERE... CHILDHOOD FRIENDS...
LOOK... LOOK INSIDE THE...THE... DID HE HAVE A *NOTEBOOK* ...?
WHY, YES HE DID.
LET'S SEE.
OH, IT'S TRUE!
HER FA... THERHATED... OUR LOVE E...VEN WORSE... WHEN...
...SHE BE...CAME A STAR... WECOULD... N'T...BE...
...CLOSEANY... MORE... COULDN'T BE...TO... GE...THER...

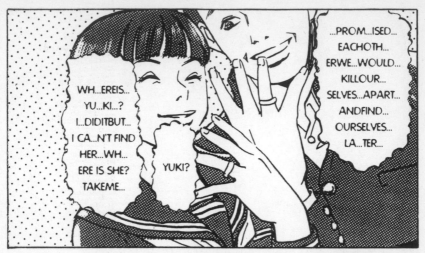

...PROM...ISED... EACHOTH... ERWE...WOULD... KILLOUR... SELVES...APART... ANDFIND... OURSELVES... LA...TER...
YUKI?
WH...EREIS... YU...KI...? I...DIDITBUT... I CA...N'T FIND HER...WH... ERE IS SHE? TAKEME...
...TA...KEME... TO...WHERE... YUKI IS... MY... NAMEIS... TOH...YA..
ヒラッ
IT JUST KIND OF REPEATS, LIKE IN-FLIGHT STEREO.
ANYTHING ELSE YOU WANT TO KNOW?
HEY! THE STIFF HAD A LOTTO TICKET. ASK HIM IF HE WANTS THIS.
NO...HE SAYS YOU CAN HAVE IT.

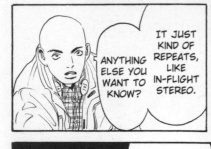

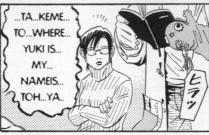

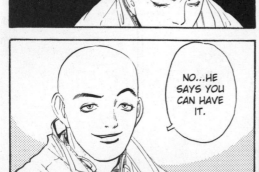

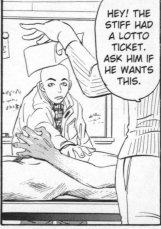

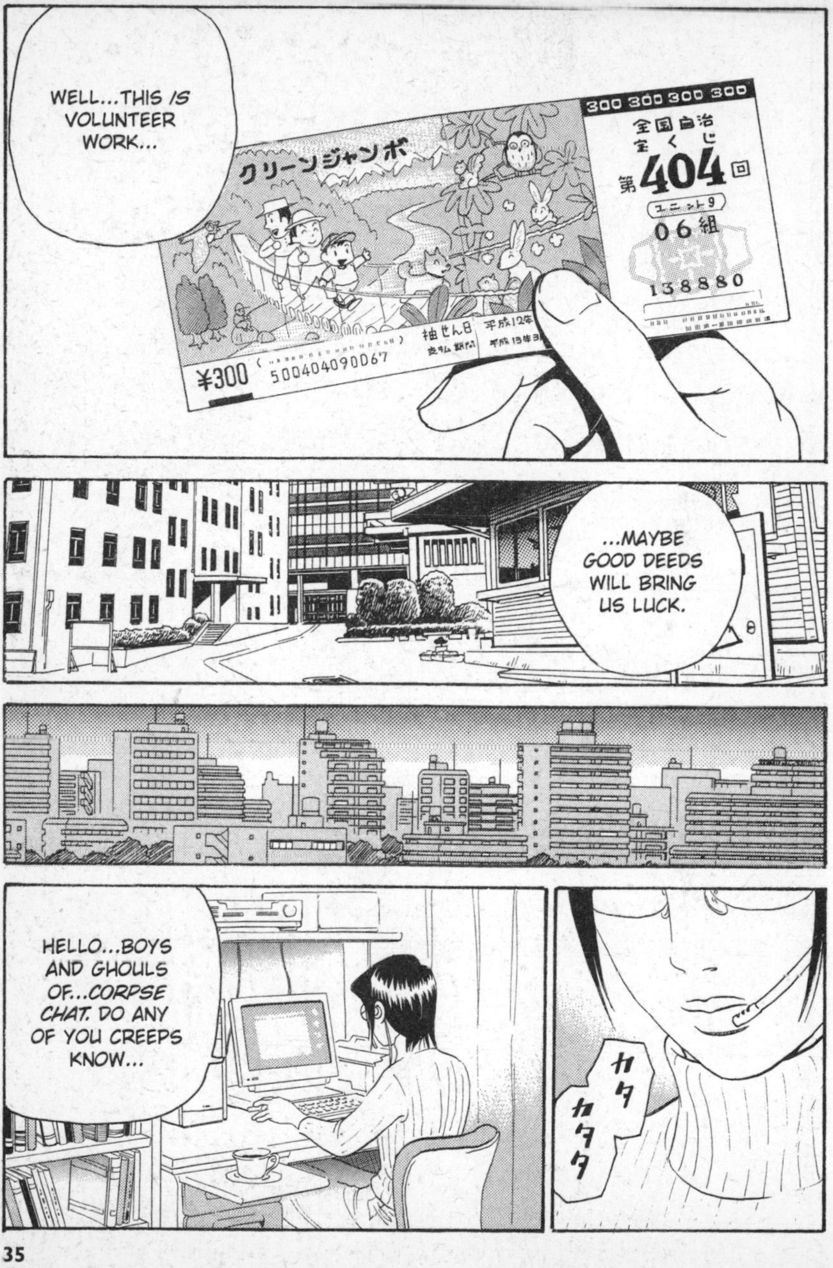
WELL...THIS *IS* VOLUNTEER WORK...
300 300 300 300
全国自治
宝くじ
第404回
ユニット9
06組
138880
クリーンジャンボ
抽せん日
¥300
500404090067
...MAYBE GOOD DEEDS WILL BRING US LUCK.
カタ
カタタ
HELLO...BOYS AND GHOULS OF...CORPSE CHAT. DO ANY OF YOU CREEPS KNOW...

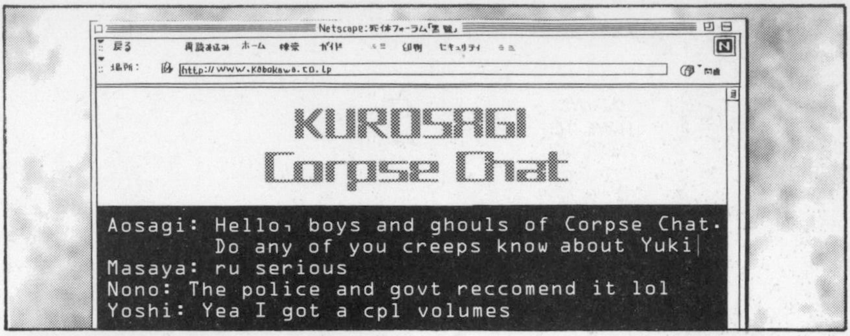
KUROSAGI
Corpse Chat
Aosagi: Hello, boys and ghouls of Corpse Chat. Do any of you creeps know about Yuki
Masaya: ru serious
Nono: The police and govt reccomend it lol
Yoshi: Yea I got a cpl volumes

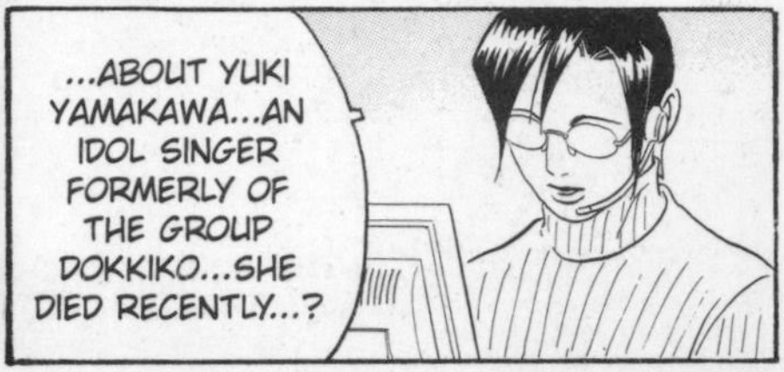
...ABOUT YUKI YAMAKAWA...AN IDOL SINGER FORMERLY OF THE GROUP DOKKIKO...SHE DIED RECENTLY...?

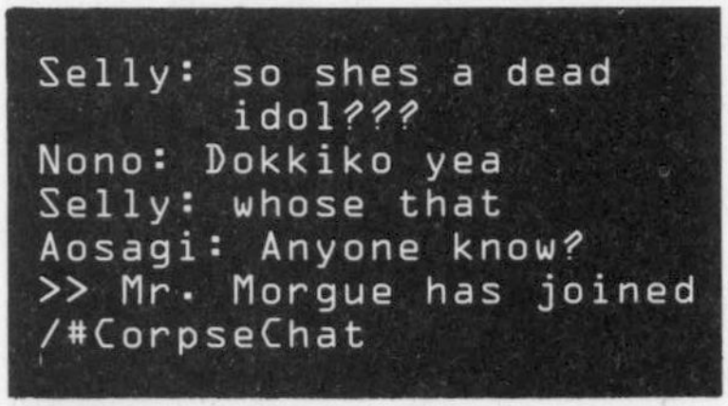
Selly: so shes a dead idol???
Nono: Dokkiko yea
Selly: whose that
Aosagi: Anyone know?
>> Mr. Morgue has joined /#CorpseChat

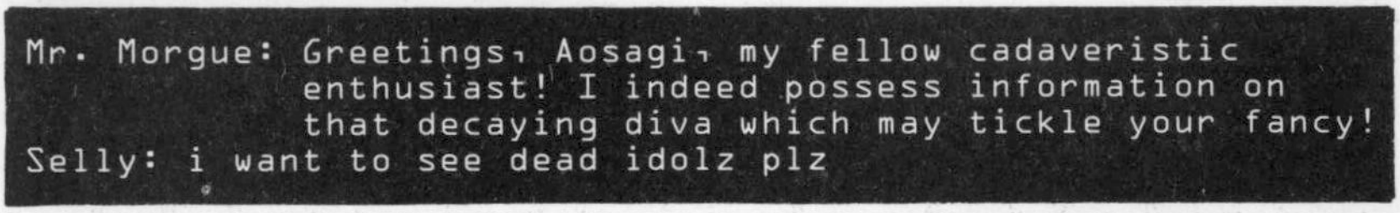
Mr. Morgue: Greetings, Aosagi, my fellow cadaveristic enthusiast! I indeed possess information on that decaying diva which may tickle your fancy!
Selly: i want to see dead idolz plz

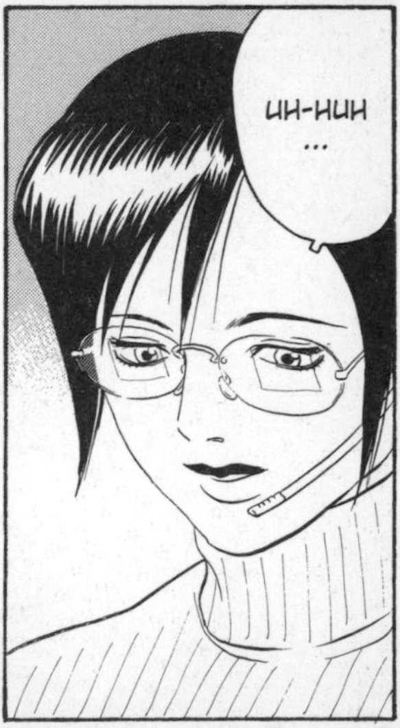
UH-HUH
...

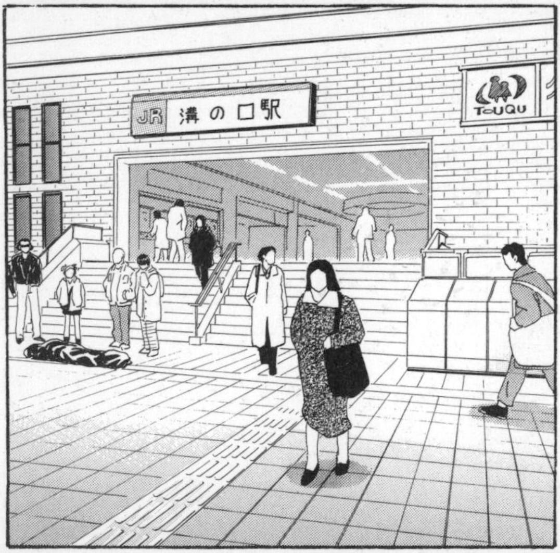
JR 溝の口駅
TOUQU

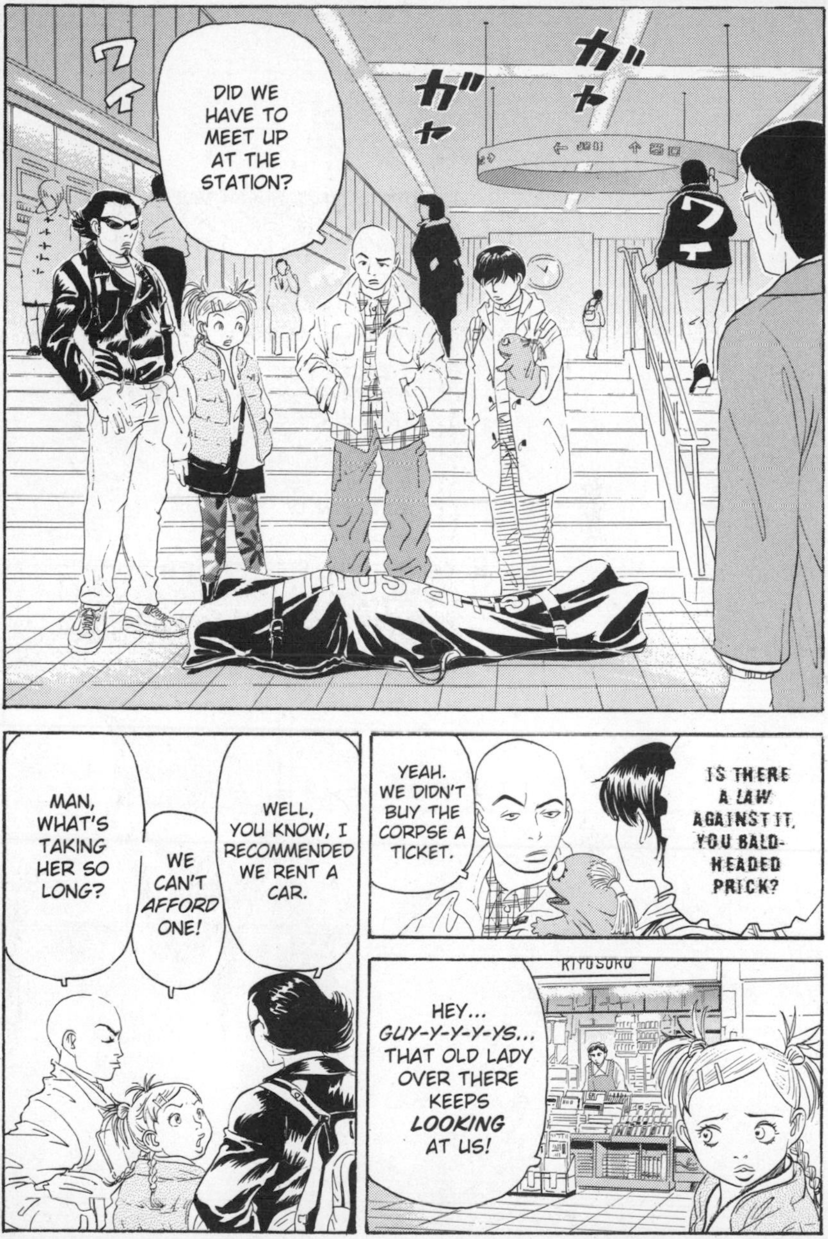
ワイ
DID WE HAVE TO MEET UP AT THE STATION?
ガヤ
ガヤ
MAN, WHAT'S TAKING HER SO LONG?
WELL, YOU KNOW, I RECOMMENDED WE RENT A CAR.
WE CAN'T *AFFORD* ONE!
YEAH. WE DIDN'T BUY THE CORPSE A TICKET.
IS THERE A *LAW* AGAINST IT, YOU BALD-HEADED PRICK?
HEY... *GUY-Y-Y-Y-YS*... THAT OLD LADY OVER THERE KEEPS *LOOKING* AT US!

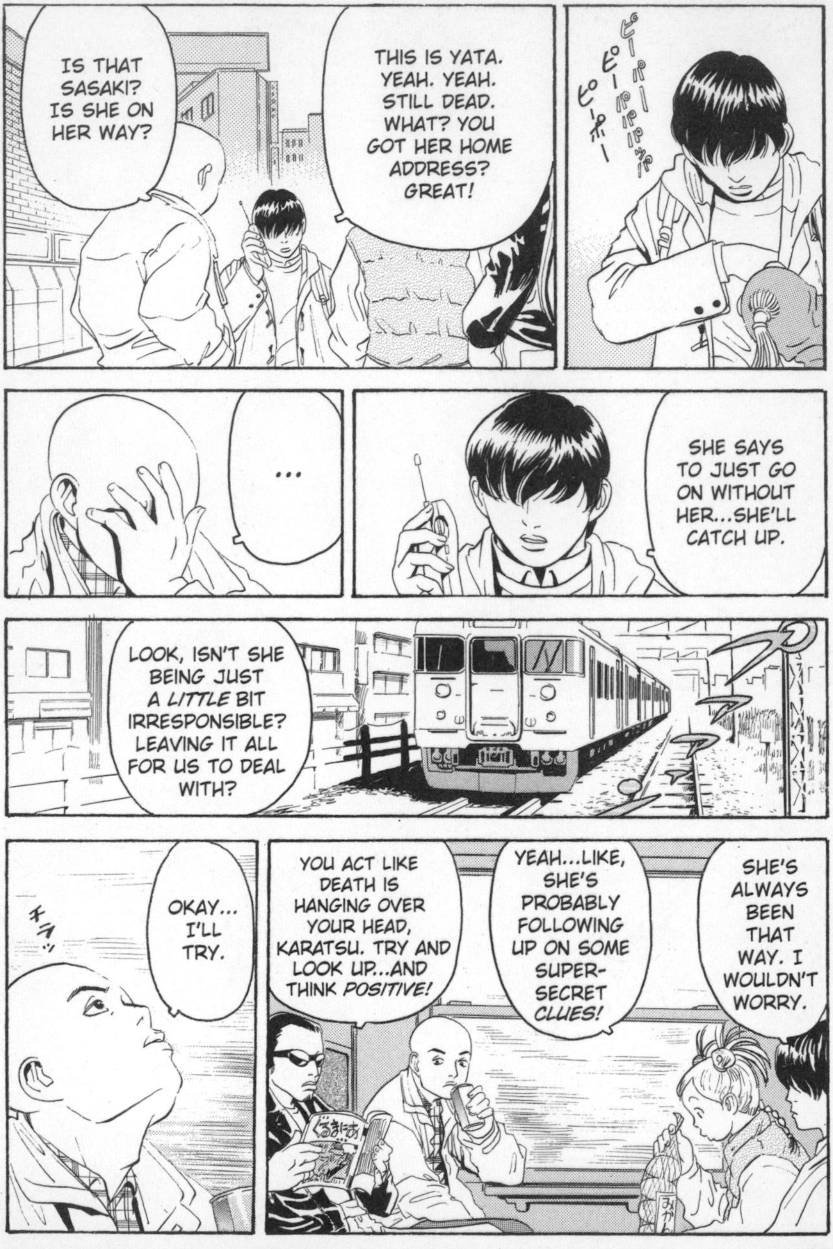
ピーパー
ピーパパパッパ
ピーポー
THIS IS YATA. YEAH. YEAH. STILL DEAD. WHAT? YOU GOT HER HOME ADDRESS? GREAT!
IS THAT SASAKI? IS SHE ON HER WAY?
SHE SAYS TO JUST GO ON WITHOUT HER...SHE'LL CATCH UP.
...
LOOK, ISN'T SHE BEING JUST A *LITTLE* BIT IRRESPONSIBLE? LEAVING IT ALL FOR US TO DEAL WITH?
SHE'S ALWAYS BEEN THAT WAY. I WOULDN'T WORRY.
YEAH...LIKE, SHE'S PROBABLY FOLLOWING UP ON SOME SUPER-SECRET *CLUES!*
YOU ACT LIKE DEATH IS HANGING OVER YOUR HEAD, KARATSU. TRY AND LOOK UP...AND THINK *POSITIVE!*
OKAY... I'LL TRY.
チラッ

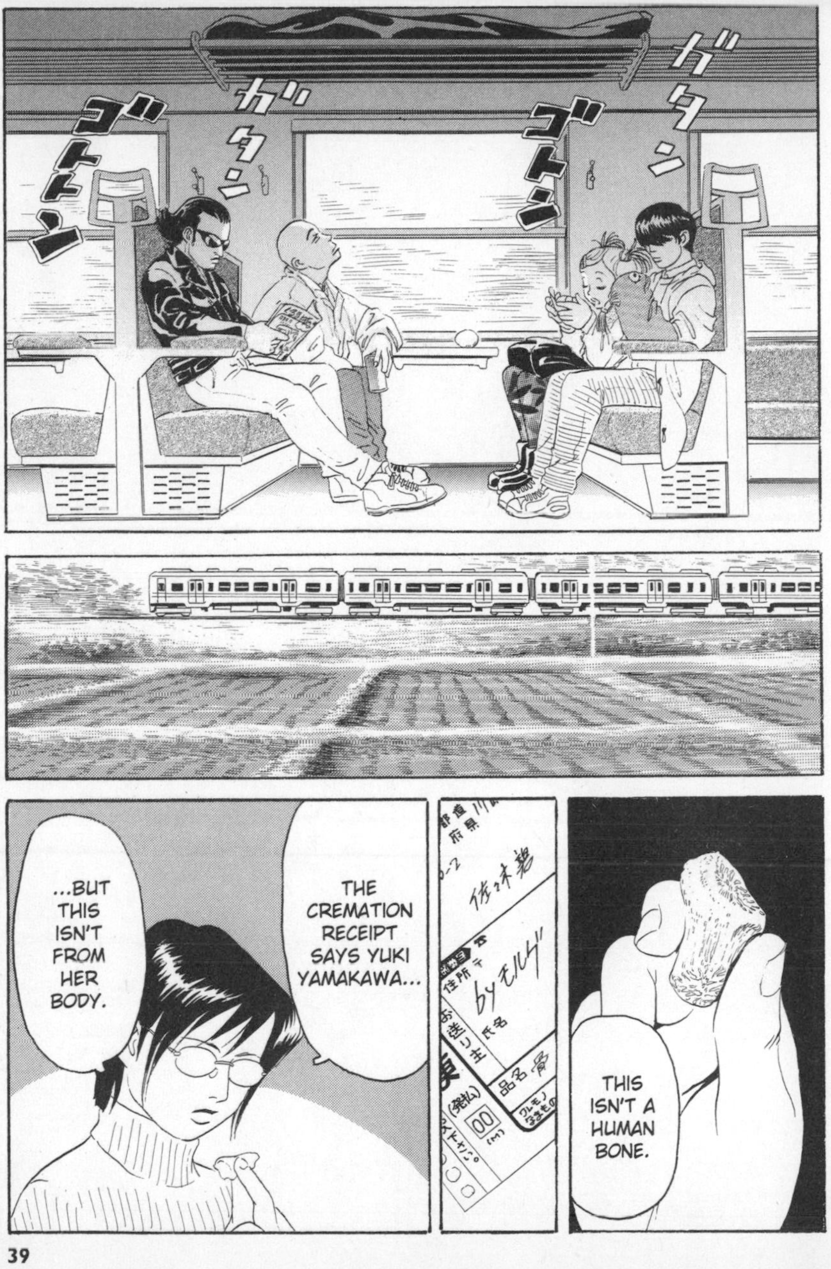
ガタン
ゴトン
ガタン
ゴトトン
THIS ISN'T A HUMAN BONE.
THE CREMATION RECEIPT SAYS YUKI YAMAKAWA...
...BUT THIS ISN'T FROM HER BODY.

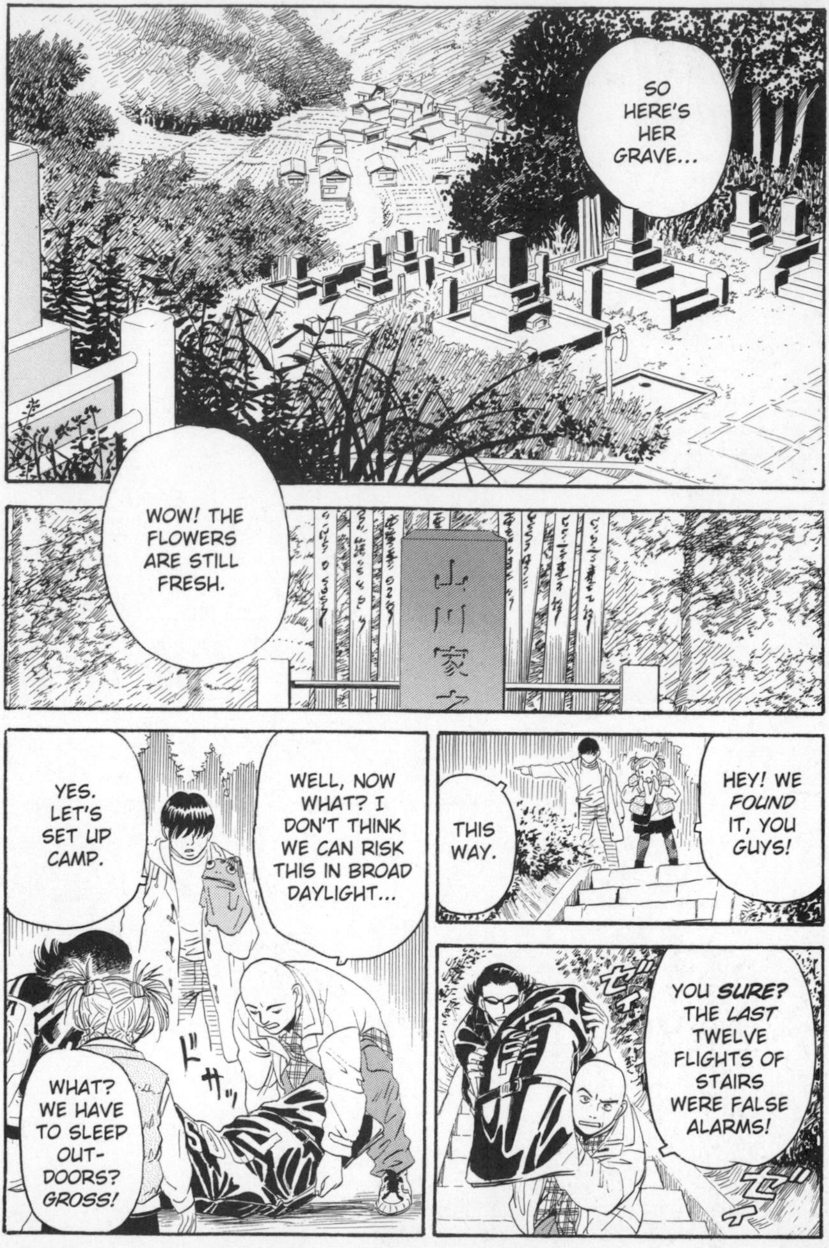
SO HERE'S HER GRAVE...
WOW! THE FLOWERS ARE STILL FRESH.
山川家
HEY! WE *FOUND* IT, YOU GUYS!
THIS WAY.
YOU ***SURE?*** THE *LAST* TWELVE FLIGHTS OF STAIRS WERE FALSE ALARMS!
ゼイ
ゼイ
WELL, NOW WHAT? I DON'T THINK WE CAN RISK THIS IN BROAD DAYLIGHT...
YES. LET'S SET UP CAMP.
ドサッ
WHAT? WE HAVE TO SLEEP OUT-DOORS? *GROSS!*

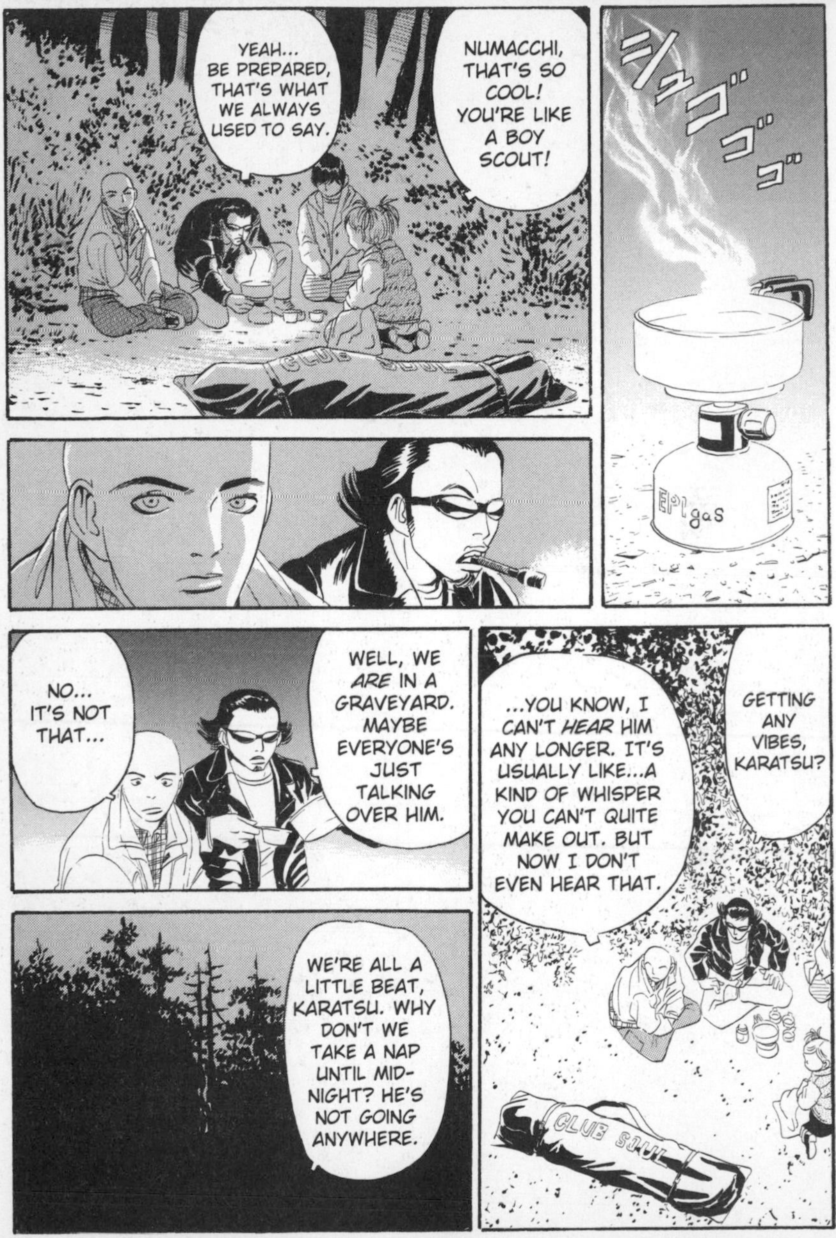
シュゴゴゴ
EPI gas
NUMACCHI, THAT'S SO COOL! YOU'RE LIKE A BOY SCOUT!
YEAH... BE PREPARED, THAT'S WHAT WE ALWAYS USED TO SAY.
CLUB SOUL
GETTING ANY VIBES, KARATSU?
...YOU KNOW, I CAN'T *HEAR* HIM ANY LONGER. IT'S USUALLY LIKE...A KIND OF WHISPER YOU CAN'T QUITE MAKE OUT. BUT NOW I DON'T EVEN HEAR THAT.
CLUB SOUL
WELL, WE *ARE* IN A GRAVEYARD. MAYBE EVERYONE'S JUST TALKING OVER HIM.
NO... IT'S NOT THAT...
WE'RE ALL A LITTLE BEAT, KARATSU. WHY DON'T WE TAKE A NAP UNTIL MID-NIGHT? HE'S NOT GOING ANYWHERE.

CLUB SOUL
モゾッ
ギッ
ヂィィィィィィ
CLUB SOUL

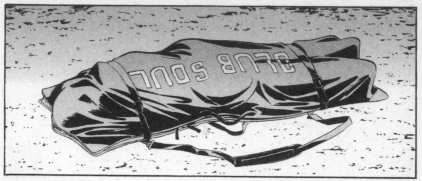

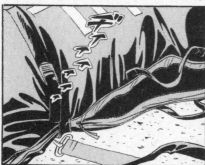

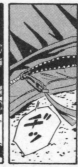

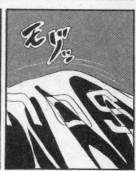

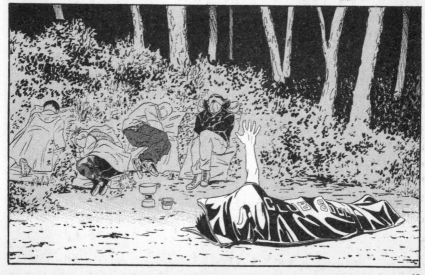

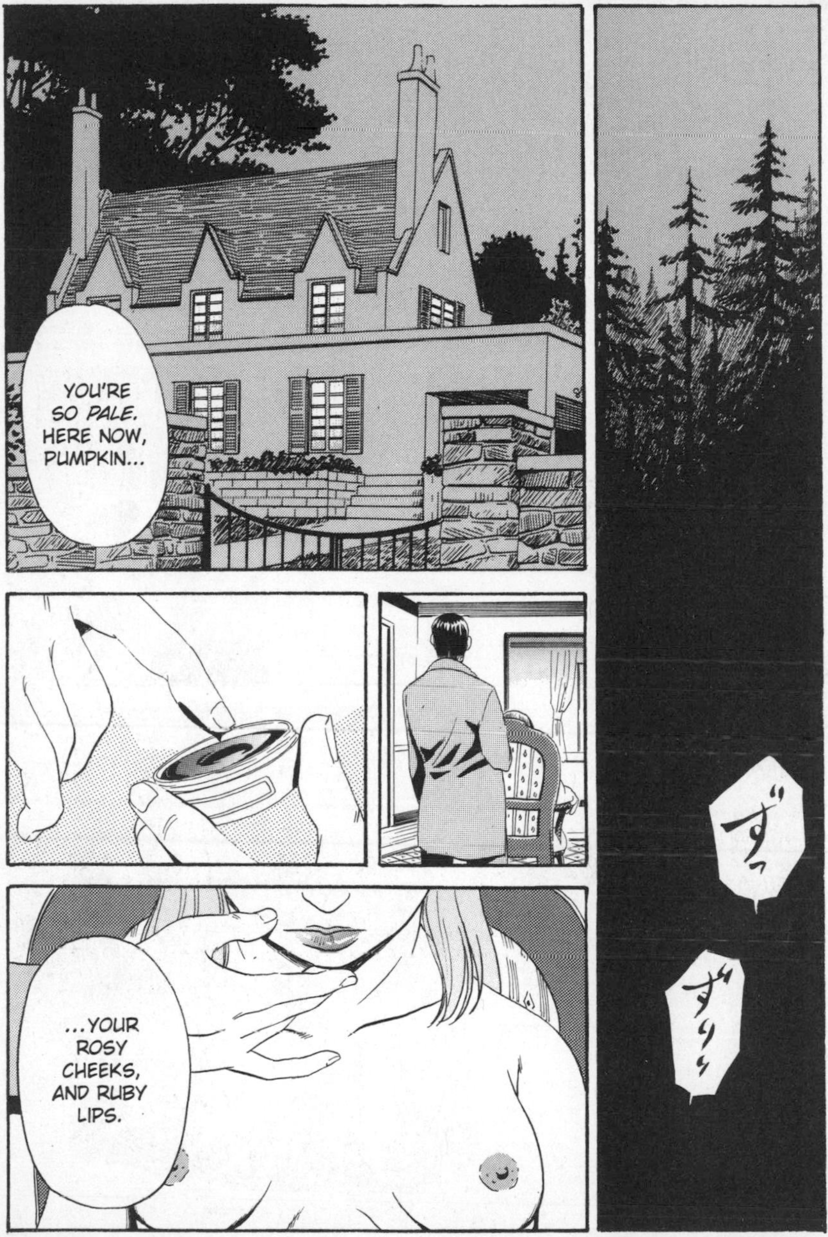
ずっ
ずりっ
YOU'RE SO *PALE*. HERE NOW, PUMPKIN...
...YOUR ROSY CHEEKS, AND RUBY LIPS.

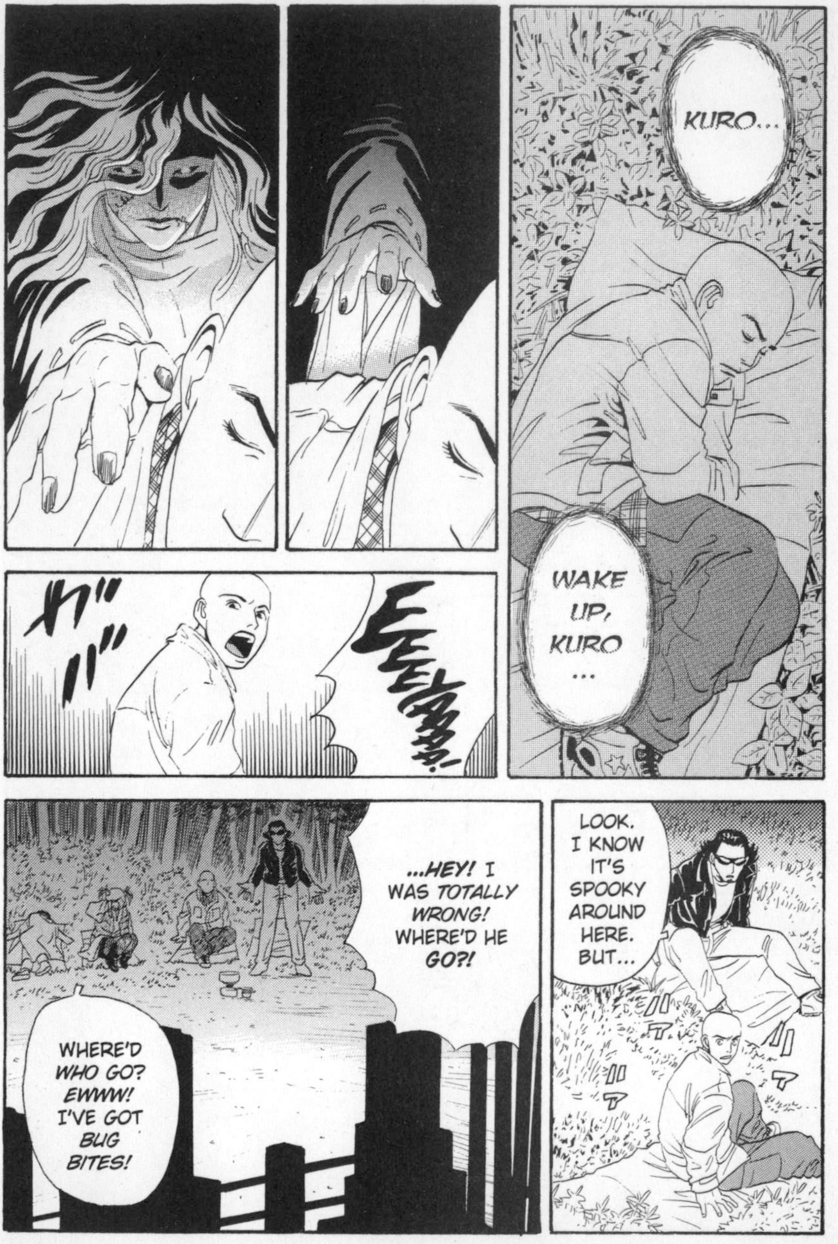
KURO...
WAKE UP, KURO ...
LOOK. I KNOW IT'S SPOOKY AROUND HERE. BUT...
...HEY! I WAS TOTALLY WRONG! WHERE'D HE GO?!
WHERE'D WHO GO? EWWW! I'VE GOT BUG BITES!

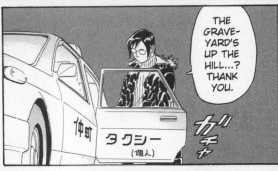

キィィッ
THE GRAVE-YARD'S UP THE HILL...? THANK YOU.
仲町
タクシー
(個人)
ガチャ
ブロロロ...
SASAKI-SAN!?
HM? WHY AREN'T YOU WITH THE BODY?
UM...
WE *WERE*, BUT, IT, UH...GOT BORED, I GUESS.
NO...IT'S BECAUSE SHE WASN'T THERE...
WHAT DID YOU FIND OUT, SASAKI?
CHECK THIS OUT--THE PRIEST WHO DID THE SERVICES AT YUKI YAMAKAWA'S FUNERAL WAS FROM *OUR SCHOOL*.

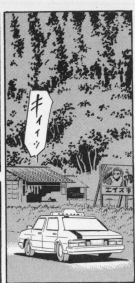

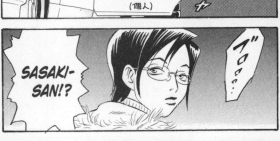

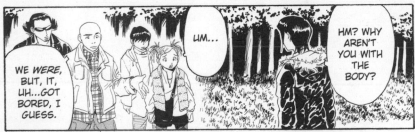

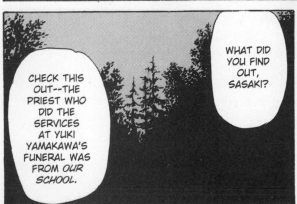

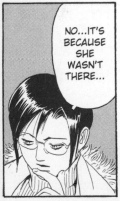

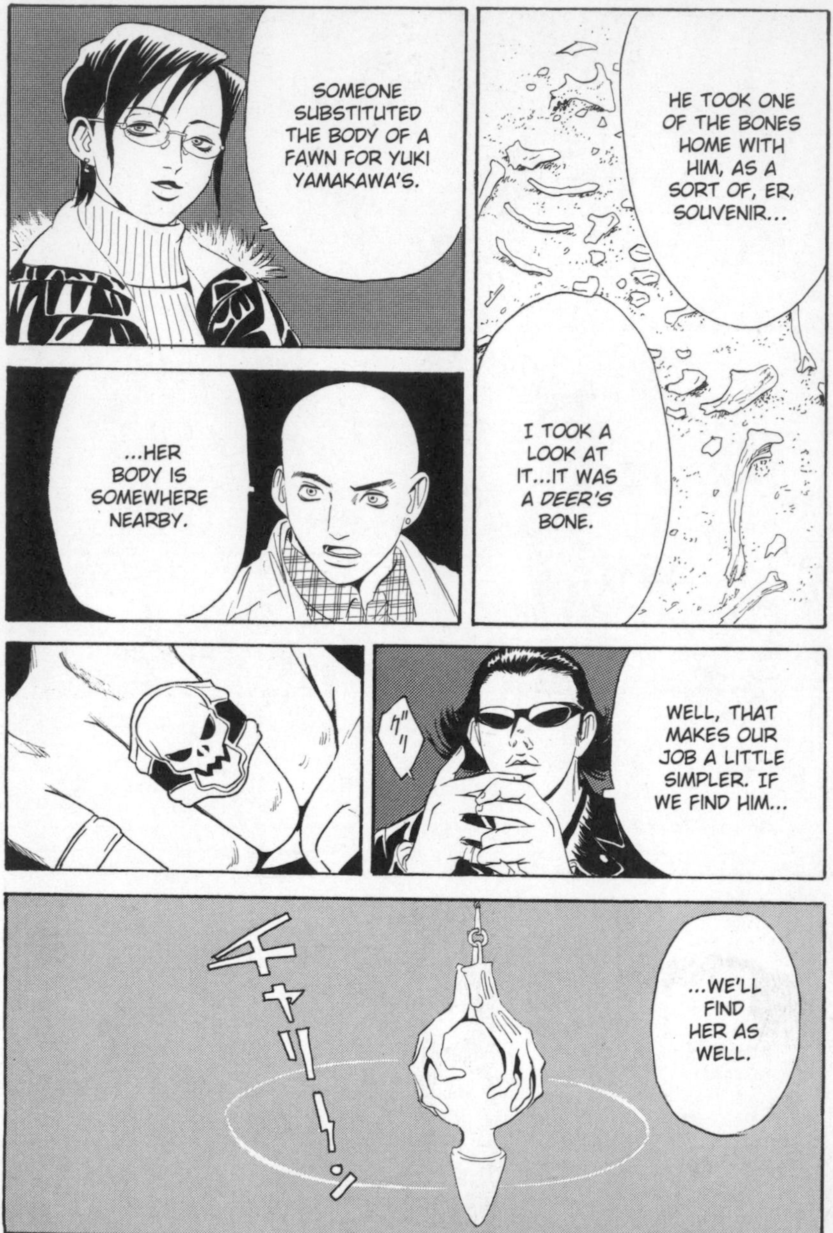
HE TOOK ONE OF THE BONES HOME WITH HIM, AS A SORT OF, ER, SOUVENIR...
I TOOK A LOOK AT IT...IT WAS A *DEER'S* BONE.
SOMEONE SUBSTITUTED THE BODY OF A FAWN FOR YUKI YAMAKAWA'S.
...HER BODY IS SOMEWHERE NEARBY.
グッ
WELL, THAT MAKES OUR JOB A LITTLE SIMPLER. IF WE FIND HIM...
...WE'LL FIND HER AS WELL.
キャリーーン

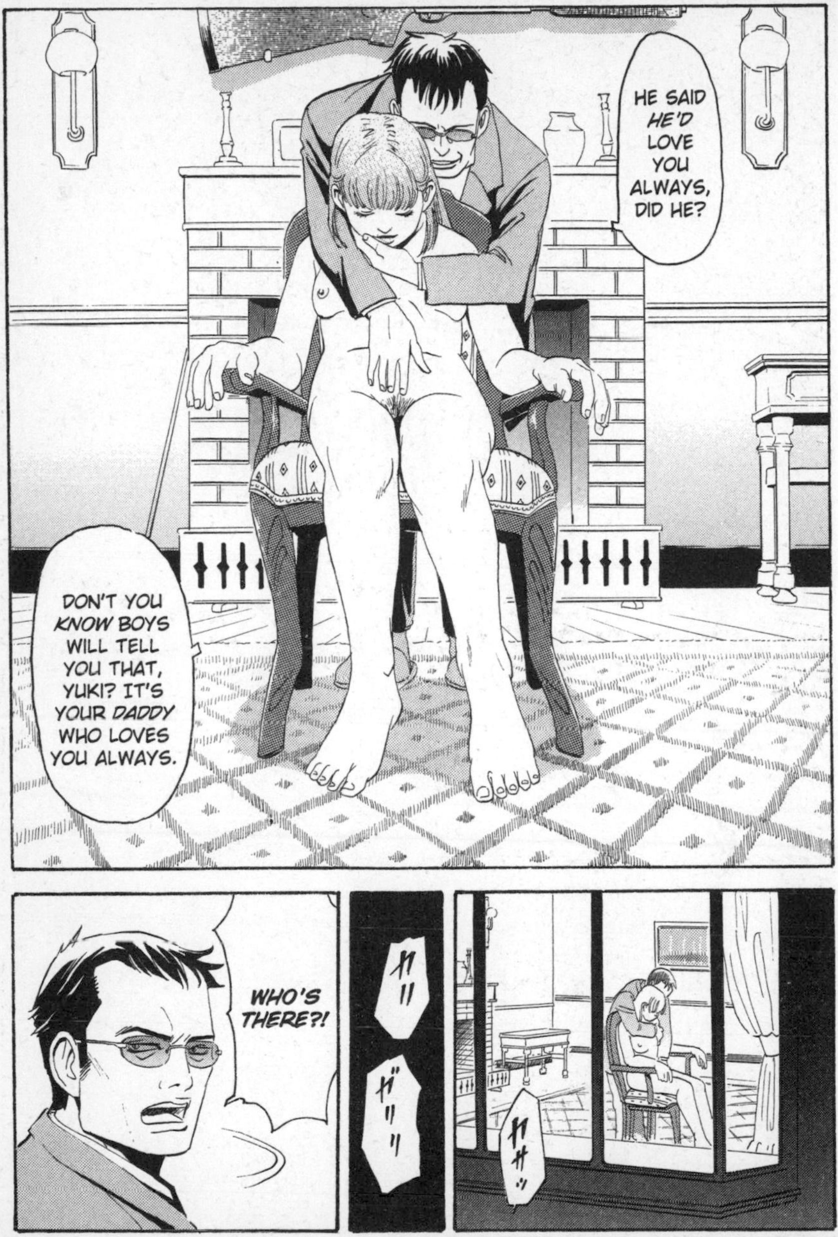
HE SAID *HE'D* LOVE YOU ALWAYS, DID HE?
DON'T YOU *KNOW* BOYS WILL TELL YOU THAT, YUKI? IT'S YOUR *DADDY* WHO LOVES YOU ALWAYS.
カサッ
カリ
ガリッ
WHO'S THERE?!

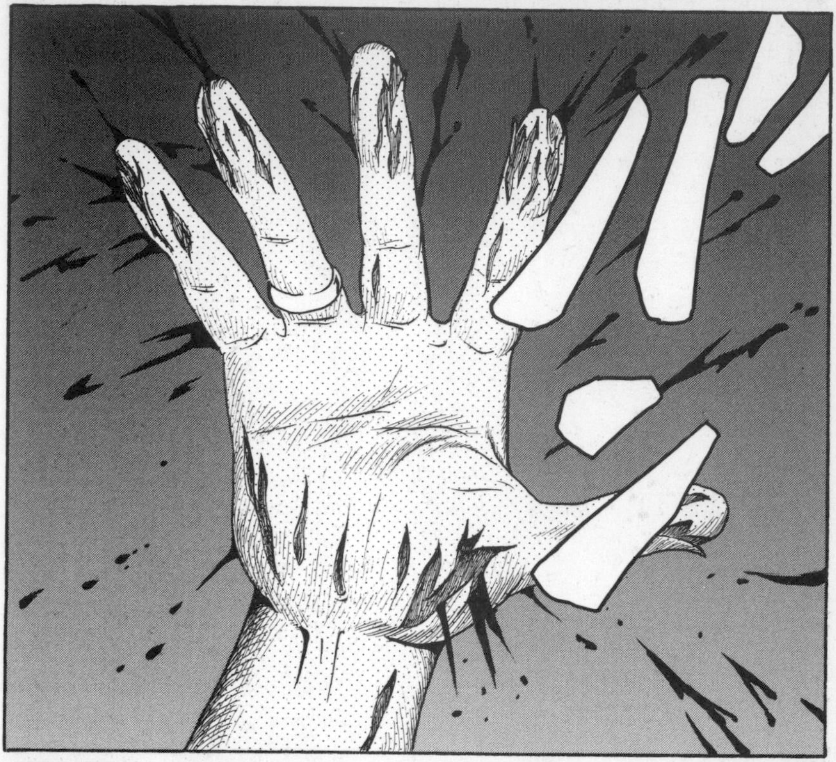

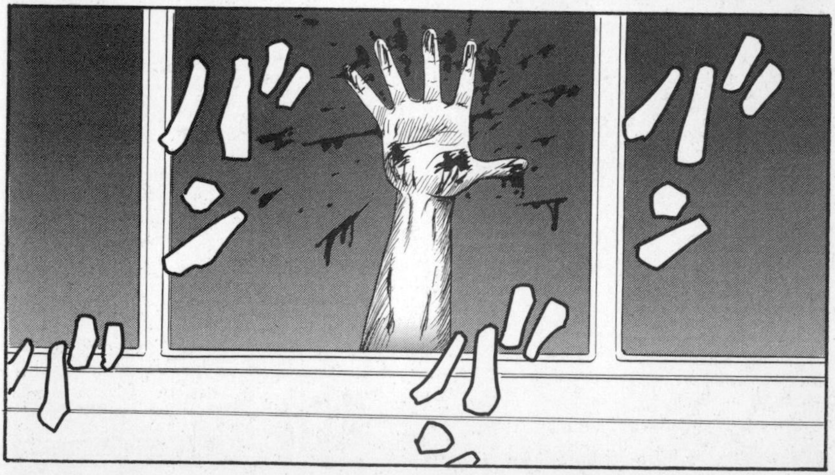
バン
バン

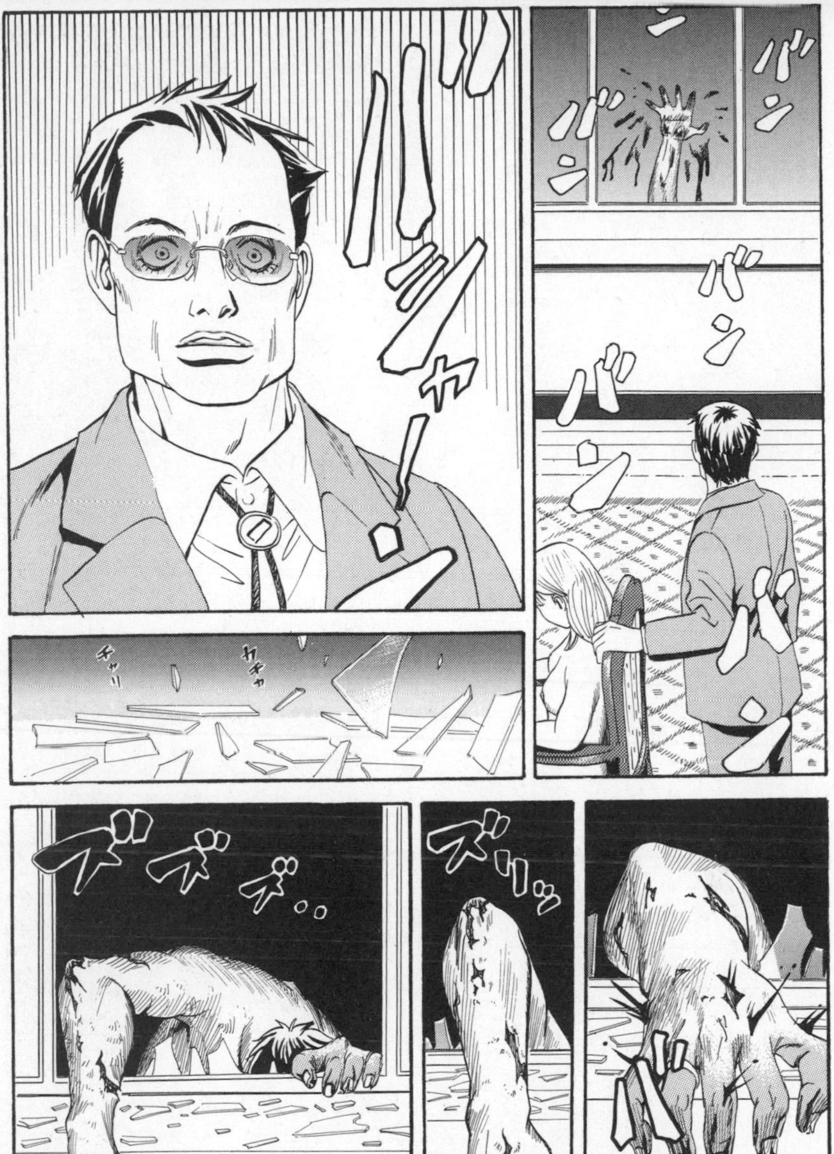
バン
バン
バン
バン
カチャ
チャリ
ズリッ
ズズズ。。

T-TO... TO...

...TOHYA.

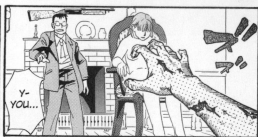

Y-YOU...

...YOU *STILL* CAN'T HAVE HER!

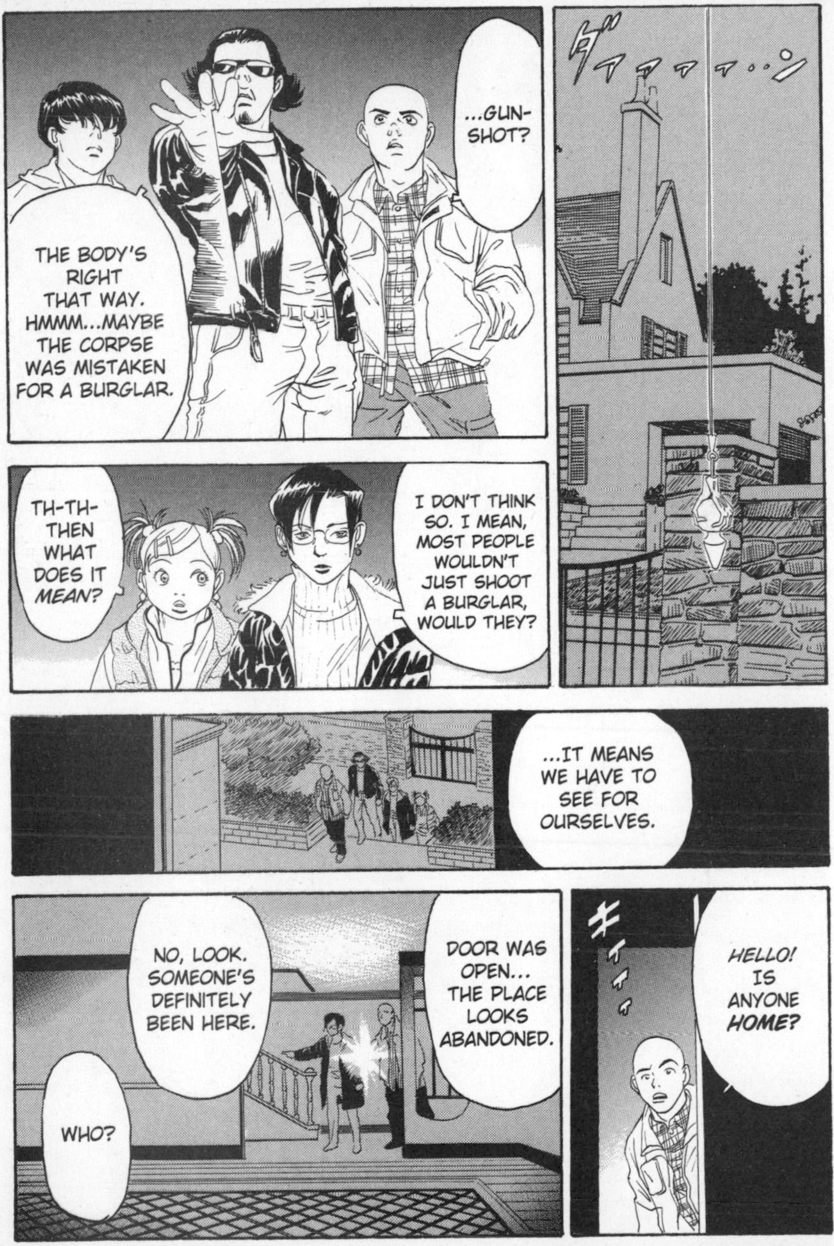
ダァァァァ・・ン
...GUN-SHOT?
THE BODY'S RIGHT THAT WAY. HMMM...MAYBE THE CORPSE WAS MISTAKEN FOR A BURGLAR.
I DON'T THINK SO. I MEAN, MOST PEOPLE WOULDN'T JUST SHOOT A BURGLAR, WOULD THEY?
TH-TH-THEN WHAT DOES IT *MEAN?*
...IT MEANS WE HAVE TO SEE FOR OURSELVES.
キィィィ
HELLO! IS ANYONE ***HOME?***
DOOR WAS OPEN... THE PLACE LOOKS ABANDONED.
NO, LOOK. SOMEONE'S DEFINITELY BEEN HERE.
WHO?

TOHYA FUJISAWA. HMM. NORMALLY, THE DEAD BLEED VERY LITTLE...

KYAAAA!

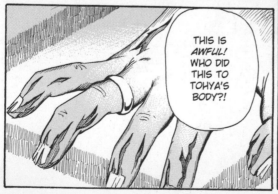

THIS IS *AWFUL!* WHO DID THIS TO TOHYA'S BODY?!

!!

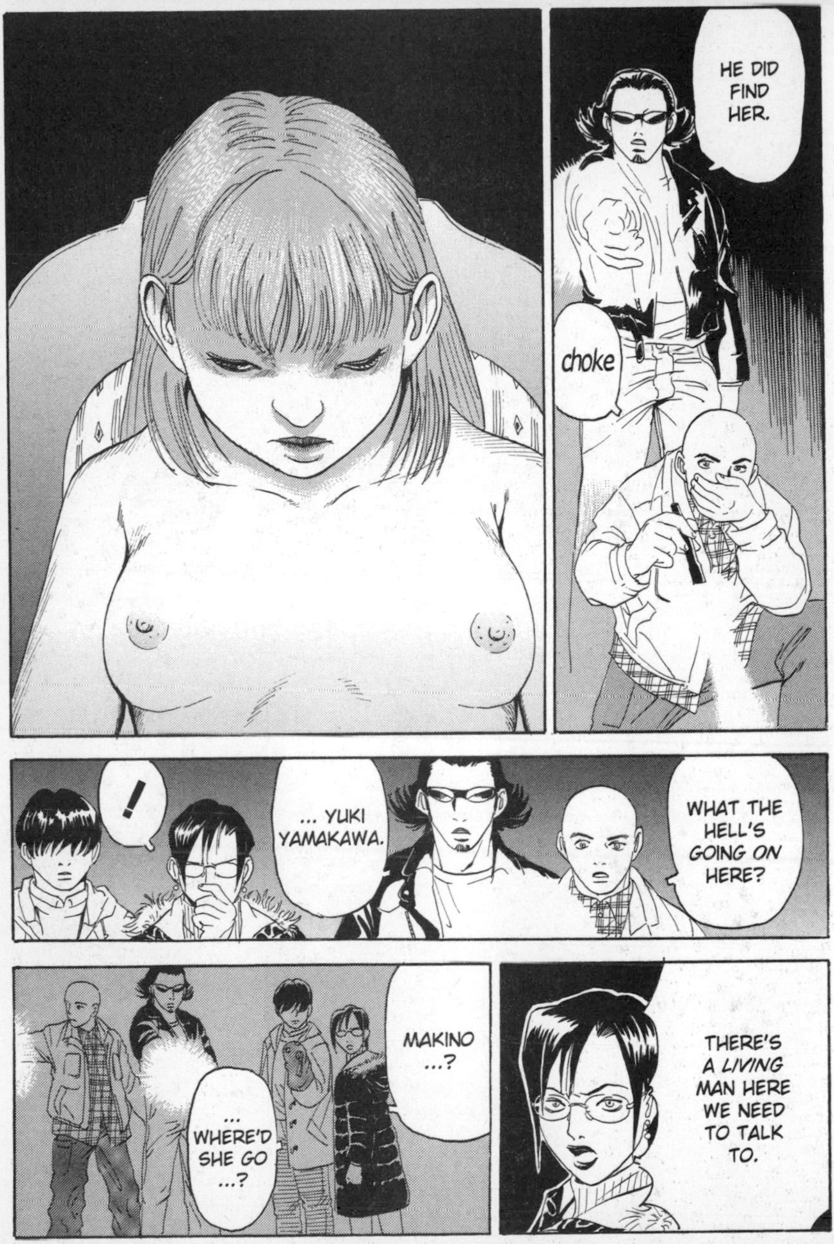
HE DID FIND HER.
choke
WHAT THE HELL'S GOING ON HERE?
... YUKI YAMAKAWA.
!
THERE'S A *LIVING* MAN HERE WE NEED TO TALK TO.
MAKINO ...?
... WHERE'D SHE GO ...?

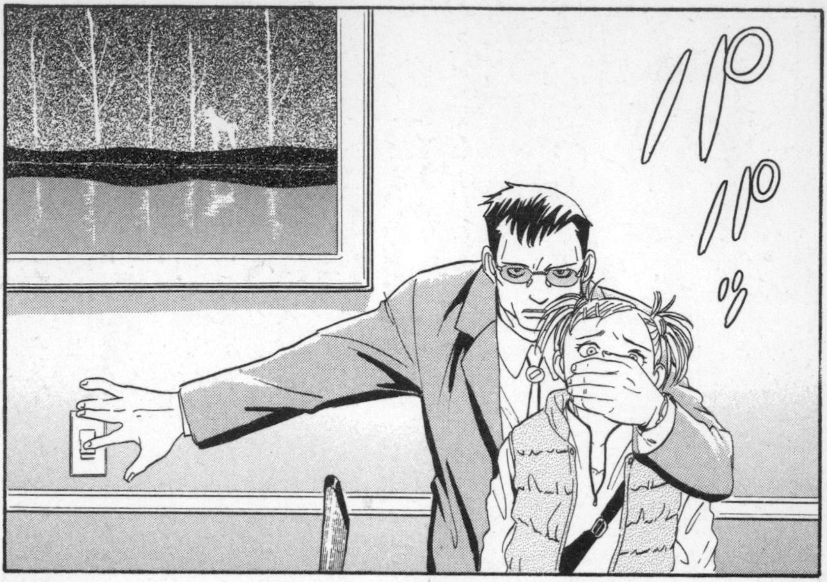
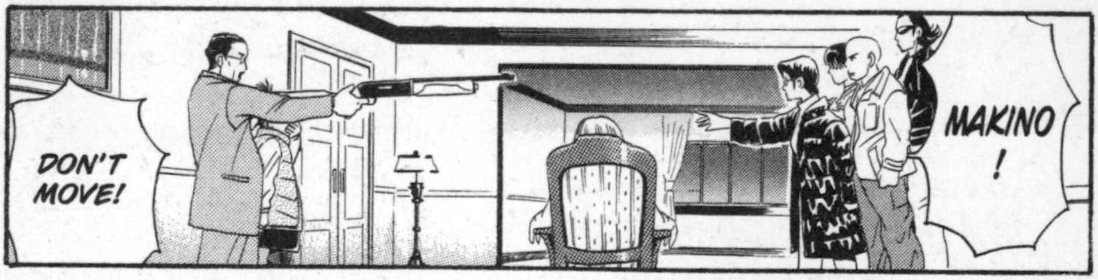
MAKINO!
DON'T MOVE!
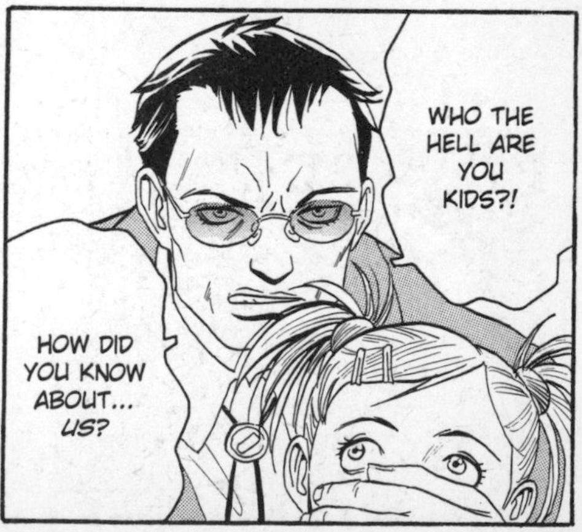
WHO THE HELL ARE YOU KIDS?!
HOW DID YOU KNOW ABOUT... US?
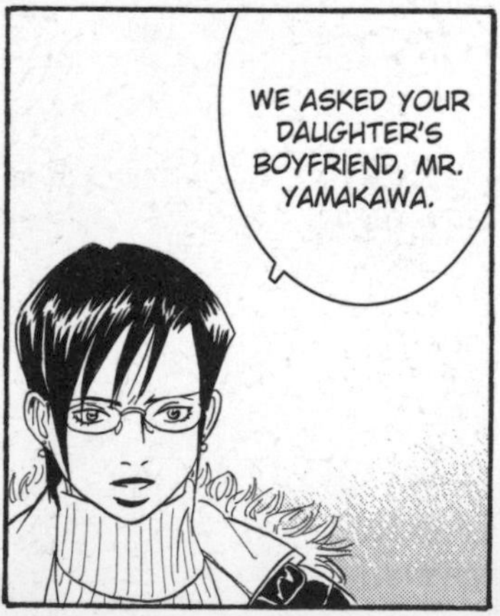
WE ASKED YOUR DAUGHTER'S BOYFRIEND, MR. YAMAKAWA.

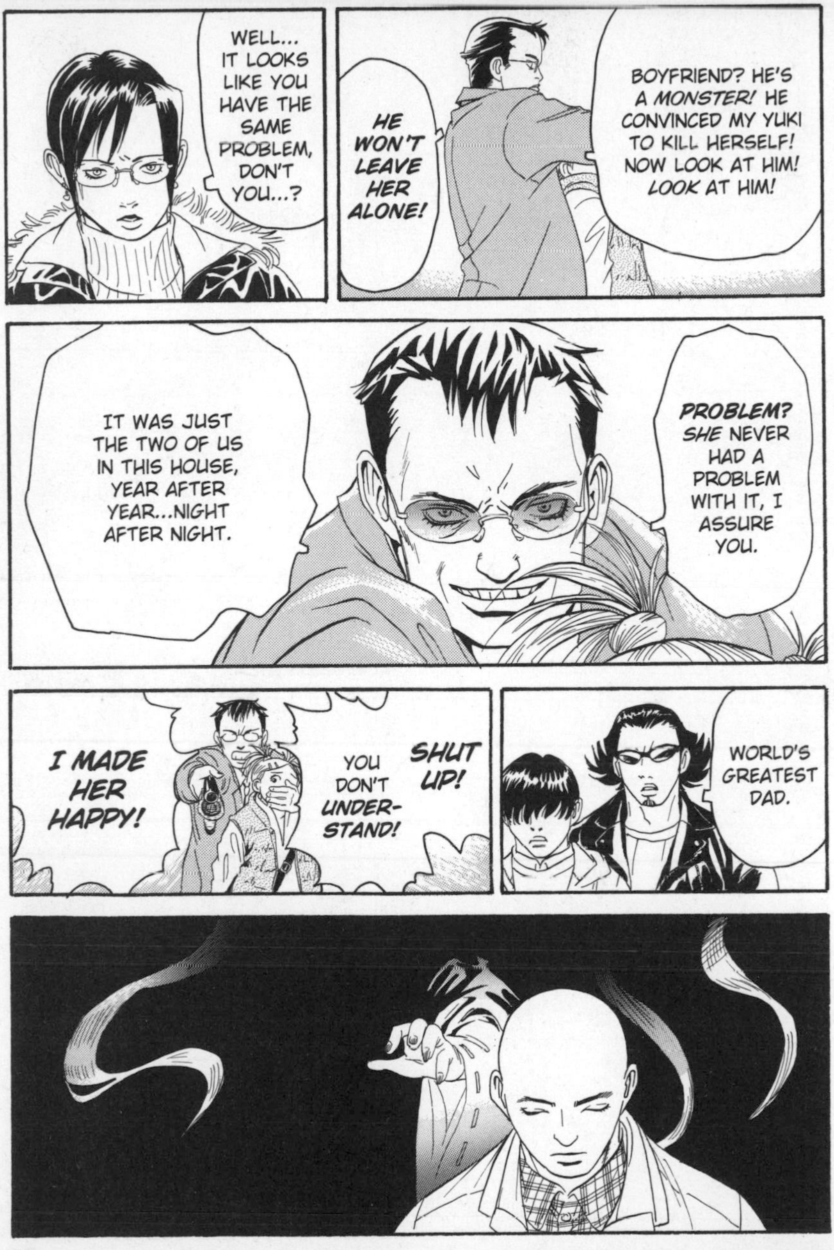
BOYFRIEND? HE'S A *MONSTER!* HE CONVINCED MY YUKI TO KILL HERSELF! NOW LOOK AT HIM! *LOOK* AT HIM!
HE WON'T LEAVE HER ALONE!
WELL... IT LOOKS LIKE YOU HAVE THE SAME PROBLEM, DON'T YOU...?
PROBLEM? SHE NEVER HAD A PROBLEM WITH IT, I ASSURE YOU.
IT WAS JUST THE TWO OF US IN THIS HOUSE, YEAR AFTER YEAR...NIGHT AFTER NIGHT.
WORLD'S GREATEST DAD.
SHUT UP!
YOU DON'T UNDER-STAND!
I MADE HER HAPPY!

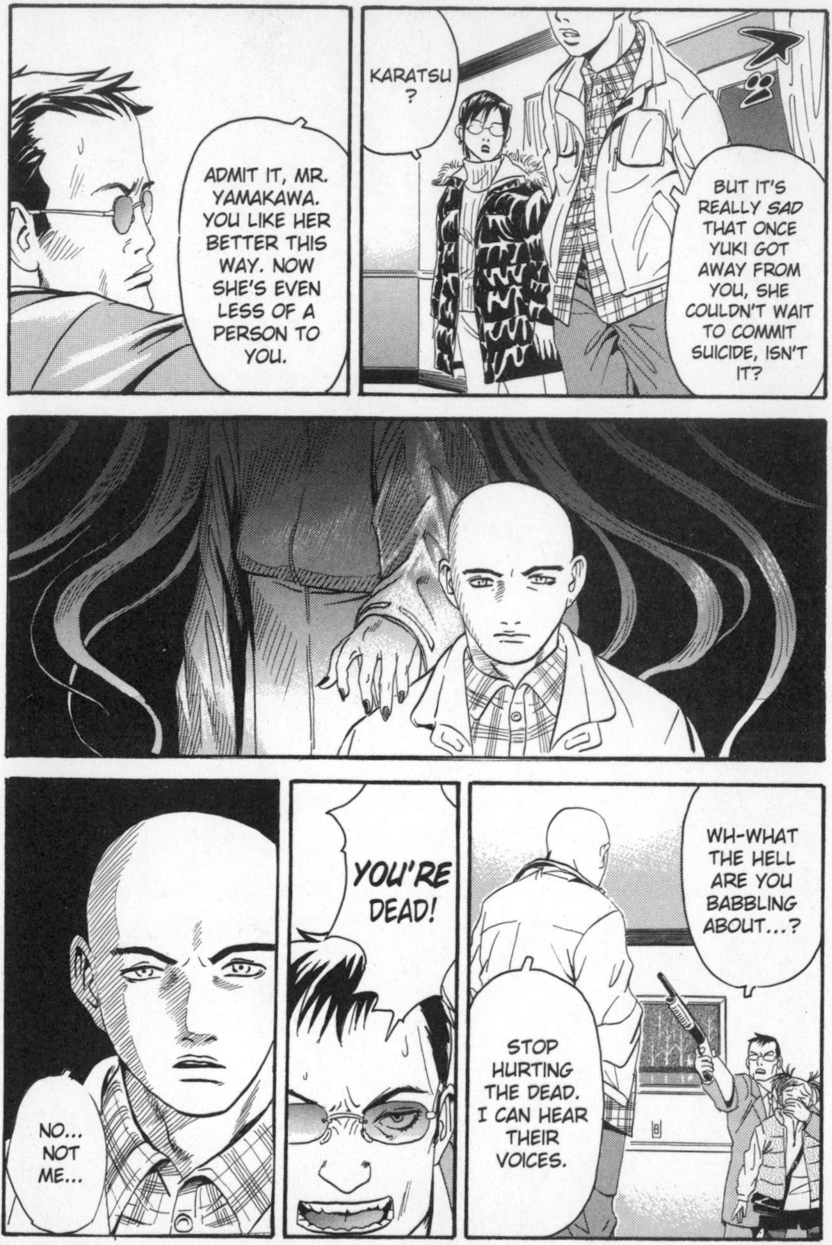
KARATSU?
BUT IT'S REALLY SAD THAT ONCE YUKI GOT AWAY FROM YOU, SHE COULDN'T WAIT TO COMMIT SUICIDE, ISN'T IT?
ADMIT IT, MR. YAMAKAWA. YOU LIKE HER BETTER THIS WAY. NOW SHE'S EVEN LESS OF A PERSON TO YOU.
WH-WHAT THE HELL ARE YOU BABBLING ABOUT...?
STOP HURTING THE DEAD. I CAN HEAR THEIR VOICES.
YOU'RE DEAD!
NO... NOT ME...

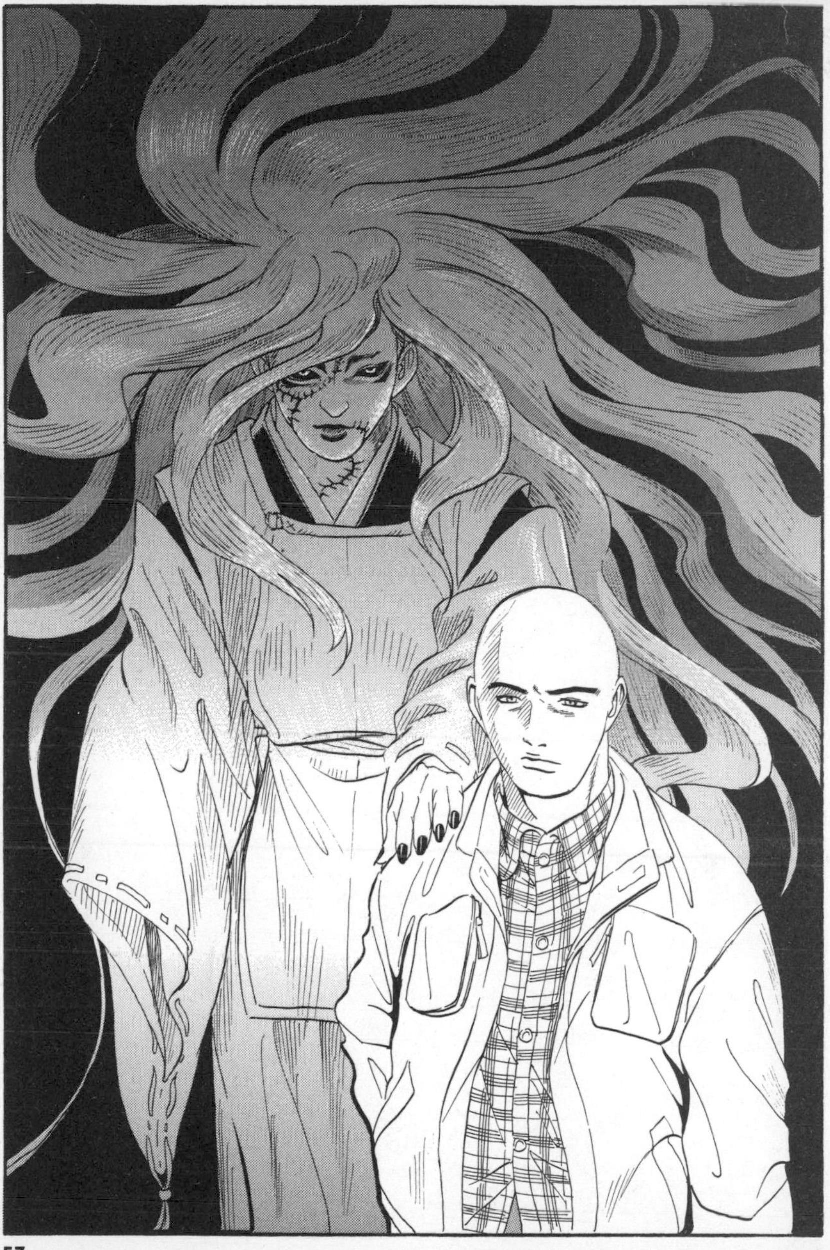

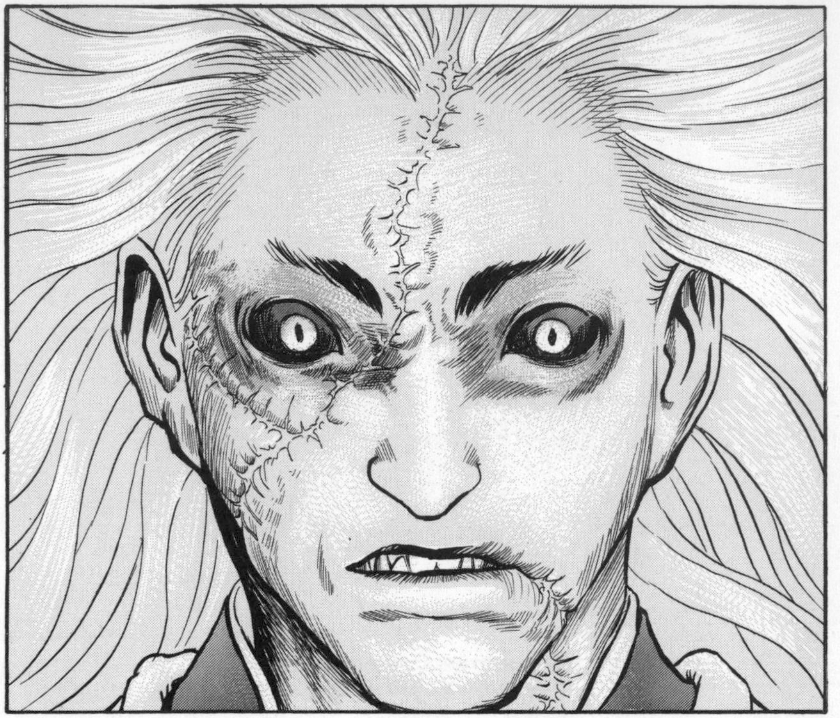

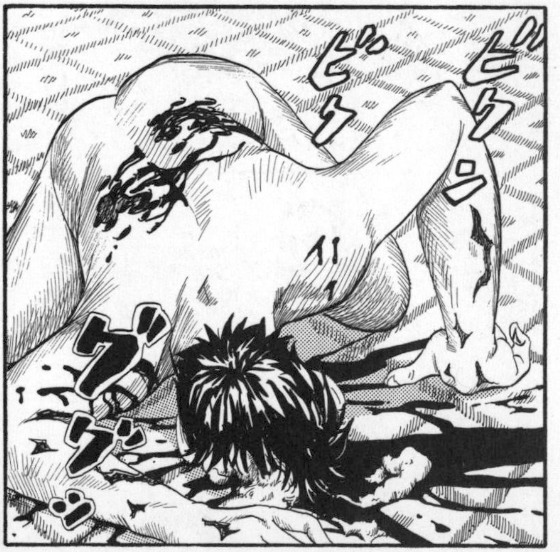

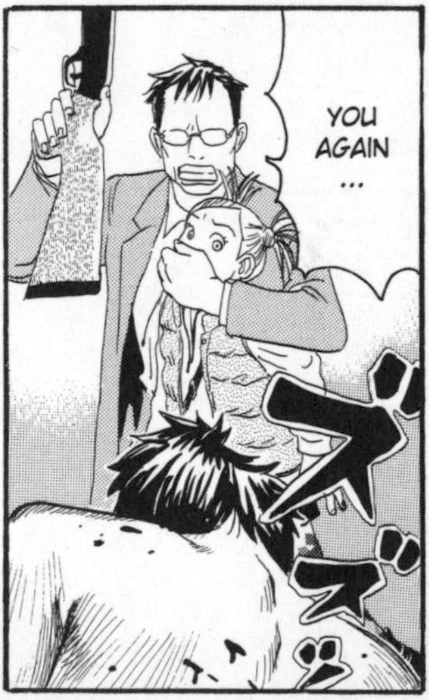
YOU AGAIN ...

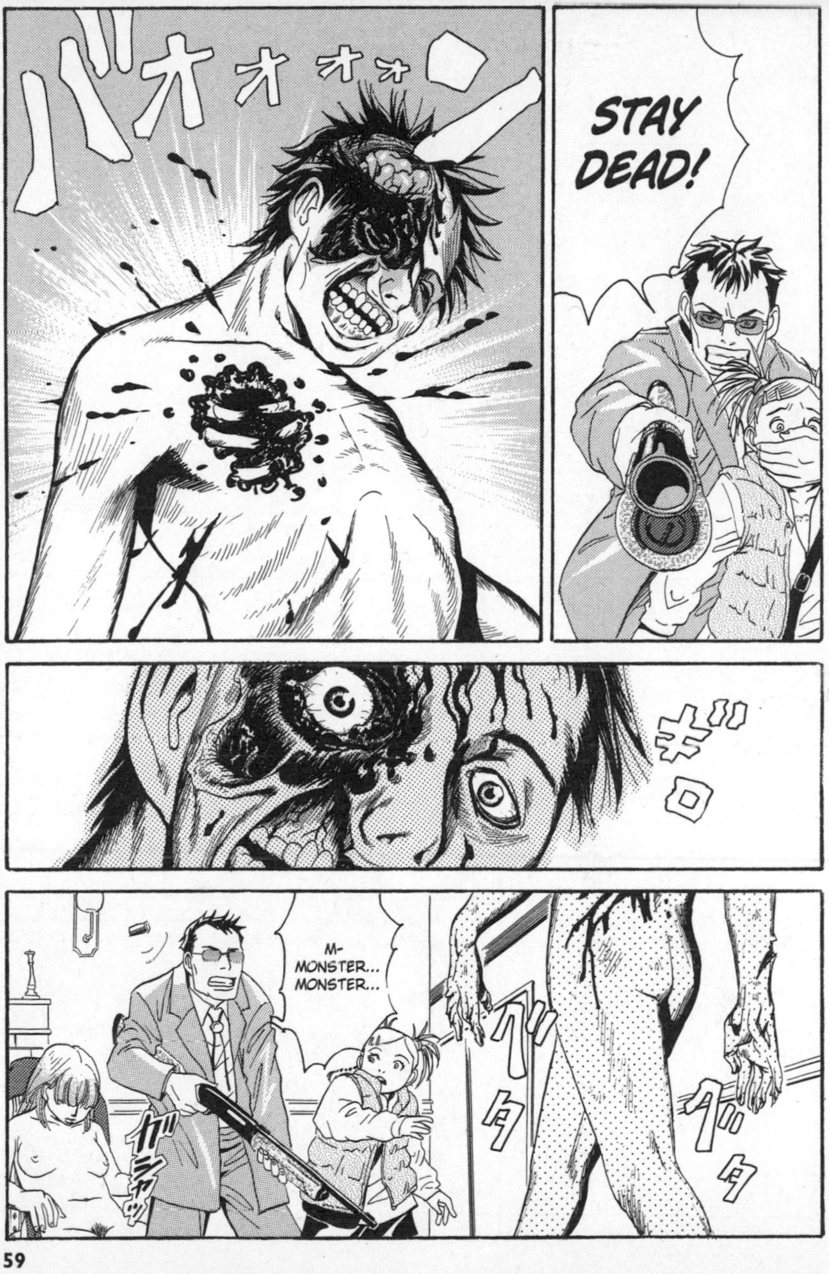
STAY DEAD!
バオオオォ
ギロ
M- MONSTER... MONSTER...
ガシャッ
グタ
グタ

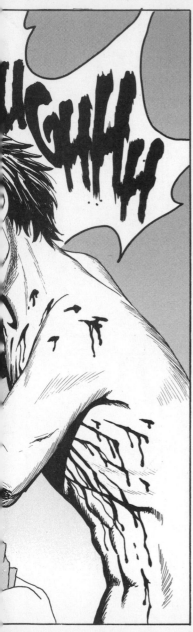

...Yuki?

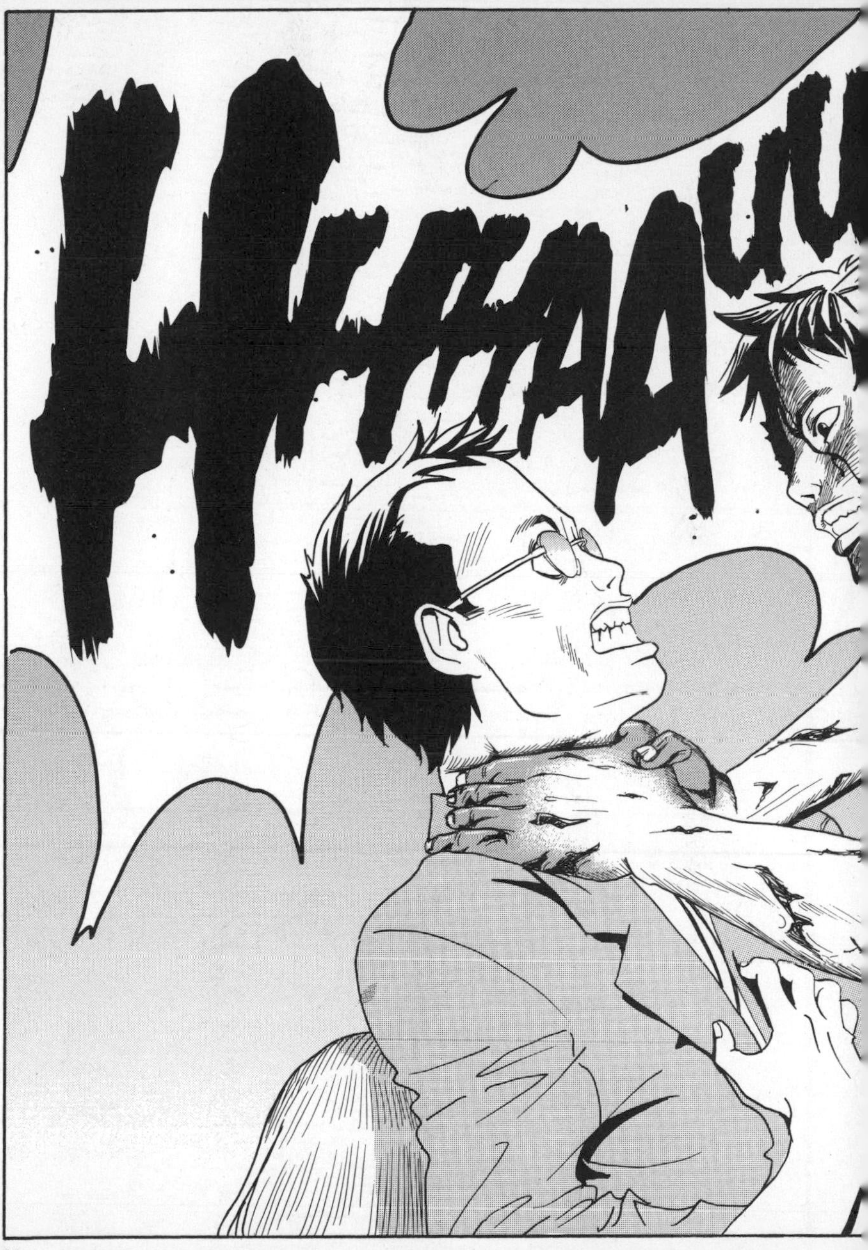
HAAAUU

hhhh hkkk ...
ハッ
ポロッ
ゲボロロッ
ベタタ
ドッ

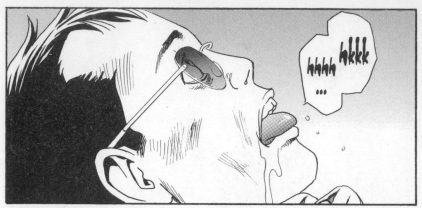

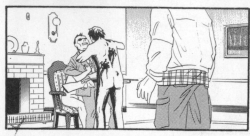

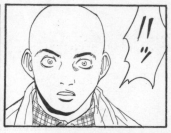

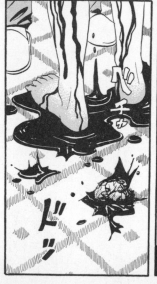

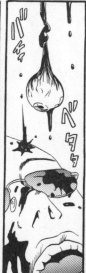

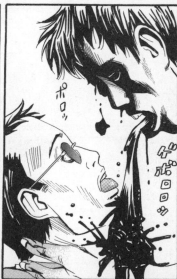

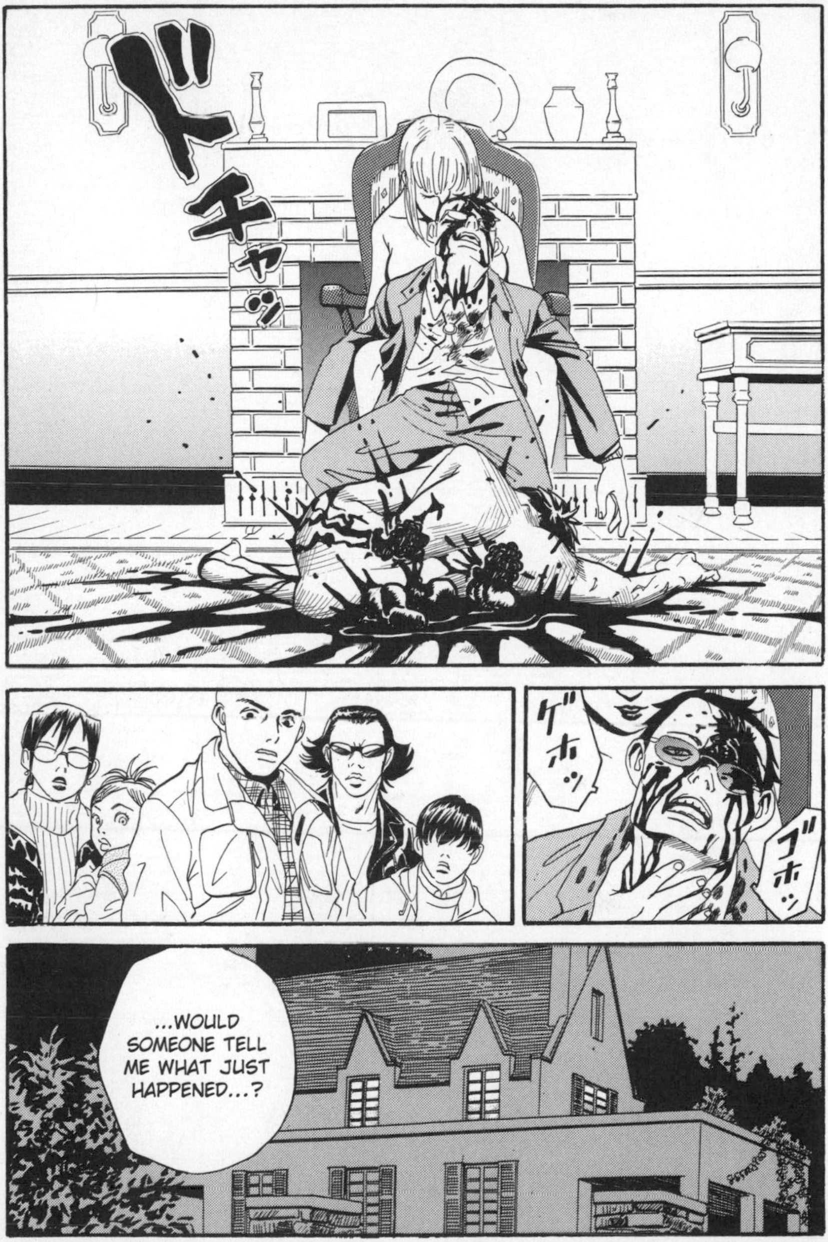
ドチャッ
ゴホッ
ゲホッ
...WOULD SOMEONE TELL ME WHAT JUST HAPPENED...?

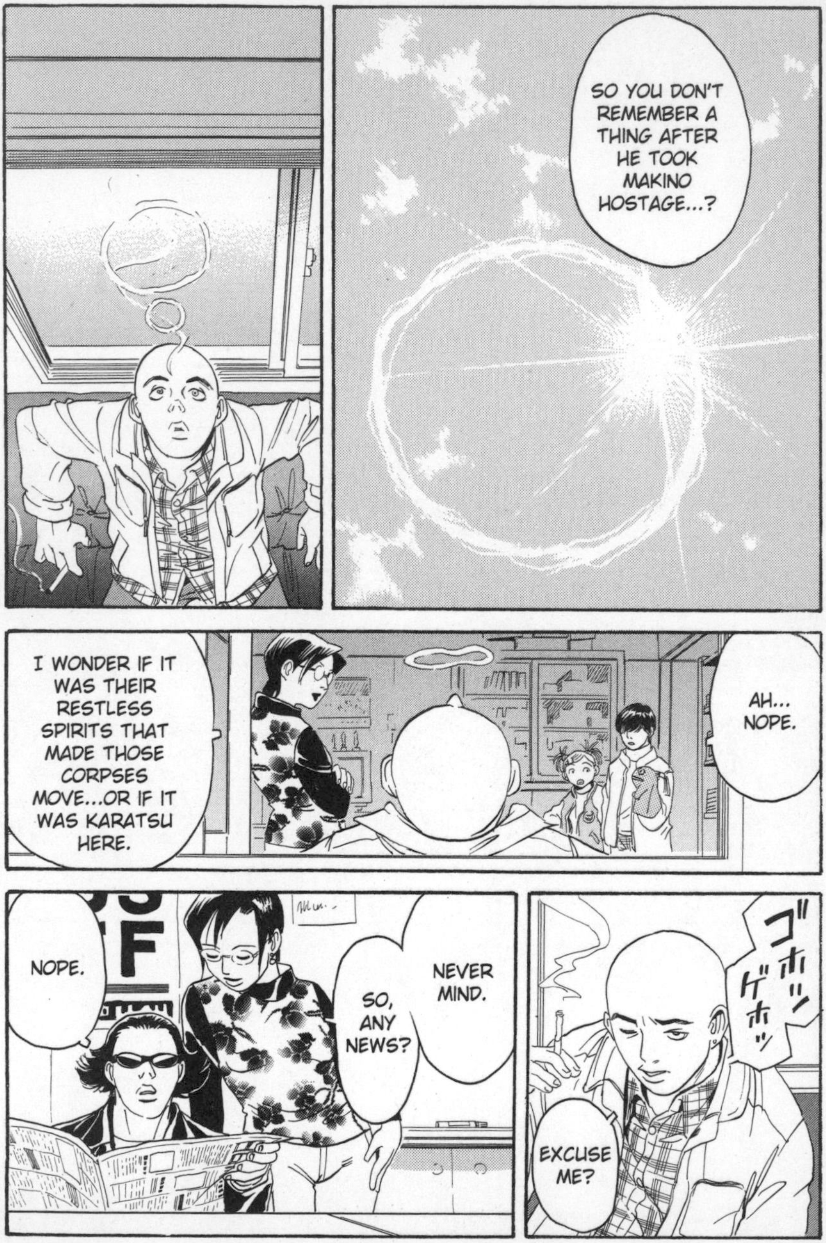
SO YOU DON'T REMEMBER A THING AFTER HE TOOK MAKINO HOSTAGE...?
AH... NOPE.
I WONDER IF IT WAS THEIR RESTLESS SPIRITS THAT MADE THOSE CORPSES MOVE...OR IF IT WAS KARATSU HERE.
ゴホッ
ゲホッ
EXCUSE ME?
NEVER MIND.
SO, ANY NEWS?
NOPE.

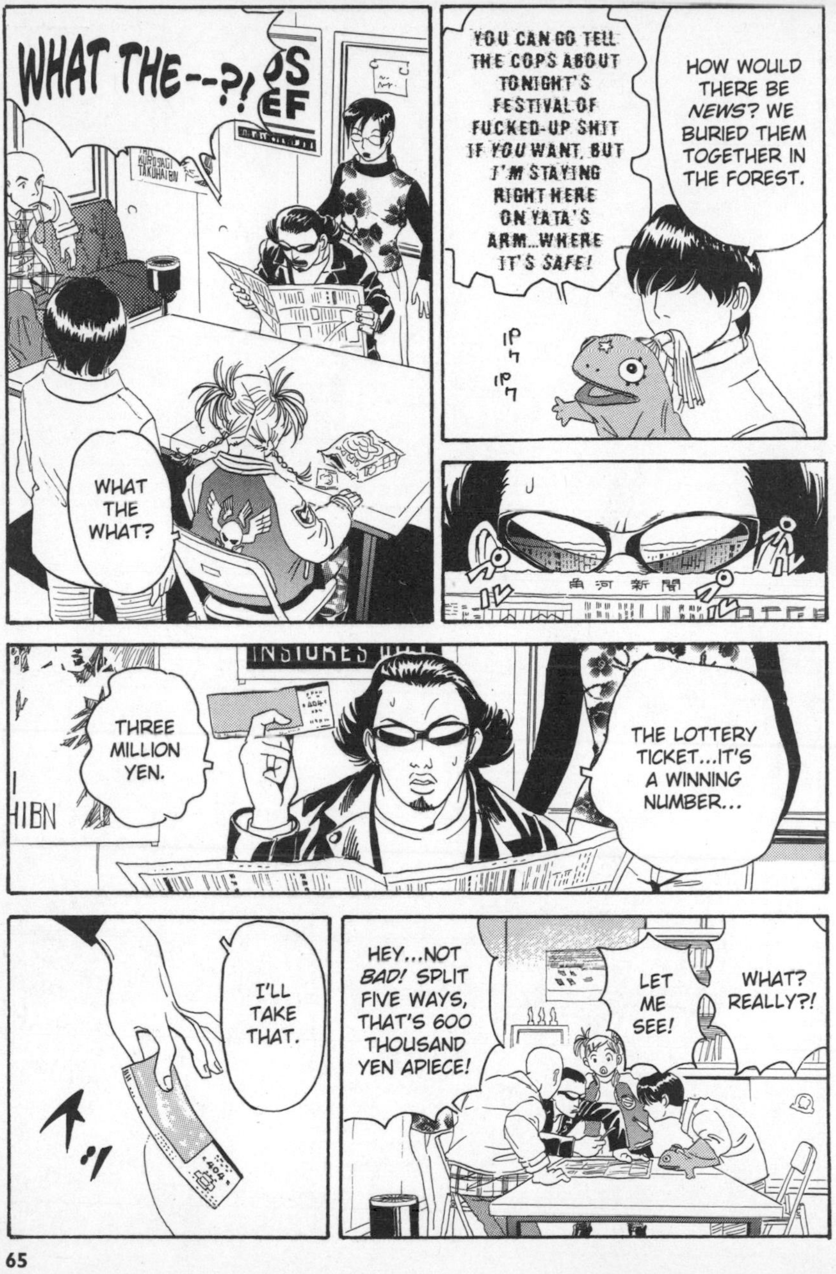
HOW WOULD THERE BE *NEWS*? WE BURIED THEM TOGETHER IN THE FOREST.
YOU CAN GO TELL THE COPS ABOUT TONIGHT'S FESTIVAL OF FUCKED-UP SHIT IF *YOU* WANT, BUT *I'M* STAYING RIGHT HERE ON YATA'S ARM...WHERE IT'S *SAFE!*
パク パク
角河新聞
WHAT THE--?!
WHAT THE WHAT?
THE LOTTERY TICKET...IT'S A WINNING NUMBER...
THREE MILLION YEN.
WHAT? REALLY?!
LET ME SEE!
HEY...NOT *BAD!* SPLIT FIVE WAYS, THAT'S 600 THOUSAND YEN APIECE!
I'LL TAKE THAT.

WE *CAN'T* GO AROUND EXPLAINING TO PEOPLE WHAT WE CAN DO...LET ALONE GET PAID FOR DOING IT.

NOT TO *LIVING* PEOPLE, THAT IS. BUT A *DEAD* MAN NOT ONLY CONFIDED IN US, HE ARRANGED A KARMIC PAYOFF.

HUNDREDS OF PEOPLE DIE IN THIS COUNTRY EVERY DAY. HOW MANY DIE THE WAY THEY WANTED TO...WITH ALL THEIR WISHES FULFILLED?

I SAY WE USE THIS MONEY AS START-UP CAPITAL...AND FIND THE OTHERS ALL AROUND US WHO NEED A LAST SERVICE FOR THEIR BODIES...

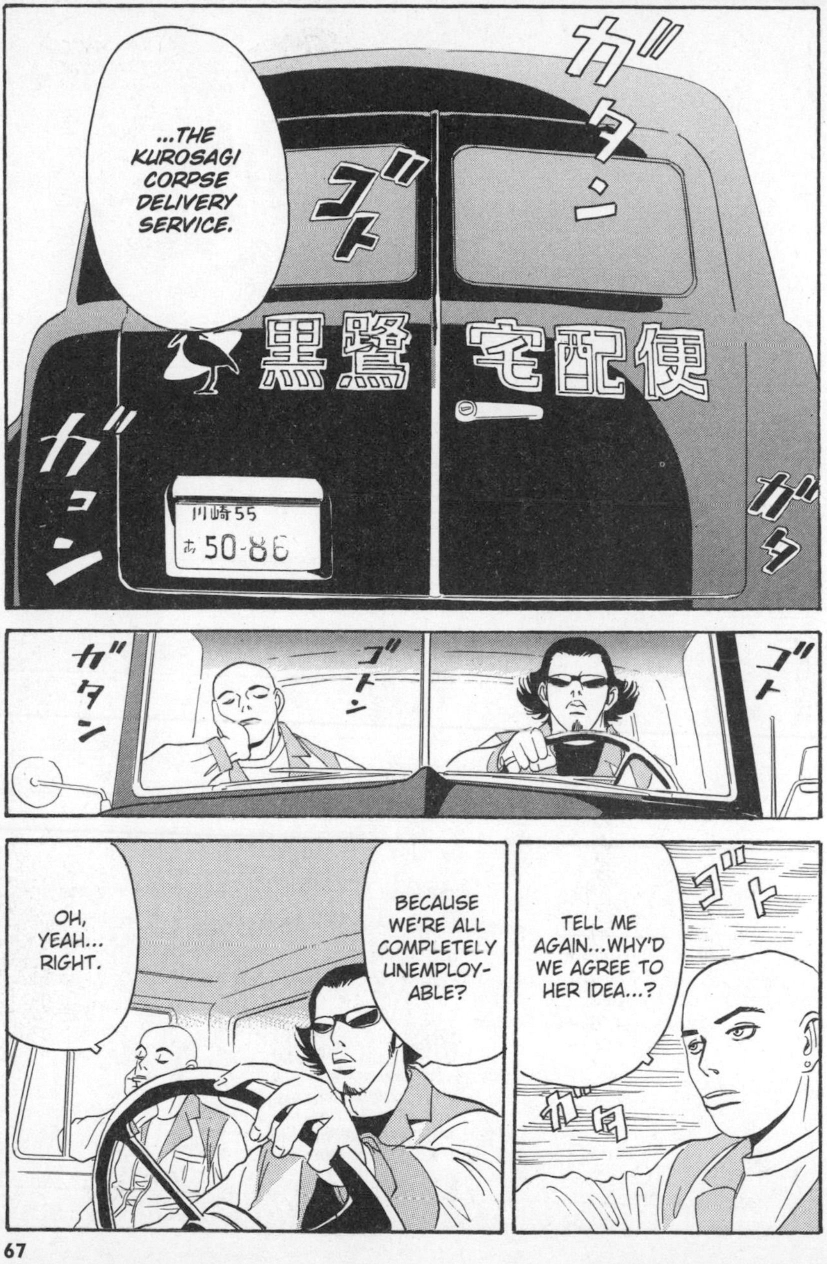
...THE KUROSAGI CORPSE DELIVERY SERVICE.
ガタン
ゴト
黒鷺 宅配便
ガッコン
ガタ
川崎55
あ 50-86
ゴト
ゴトン
ガタン
ゴト
TELL ME AGAIN...WHY'D WE AGREE TO HER IDEA...?
ガタ
BECAUSE WE'RE ALL COMPLETELY UNEMPLOY-ABLE?
OH, YEAH... RIGHT.

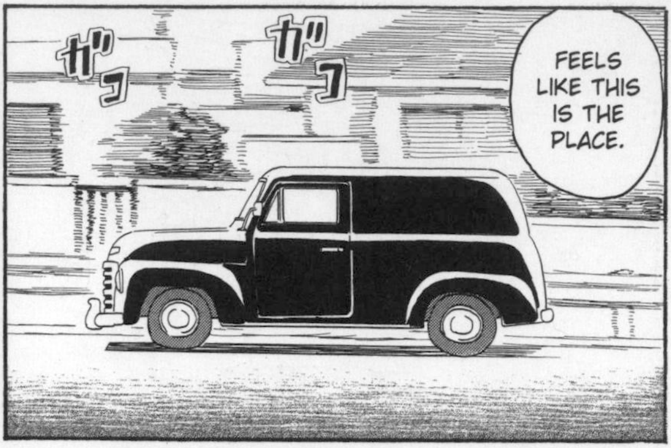
ガコ
ガコ
FEELS LIKE THIS IS THE PLACE.

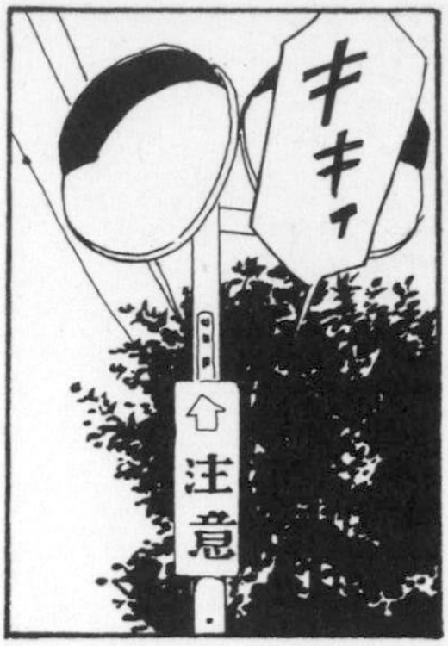
キキィ
注意

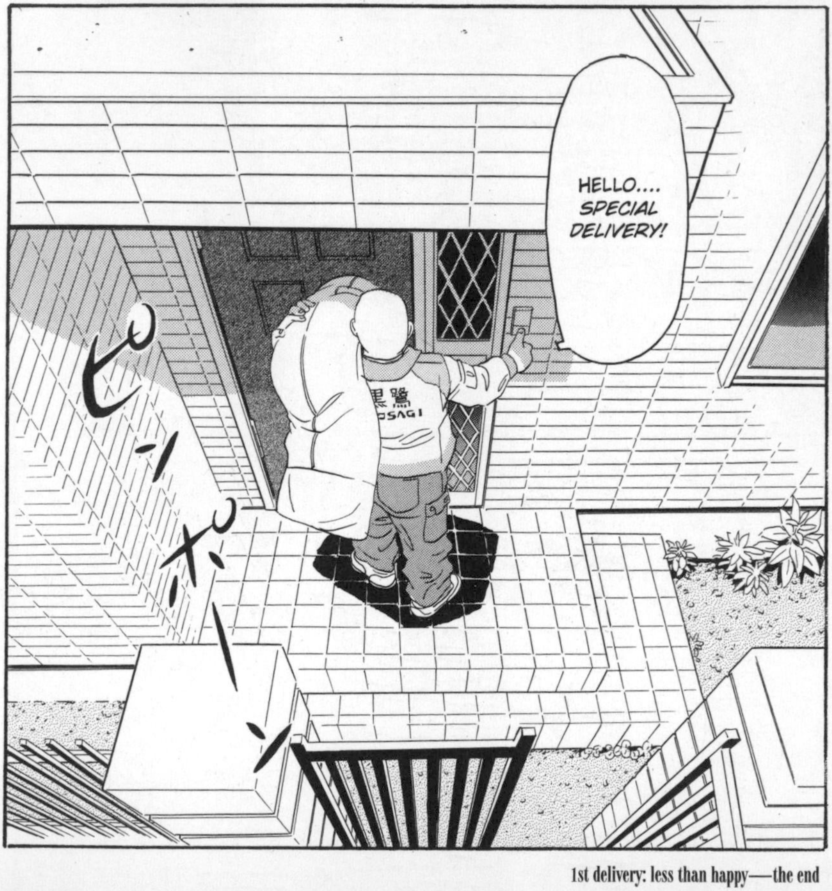
HELLO.... SPECIAL DELIVERY!
ピンポーン
黒鷺

1st delivery: less than happy—the end

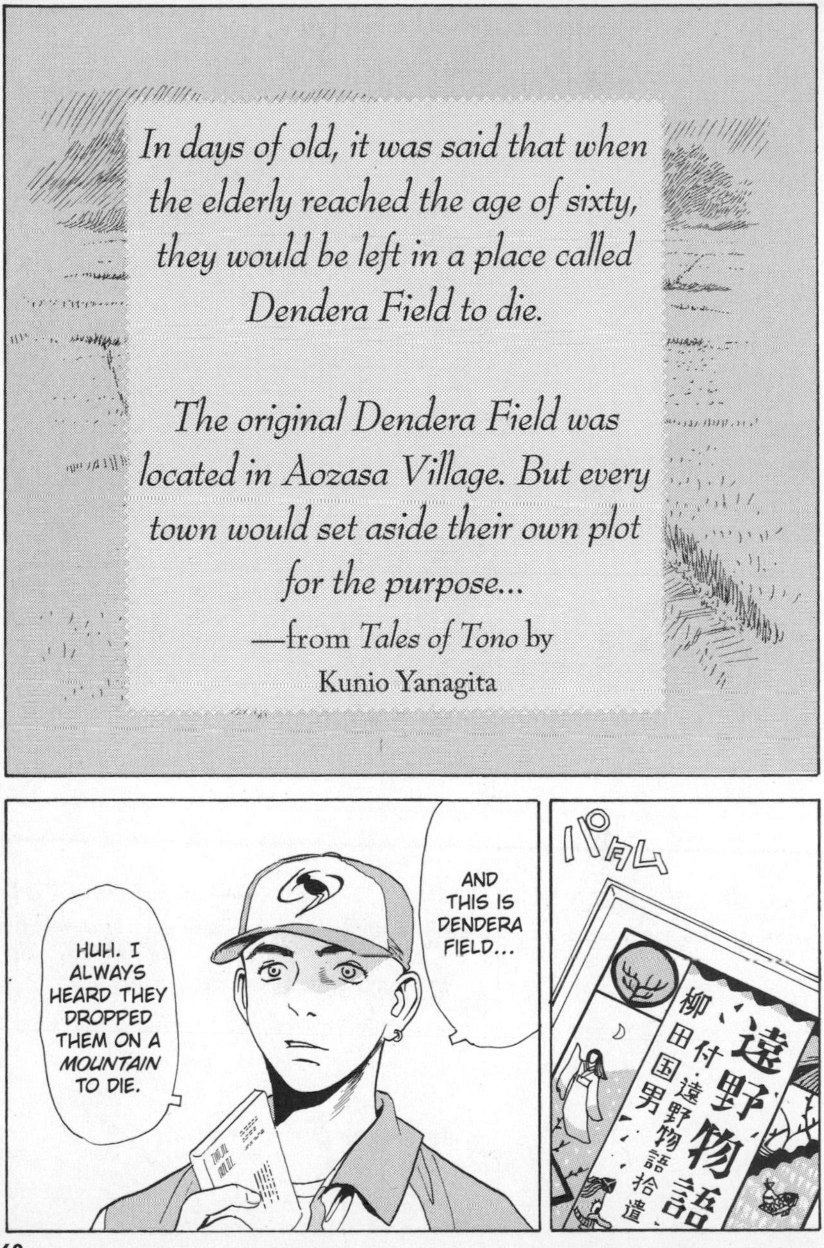
In days of old, it was said that when the elderly reached the age of sixty, they would be left in a place called Dendera Field to die.
The original Dendera Field was located in Aozasa Village. But every town would set aside their own plot for the purpose...
—from *Tales of Tono* by Kunio Yanagita
パタム
遠野物語
付・遠野物語拾遺
柳田国男
AND THIS IS DENDERA FIELD...
HUH. I ALWAYS HEARD THEY DROPPED THEM ON A *MOUNTAIN* TO DIE.

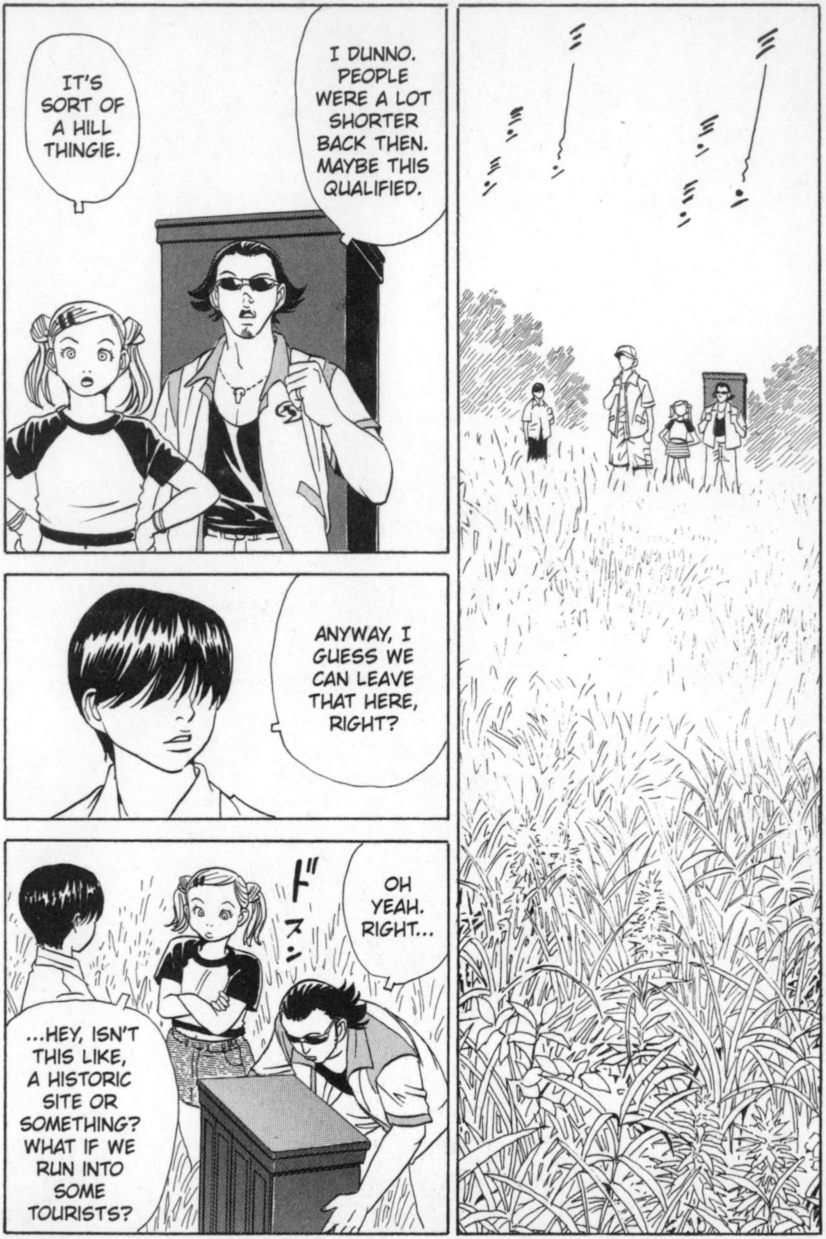
I DUNNO. PEOPLE WERE A LOT SHORTER BACK THEN. MAYBE THIS QUALIFIED.
IT'S SORT OF A HILL THINGIE.
ANYWAY, I GUESS WE CAN LEAVE THAT HERE, RIGHT?
OH YEAH. RIGHT...
ドスン
...HEY, ISN'T THIS LIKE, A HISTORIC SITE OR SOMETHING? WHAT IF WE RUN INTO SOME TOURISTS?

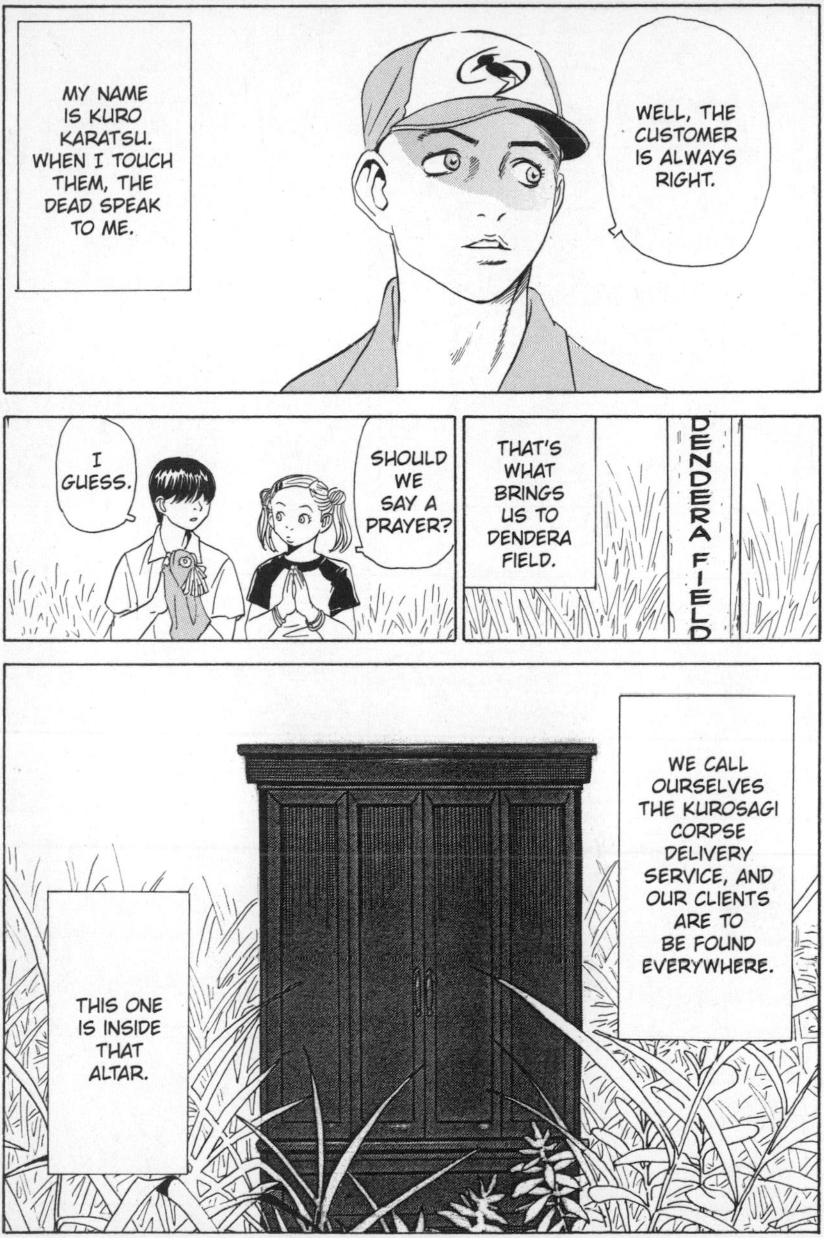
WELL, THE CUSTOMER IS ALWAYS RIGHT.
MY NAME IS KURO KARATSU. WHEN I TOUCH THEM, THE DEAD SPEAK TO ME.
DENDERA FIELD
THAT'S WHAT BRINGS US TO DENDERA FIELD.
SHOULD WE SAY A PRAYER?
I GUESS.
WE CALL OURSELVES THE KUROSAGI CORPSE DELIVERY SERVICE, AND OUR CLIENTS ARE TO BE FOUND EVERYWHERE.
THIS ONE IS INSIDE THAT ALTAR.

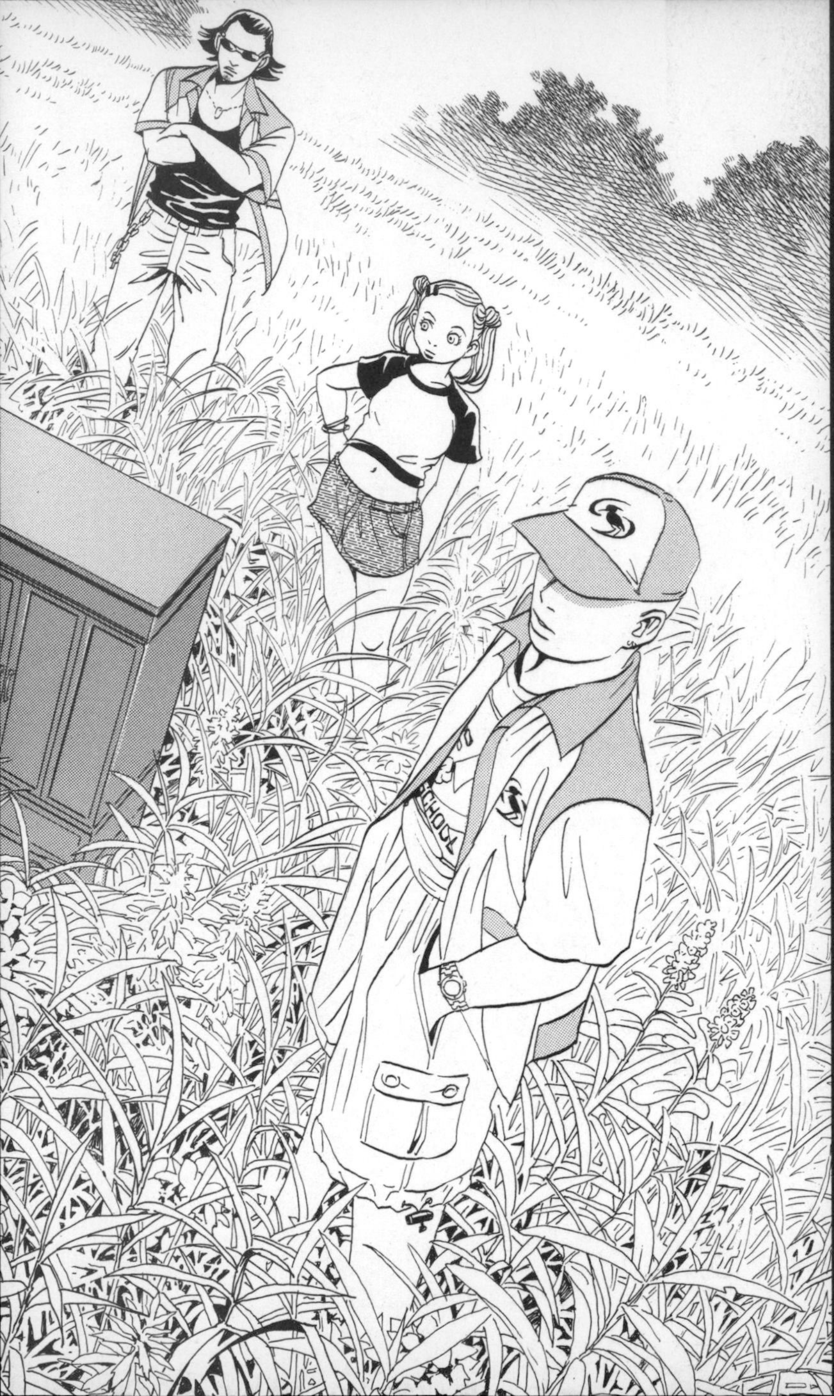

lonely people

2nd doll:
ロンリィ・ピーポー

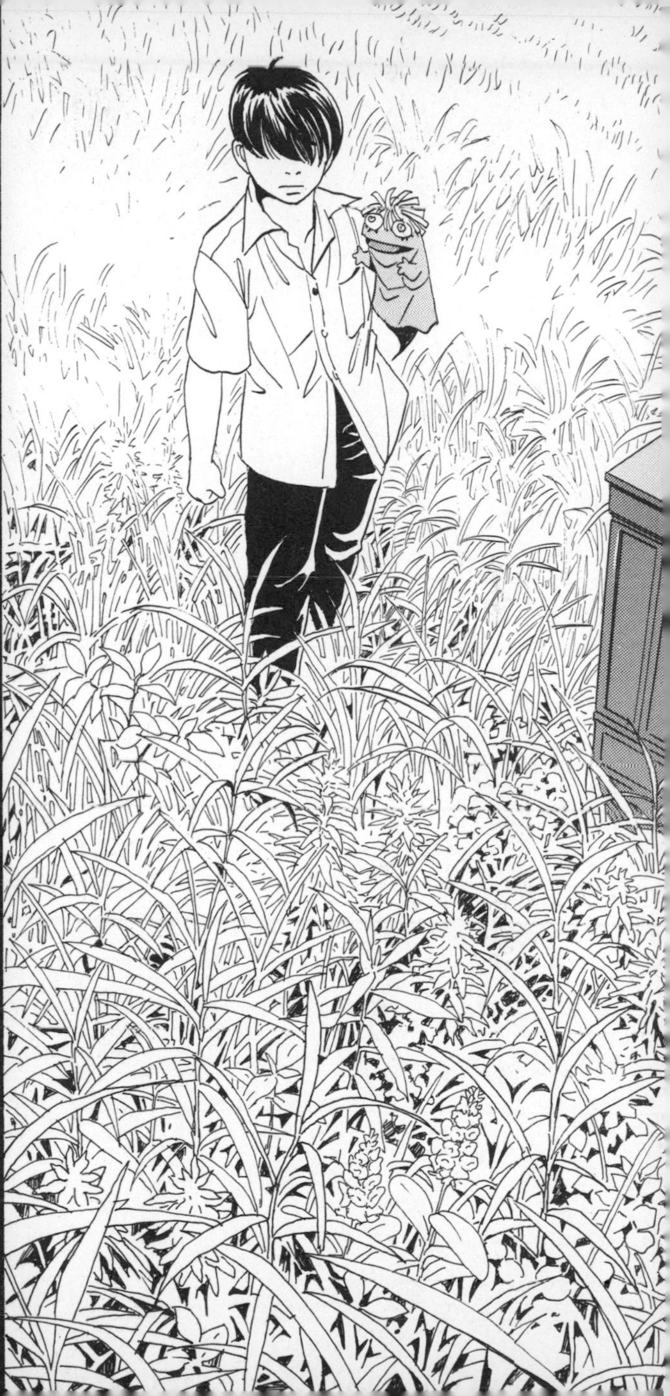

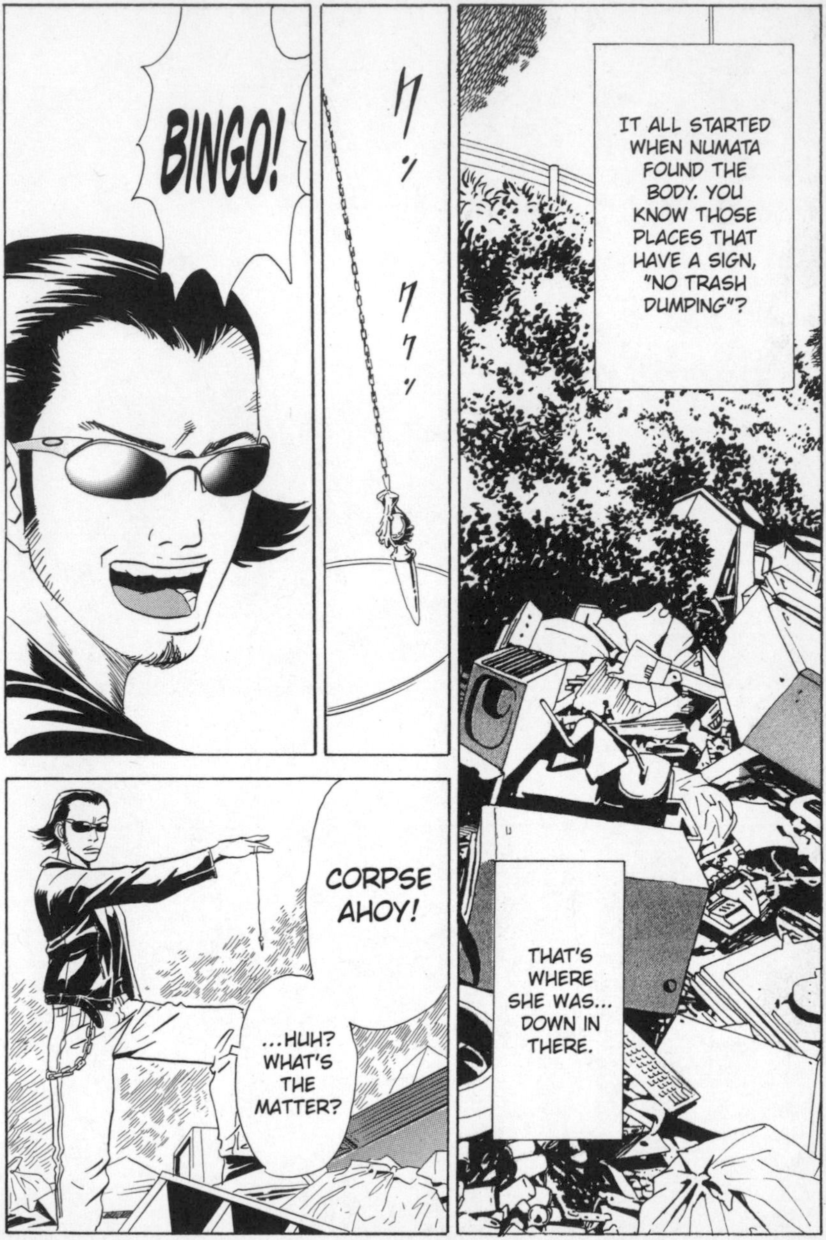
IT ALL STARTED WHEN NUMATA FOUND THE BODY. YOU KNOW THOSE PLACES THAT HAVE A SIGN, "NO TRASH DUMPING"?
THAT'S WHERE SHE WAS... DOWN IN THERE.
クッ
ククッ
BINGO!
CORPSE AHOY!
...HUH? WHAT'S THE MATTER?

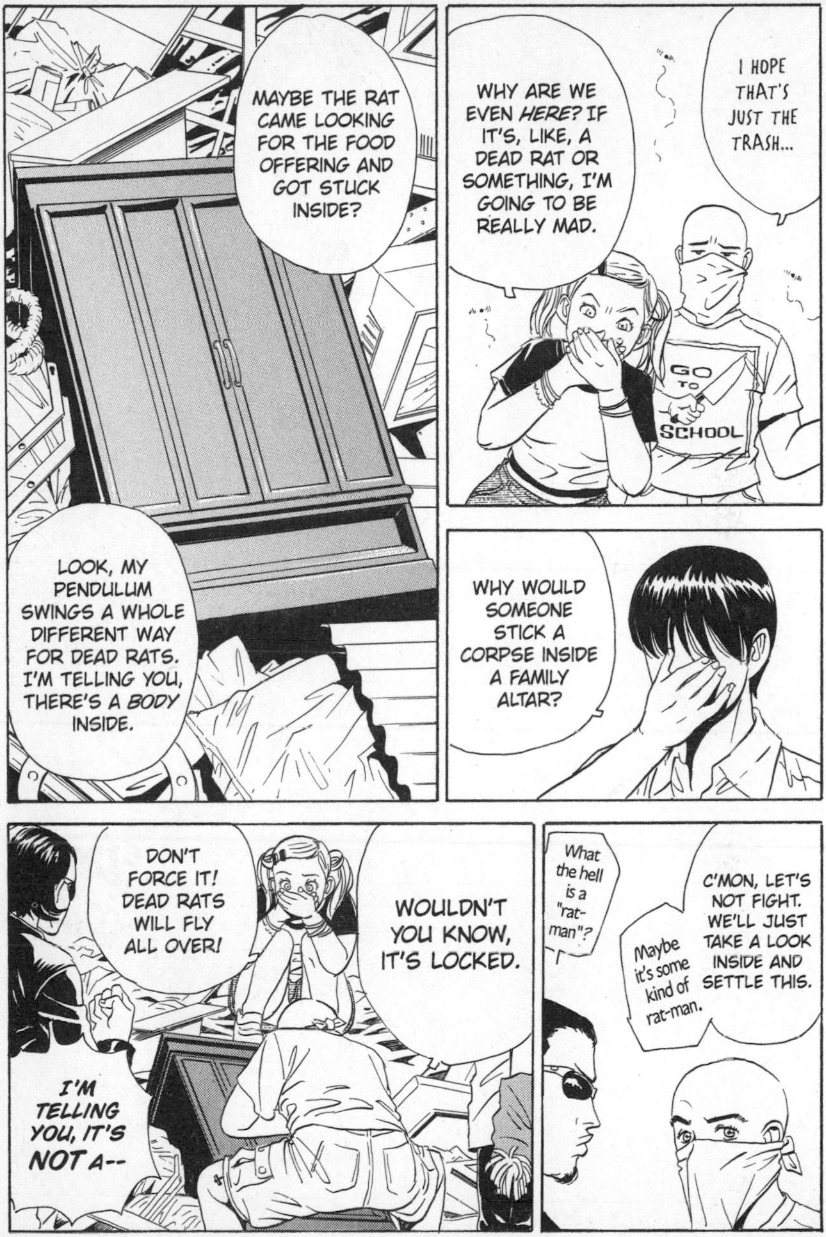
I HOPE THAT'S JUST THE TRASH...
WHY ARE WE EVEN *HERE*? IF IT'S, LIKE, A DEAD RAT OR SOMETHING, I'M GOING TO BE REALLY MAD.
GO TO SCHOOL
WHY WOULD SOMEONE STICK A CORPSE INSIDE A FAMILY ALTAR?
MAYBE THE RAT CAME LOOKING FOR THE FOOD OFFERING AND GOT STUCK INSIDE?
LOOK, MY PENDULUM SWINGS A WHOLE DIFFERENT WAY FOR DEAD RATS. I'M TELLING YOU, THERE'S A *BODY* INSIDE.
C'MON, LET'S NOT FIGHT. WE'LL JUST TAKE A LOOK INSIDE AND SETTLE THIS.
Maybe it's some kind of rat-man.
What the hell is a "rat-man"?
WOULDN'T YOU KNOW, IT'S LOCKED.
DON'T FORCE IT! DEAD RATS WILL FLY ALL OVER!
I'M TELLING YOU, IT'S ***NOT*** *A--*

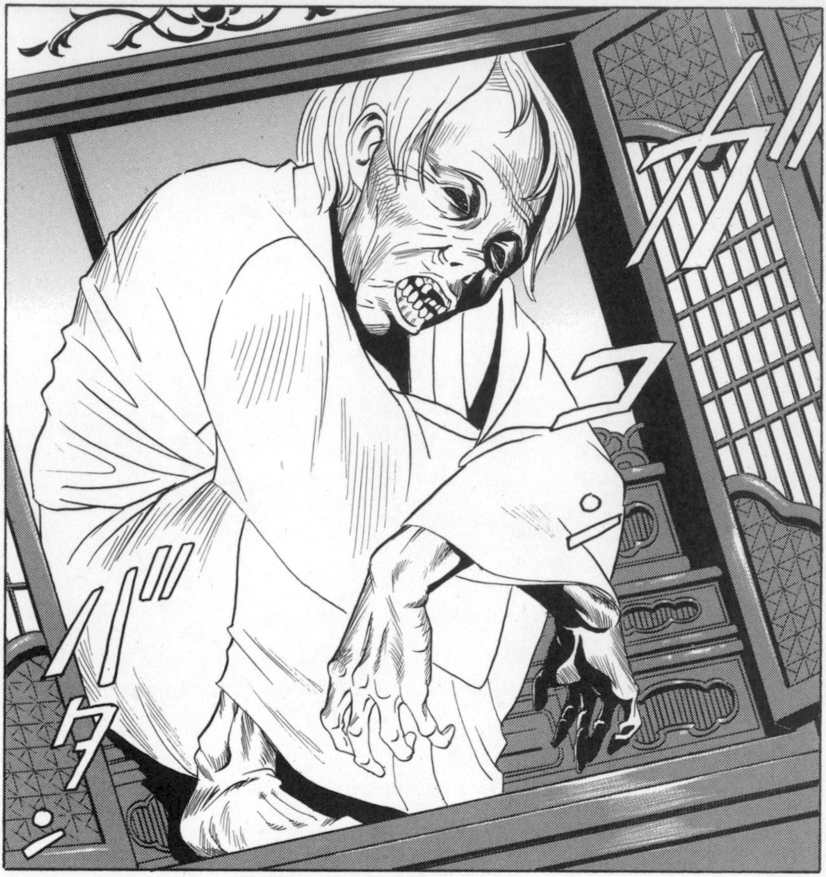

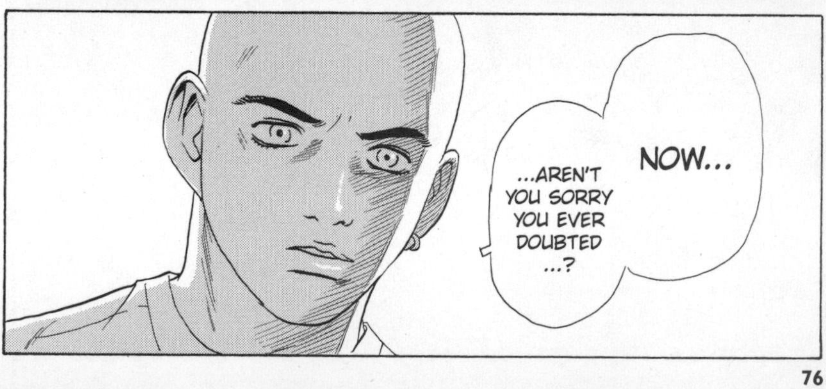
NOW...
...AREN'T YOU SORRY YOU EVER DOUBTED ...?

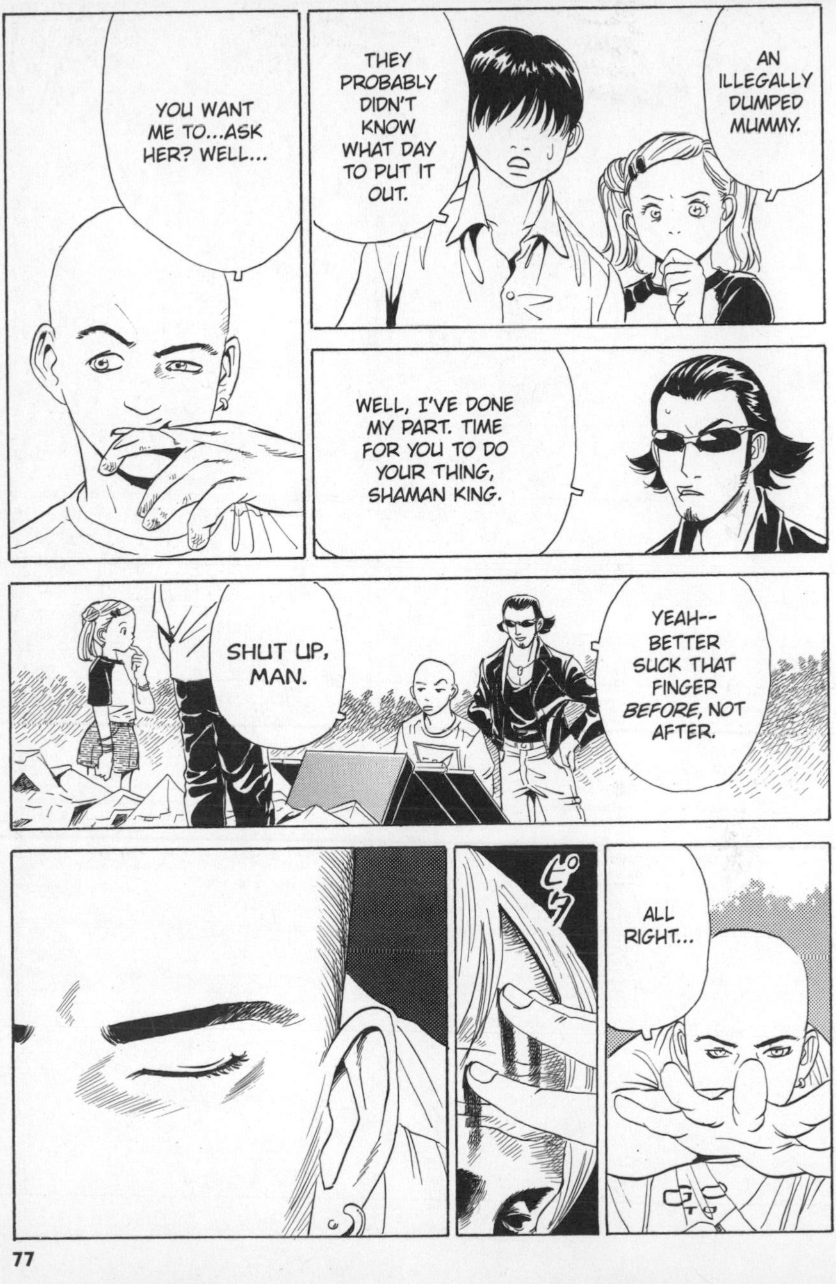
AN ILLEGALLY DUMPED MUMMY.
THEY PROBABLY DIDN'T KNOW WHAT DAY TO PUT IT OUT.
WELL, I'VE DONE MY PART. TIME FOR YOU TO DO YOUR THING, SHAMAN KING.
YOU WANT ME TO...ASK HER? WELL...
YEAH-- BETTER SUCK THAT FINGER *BEFORE*, NOT AFTER.
SHUT UP, MAN.
ALL RIGHT...

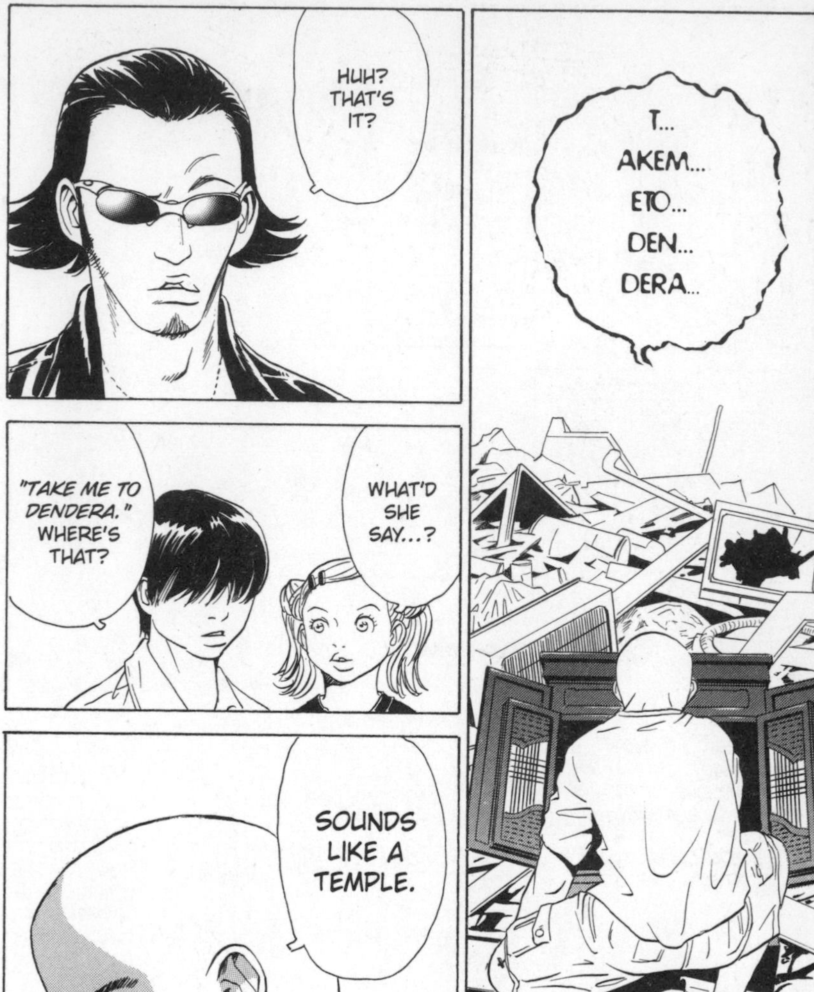
T... AKEM... ETO... DEN... DERA...
HUH? THAT'S IT?
WHAT'D SHE SAY...?
"TAKE ME TO DENDERA." WHERE'S THAT?
SOUNDS LIKE A TEMPLE.

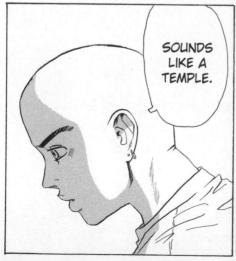

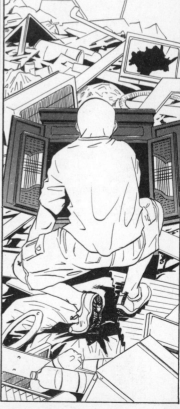

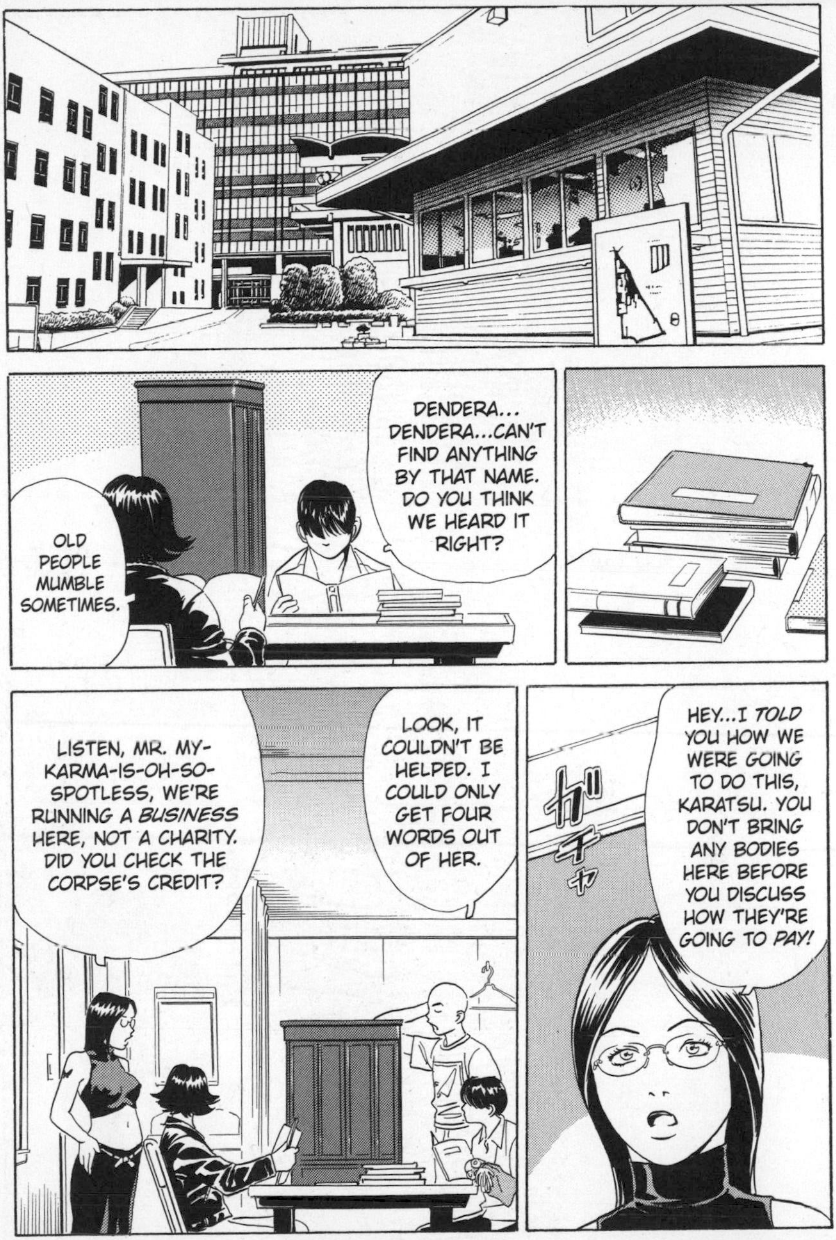
DENDERA... DENDERA...CAN'T FIND ANYTHING BY THAT NAME. DO YOU THINK WE HEARD IT RIGHT?
OLD PEOPLE MUMBLE SOMETIMES.
ガチャ
HEY...I *TOLD* YOU HOW WE WERE GOING TO DO THIS, KARATSU. YOU DON'T BRING ANY BODIES HERE BEFORE YOU DISCUSS HOW THEY'RE GOING TO *PAY!*
LOOK, IT COULDN'T BE HELPED. I COULD ONLY GET FOUR WORDS OUT OF HER.
LISTEN, MR. MY-KARMA-IS-OH-SO-SPOTLESS, WE'RE RUNNING A *BUSINESS* HERE, NOT A CHARITY. DID YOU CHECK THE CORPSE'S CREDIT?

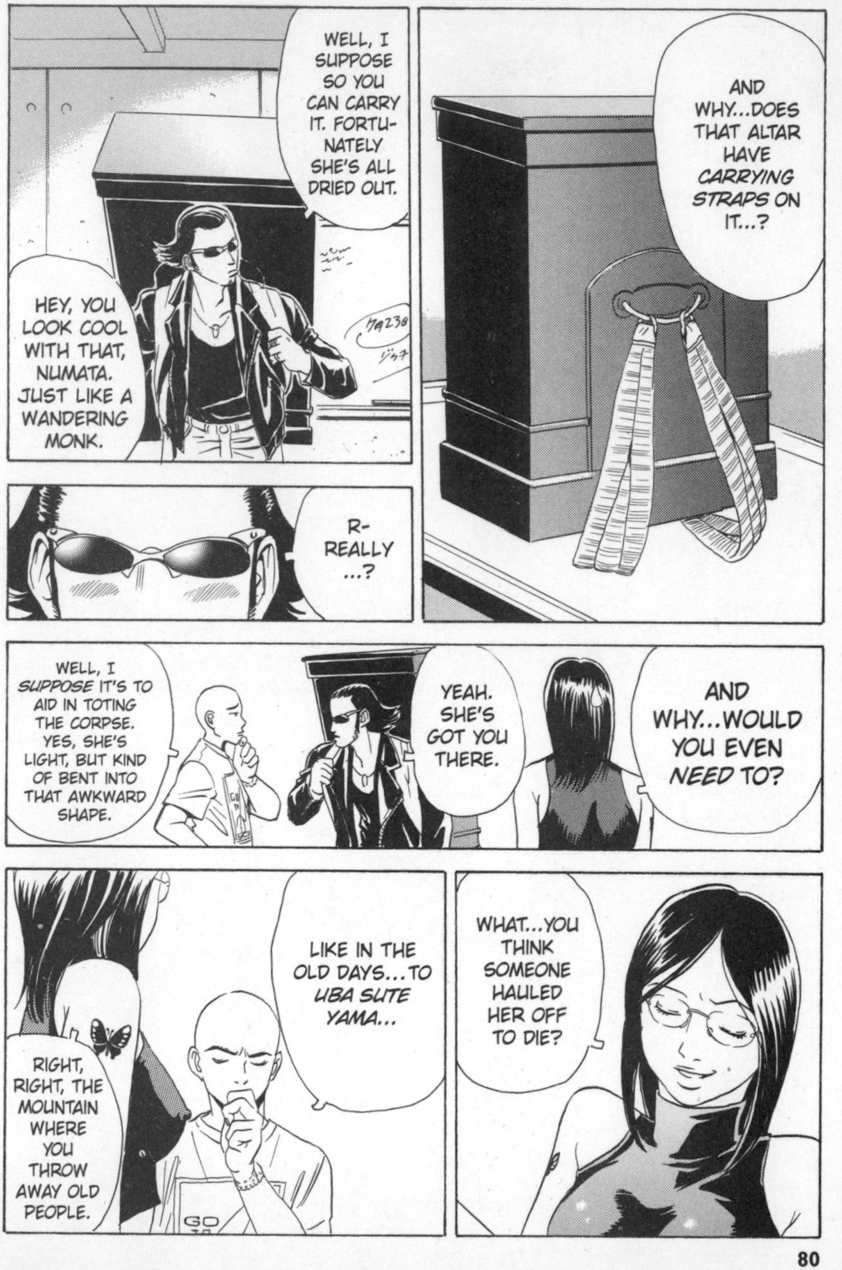
AND WHY...DOES THAT ALTAR HAVE CARRYING STRAPS ON IT...?
WELL, I SUPPOSE SO YOU CAN CARRY IT. FORTU-NATELY SHE'S ALL DRIED OUT.
HEY, YOU LOOK COOL WITH THAT, NUMATA. JUST LIKE A WANDERING MONK.
R-REALLY ...?
AND WHY...WOULD YOU EVEN NEED TO?
YEAH. SHE'S GOT YOU THERE.
WELL, I SUPPOSE IT'S TO AID IN TOTING THE CORPSE. YES, SHE'S LIGHT, BUT KIND OF BENT INTO THAT AWKWARD SHAPE.
WHAT...YOU THINK SOMEONE HAULED HER OFF TO DIE?
LIKE IN THE OLD DAYS...TO UBA SUTE YAMA...
RIGHT, RIGHT, THE MOUNTAIN WHERE YOU THROW AWAY OLD PEOPLE.

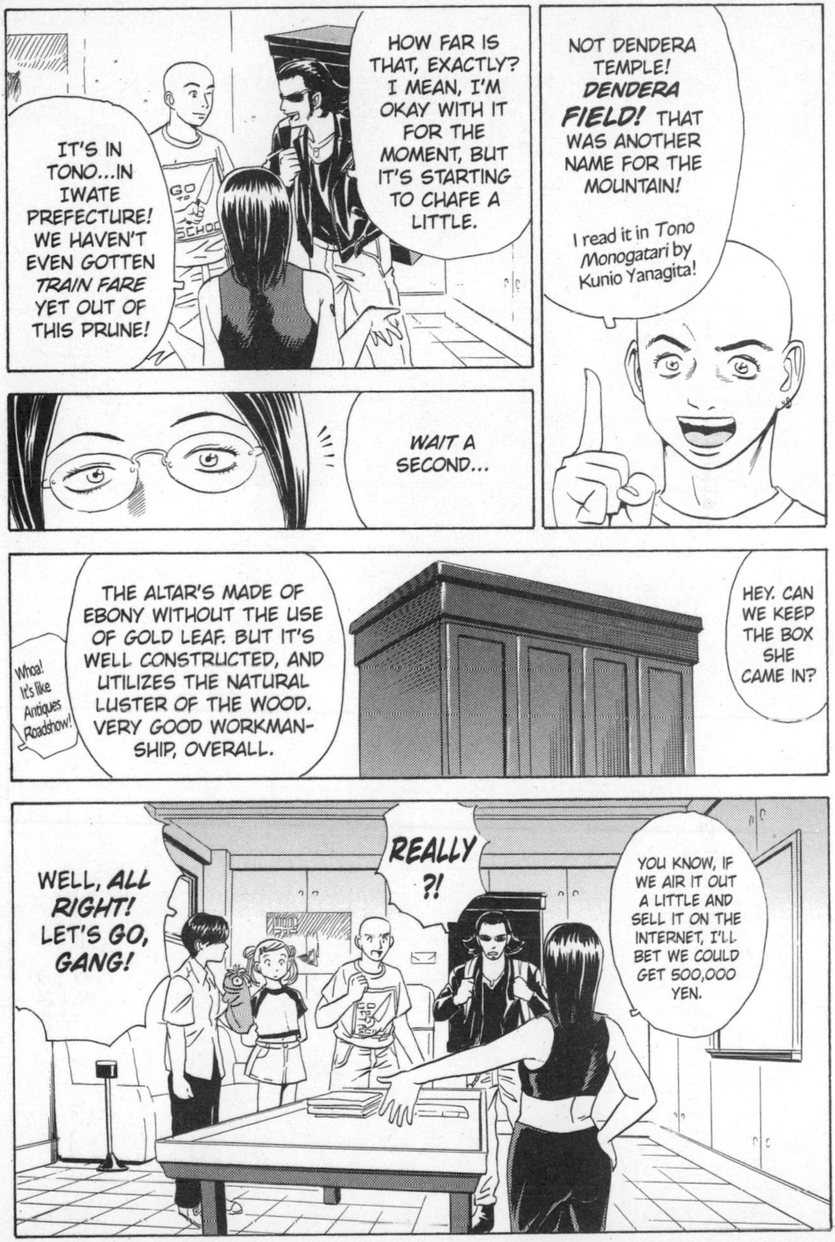
NOT DENDERA TEMPLE! DENDERA FIELD! THAT WAS ANOTHER NAME FOR THE MOUNTAIN!
I read it in Tono Monogatari by Kunio Yanagita!
HOW FAR IS THAT, EXACTLY? I MEAN, I'M OKAY WITH IT FOR THE MOMENT, BUT IT'S STARTING TO CHAFE A LITTLE.
IT'S IN TONO...IN IWATE PREFECTURE! WE HAVEN'T EVEN GOTTEN TRAIN FARE YET OUT OF THIS PRUNE!
WAIT A SECOND...
HEY. CAN WE KEEP THE BOX SHE CAME IN?
THE ALTAR'S MADE OF EBONY WITHOUT THE USE OF GOLD LEAF. BUT IT'S WELL CONSTRUCTED, AND UTILIZES THE NATURAL LUSTER OF THE WOOD. VERY GOOD WORKMANSHIP, OVERALL.
Whoa! It's like Antiques Roadshow!
YOU KNOW, IF WE AIR IT OUT A LITTLE AND SELL IT ON THE INTERNET, I'LL BET WE COULD GET 500,000 YEN.
REALLY ?!
WELL, ALL RIGHT! LET'S GO, GANG!

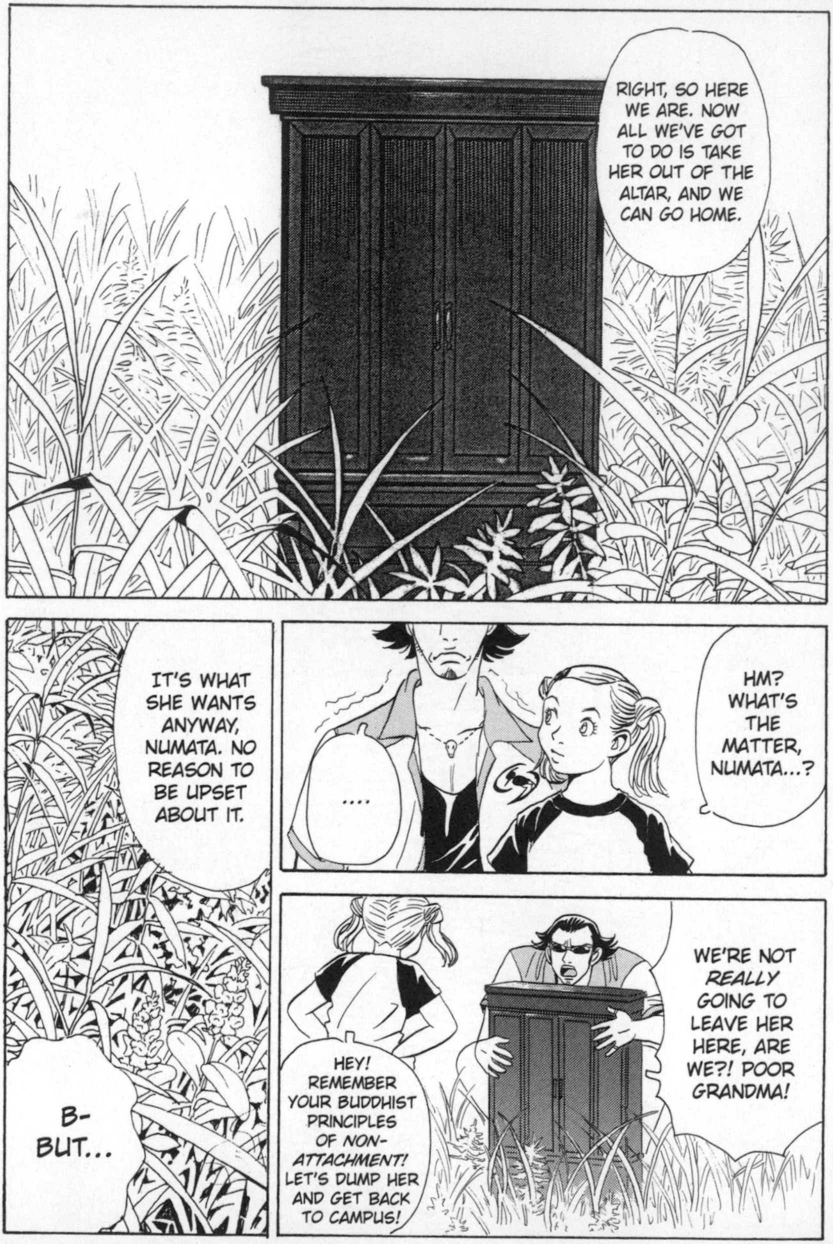
RIGHT, SO HERE WE ARE. NOW ALL WE'VE GOT TO DO IS TAKE HER OUT OF THE ALTAR, AND WE CAN GO HOME.
HM? WHAT'S THE MATTER, NUMATA...?
....
WE'RE NOT *REALLY* GOING TO LEAVE HER HERE, ARE WE?! POOR GRANDMA!
HEY! REMEMBER YOUR BUDDHIST PRINCIPLES OF *NON-ATTACHMENT!* LET'S DUMP HER AND GET BACK TO CAMPUS!
IT'S WHAT SHE WANTS ANYWAY, NUMATA. NO REASON TO BE UPSET ABOUT IT.
B-BUT...

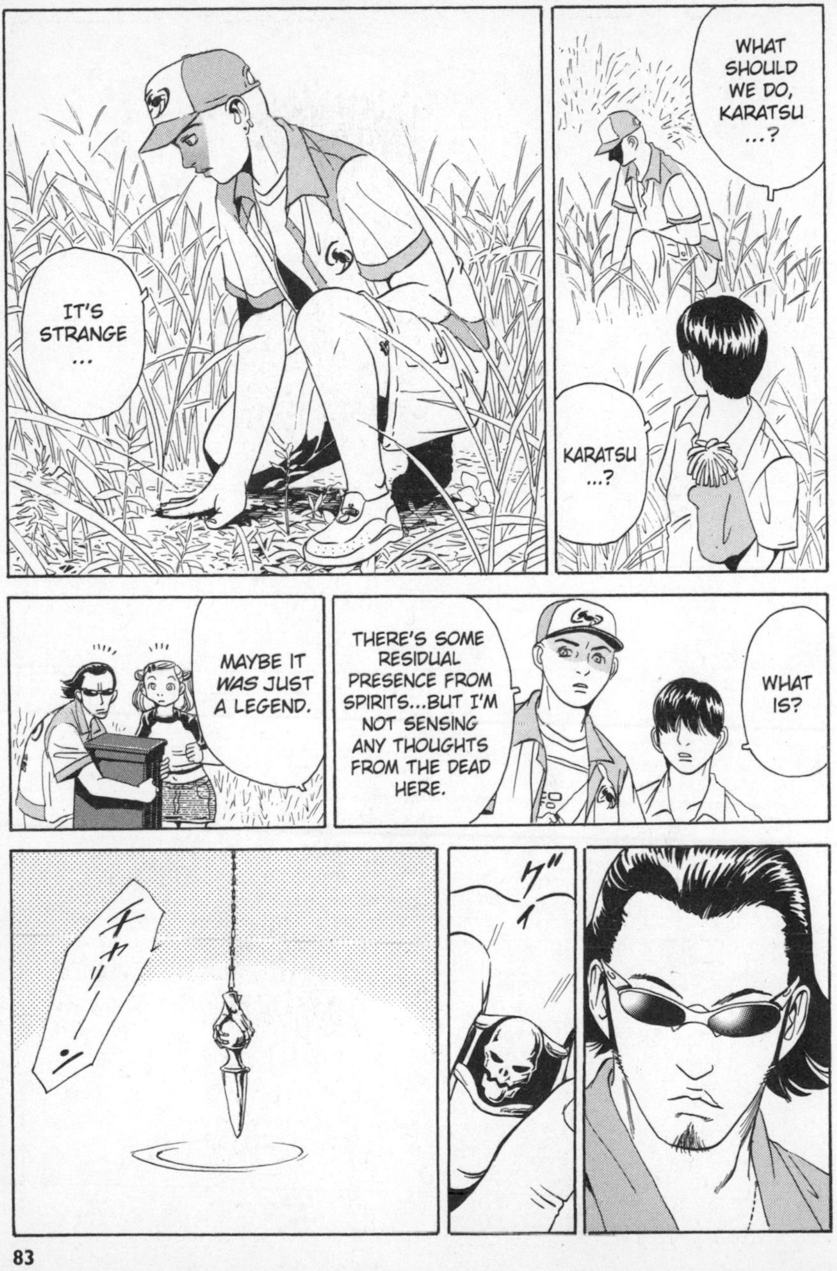
WHAT SHOULD WE DO, KARATSU ...?
KARATSU ...?
IT'S STRANGE ...
WHAT IS?
THERE'S SOME RESIDUAL PRESENCE FROM SPIRITS...BUT I'M NOT SENSING ANY THOUGHTS FROM THE DEAD HERE.
MAYBE IT *WAS* JUST A LEGEND.
グイ

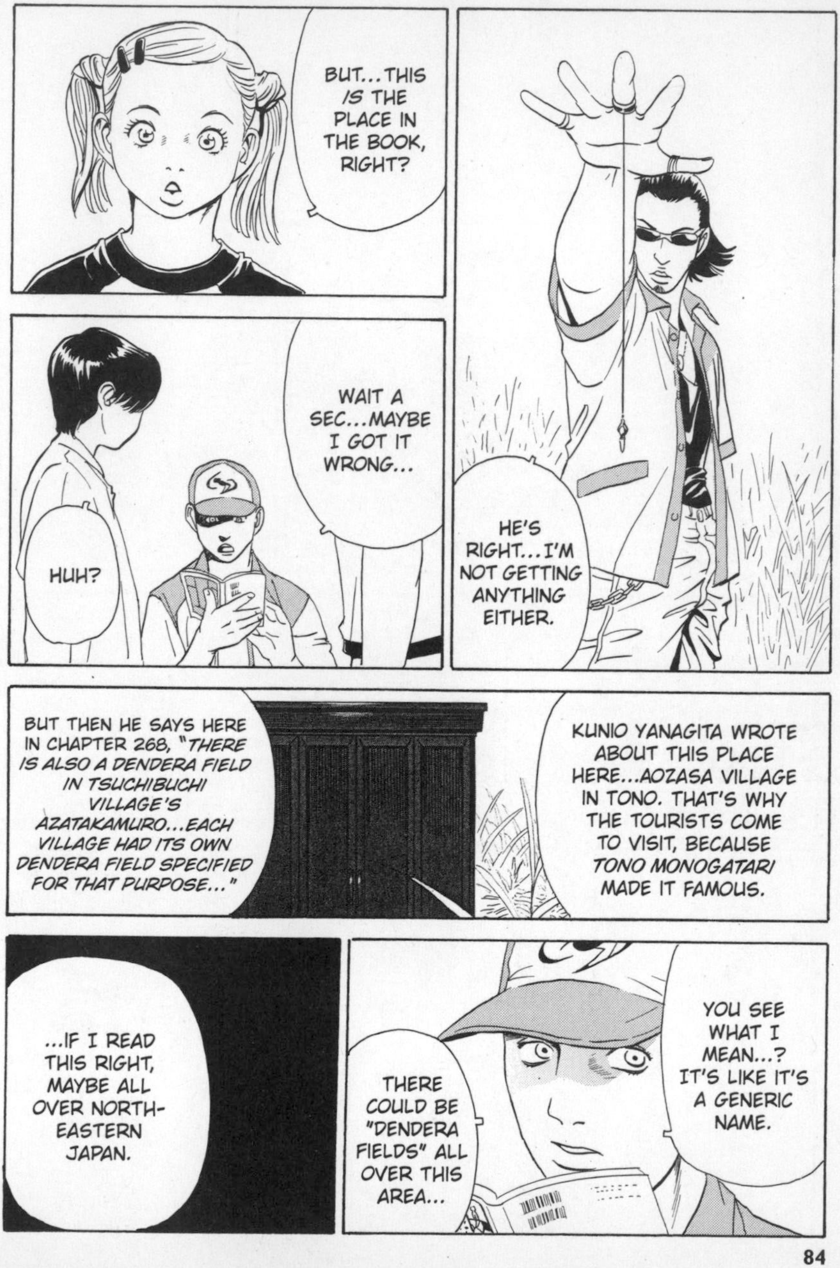
HE'S RIGHT... I'M NOT GETTING ANYTHING EITHER.
BUT... THIS IS THE PLACE IN THE BOOK, RIGHT?
WAIT A SEC... MAYBE I GOT IT WRONG...
HUH?
KUNIO YANAGITA WROTE ABOUT THIS PLACE HERE... AOZASA VILLAGE IN TONO. THAT'S WHY THE TOURISTS COME TO VISIT, BECAUSE TONO MONOGATARI MADE IT FAMOUS.
BUT THEN HE SAYS HERE IN CHAPTER 268, "THERE IS ALSO A DENDERA FIELD IN TSUCHIBUCHI VILLAGE'S AZATAKAMURO... EACH VILLAGE HAD ITS OWN DENDERA FIELD SPECIFIED FOR THAT PURPOSE..."
YOU SEE WHAT I MEAN...? IT'S LIKE IT'S A GENERIC NAME.
THERE COULD BE "DENDERA FIELDS" ALL OVER THIS AREA...
...IF I READ THIS RIGHT, MAYBE ALL OVER NORTH-EASTERN JAPAN.

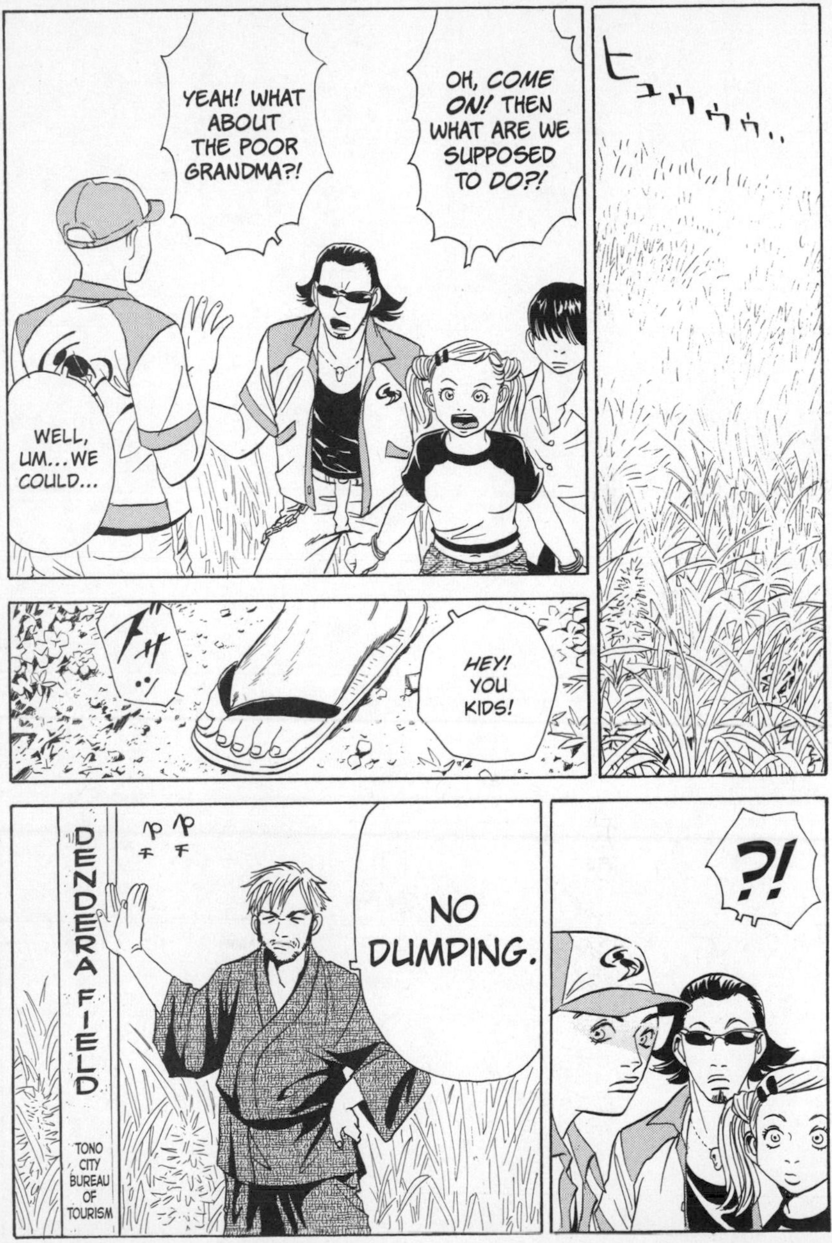
ヒュウウウ..
OH, COME ON! THEN WHAT ARE WE SUPPOSED TO DO?!
YEAH! WHAT ABOUT THE POOR GRANDMA?!
WELL, UM...WE COULD...
HEY! YOU KIDS!
ザッ
?!
NO DUMPING.
ペチ ペチ
DENDERA FIELD
TONO CITY BUREAU OF TOURISM

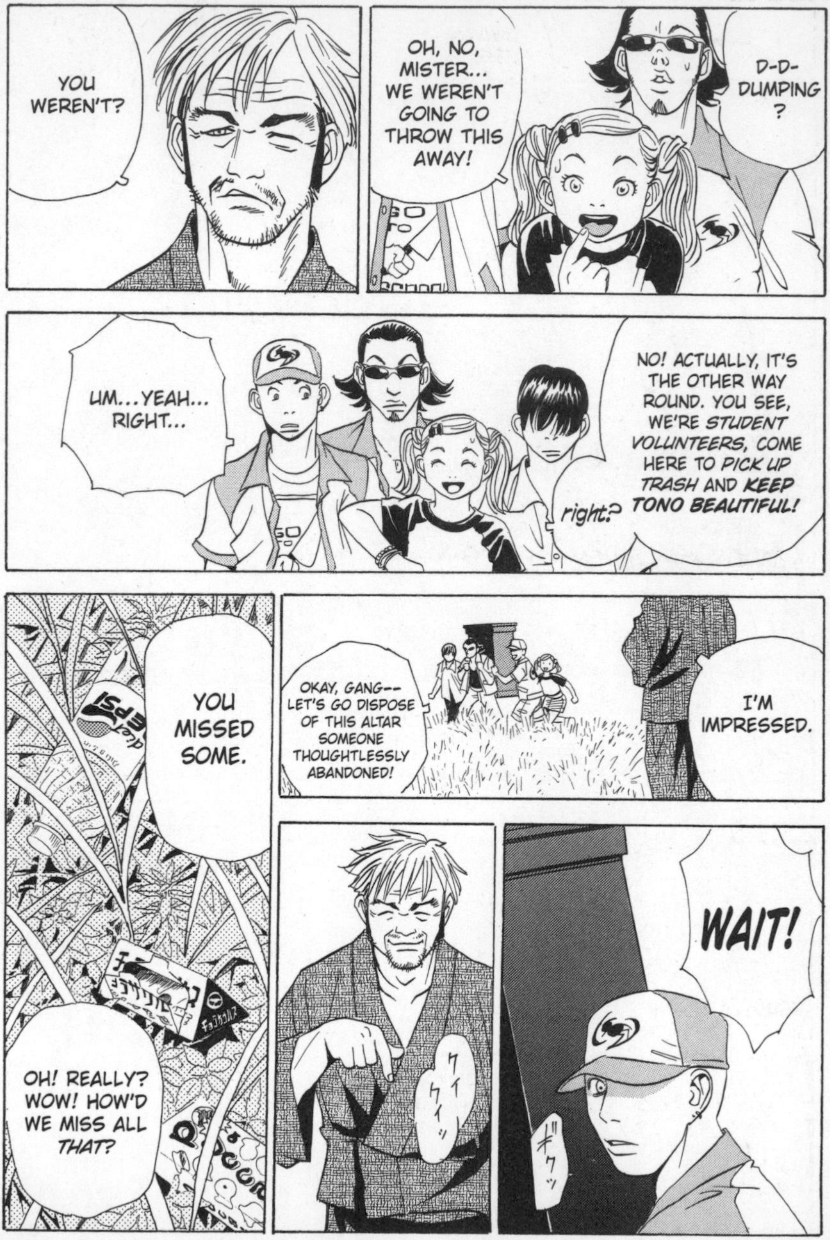
OH, NO, MISTER... WE WEREN'T GOING TO THROW THIS AWAY!
D-D-DUMPING?
YOU WEREN'T?
NO! ACTUALLY, IT'S THE OTHER WAY ROUND. YOU SEE, WE'RE *STUDENT VOLUNTEERS*, COME HERE TO *PICK UP TRASH* AND ***KEEP TONO BEAUTIFUL!***
right?
UM...YEAH... RIGHT...
I'M IMPRESSED.
OKAY, GANG-- LET'S GO DISPOSE OF THIS ALTAR SOMEONE THOUGHTLESSLY ABANDONED!
WAIT!
ギクッ
クイ クイッ
YOU MISSED SOME.
OH! REALLY? WOW! HOW'D WE MISS ALL *THAT*?

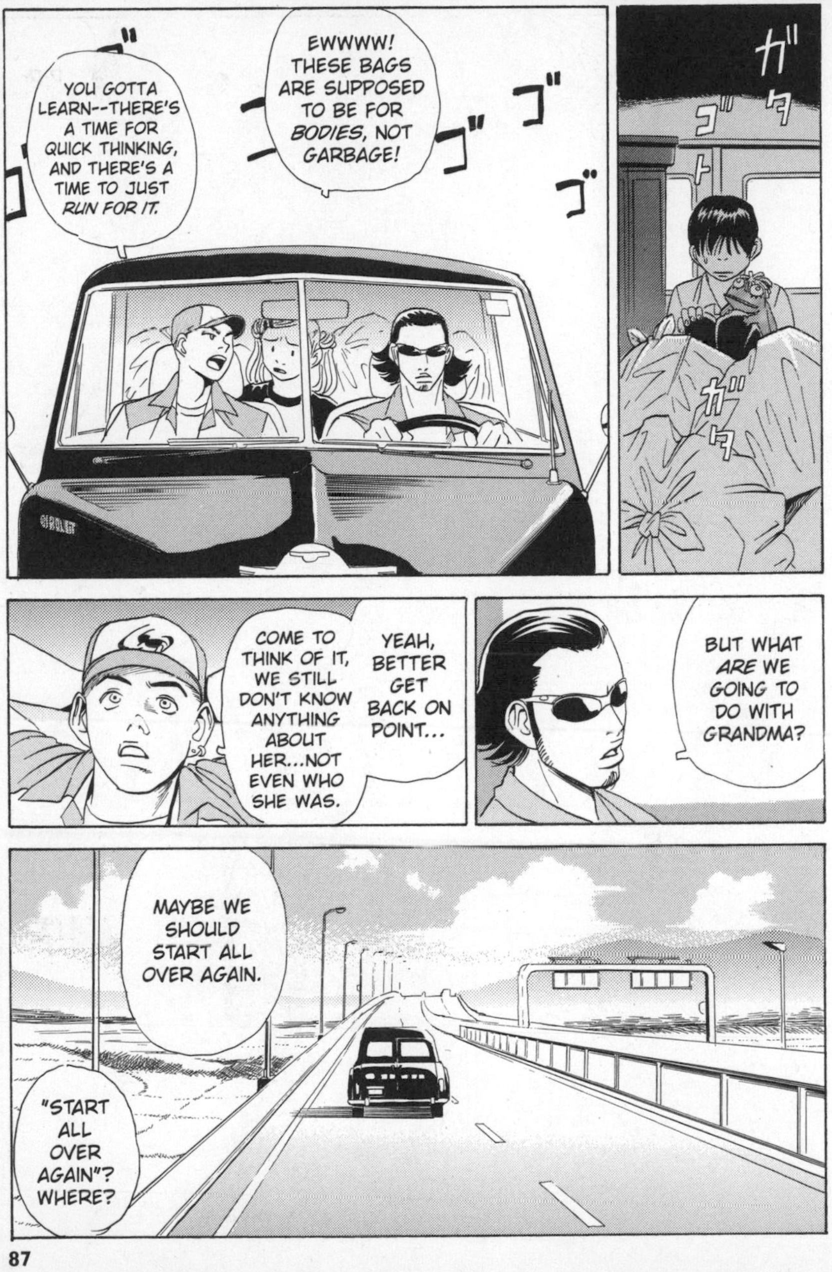
ガタ
ゴト
ガタ
EWWWW! THESE BAGS ARE SUPPOSED TO BE FOR *BODIES*, NOT GARBAGE!
YOU GOTTA LEARN--THERE'S A TIME FOR QUICK THINKING, AND THERE'S A TIME TO JUST *RUN FOR IT.*
ゴ
ゴ
ゴ
BUT WHAT *ARE* WE GOING TO DO WITH GRANDMA?
YEAH, BETTER GET BACK ON POINT...
COME TO THINK OF IT, WE STILL DON'T KNOW ANYTHING ABOUT HER...NOT EVEN WHO SHE WAS.
MAYBE WE SHOULD START ALL OVER AGAIN.
"START ALL OVER AGAIN"? WHERE?

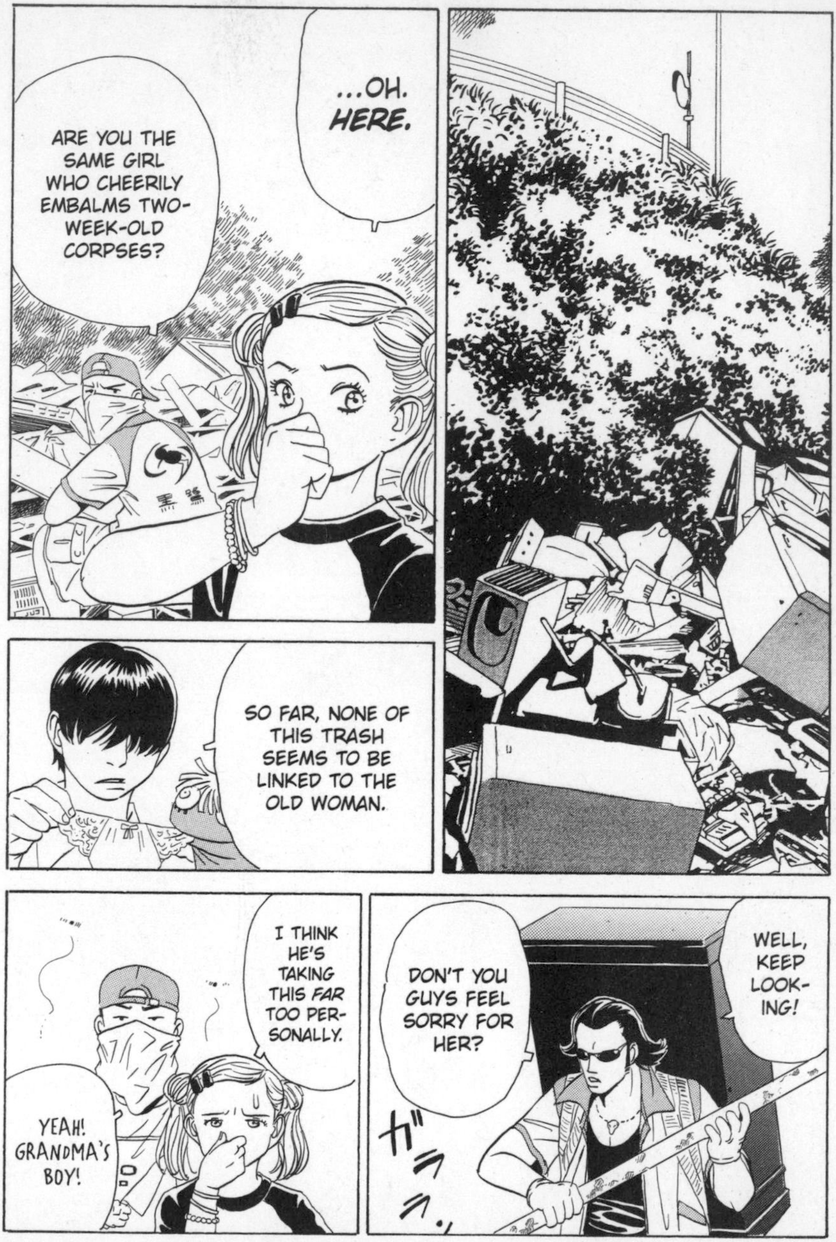
...OH. *HERE.*
ARE YOU THE SAME GIRL WHO CHEERILY EMBALMS TWO-WEEK-OLD CORPSES?
SO FAR, NONE OF THIS TRASH SEEMS TO BE LINKED TO THE OLD WOMAN.
WELL, KEEP LOOKING!
DON'T YOU GUYS FEEL SORRY FOR HER?
I THINK HE'S TAKING THIS *FAR* TOO PERSONALLY.
YEAH! GRANDMA'S BOY!

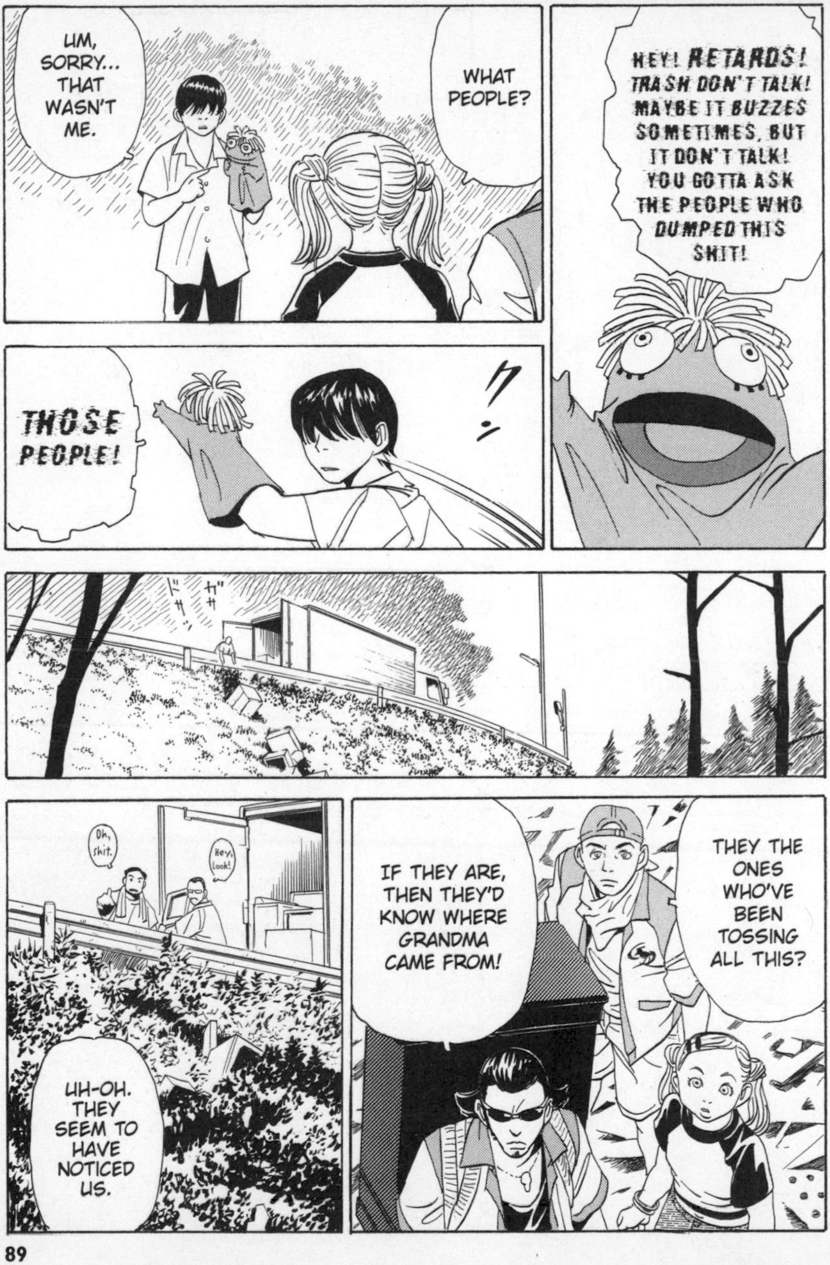
HEY! RETARDS! TRASH DON'T TALK! MAYBE IT BUZZES SOMETIMES, BUT IT DON'T TALK! YOU GOTTA ASK THE PEOPLE WHO DUMPED THIS SHIT!
WHAT PEOPLE?
UM, SORRY... THAT WASN'T ME.
THOSE PEOPLE!
THEY THE ONES WHO'VE BEEN TOSSING ALL THIS?
IF THEY ARE, THEN THEY'D KNOW WHERE GRANDMA CAME FROM!
Hey, look!
Oh, shit.
UH-OH. THEY SEEM TO HAVE NOTICED US.

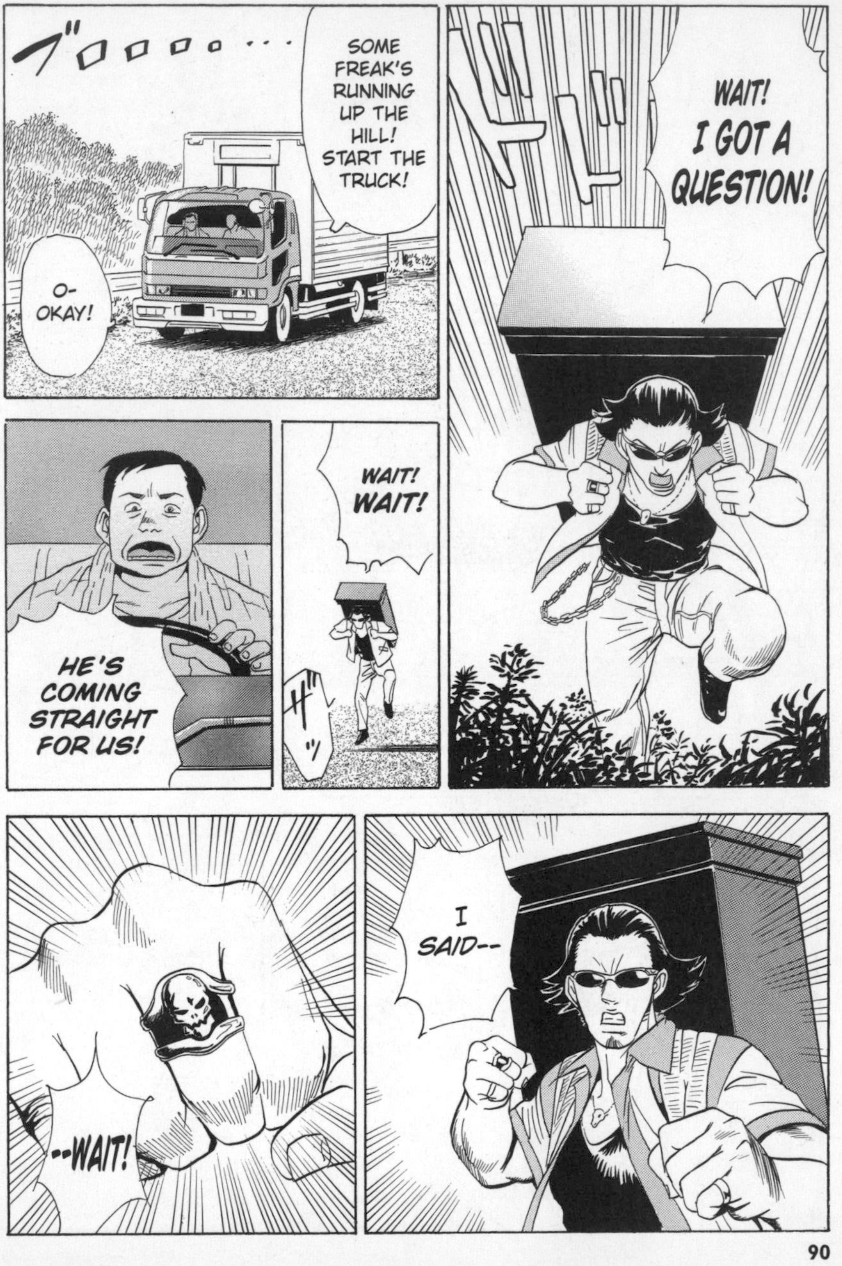
WAIT! I GOT A QUESTION!
ブロロロロ...
SOME FREAK'S RUNNING UP THE HILL! START THE TRUCK!
O- OKAY!
WAIT! WAIT!
ザッ
HE'S COMING STRAIGHT FOR US!
I SAID--
--WAIT!

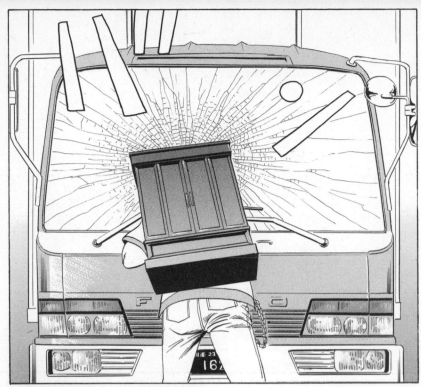

LOOK, THIS WON'T TAKE LONG. DO YOU MIND?

N-n-n-n-not at all...

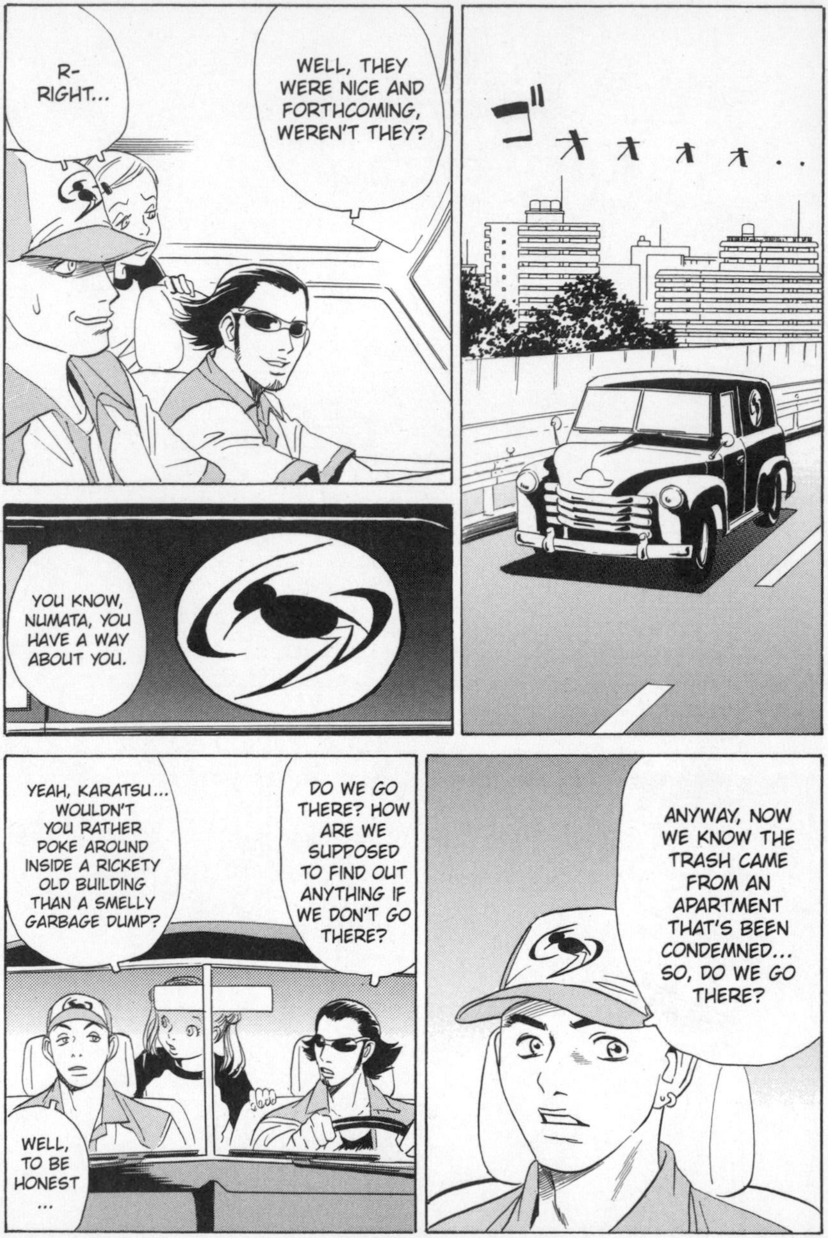
ゴォォォォ..
WELL, THEY WERE NICE AND FORTHCOMING, WEREN'T THEY?
R- RIGHT...
YOU KNOW, NUMATA, YOU HAVE A WAY ABOUT YOU.
ANYWAY, NOW WE KNOW THE TRASH CAME FROM AN APARTMENT THAT'S BEEN CONDEMNED... SO, DO WE GO THERE?
DO WE GO THERE? HOW ARE WE SUPPOSED TO FIND OUT ANYTHING IF WE DON'T GO THERE?
YEAH, KARATSU... WOULDN'T YOU RATHER POKE AROUND INSIDE A RICKETY OLD BUILDING THAN A SMELLY GARBAGE DUMP?
WELL, TO BE HONEST ...

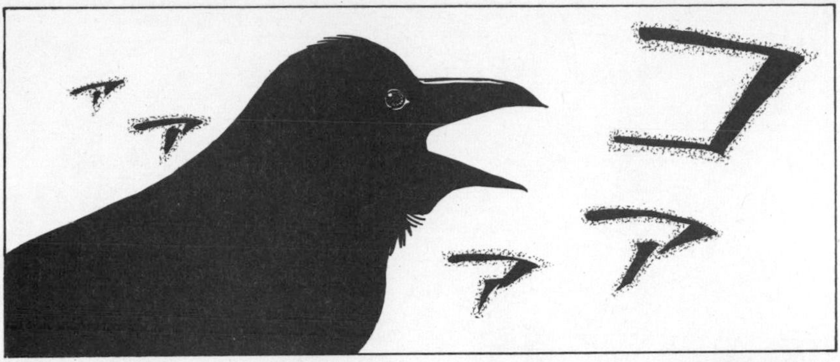
コアァ
アア
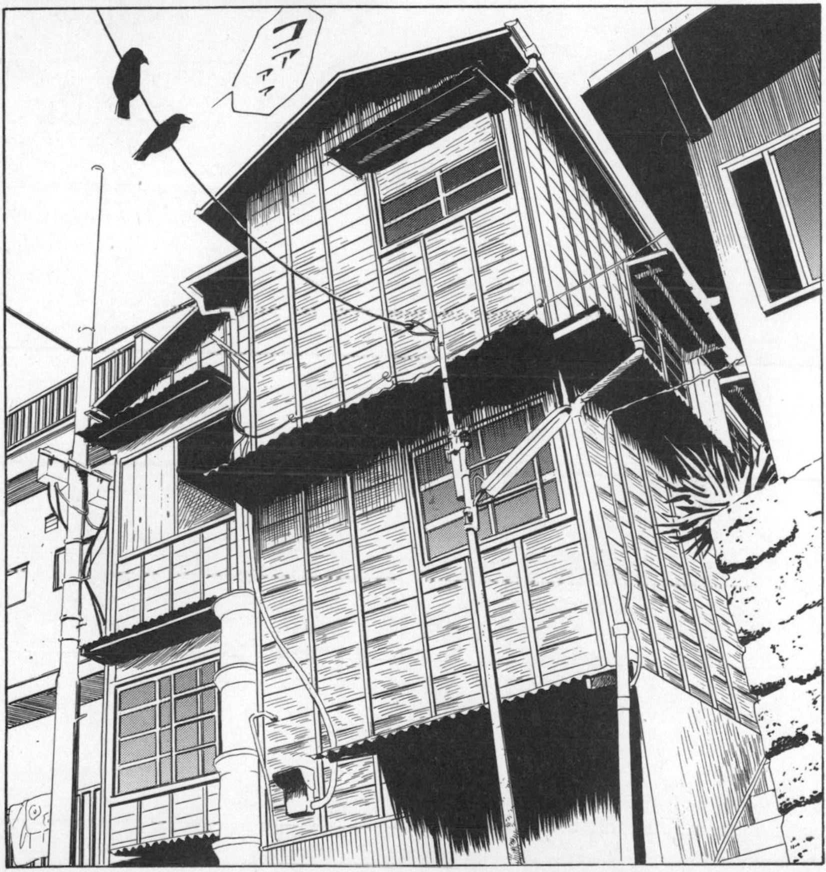
コァァァ

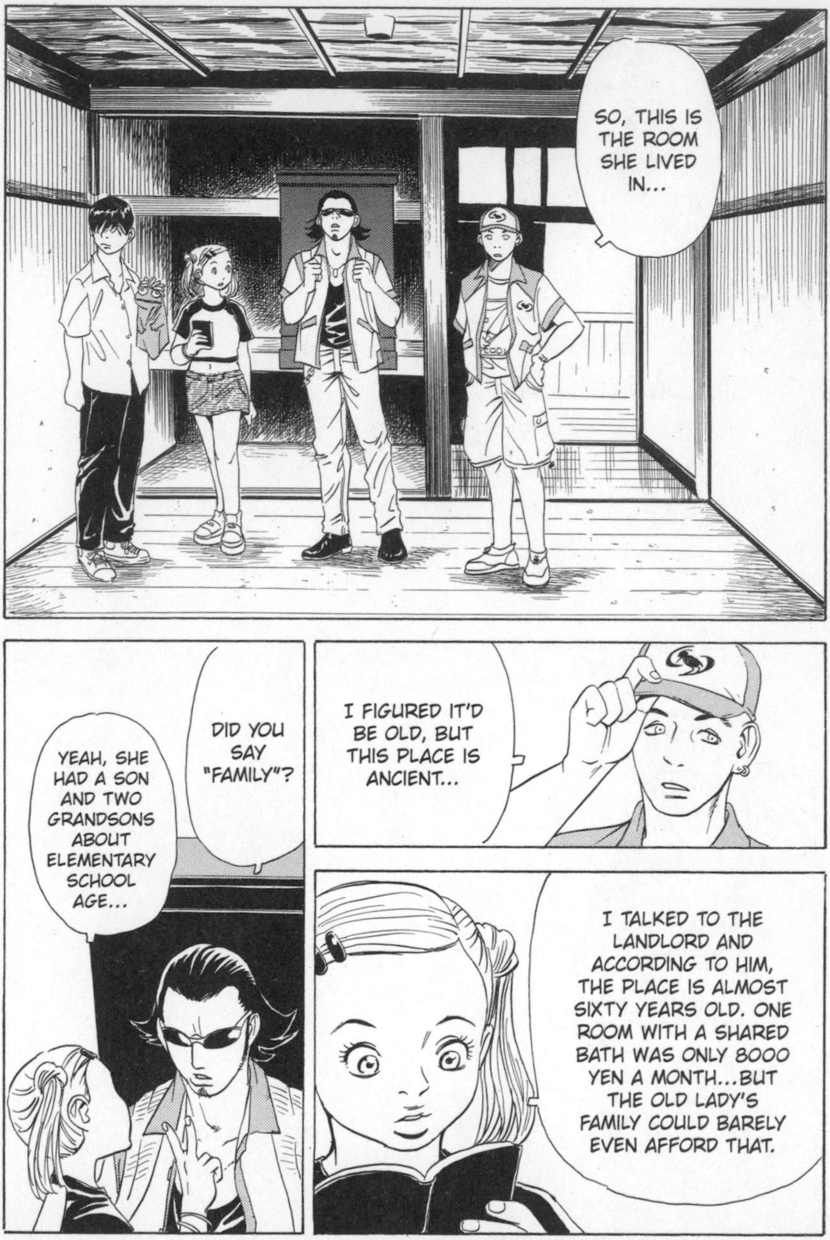
SO, THIS IS THE ROOM SHE LIVED IN...
I FIGURED IT'D BE OLD, BUT THIS PLACE IS ANCIENT...
I TALKED TO THE LANDLORD AND ACCORDING TO HIM, THE PLACE IS ALMOST SIXTY YEARS OLD. ONE ROOM WITH A SHARED BATH WAS ONLY 8000 YEN A MONTH...BUT THE OLD LADY'S FAMILY COULD BARELY EVEN AFFORD THAT.
DID YOU SAY "FAMILY"?
YEAH, SHE HAD A SON AND TWO GRANDSONS ABOUT ELEMENTARY SCHOOL AGE...

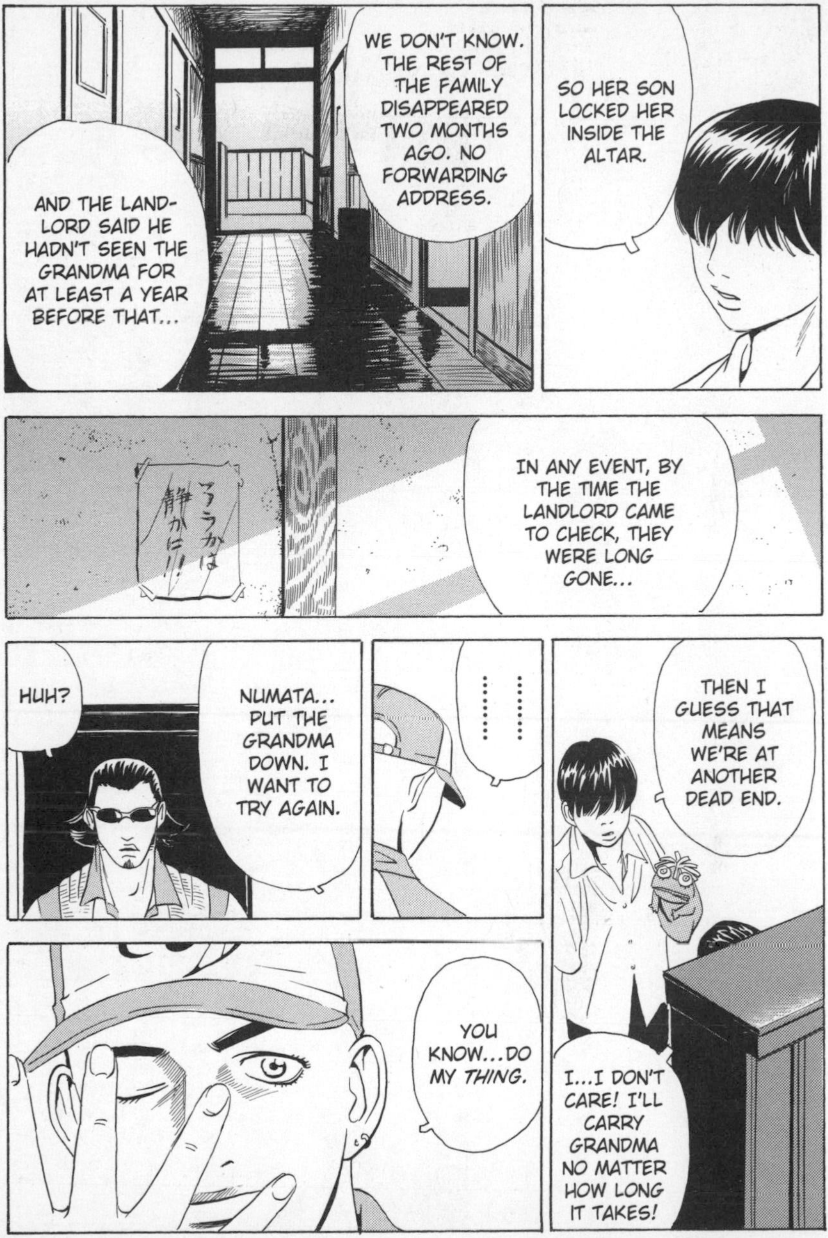
SO HER SON LOCKED HER INSIDE THE ALTAR.
WE DON'T KNOW. THE REST OF THE FAMILY DISAPPEARED TWO MONTHS AGO. NO FORWARDING ADDRESS.
AND THE LAND-LORD SAID HE HADN'T SEEN THE GRANDMA FOR AT LEAST A YEAR BEFORE THAT...
IN ANY EVENT, BY THE TIME THE LANDLORD CAME TO CHECK, THEY WERE LONG GONE...
THEN I GUESS THAT MEANS WE'RE AT ANOTHER DEAD END.
I...I DON'T CARE! I'LL CARRY GRANDMA NO MATTER HOW LONG IT TAKES!
......
NUMATA... PUT THE GRANDMA DOWN. I WANT TO TRY AGAIN.
HUH?
YOU KNOW...DO MY *THING*.

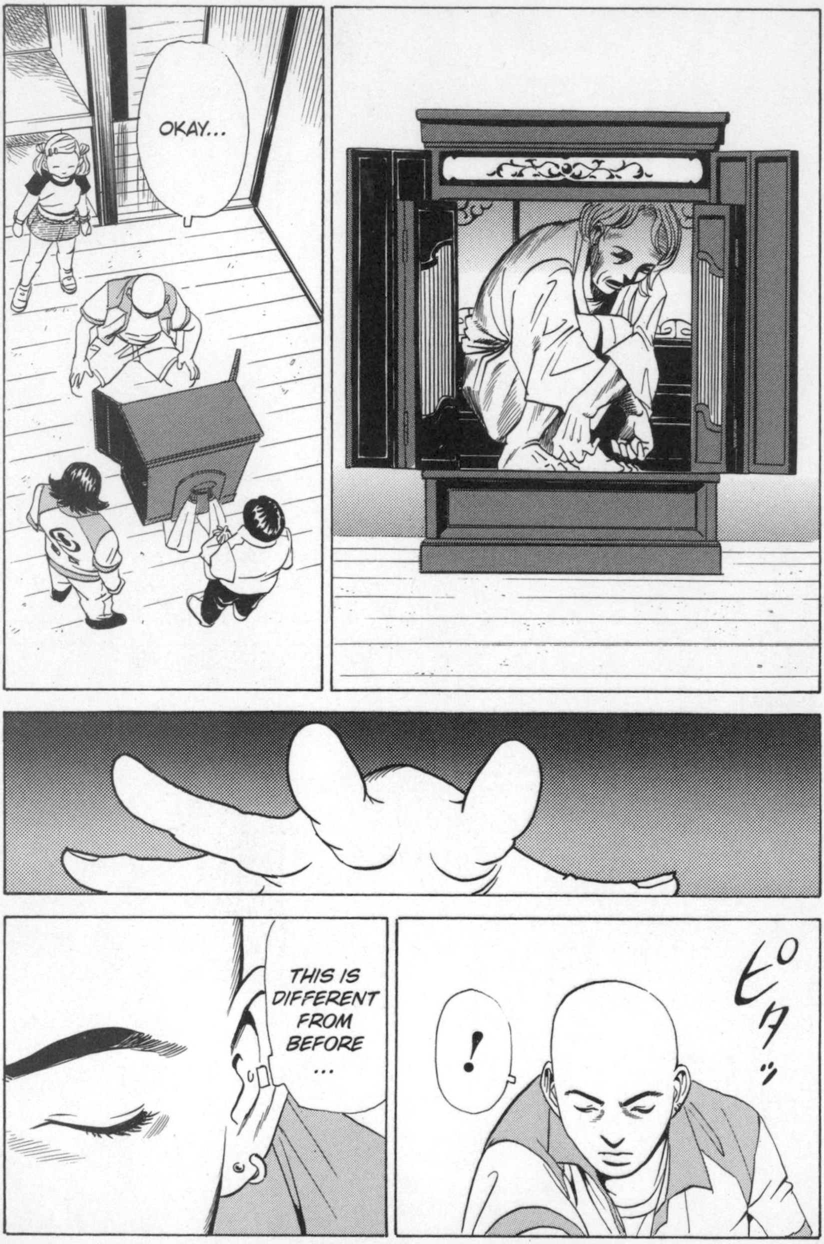
OKAY...
!
ピタッ
THIS IS DIFFERENT FROM BEFORE ...

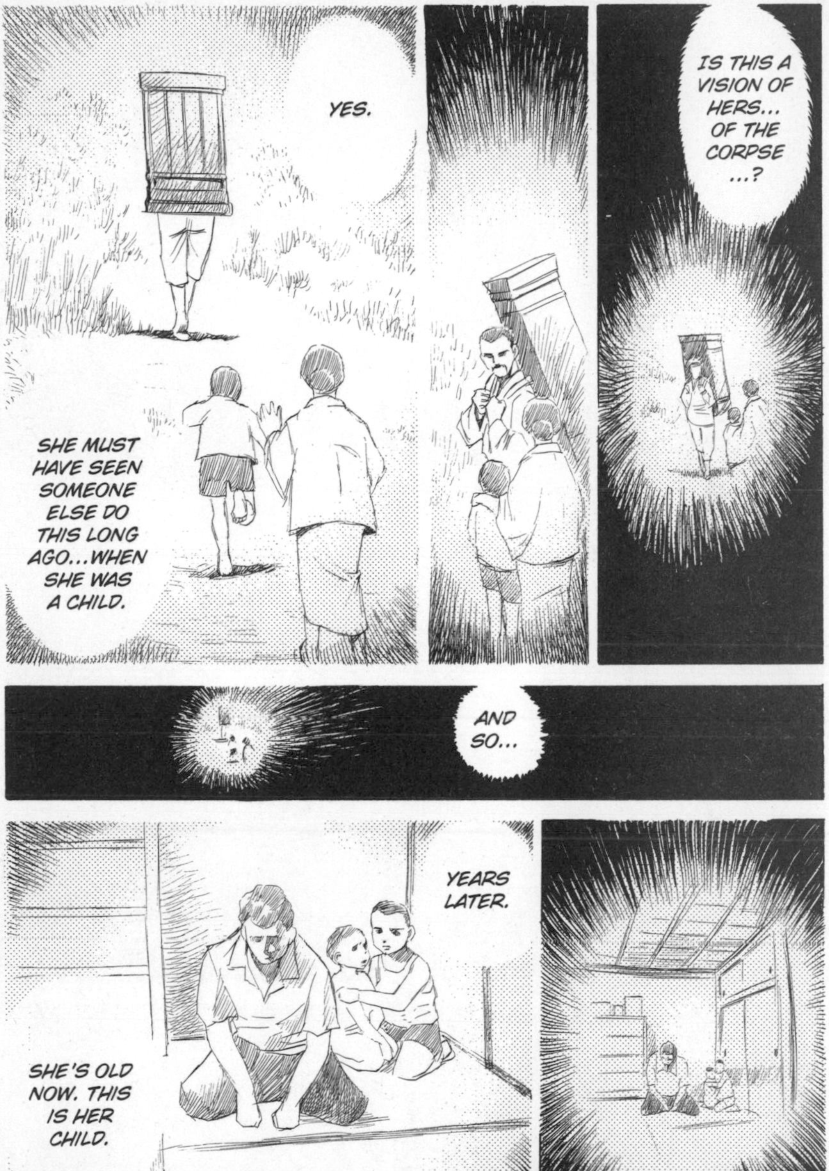
IS THIS A VISION OF HERS... OF THE CORPSE ...?
YES.
SHE MUST HAVE SEEN SOMEONE ELSE DO THIS LONG AGO...WHEN SHE WAS A CHILD.
AND SO...
YEARS LATER.
SHE'S OLD NOW. THIS IS HER CHILD.

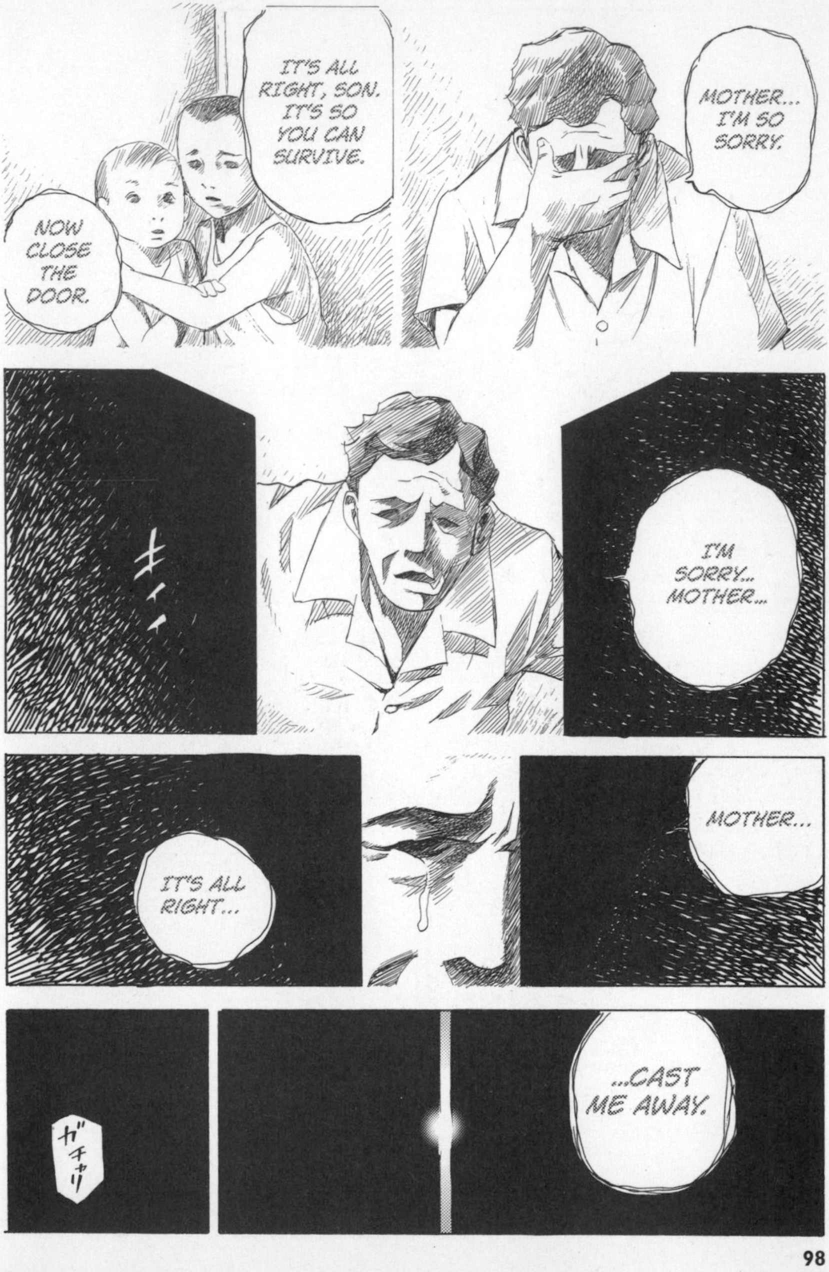
MOTHER... I'M SO SORRY.
IT'S ALL RIGHT, SON. IT'S SO YOU CAN SURVIVE.
NOW CLOSE THE DOOR.
I'M SORRY... MOTHER...
キィ
MOTHER...
IT'S ALL RIGHT...
...CAST ME AWAY.
ガチャリ

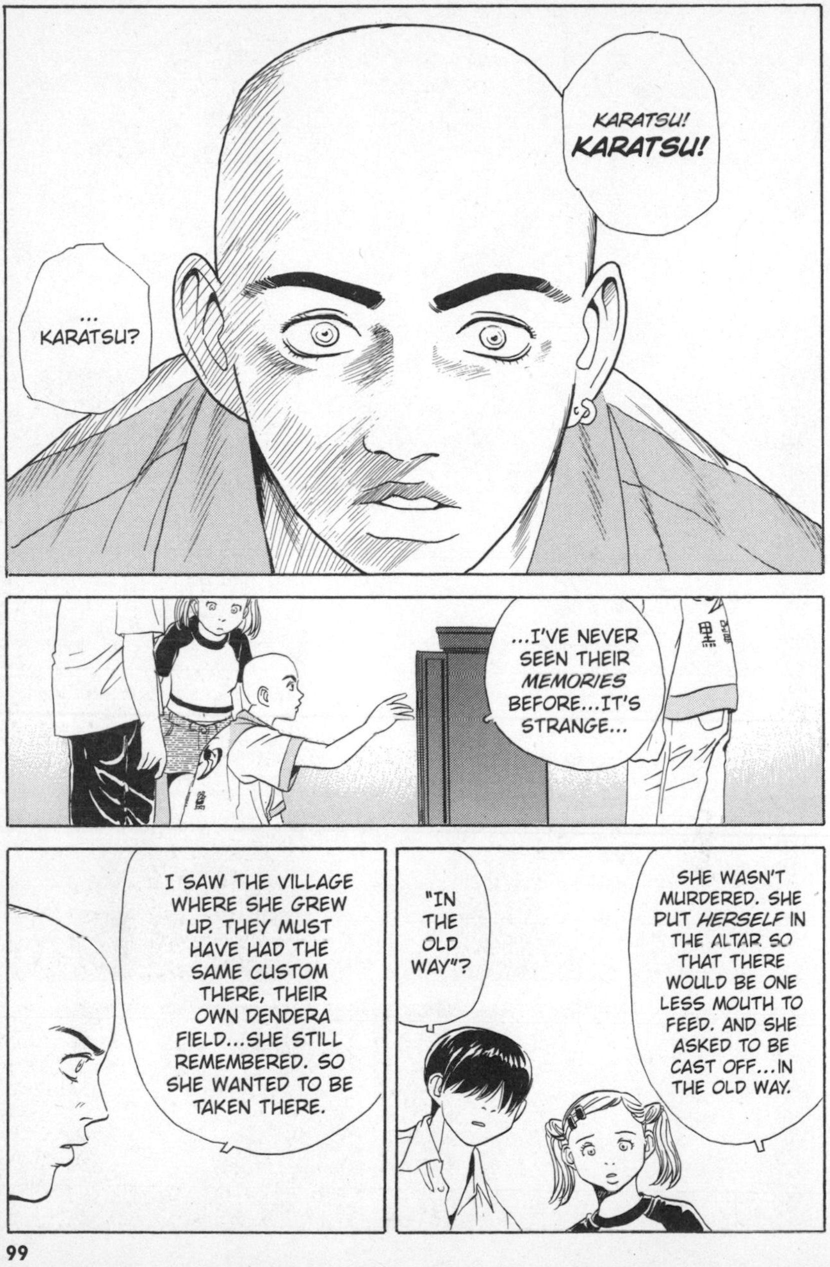
KARATSU! KARATSU!
...KARATSU?
...I'VE NEVER SEEN THEIR MEMORIES BEFORE...IT'S STRANGE...
SHE WASN'T MURDERED. SHE PUT HERSELF IN THE ALTAR SO THAT THERE WOULD BE ONE LESS MOUTH TO FEED. AND SHE ASKED TO BE CAST OFF...IN THE OLD WAY.
"IN THE OLD WAY"?
I SAW THE VILLAGE WHERE SHE GREW UP. THEY MUST HAVE HAD THE SAME CUSTOM THERE, THEIR OWN DENDERA FIELD...SHE STILL REMEMBERED. SO SHE WANTED TO BE TAKEN THERE.

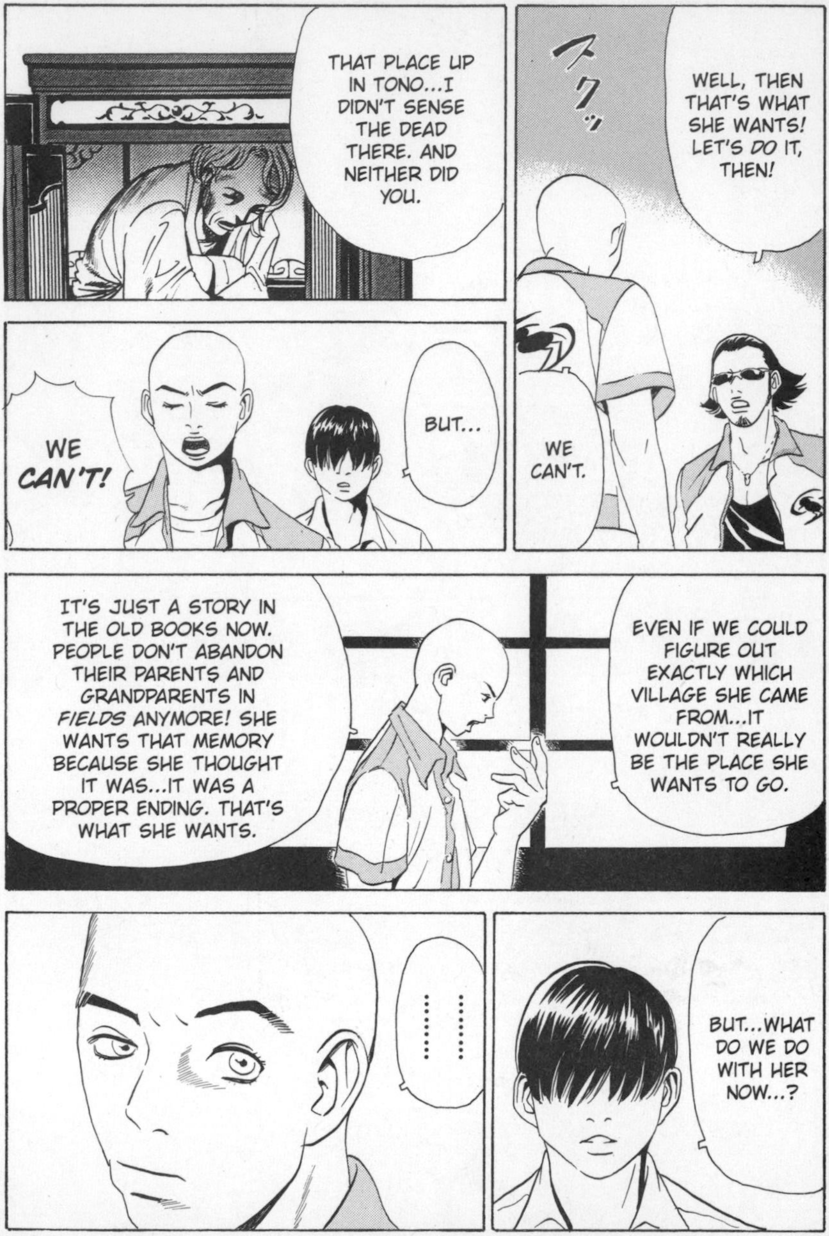
スクッ
WELL, THEN THAT'S WHAT SHE WANTS! LET'S *DO* IT, THEN!
WE CAN'T.
THAT PLACE UP IN TONO...I DIDN'T SENSE THE DEAD THERE. AND NEITHER DID YOU.
BUT...
WE ***CAN'T!***
EVEN IF WE COULD FIGURE OUT EXACTLY WHICH VILLAGE SHE CAME FROM...IT WOULDN'T REALLY BE THE PLACE SHE WANTS TO GO.
IT'S JUST A STORY IN THE OLD BOOKS NOW. PEOPLE DON'T ABANDON THEIR PARENTS AND GRANDPARENTS IN *FIELDS* ANYMORE! SHE WANTS THAT MEMORY BECAUSE SHE THOUGHT IT WAS...IT WAS A PROPER ENDING. THAT'S WHAT SHE WANTS.
BUT...WHAT DO WE DO WITH HER NOW...?
......

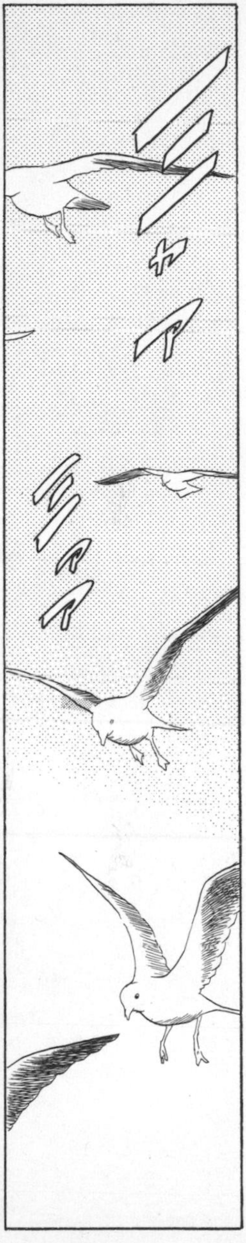
ミャア
ミャァァ
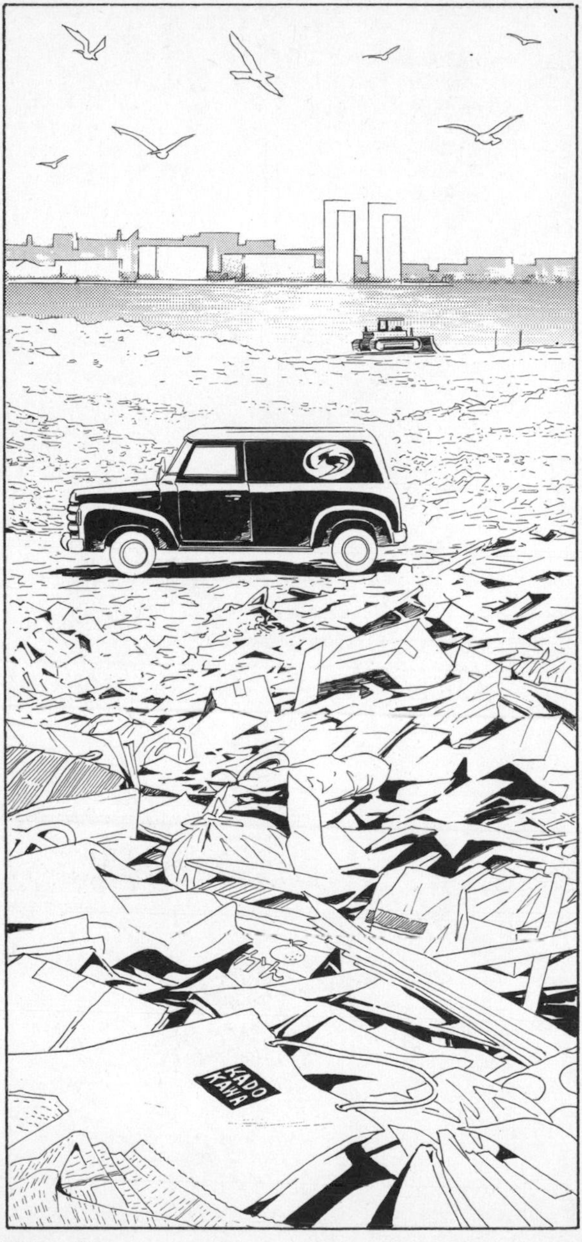
KADO
KAWA

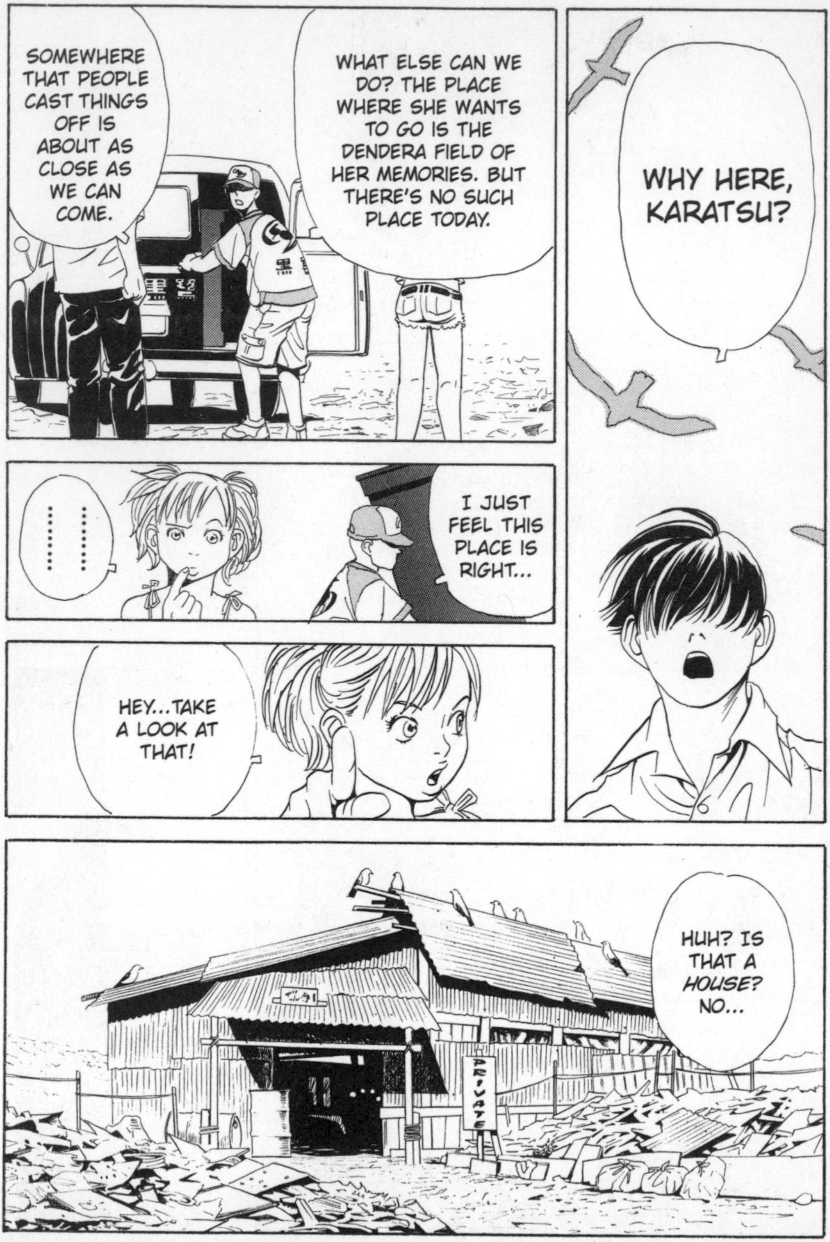
WHY HERE, KARATSU?
WHAT ELSE CAN WE DO? THE PLACE WHERE SHE WANTS TO GO IS THE DENDERA FIELD OF HER MEMORIES. BUT THERE'S NO SUCH PLACE TODAY.
SOMEWHERE THAT PEOPLE CAST THINGS OFF IS ABOUT AS CLOSE AS WE CAN COME.
I JUST FEEL THIS PLACE IS RIGHT...
......
HEY...TAKE A LOOK AT THAT!
HUH? IS THAT A *HOUSE?* NO...
PRIVATE

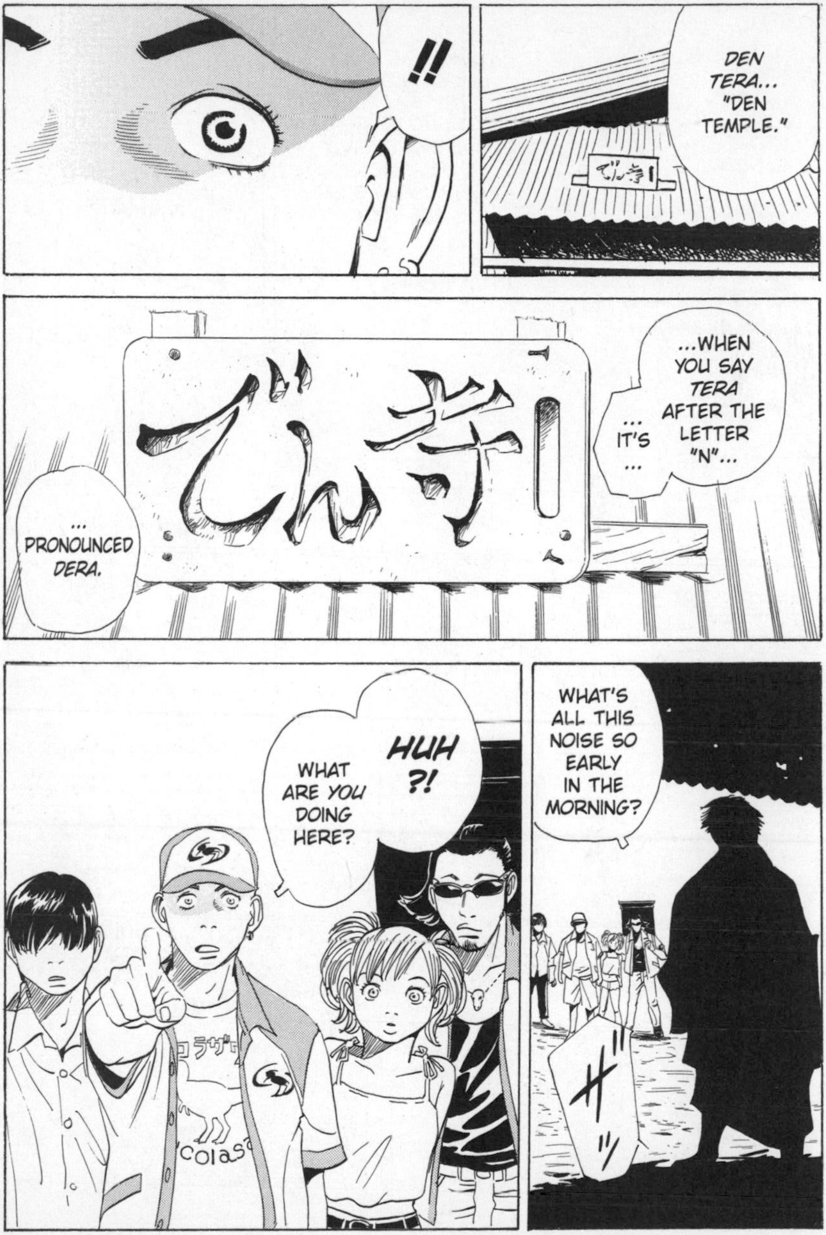
DEN TERA... "DEN TEMPLE."
!!
...WHEN YOU SAY TERA AFTER THE LETTER "N"...
...IT'S...
...PRONOUNCED DERA.
WHAT'S ALL THIS NOISE SO EARLY IN THE MORNING?
HUH?!
WHAT ARE YOU DOING HERE?

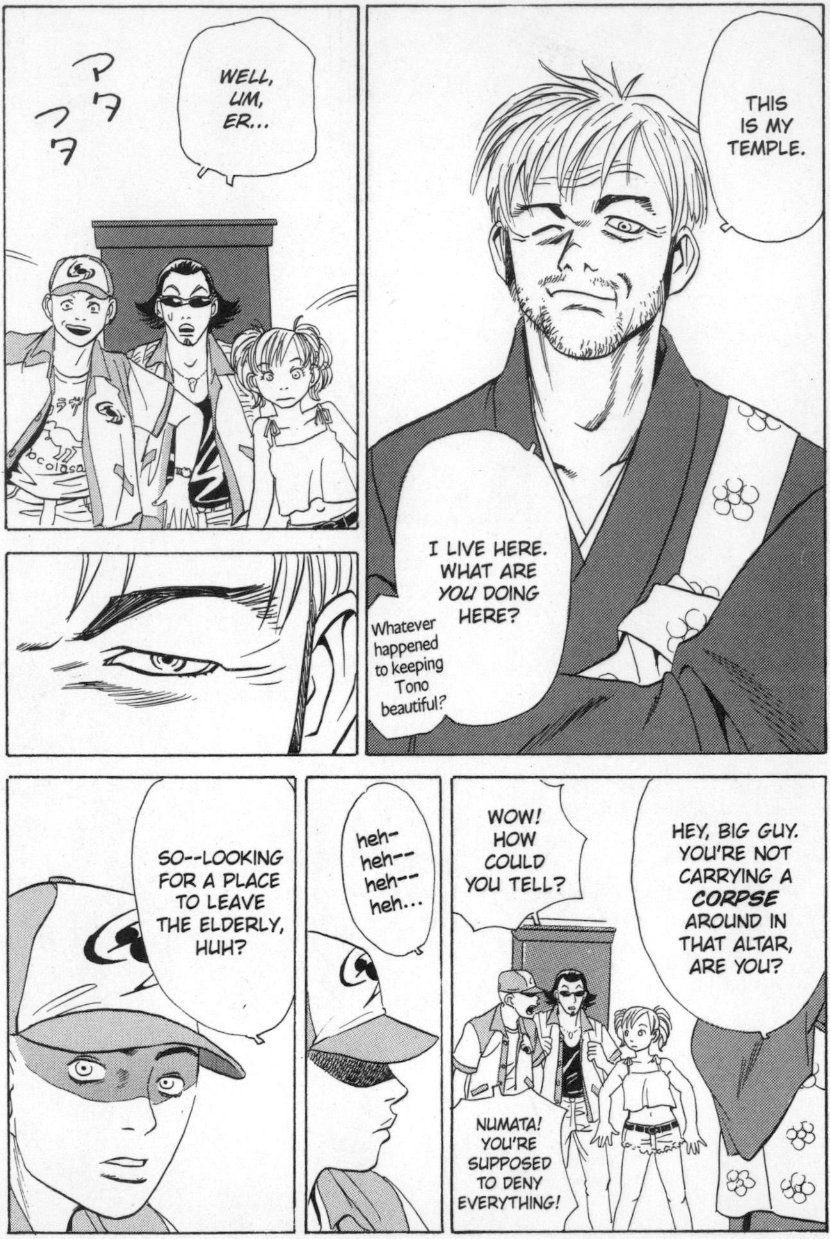
THIS IS MY TEMPLE.
I LIVE HERE. WHAT ARE *YOU* DOING HERE?
Whatever happened to keeping Tono beautiful?
WELL, UM, ER...
アワワワ
HEY, BIG GUY. YOU'RE NOT CARRYING A ***CORPSE*** AROUND IN THAT ALTAR, ARE YOU?
WOW! HOW COULD YOU TELL?
NUMATA! YOU'RE SUPPOSED TO DENY EVERYTHING!
heh-heh--heh--heh...
SO--LOOKING FOR A PLACE TO LEAVE THE ELDERLY, HUH?

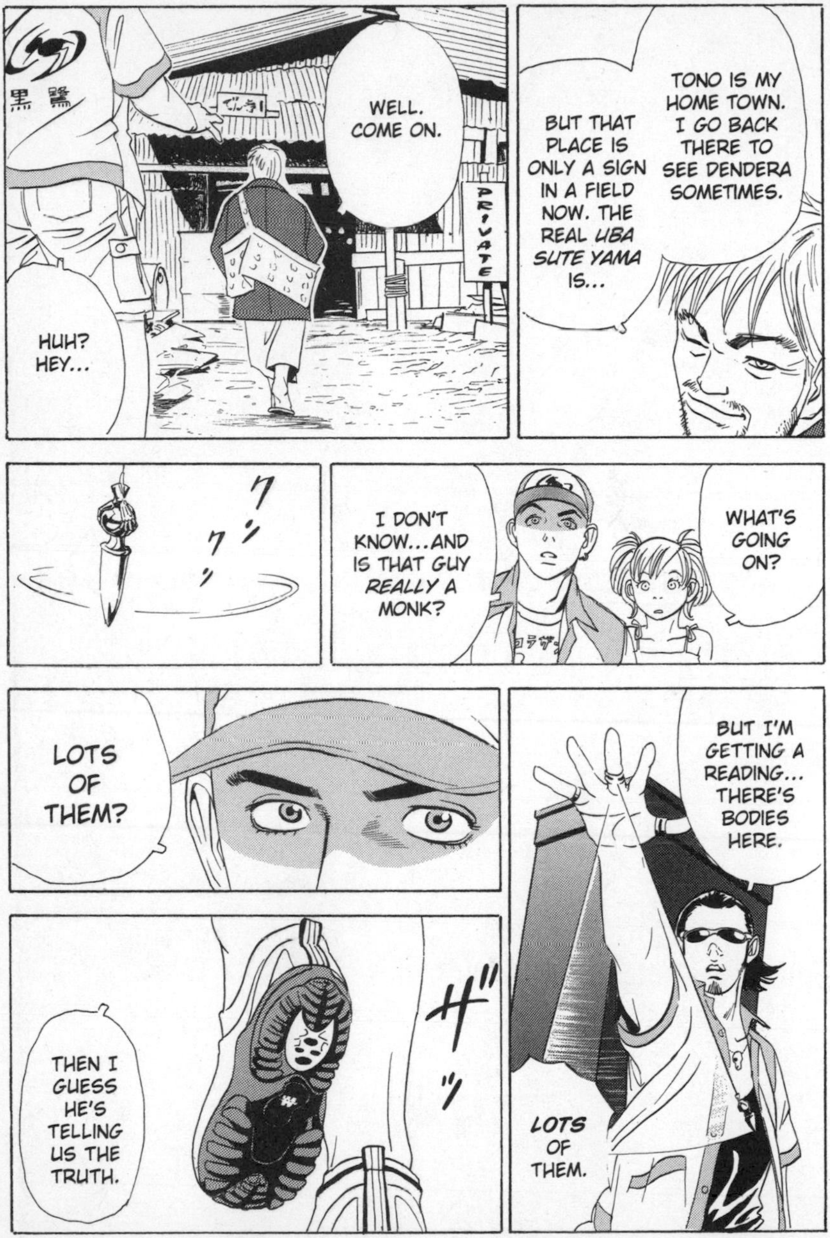
TONO IS MY HOME TOWN. I GO BACK THERE TO SEE DENDERA SOMETIMES.
BUT THAT PLACE IS ONLY A SIGN IN A FIELD NOW. THE REAL *UBA SUTE YAMA* IS...
WELL. COME ON.
PRIVATE
黒鷺
HUH? HEY...
WHAT'S GOING ON?
I DON'T KNOW...AND IS THAT GUY *REALLY* A MONK?
クン
クン
BUT I'M GETTING A READING... THERE'S BODIES HERE.
LOTS OF THEM.
LOTS OF THEM?
ザッ
THEN I GUESS HE'S TELLING US THE TRUTH.

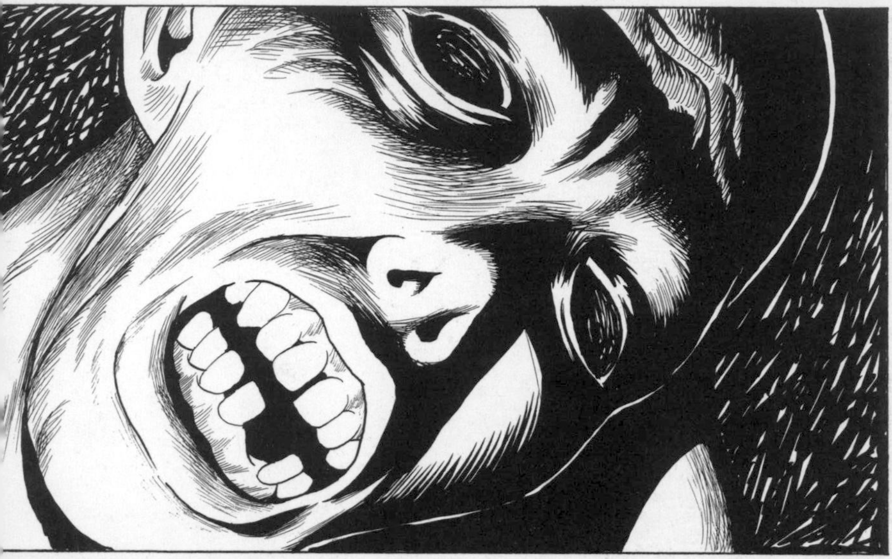
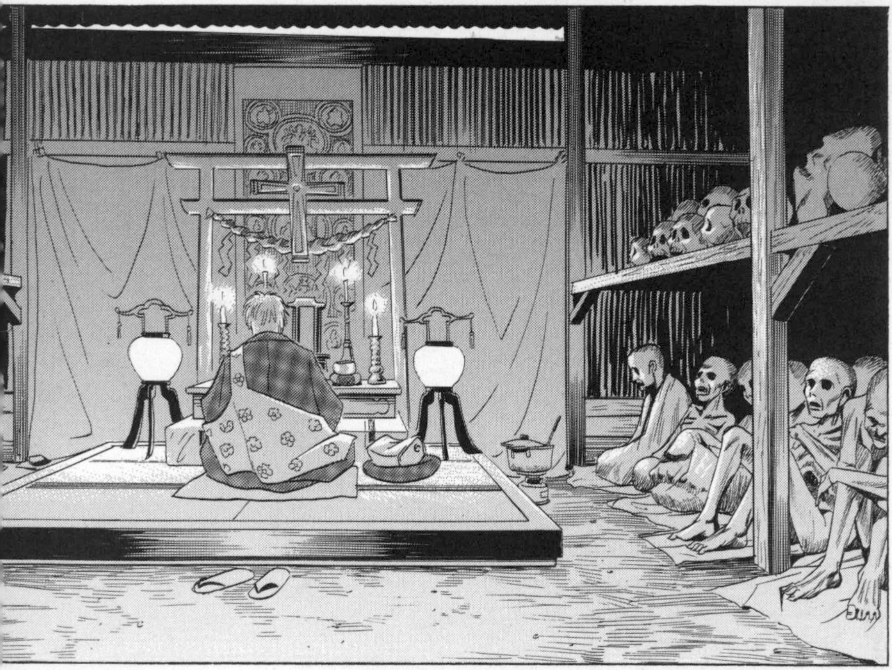

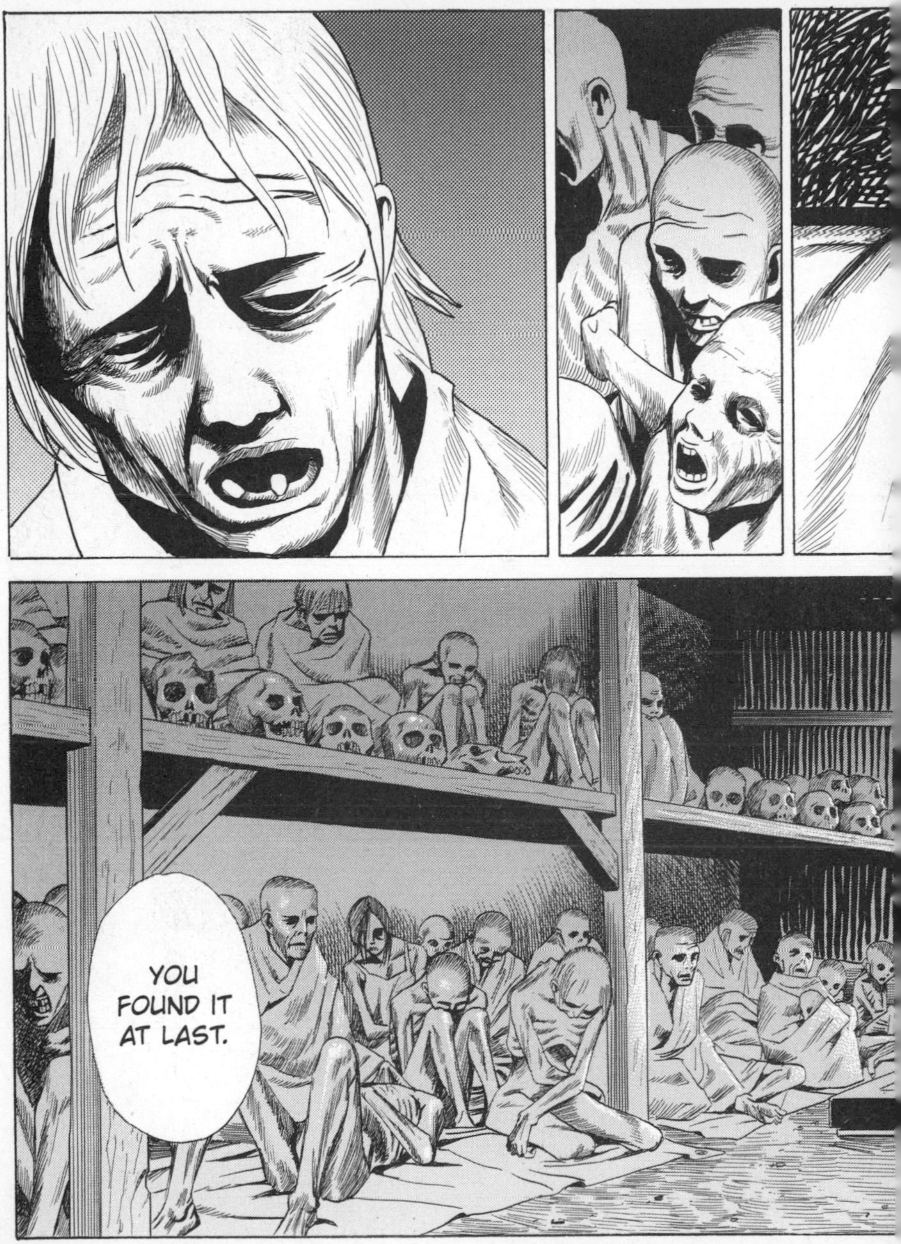
YOU FOUND IT AT LAST.

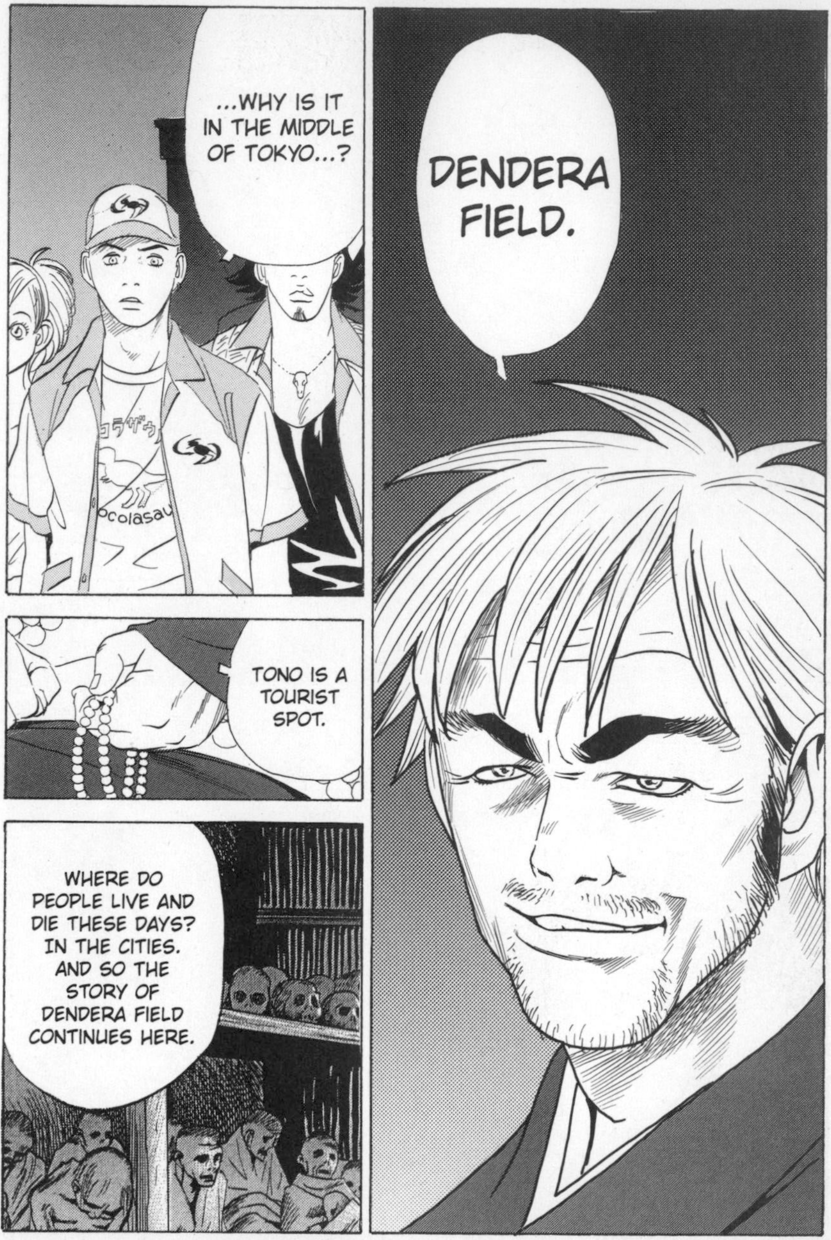
DENDERA FIELD.
...WHY IS IT IN THE MIDDLE OF TOKYO...?
ocolasau
TONO IS A TOURIST SPOT.
WHERE DO PEOPLE LIVE AND DIE THESE DAYS? IN THE CITIES. AND SO THE STORY OF DENDERA FIELD CONTINUES HERE.

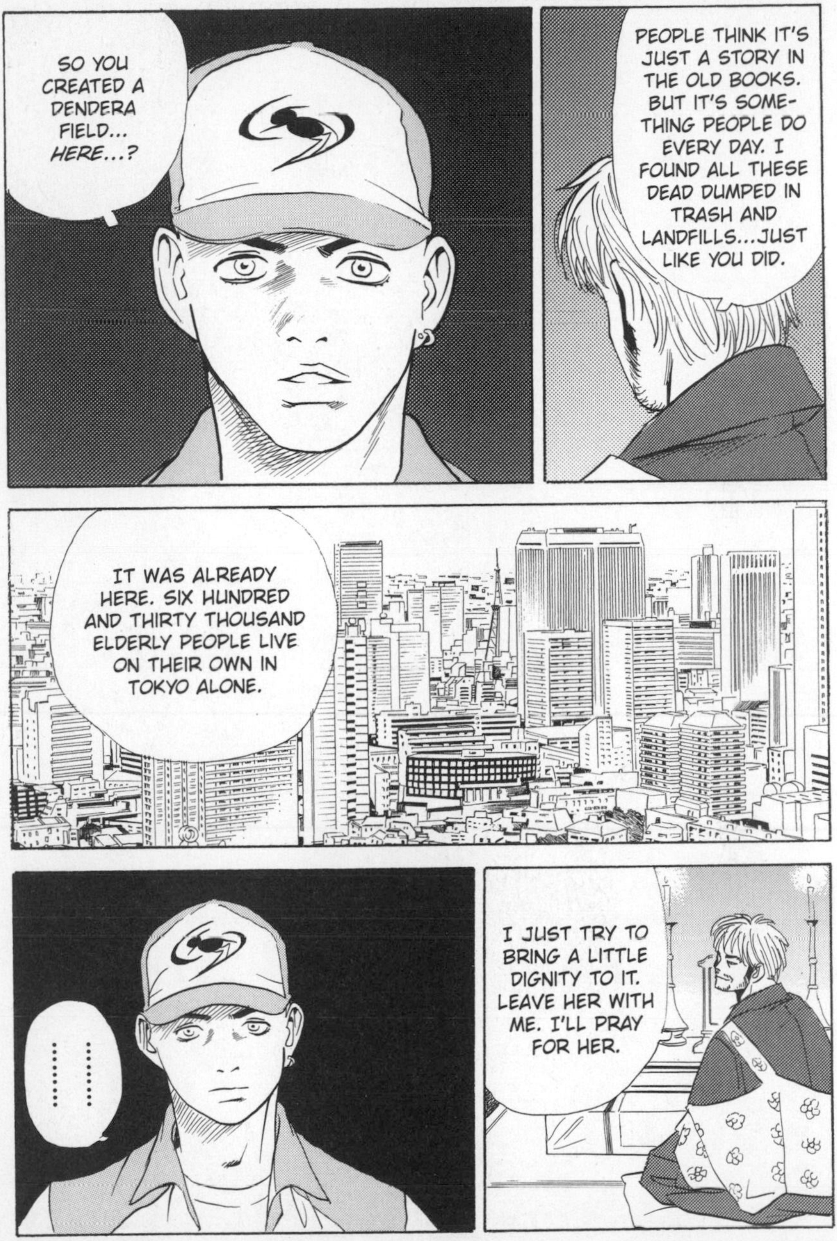
PEOPLE THINK IT'S JUST A STORY IN THE OLD BOOKS. BUT IT'S SOMETHING PEOPLE DO EVERY DAY. I FOUND ALL THESE DEAD DUMPED IN TRASH AND LANDFILLS...JUST LIKE YOU DID.
SO YOU CREATED A DENDERA FIELD... *HERE...?*
IT WAS ALREADY HERE. SIX HUNDRED AND THIRTY THOUSAND ELDERLY PEOPLE LIVE ON THEIR OWN IN TOKYO ALONE.
I JUST TRY TO BRING A LITTLE DIGNITY TO IT. LEAVE HER WITH ME. I'LL PRAY FOR HER.
......

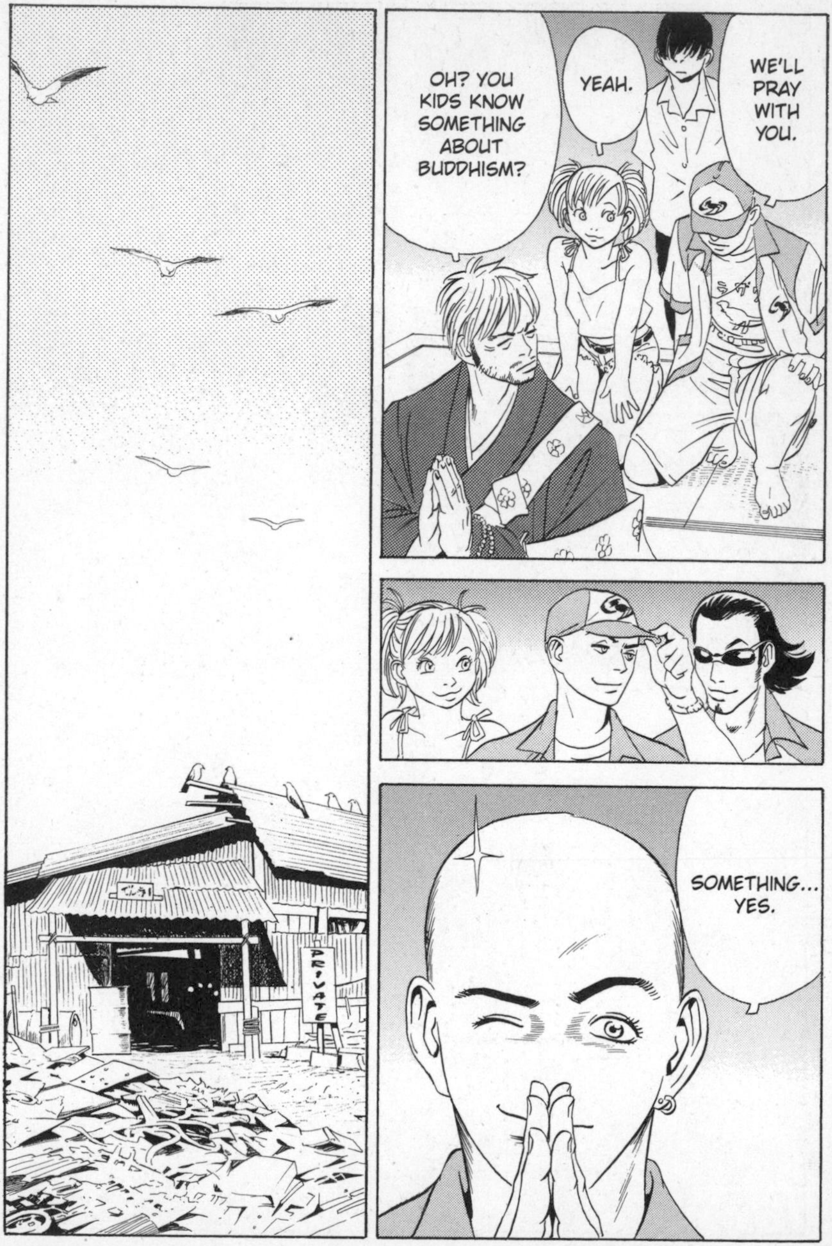
PRIVATE
OH? YOU KIDS KNOW SOMETHING ABOUT BUDDHISM?
YEAH.
WE'LL PRAY WITH YOU.
SOMETHING... YES.

2nd delivery: lonely people—the end

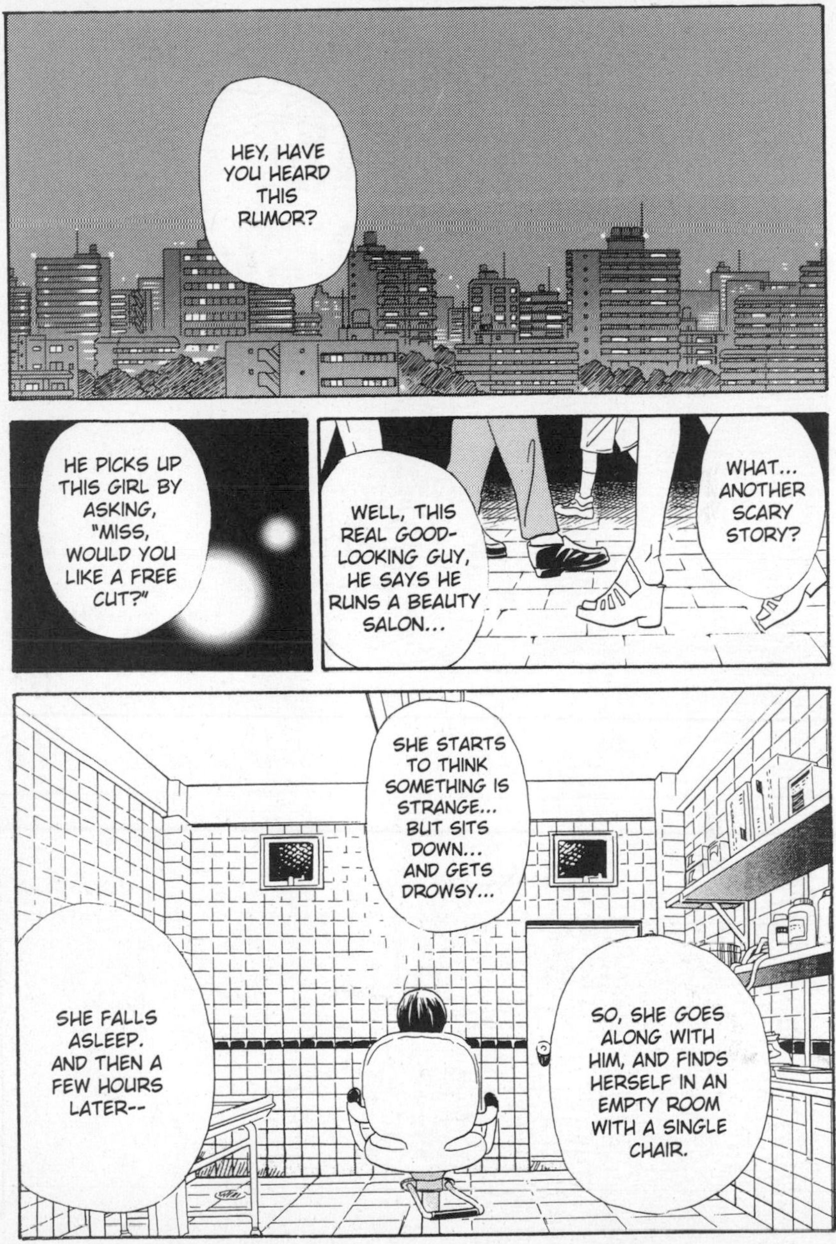
HEY, HAVE YOU HEARD THIS RUMOR?
WHAT... ANOTHER SCARY STORY?
WELL, THIS REAL GOOD-LOOKING GUY, HE SAYS HE RUNS A BEAUTY SALON...
HE PICKS UP THIS GIRL BY ASKING, "MISS, WOULD YOU LIKE A FREE CUT?"
SO, SHE GOES ALONG WITH HIM, AND FINDS HERSELF IN AN EMPTY ROOM WITH A SINGLE CHAIR.
SHE STARTS TO THINK SOMETHING IS STRANGE... BUT SITS DOWN... AND GETS DROWSY...
SHE FALLS ASLEEP. AND THEN A FEW HOURS LATER--

--WOW, YOU'RE AWAKE. SO WHAT DO YOU THINK OF YOUR NEW CUT?

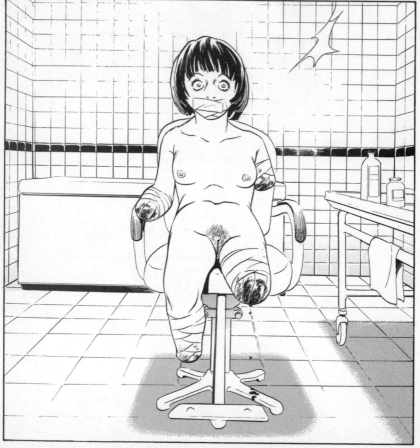

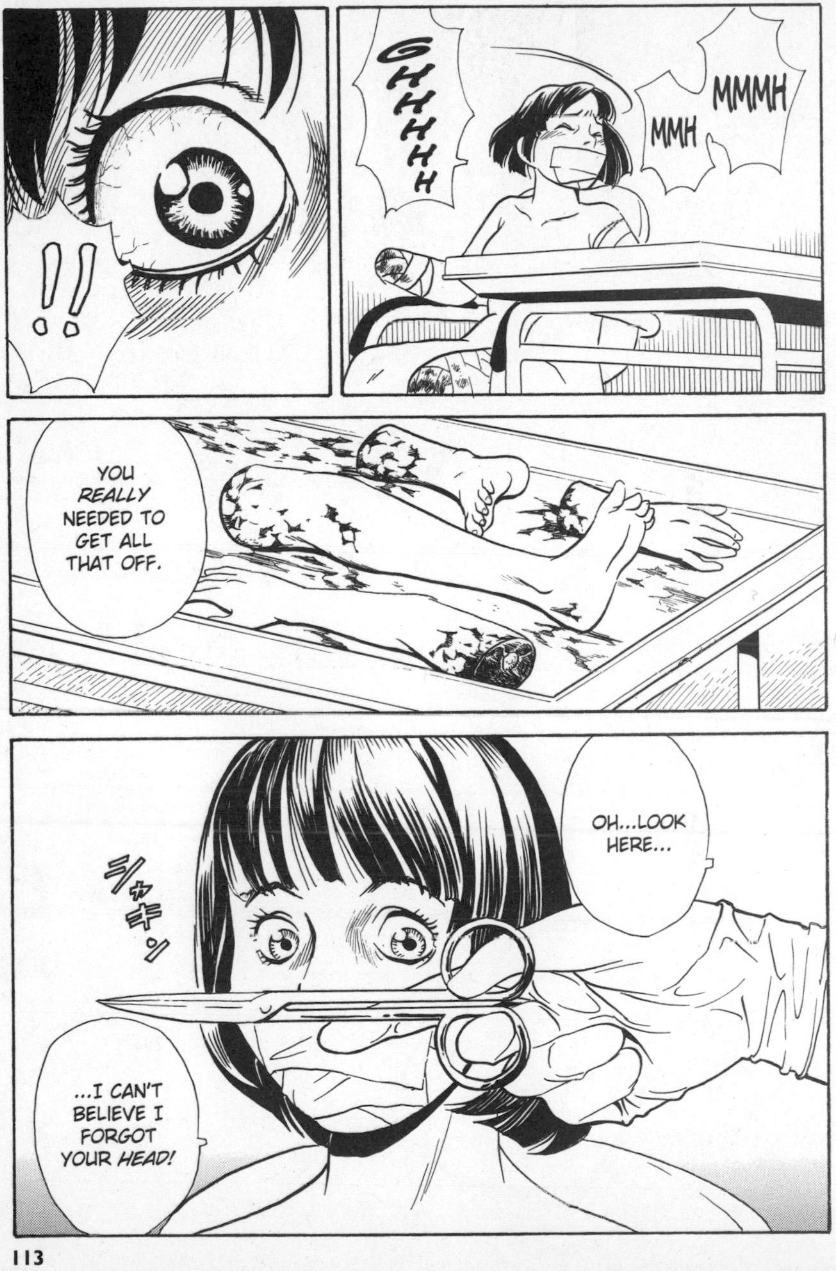
MMMH
MMH
GHHHHHH
!!
YOU *REALLY* NEEDED TO GET ALL THAT OFF.
OH...LOOK HERE...
シャキッ
...I CAN'T BELIEVE I FORGOT YOUR *HEAD!*

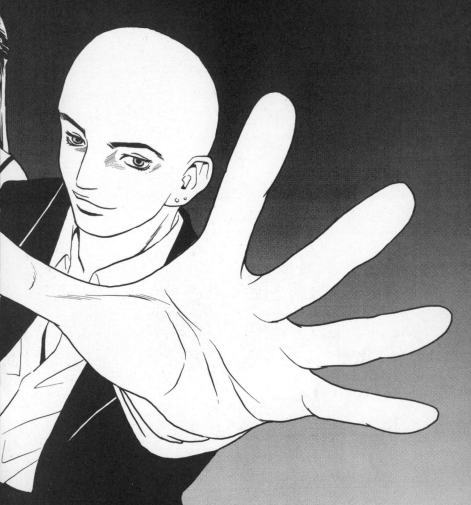

3rd delivery

失恋魔術師

magician of lost love

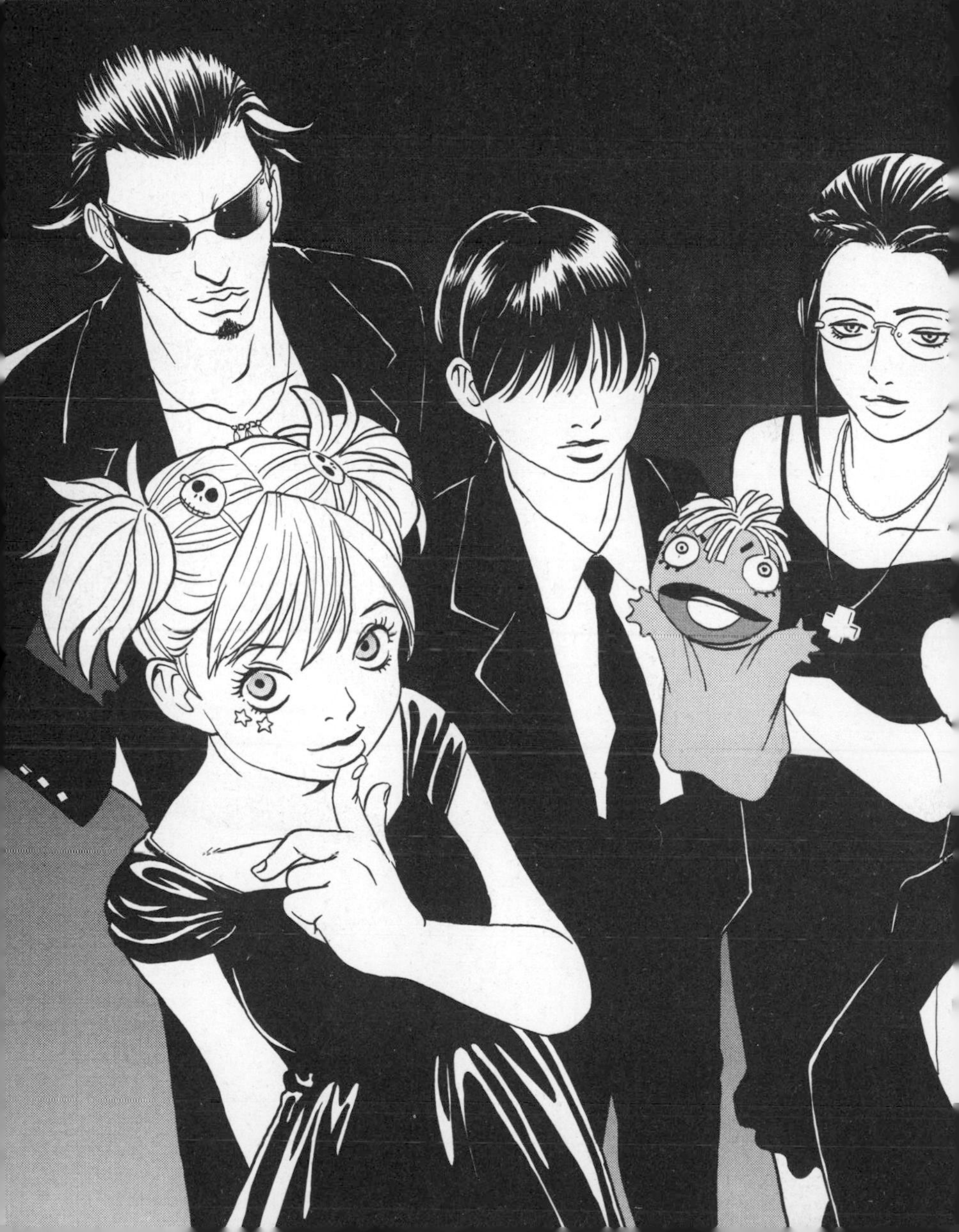

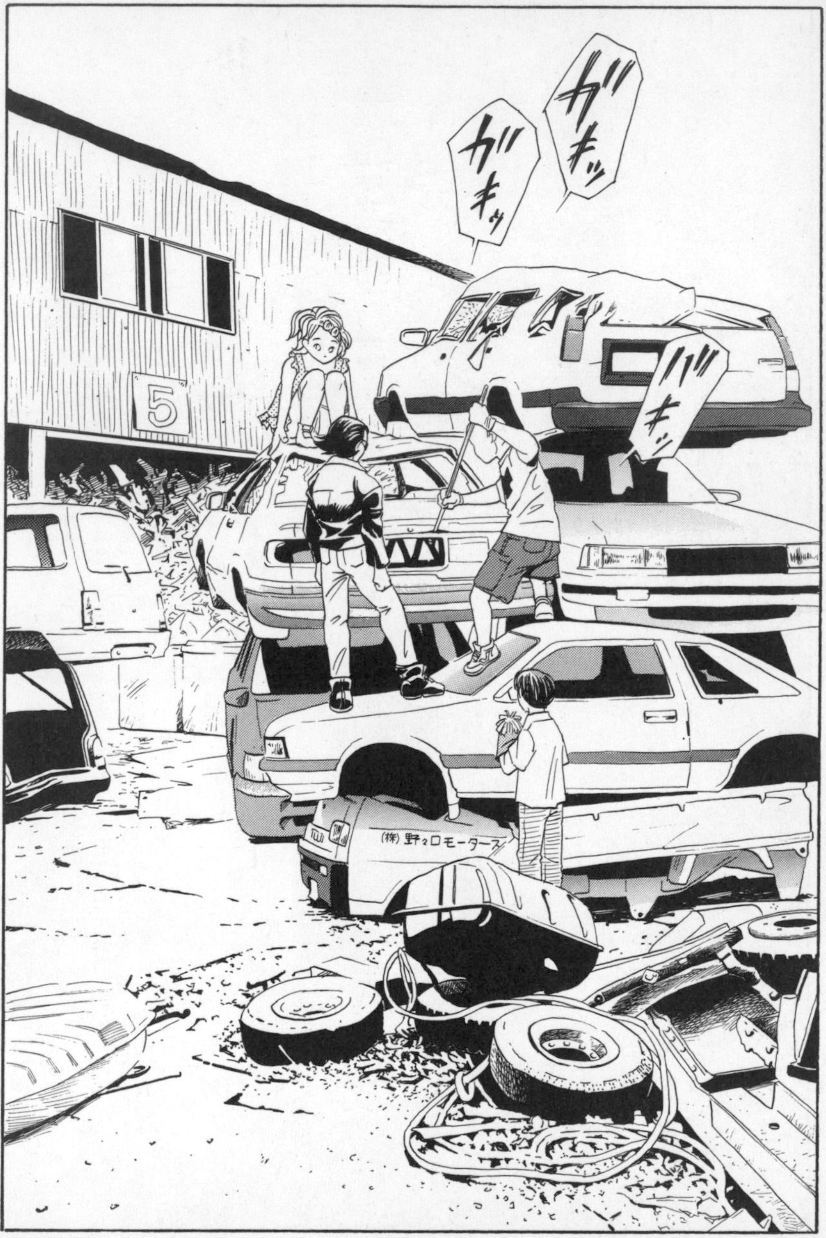
ガギッ
ガギッ
バキッ
(株)野々口モーターズ

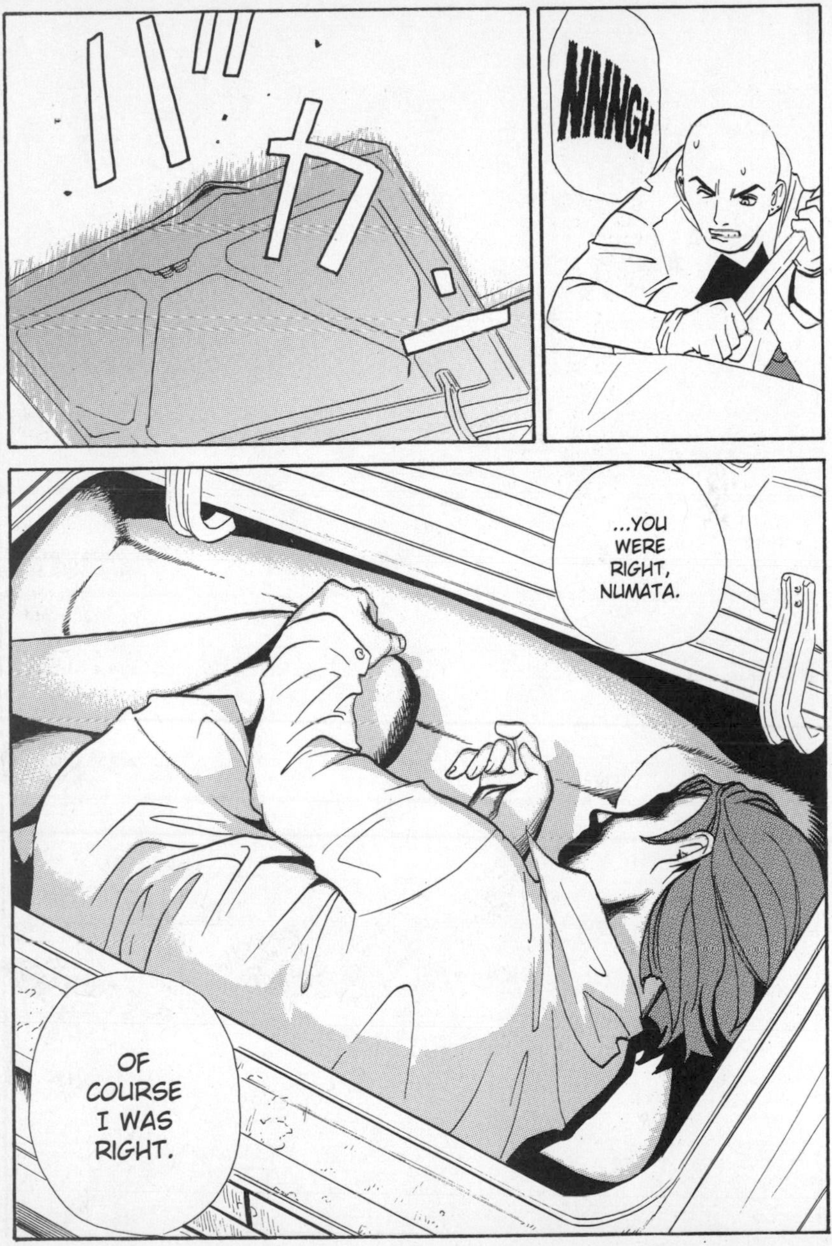
NNNGH
バカ
...YOU WERE RIGHT, NUMATA.
OF COURSE I WAS RIGHT.

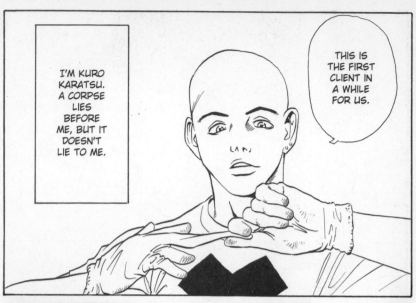

THIS IS THE FIRST CLIENT IN A WHILE FOR US.
I'M KURO KARATSU. A CORPSE LIES BEFORE ME, BUT IT DOESN'T LIE TO ME.
IT TELLS ME ITS TROUBLES AND ITS CARES.
ALL THE THINGS THAT MAKE IT REST UNEASY ...
... KEEPS ITS SOUL BOUND TO THIS FLESH.
WE MAKE A LIVING OFF THESE DEAD, MY FRIENDS AND I.

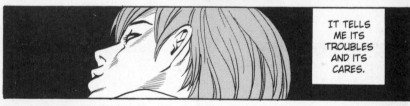

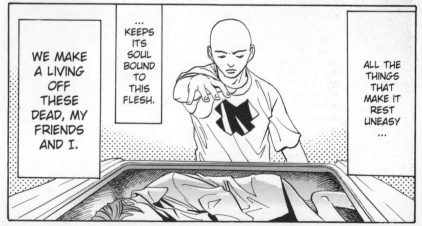

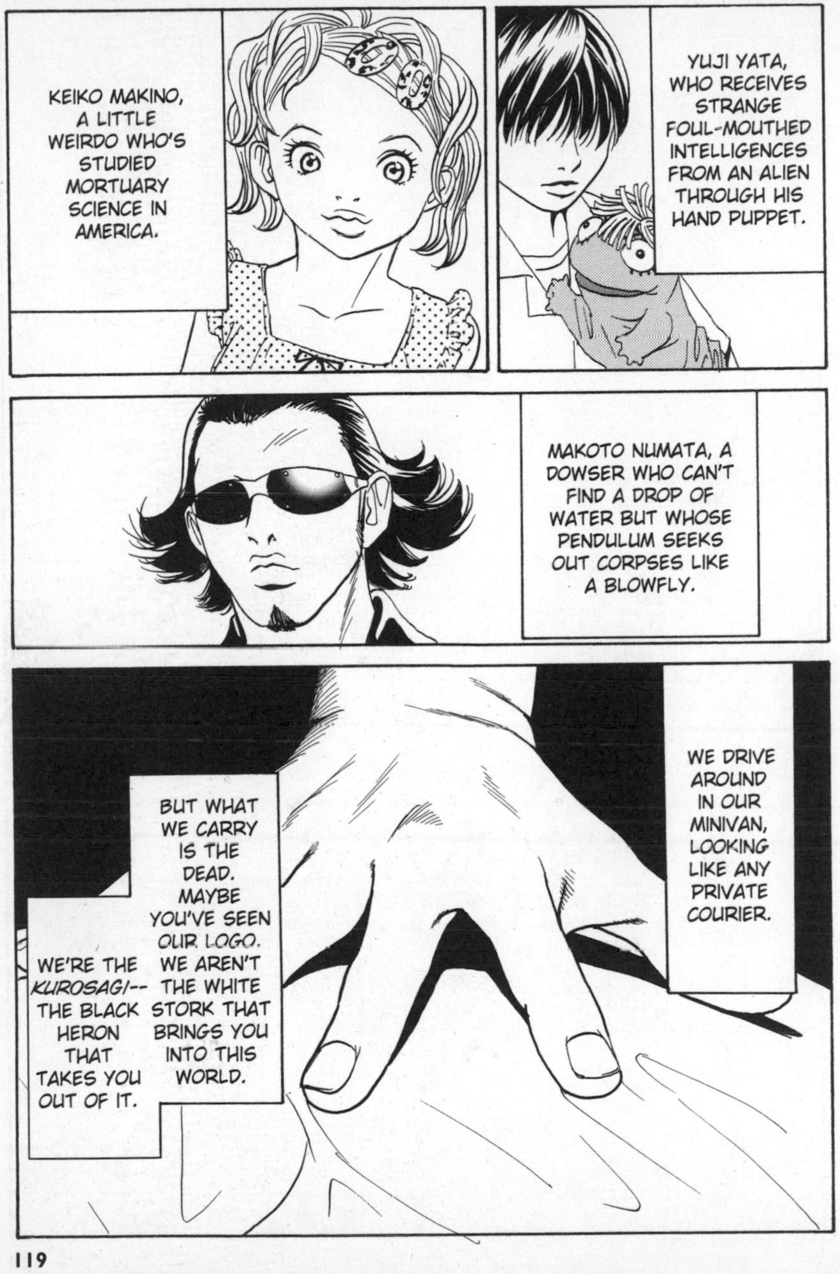
YUJI YATA, WHO RECEIVES STRANGE FOUL-MOUTHED INTELLIGENCES FROM AN ALIEN THROUGH HIS HAND PUPPET.
KEIKO MAKINO, A LITTLE WEIRDO WHO'S STUDIED MORTUARY SCIENCE IN AMERICA.
MAKOTO NUMATA, A DOWSER WHO CAN'T FIND A DROP OF WATER BUT WHOSE PENDULUM SEEKS OUT CORPSES LIKE A BLOWFLY.
WE DRIVE AROUND IN OUR MINIVAN, LOOKING LIKE ANY PRIVATE COURIER.
BUT WHAT WE CARRY IS THE DEAD. MAYBE YOU'VE SEEN OUR LOGO. WE AREN'T THE WHITE STORK THAT BRINGS YOU INTO THIS WORLD.
WE'RE THE *KUROSAGI*-- THE BLACK HERON THAT TAKES YOU OUT OF IT.

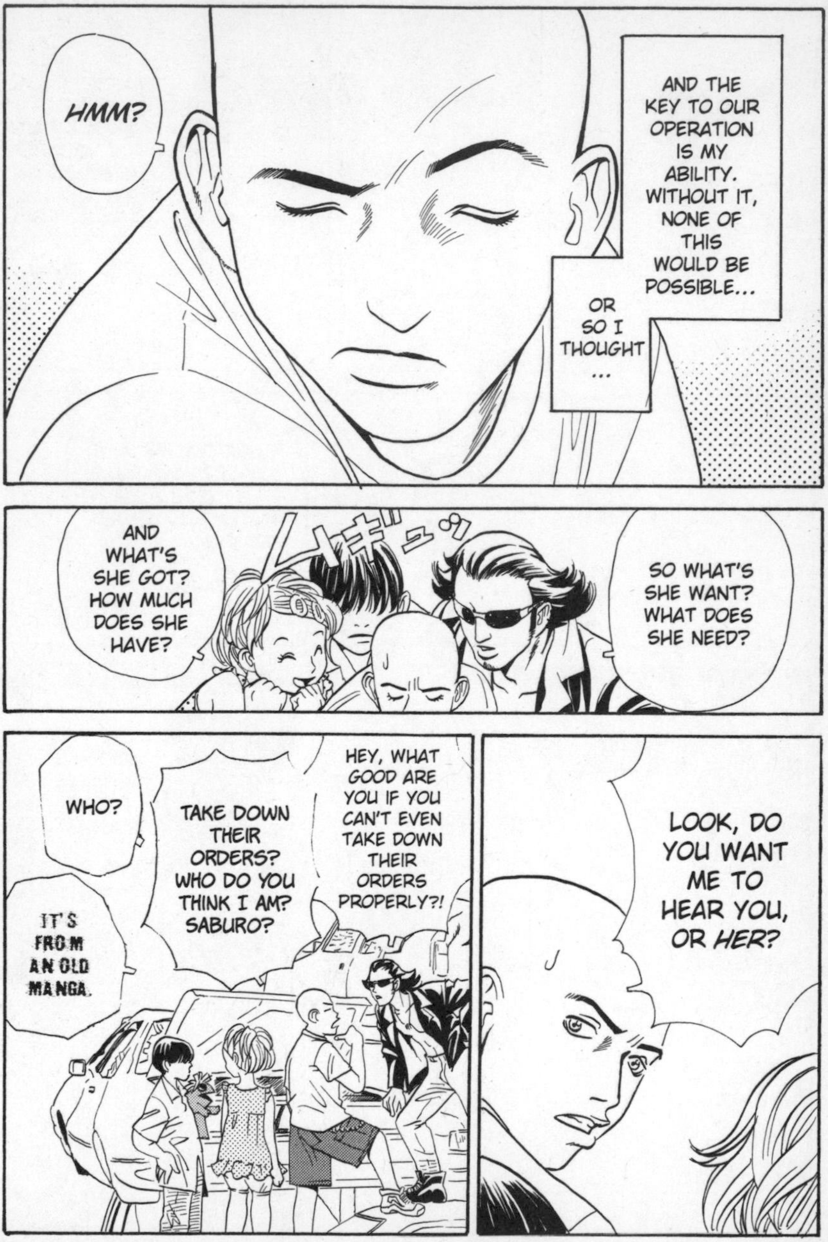
AND THE KEY TO OUR OPERATION IS MY ABILITY. WITHOUT IT, NONE OF THIS WOULD BE POSSIBLE...
OR SO I THOUGHT ...
HMM?
SO WHAT'S SHE WANT? WHAT DOES SHE NEED?
AND WHAT'S SHE GOT? HOW MUCH DOES SHE HAVE?
LOOK, DO YOU WANT ME TO HEAR YOU, OR *HER*?
HEY, WHAT GOOD ARE YOU IF YOU CAN'T EVEN TAKE DOWN THEIR ORDERS PROPERLY?!
TAKE DOWN THEIR ORDERS? WHO DO YOU THINK I AM? SABURO?
WHO?
IT'S FROM AN OLD MANGA.

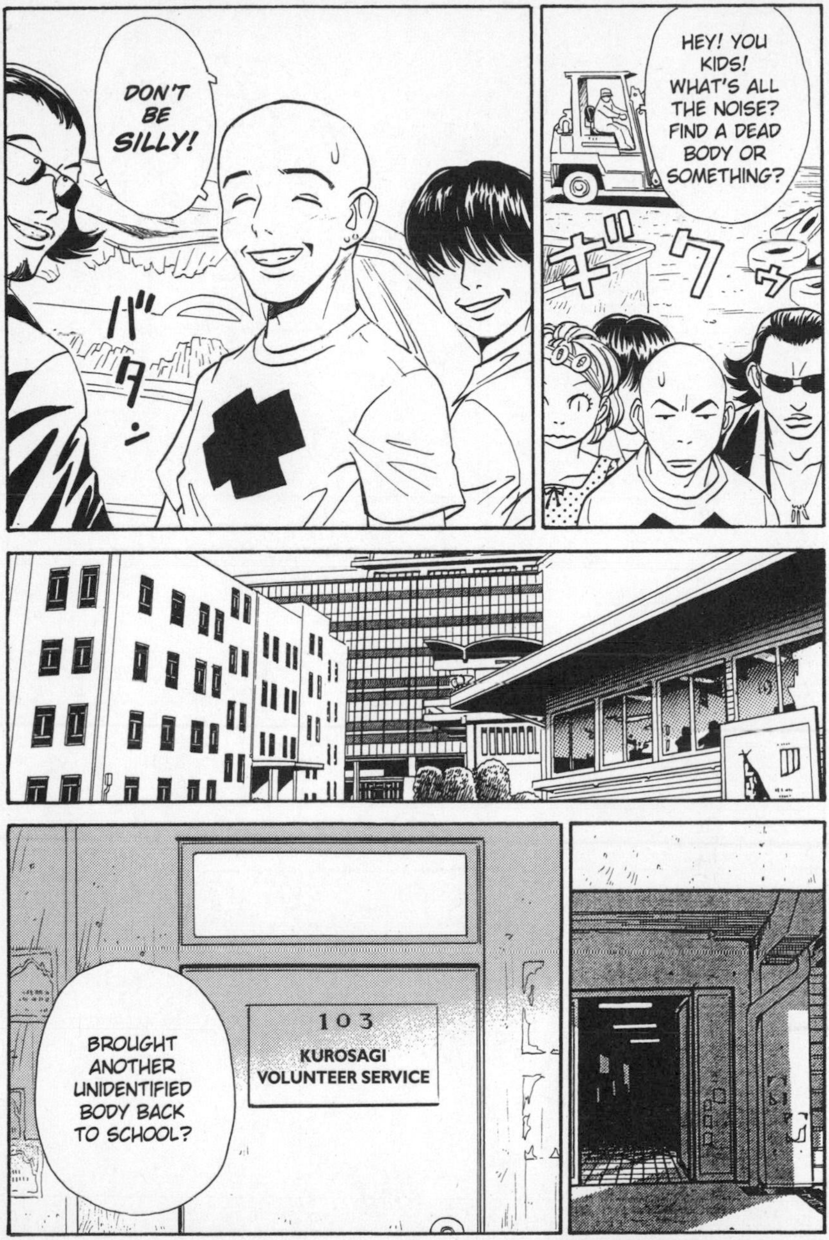
HEY! YOU KIDS! WHAT'S ALL THE NOISE? FIND A DEAD BODY OR SOMETHING?
ギクゥ
DON'T BE SILLY!
バタン
103
KUROSAGI VOLUNTEER SERVICE
BROUGHT ANOTHER UNIDENTIFIED BODY BACK TO SCHOOL?

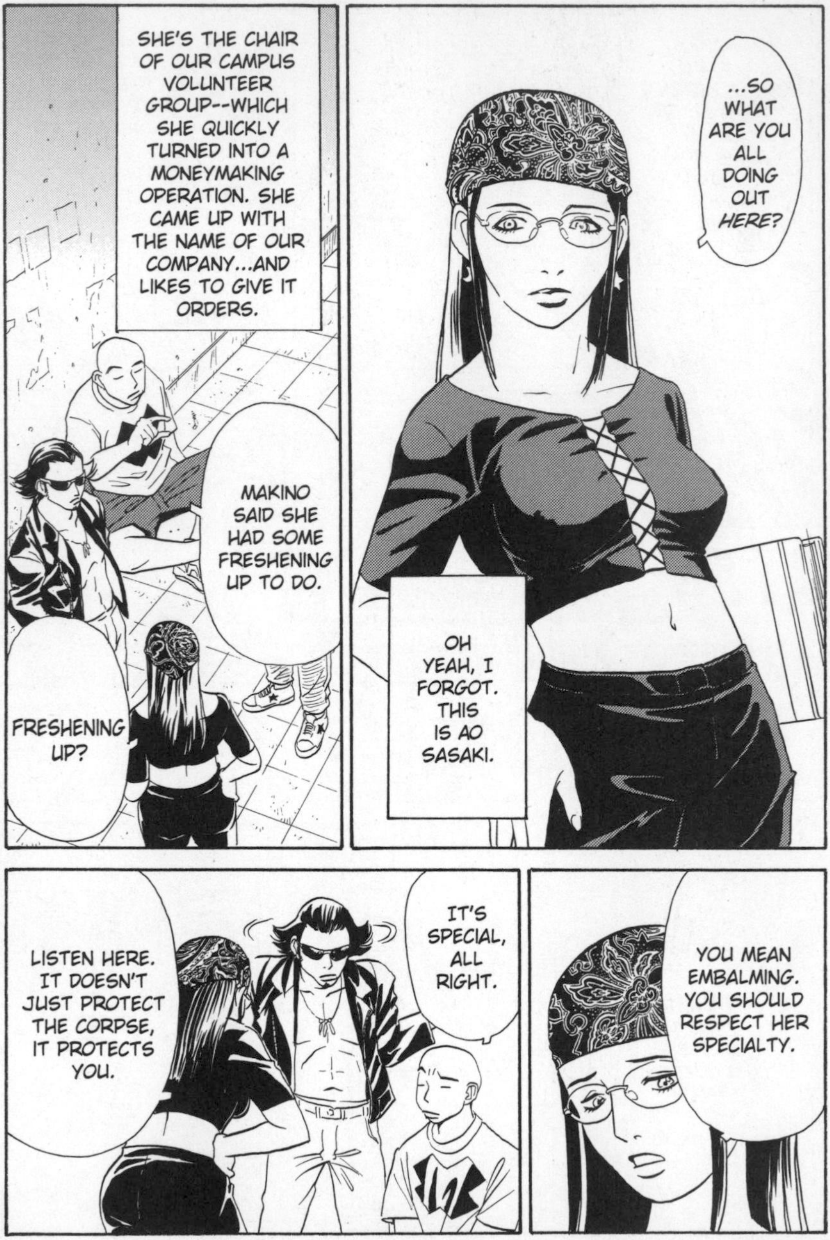
...SO WHAT ARE YOU ALL DOING OUT HERE?
OH YEAH, I FORGOT. THIS IS AO SASAKI.
SHE'S THE CHAIR OF OUR CAMPUS VOLUNTEER GROUP--WHICH SHE QUICKLY TURNED INTO A MONEYMAKING OPERATION. SHE CAME UP WITH THE NAME OF OUR COMPANY...AND LIKES TO GIVE IT ORDERS.
MAKINO SAID SHE HAD SOME FRESHENING UP TO DO.
FRESHENING UP?
YOU MEAN EMBALMING. YOU SHOULD RESPECT HER SPECIALTY.
IT'S SPECIAL, ALL RIGHT.
LISTEN HERE. IT DOESN'T JUST PROTECT THE CORPSE, IT PROTECTS YOU.

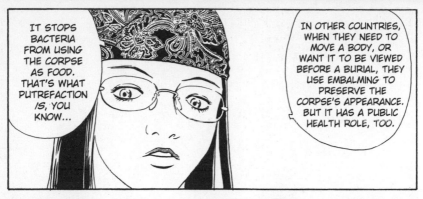

IN OTHER COUNTRIES, WHEN THEY NEED TO MOVE A BODY, OR WANT IT TO BE VIEWED BEFORE A BURIAL, THEY USE EMBALMING TO PRESERVE THE CORPSE'S APPEARANCE. BUT IT HAS A PUBLIC HEALTH ROLE, TOO.
IT STOPS BACTERIA FROM USING THE CORPSE AS FOOD. THAT'S WHAT PUTREFACTION *IS*, YOU KNOW...
I'VE GOT TO *TOUCH* THEM...
A SMALL AMOUNT OF CONTACT IS FINE.
BUT IF IT'S SO DANGEROUS, IS IT SAFE TO LET MAKINO HANDLE IT ON HER OWN?
DON'T BE A FOOL. SHE'S ONE OF THE FEW PEOPLE IN THE COUNTRY WHO STUDIED AND WAS LICENSED TO BE AN EMBALMER IN THE UNITED STATES.
WHEN IT COMES TO HANDLING OUR CLIENTS, THERE'S NO ONE I'D TRUST MORE.

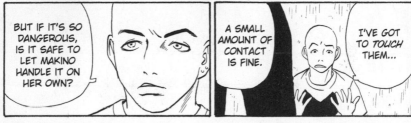

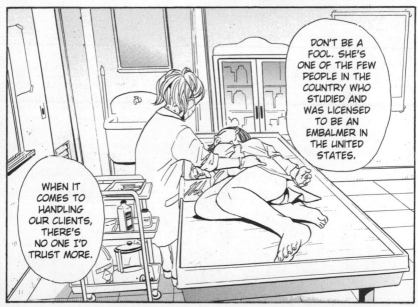

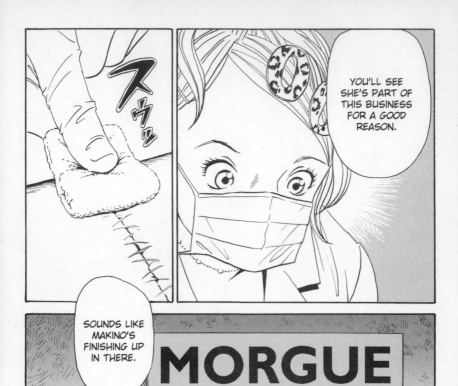

YOU'LL SEE SHE'S PART OF THIS BUSINESS FOR A GOOD REASON.
スゥッ
SOUNDS LIKE MAKINO'S FINISHING UP IN THERE.
MORGUE
MORGUE
ガチャ
UH... WELL... HOW DID IT GO...?
DID YOU TAKE CARE OF THE BODY?
IT'S NOT REALLY A BODY...
HERE... TAKE A LOOK.

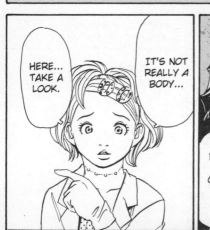

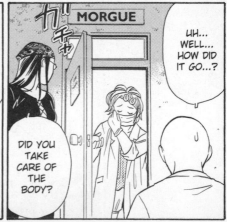

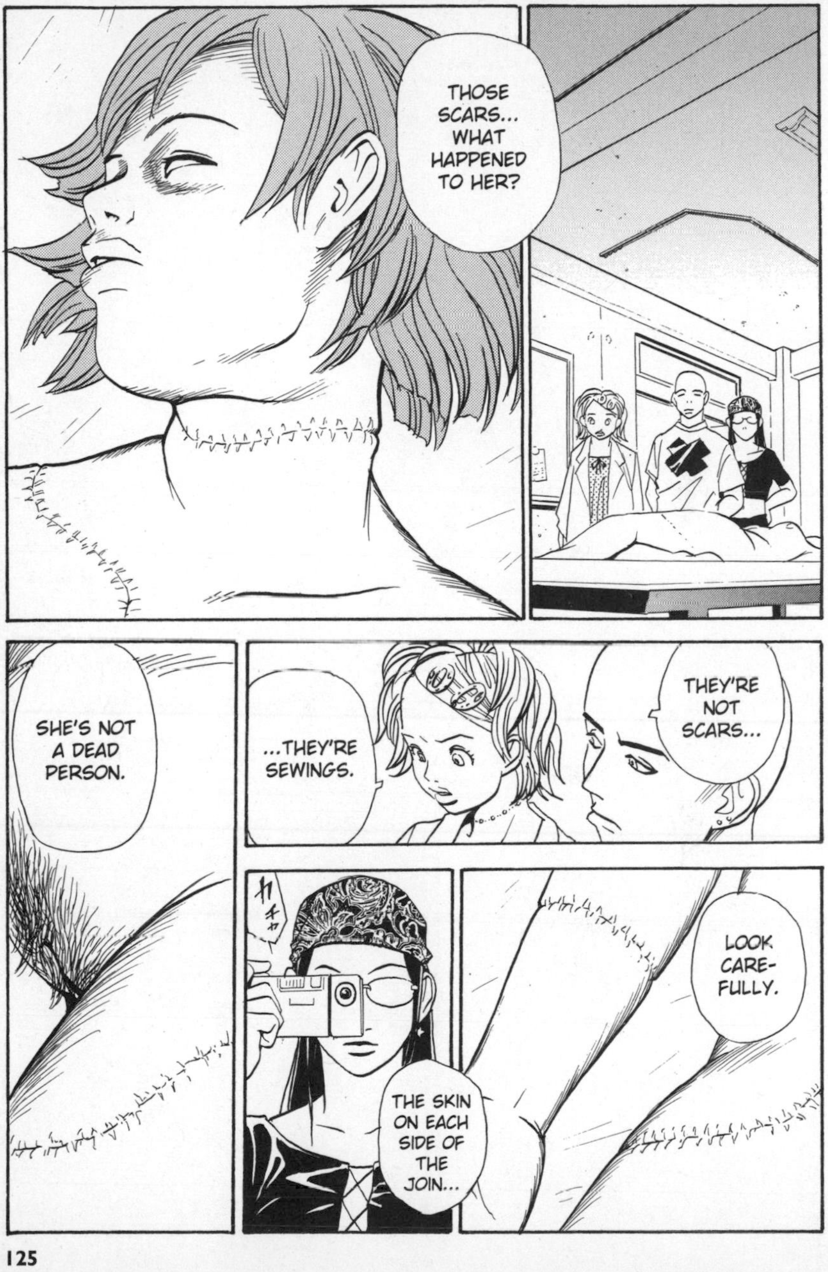
THOSE SCARS... WHAT HAPPENED TO HER?
THEY'RE NOT SCARS...
...THEY'RE SEWINGS.
LOOK CARE-FULLY.
カチャ
THE SKIN ON EACH SIDE OF THE JOIN...
SHE'S NOT A DEAD PERSON.

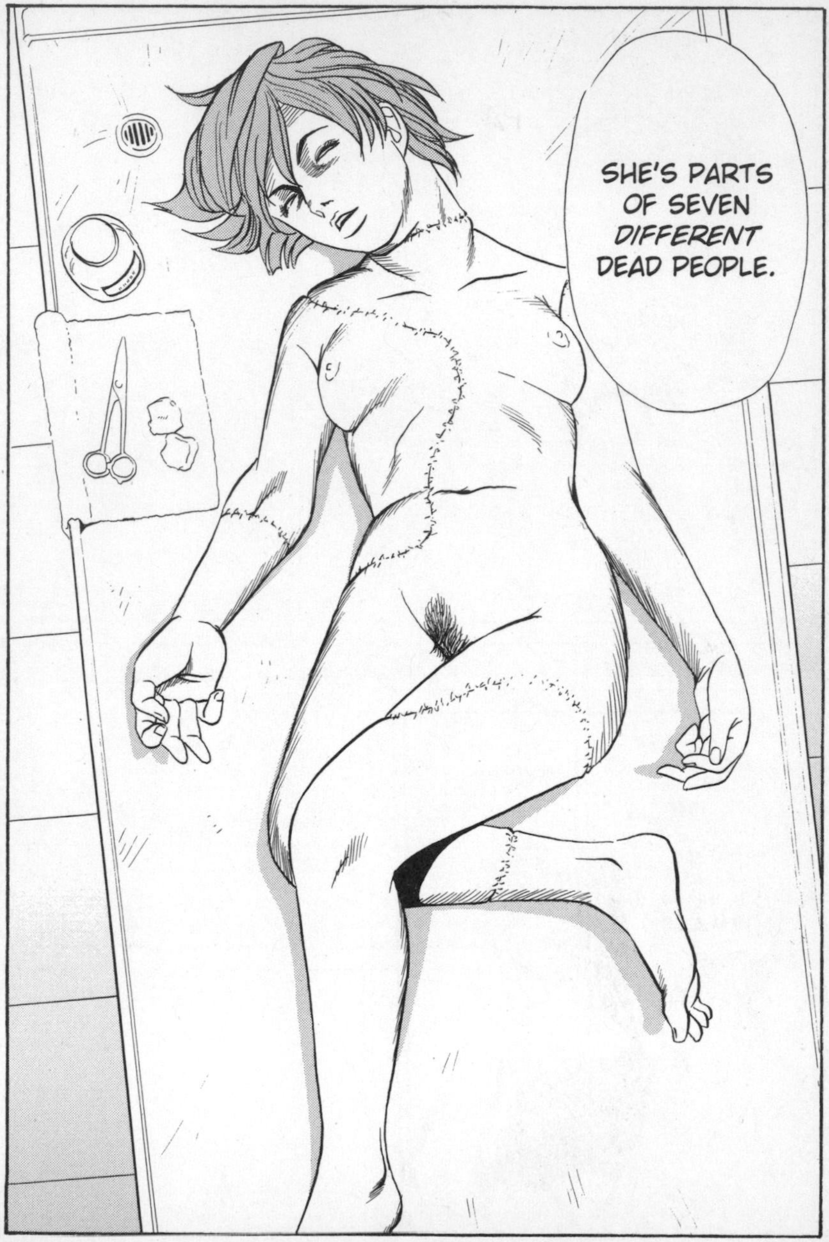
SHE'S PARTS OF SEVEN *DIFFERENT* DEAD PEOPLE.

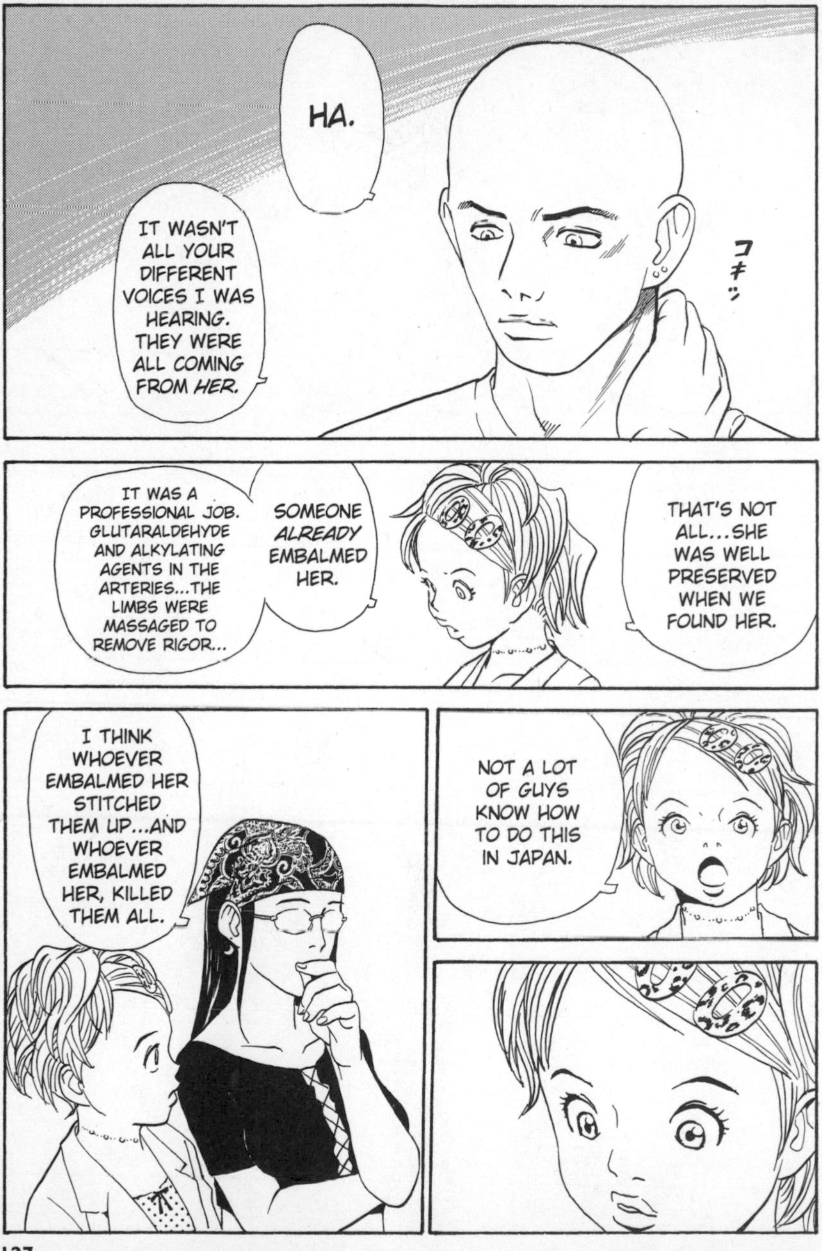
HA.
コキッ
IT WASN'T ALL YOUR DIFFERENT VOICES I WAS HEARING. THEY WERE ALL COMING FROM *HER*.
THAT'S NOT ALL...SHE WAS WELL PRESERVED WHEN WE FOUND HER.
SOMEONE *ALREADY* EMBALMED HER.
IT WAS A PROFESSIONAL JOB. GLUTARALDEHYDE AND ALKYLATING AGENTS IN THE ARTERIES...THE LIMBS WERE MASSAGED TO REMOVE RIGOR...
NOT A LOT OF GUYS KNOW HOW TO DO THIS IN JAPAN.
I THINK WHOEVER EMBALMED HER STITCHED THEM UP...AND WHOEVER EMBALMED HER, KILLED THEM ALL.

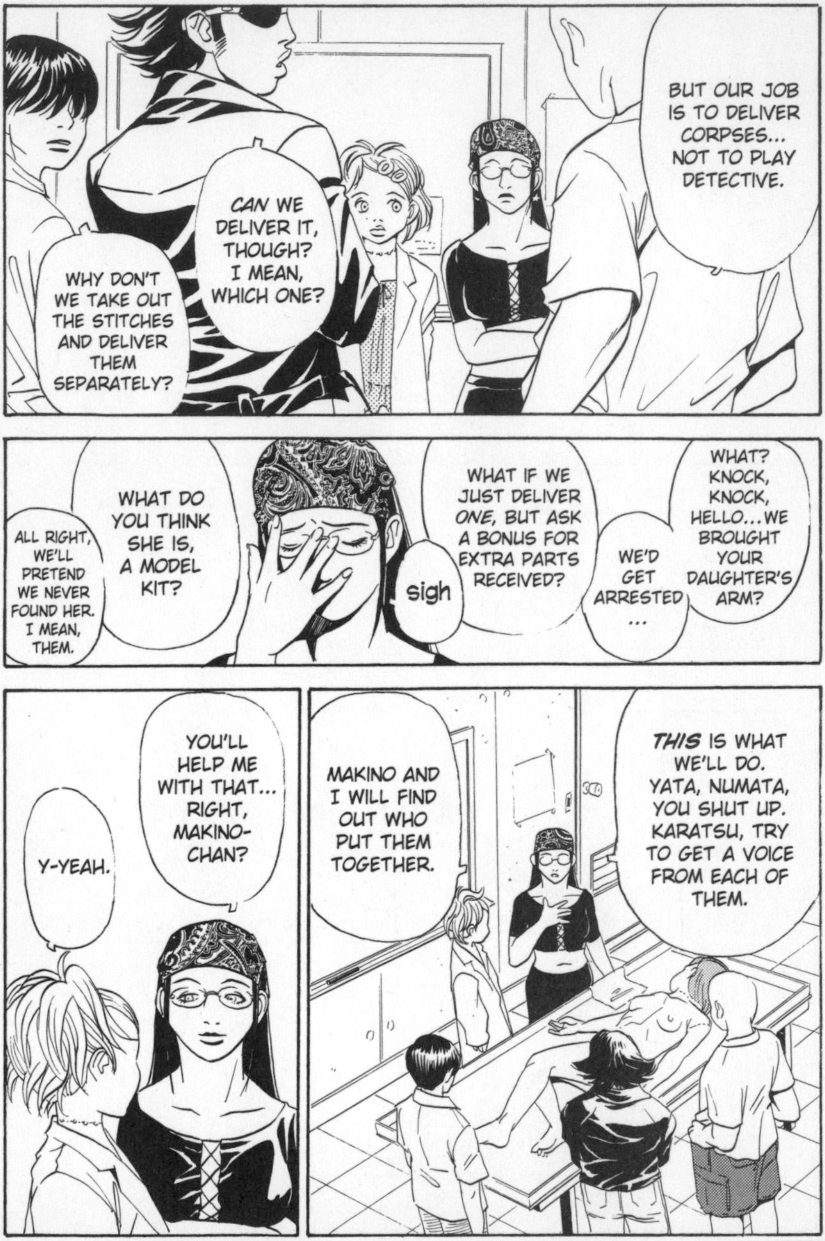
BUT OUR JOB IS TO DELIVER CORPSES... NOT TO PLAY DETECTIVE.
CAN WE DELIVER IT, THOUGH? I MEAN, WHICH ONE?
WHY DON'T WE TAKE OUT THE STITCHES AND DELIVER THEM SEPARATELY?
WHAT IF WE JUST DELIVER *ONE*, BUT ASK A BONUS FOR EXTRA PARTS RECEIVED?
WHAT? KNOCK, KNOCK, HELLO...WE BROUGHT YOUR DAUGHTER'S ARM?
WE'D GET ARRESTED ...
sigh
WHAT DO YOU THINK SHE IS, A MODEL KIT?
ALL RIGHT, WE'LL PRETEND WE NEVER FOUND HER. I MEAN, THEM.
THIS IS WHAT WE'LL DO. YATA, NUMATA, YOU SHUT UP. KARATSU, TRY TO GET A VOICE FROM EACH OF THEM.
MAKINO AND I WILL FIND OUT WHO PUT THEM TOGETHER.
YOU'LL HELP ME WITH THAT... RIGHT, MAKINO-CHAN?
Y-YEAH.

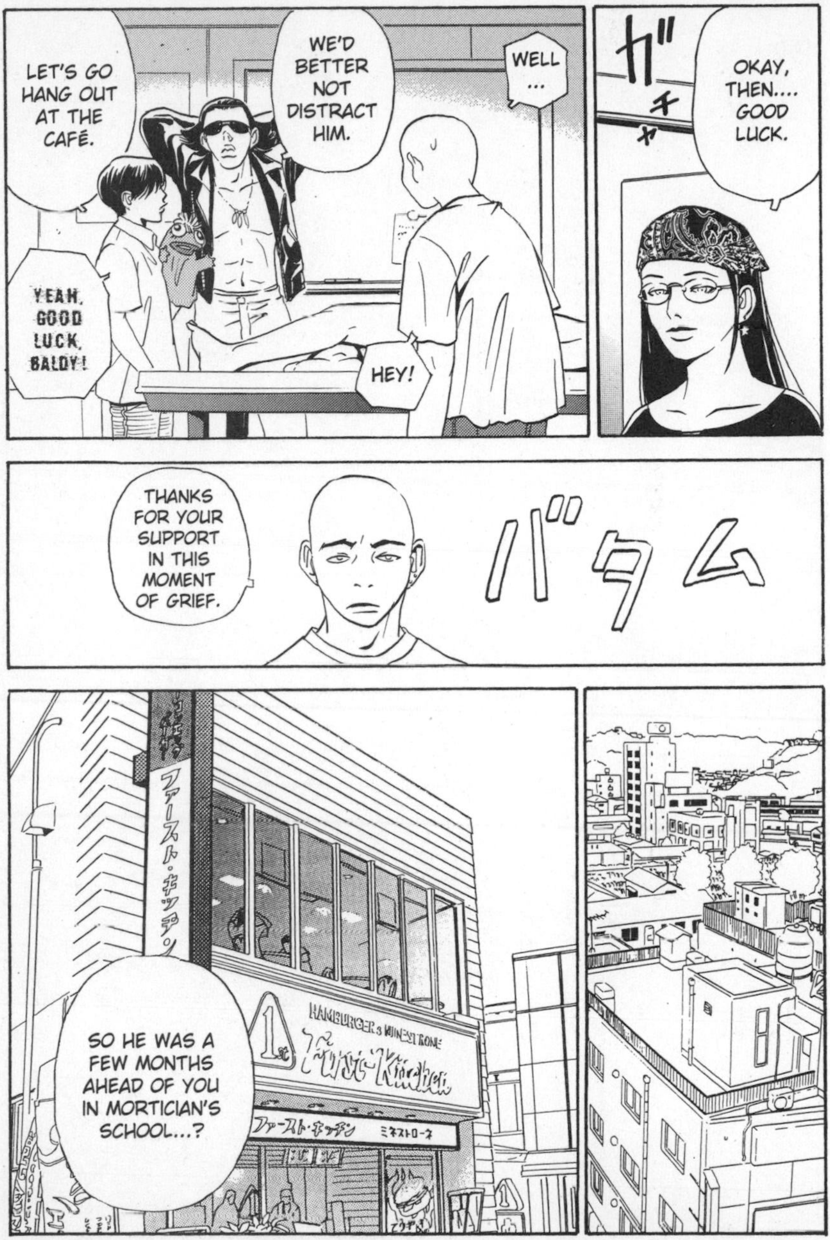
ガチャ
OKAY, THEN.... GOOD LUCK.
WELL ...
WE'D BETTER NOT DISTRACT HIM.
LET'S GO HANG OUT AT THE CAFÉ.
YEAH, GOOD LUCK, BALDY!
HEY!
バタム
THANKS FOR YOUR SUPPORT IN THIS MOMENT OF GRIEF.
ファースト・キッチン
HAMBURGER & MINESTRONE
1st
First Kitchen
ファースト・キッチン
ミネストローネ
SO HE WAS A FEW MONTHS AHEAD OF YOU IN MORTICIAN'S SCHOOL...?

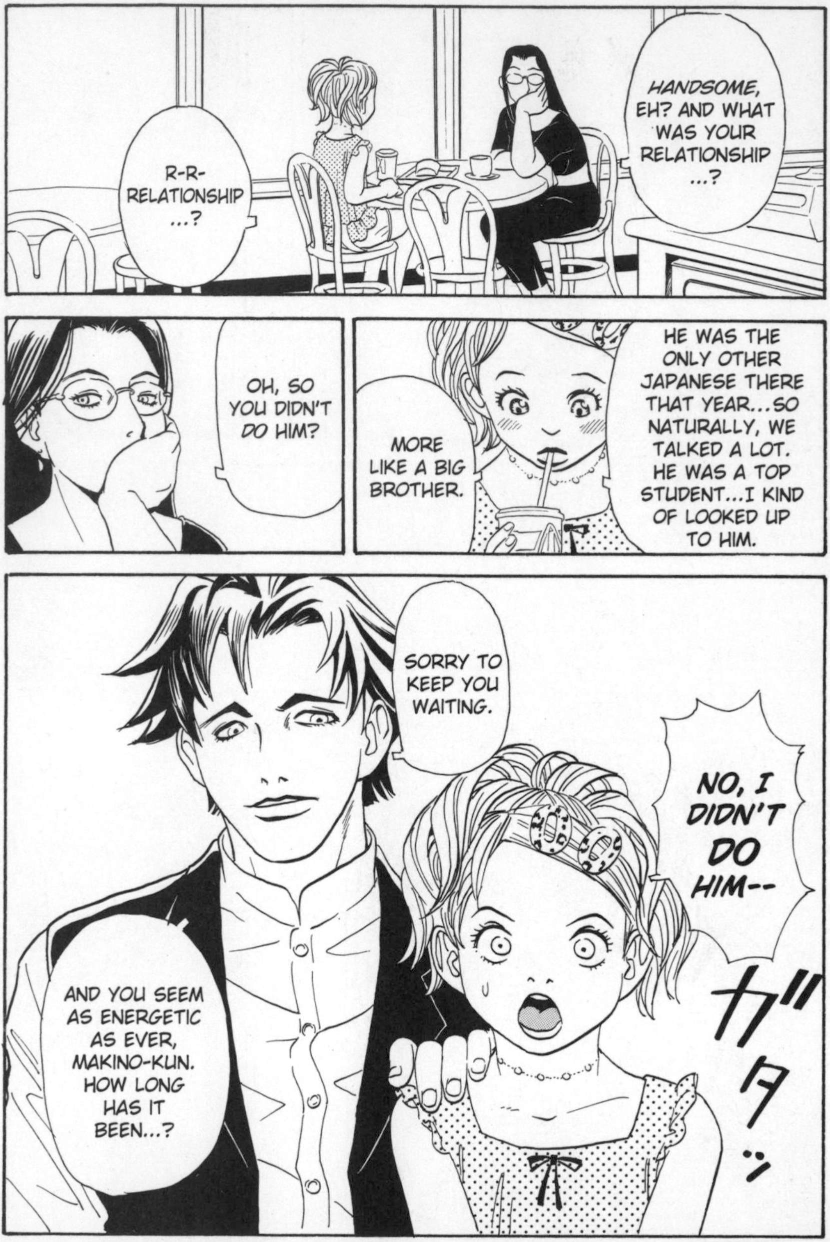
HANDSOME, EH? AND WHAT WAS YOUR RELATIONSHIP ...?
R-R-RELATIONSHIP ...?
HE WAS THE ONLY OTHER JAPANESE THERE THAT YEAR...SO NATURALLY, WE TALKED A LOT. HE WAS A TOP STUDENT...I KIND OF LOOKED UP TO HIM.
MORE LIKE A BIG BROTHER.
OH, SO YOU DIDN'T DO HIM?
NO, I DIDN'T DO HIM--
ガタッ
SORRY TO KEEP YOU WAITING.
AND YOU SEEM AS ENERGETIC AS EVER, MAKINO-KUN. HOW LONG HAS IT BEEN...?

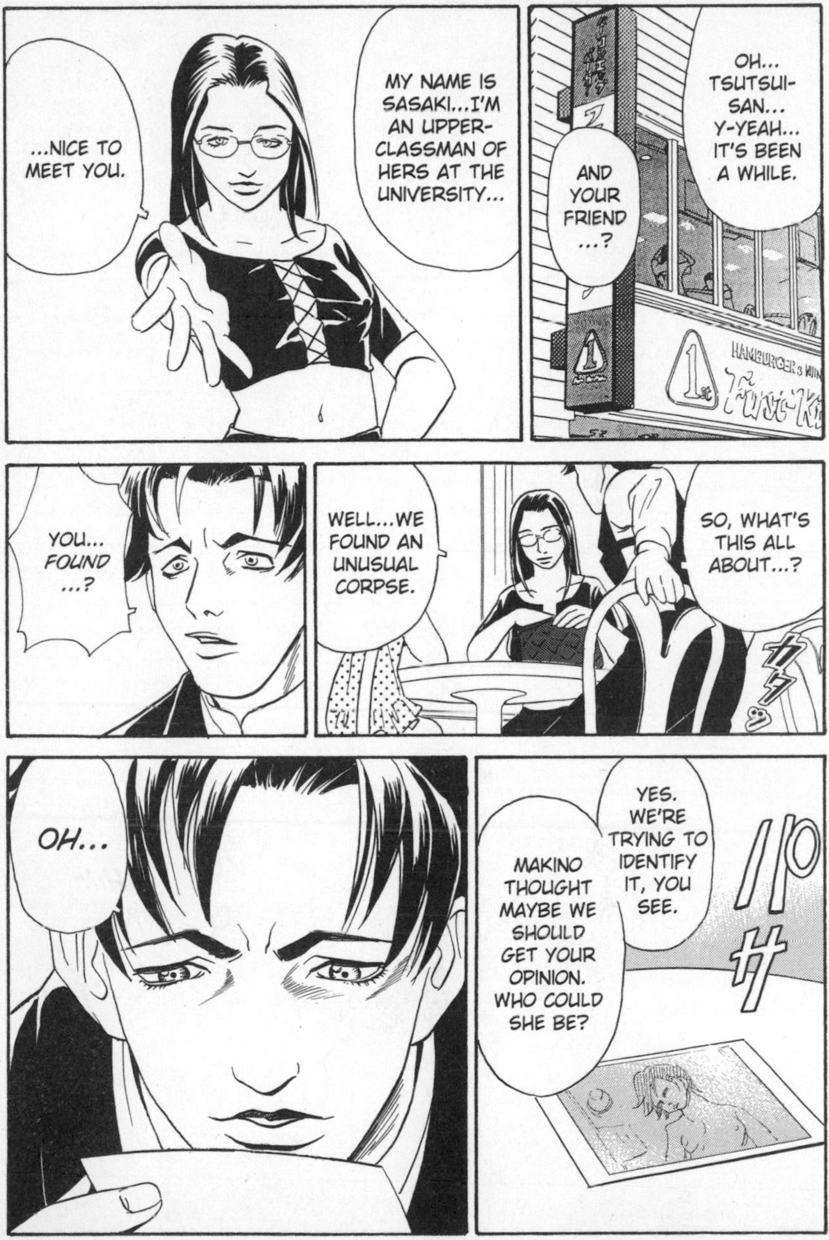
OH... TSUTSUI-SAN... Y-YEAH... IT'S BEEN A WHILE.
AND YOUR FRIEND ...?
MY NAME IS SASAKI...I'M AN UPPER-CLASSMAN OF HERS AT THE UNIVERSITY...
...NICE TO MEET YOU.
SO, WHAT'S THIS ALL ABOUT...?
WELL...WE FOUND AN UNUSUAL CORPSE.
YOU... FOUND ...?
YES. WE'RE TRYING TO IDENTIFY IT, YOU SEE.
MAKINO THOUGHT MAYBE WE SHOULD GET YOUR OPINION. WHO COULD SHE BE?
OH...

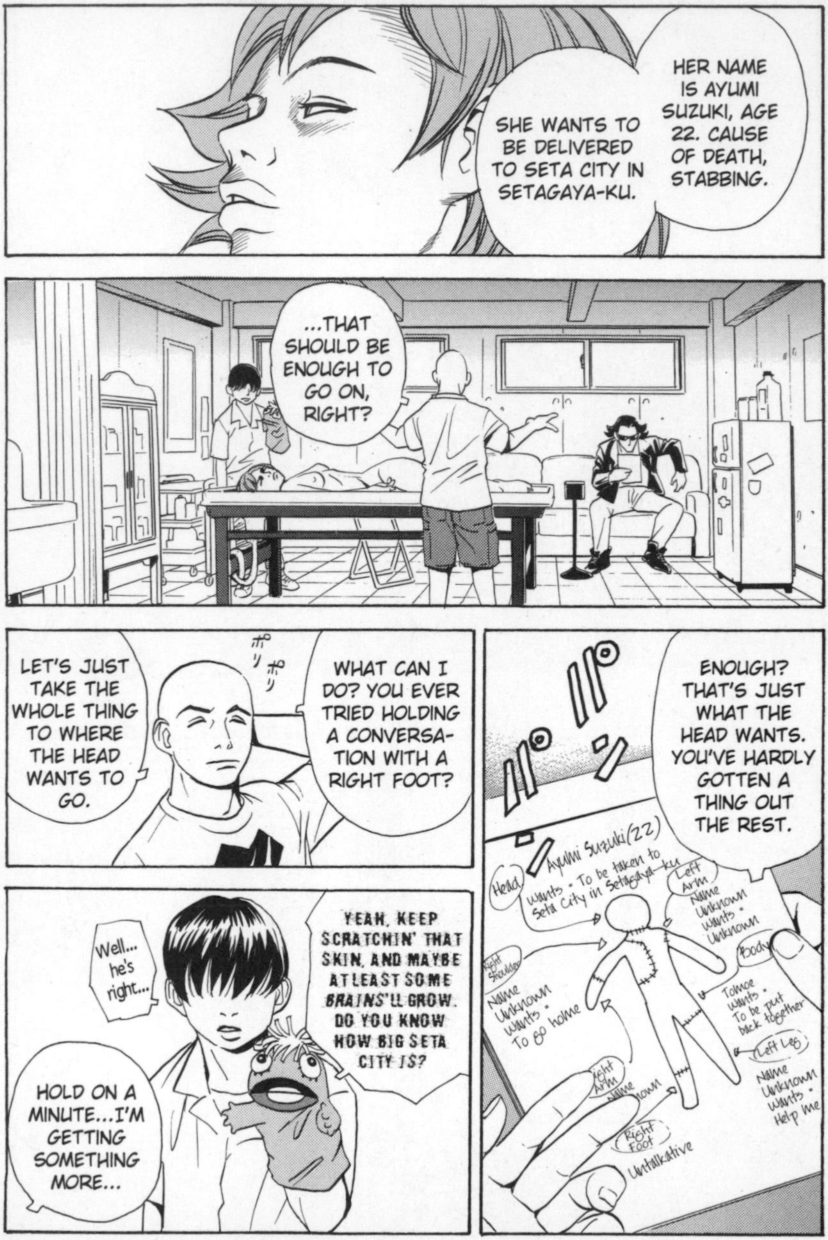
HER NAME IS AYUMI SUZUKI, AGE 22. CAUSE OF DEATH, STABBING.
SHE WANTS TO BE DELIVERED TO SETA CITY IN SETAGAYA-KU.
...THAT SHOULD BE ENOUGH TO GO ON, RIGHT?
ENOUGH? THAT'S JUST WHAT THE HEAD WANTS. YOU'VE HARDLY GOTTEN A THING OUT THE REST.
Ayumi Suzuki (22)
Head
Wants = To be taken to Seta City in Setagaya-ku
Left Arm
Name Unknown
Wants = Unknown
Right Shoulder
Name Unknown
Wants = To go home
Body
Tomoe
Wants = To be put back together
Left Leg
Name Unknown
Wants = Help me
Right Arm
Right Foot
Untalkative
WHAT CAN I DO? YOU EVER TRIED HOLDING A CONVERSATION WITH A RIGHT FOOT?
LET'S JUST TAKE THE WHOLE THING TO WHERE THE HEAD WANTS TO GO.
YEAH, KEEP SCRATCHIN' THAT SKIN, AND MAYBE AT LEAST SOME BRAINS'LL GROW. DO YOU KNOW HOW BIG SETA CITY IS?
Well... he's right...
HOLD ON A MINUTE...I'M GETTING SOMETHING MORE...

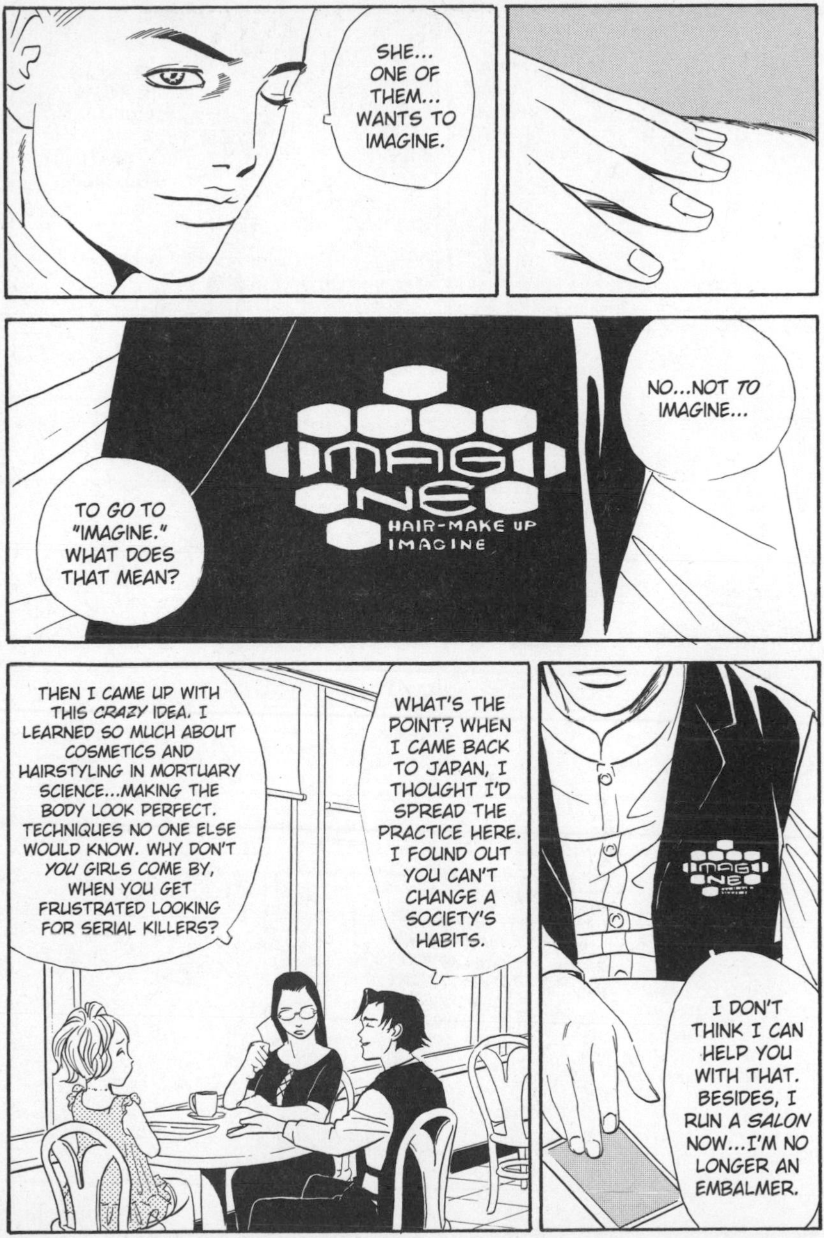
SHE... ONE OF THEM... WANTS TO IMAGINE.
NO...NOT *TO* IMAGINE...
TO GO TO "IMAGINE." WHAT DOES THAT MEAN?
HAIR-MAKE UP
IMAGINE
I DON'T THINK I CAN HELP YOU WITH THAT. BESIDES, I RUN A *SALON* NOW...I'M NO LONGER AN EMBALMER.
WHAT'S THE POINT? WHEN I CAME BACK TO JAPAN, I THOUGHT I'D SPREAD THE PRACTICE HERE. I FOUND OUT YOU CAN'T CHANGE A SOCIETY'S HABITS.
THEN I CAME UP WITH THIS *CRAZY* IDEA. I LEARNED SO MUCH ABOUT COSMETICS AND HAIRSTYLING IN MORTUARY SCIENCE...MAKING THE BODY LOOK PERFECT. TECHNIQUES NO ONE ELSE WOULD KNOW. WHY DON'T *YOU* GIRLS COME BY, WHEN YOU GET FRUSTRATED LOOKING FOR SERIAL KILLERS?

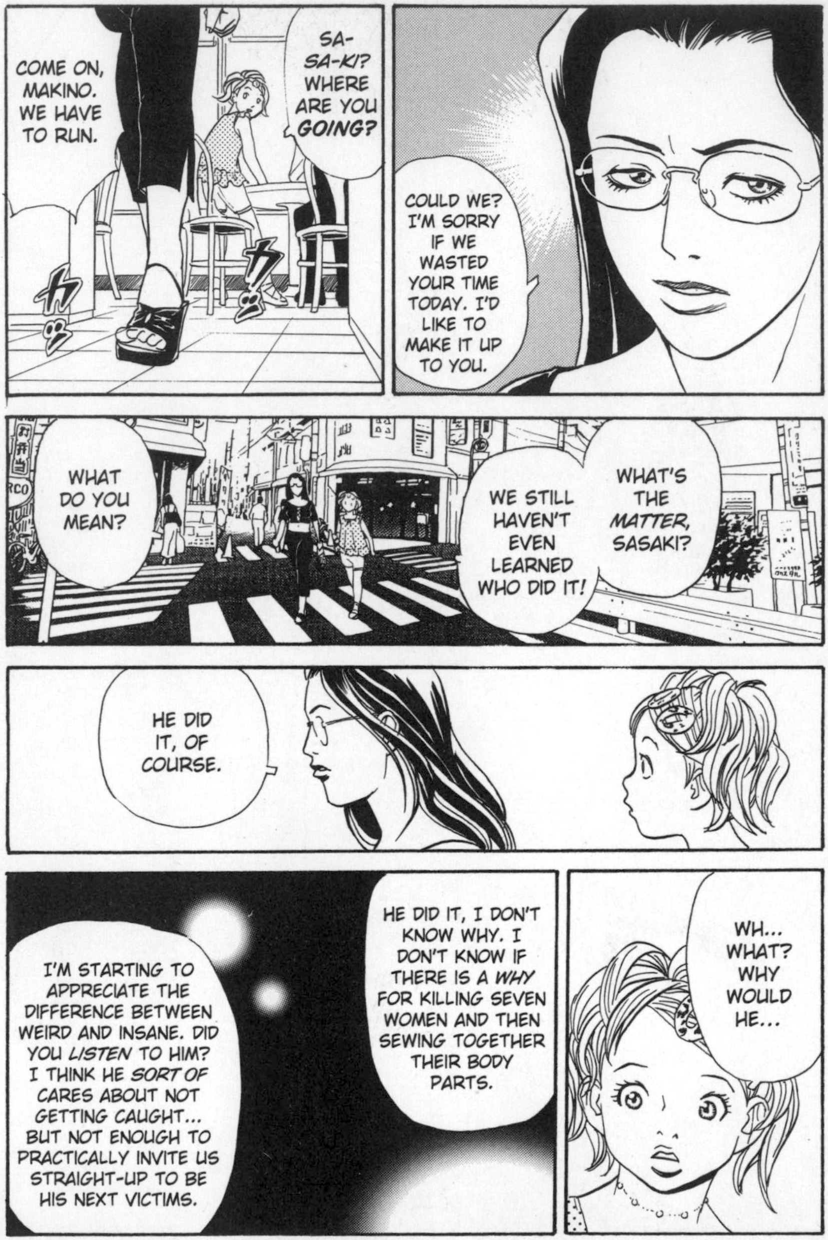
COULD WE? I'M SORRY IF WE WASTED YOUR TIME TODAY. I'D LIKE TO MAKE IT UP TO YOU.
SA-SA-KI? WHERE ARE YOU *GOING?*
COME ON, MAKINO. WE HAVE TO RUN.
WHAT'S THE *MATTER,* SASAKI?
WE STILL HAVEN'T EVEN LEARNED WHO DID IT!
WHAT DO YOU MEAN?
HE DID IT, OF COURSE.
WH... WHAT? WHY WOULD HE...
HE DID IT, I DON'T KNOW WHY. I DON'T KNOW IF THERE IS A *WHY* FOR KILLING SEVEN WOMEN AND THEN SEWING TOGETHER THEIR BODY PARTS.
I'M STARTING TO APPRECIATE THE DIFFERENCE BETWEEN WEIRD AND INSANE. DID YOU *LISTEN* TO HIM? I THINK HE *SORT OF* CARES ABOUT NOT GETTING CAUGHT... BUT NOT ENOUGH TO PRACTICALLY INVITE US STRAIGHT-UP TO BE HIS NEXT VICTIMS.

!!

"SERIAL KILLER?" WHEN DID WE EVER SAY *SERIAL KILLER*? WE NEVER MENTIONED PARTS HAD BEEN SEWN TOGETHER...OTHERWISE, THERE'S ONLY *ONE* BODY IN THAT PHOTO.

YOU KNOW, I DON'T WANT TO GET THE *LAW* INVOLVED WITH OUR BUSINESS. AND DO YOU KNOW WHY?

......

BECAUSE WE'LL ONLY GET PAID FOR *JUSTICE*.

...HE CUTS HAIR, TOO...?

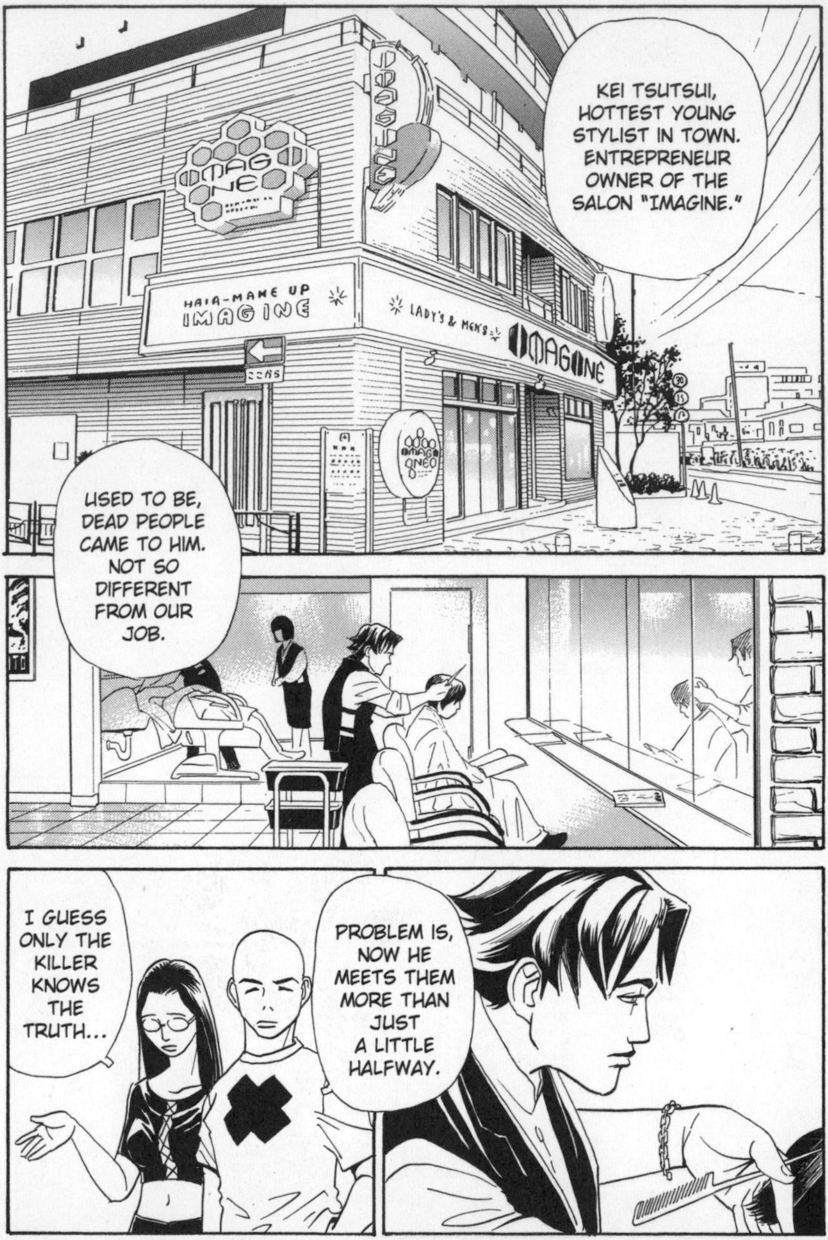
KEI TSUTSUI, HOTTEST YOUNG STYLIST IN TOWN. ENTREPRENEUR OWNER OF THE SALON "IMAGINE."
USED TO BE, DEAD PEOPLE CAME TO HIM. NOT SO DIFFERENT FROM OUR JOB.
PROBLEM IS, NOW HE MEETS THEM MORE THAN JUST A LITTLE HALFWAY.
I GUESS ONLY THE KILLER KNOWS THE TRUTH...

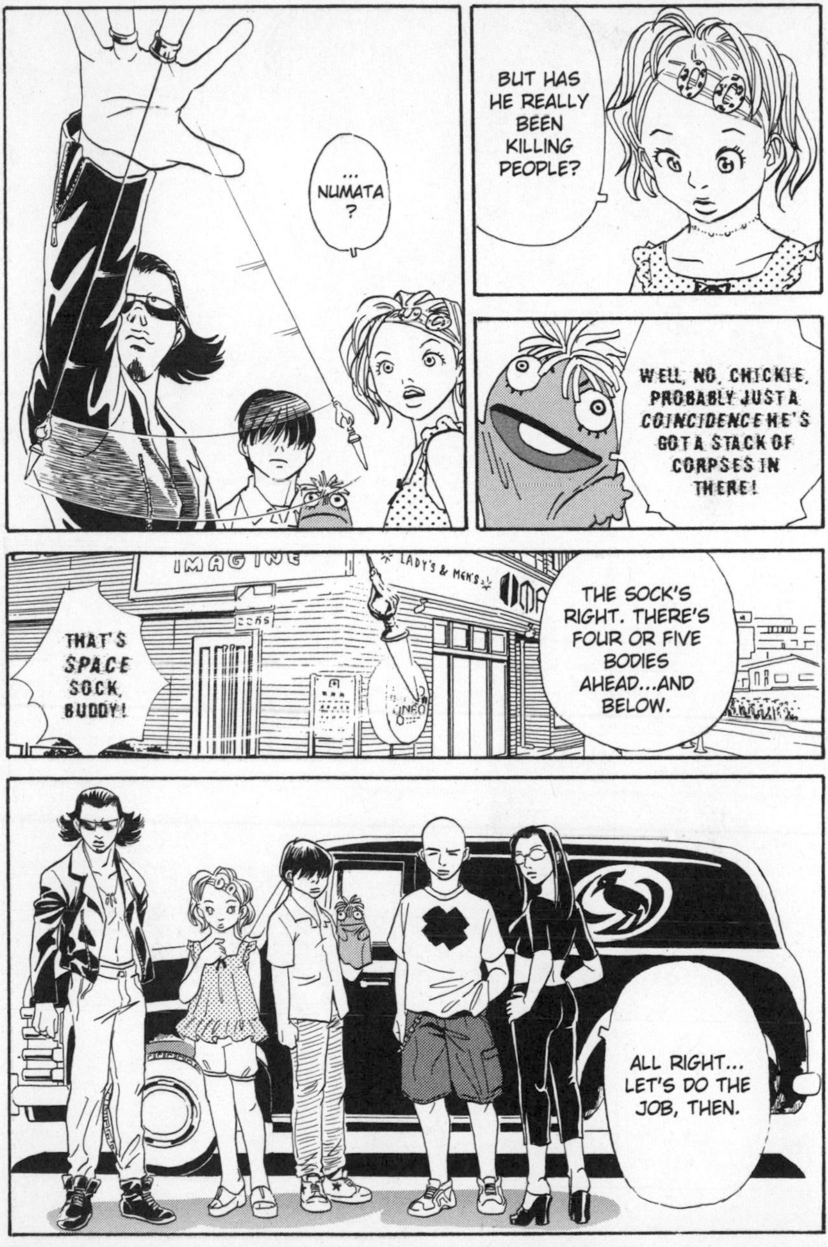
BUT HAS HE REALLY BEEN KILLING PEOPLE?
WELL, NO, CHICKIE, PROBABLY JUST A COINCIDENCE HE'S GOT A STACK OF CORPSES IN THERE!
... NUMATA ?
IMAGINE
LADY'S & MEN'S
THE SOCK'S RIGHT. THERE'S FOUR OR FIVE BODIES AHEAD...AND BELOW.
THAT'S SPACE SOCK, BUDDY!
ALL RIGHT... LET'S DO THE JOB, THEN.

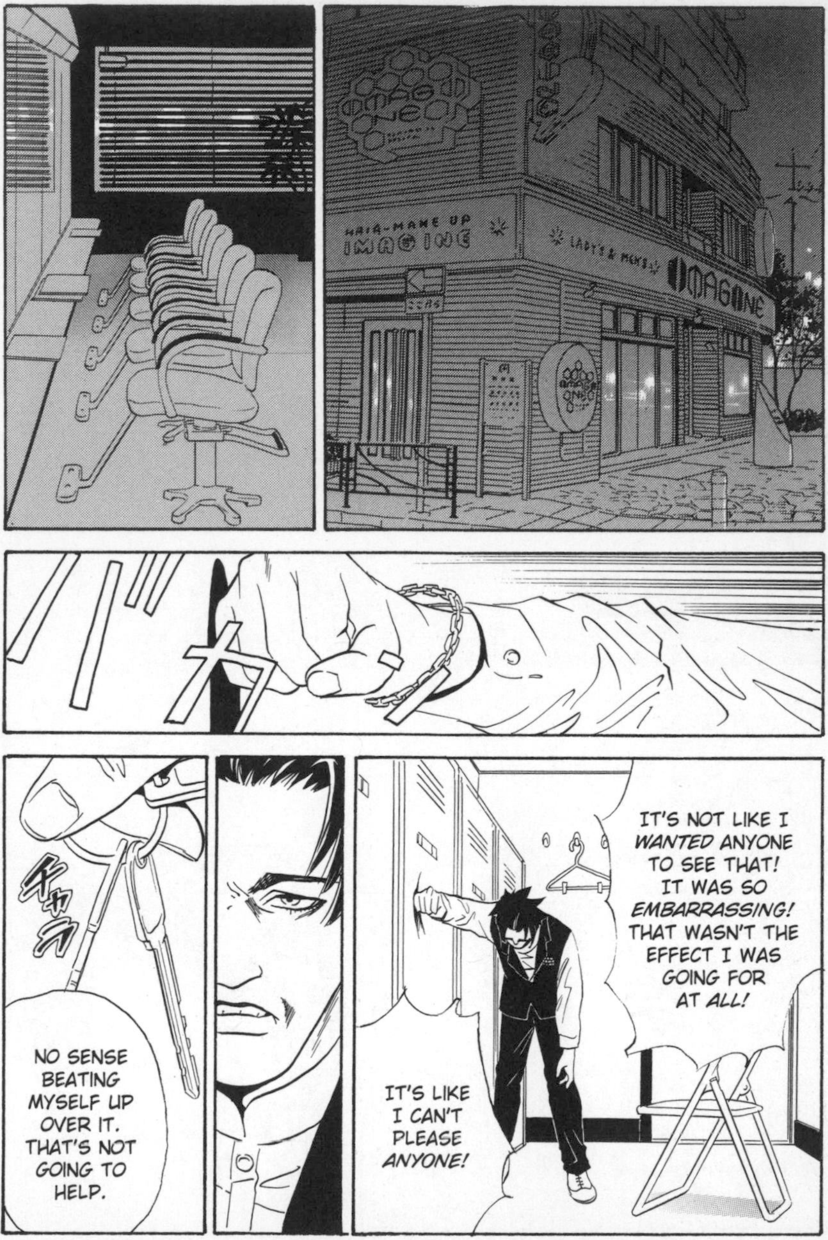
IT'S NOT LIKE I *WANTED* ANYONE TO SEE THAT! IT WAS SO *EMBARRASSING!* THAT WASN'T THE EFFECT I WAS GOING FOR AT *ALL!*
IT'S LIKE I CAN'T PLEASE *ANYONE!*
NO SENSE BEATING MYSELF UP OVER IT. THAT'S NOT GOING TO HELP.

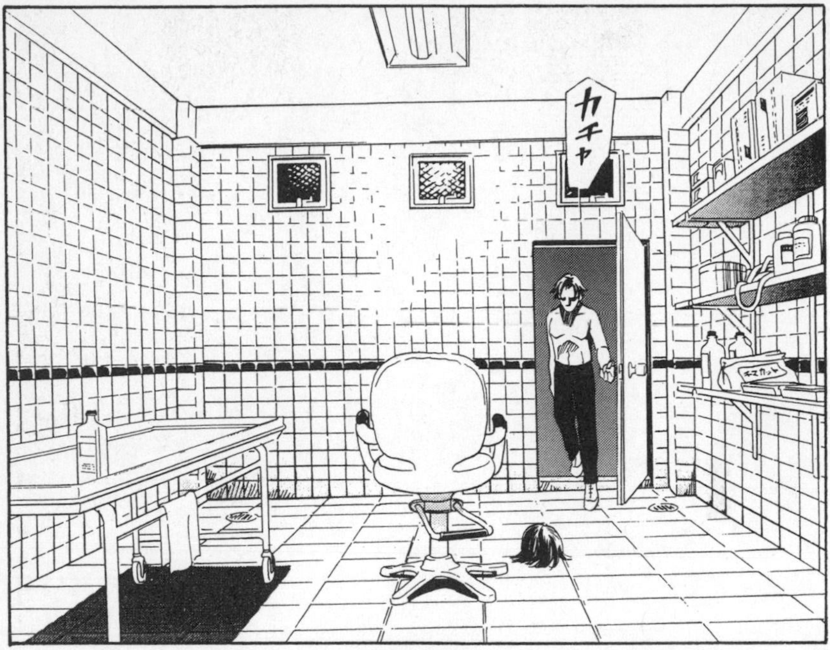
カチャ

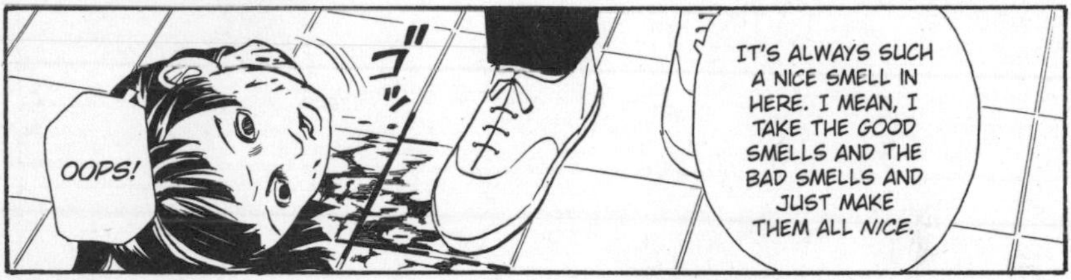
IT'S ALWAYS SUCH A NICE SMELL IN HERE. I MEAN, I TAKE THE GOOD SMELLS AND THE BAD SMELLS AND JUST MAKE THEM ALL *NICE*.
ゴッ
OOPS!

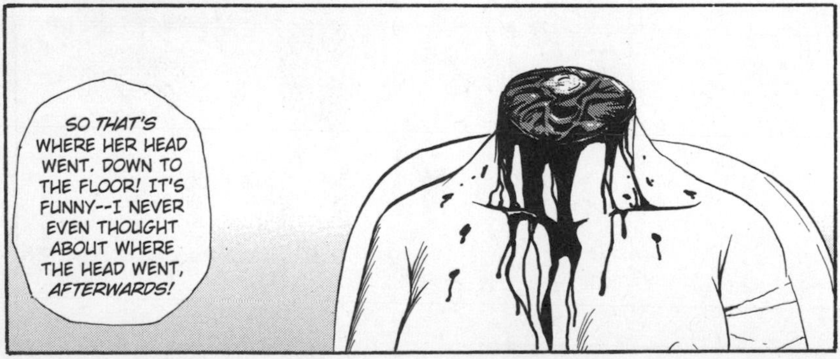
SO *THAT'S* WHERE HER HEAD WENT. DOWN TO THE FLOOR! IT'S FUNNY--I NEVER EVEN THOUGHT ABOUT WHERE THE HEAD WENT, *AFTERWARDS!*

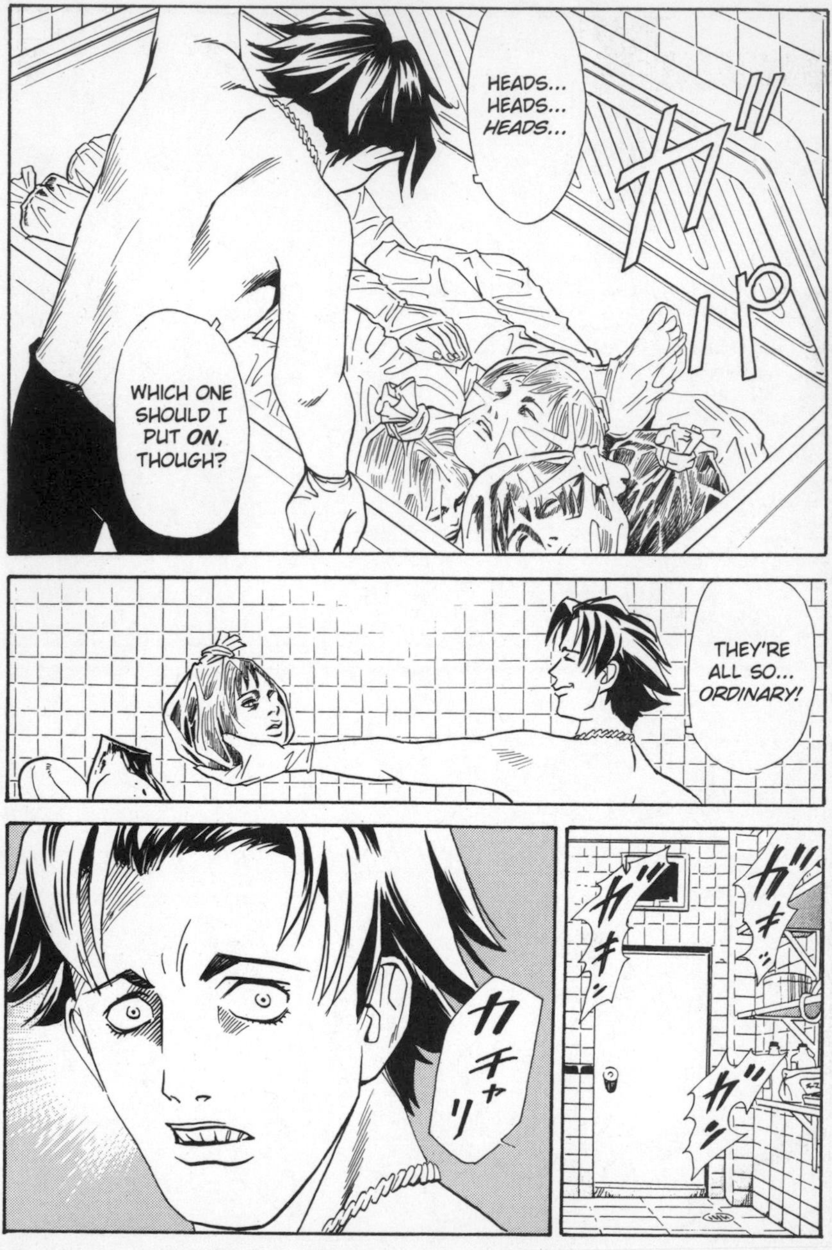
HEADS... HEADS... HEADS...
WHICH ONE SHOULD I PUT ON, THOUGH?
THEY'RE ALL SO... ORDINARY!
ガキッ
ガキン
ガン
カチャリ

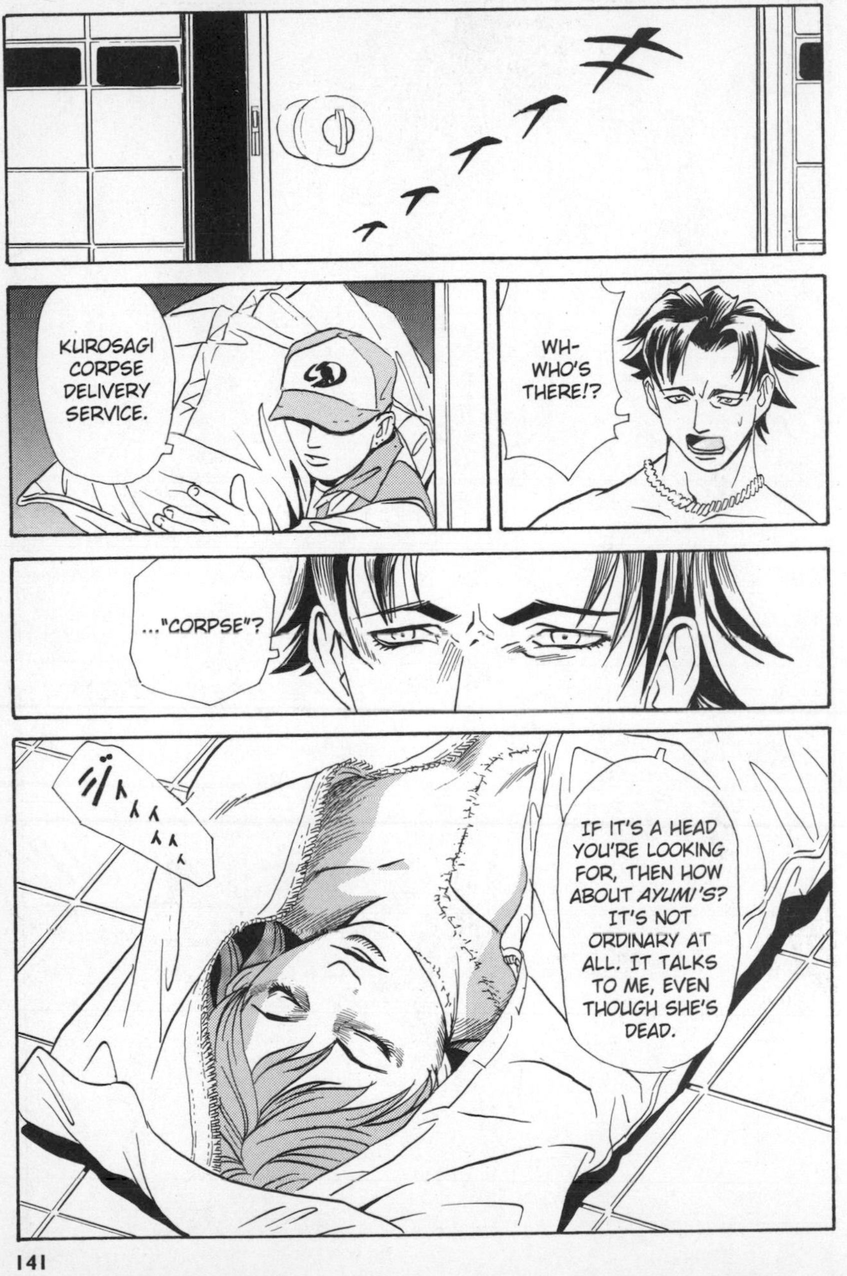
WH- WHO'S THERE!?
KUROSAGI CORPSE DELIVERY SERVICE.
..."CORPSE"?
IF IT'S A HEAD YOU'RE LOOKING FOR, THEN HOW ABOUT *AYUMI'S*? IT'S NOT ORDINARY AT ALL. IT TALKS TO ME, EVEN THOUGH SHE'S DEAD.

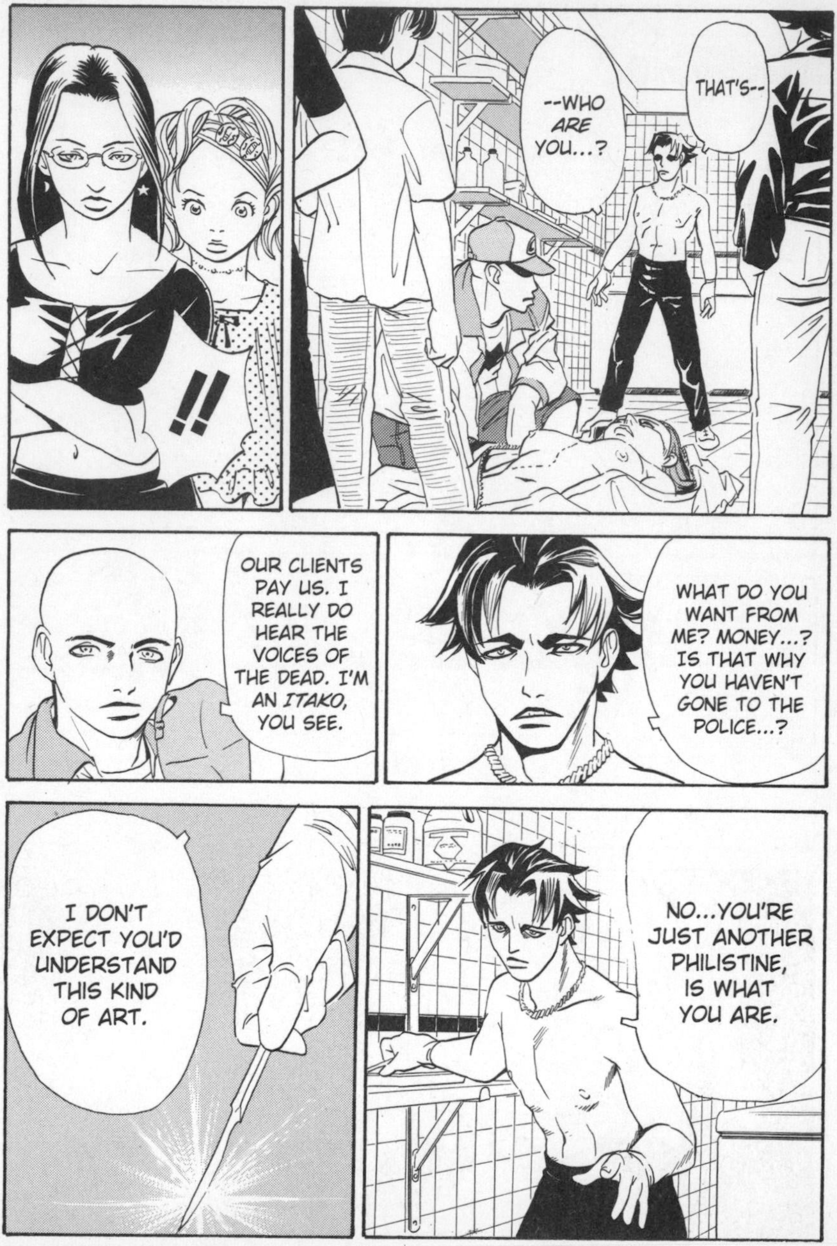
THAT'S--
--WHO *ARE* YOU...?
!!
WHAT DO YOU WANT FROM ME? MONEY...? IS THAT WHY YOU HAVEN'T GONE TO THE POLICE...?
OUR CLIENTS PAY US. I REALLY DO HEAR THE VOICES OF THE DEAD. I'M AN *ITAKO*, YOU SEE.
NO...YOU'RE JUST ANOTHER PHILISTINE, IS WHAT YOU ARE.
I DON'T EXPECT YOU'D UNDERSTAND THIS KIND OF ART.

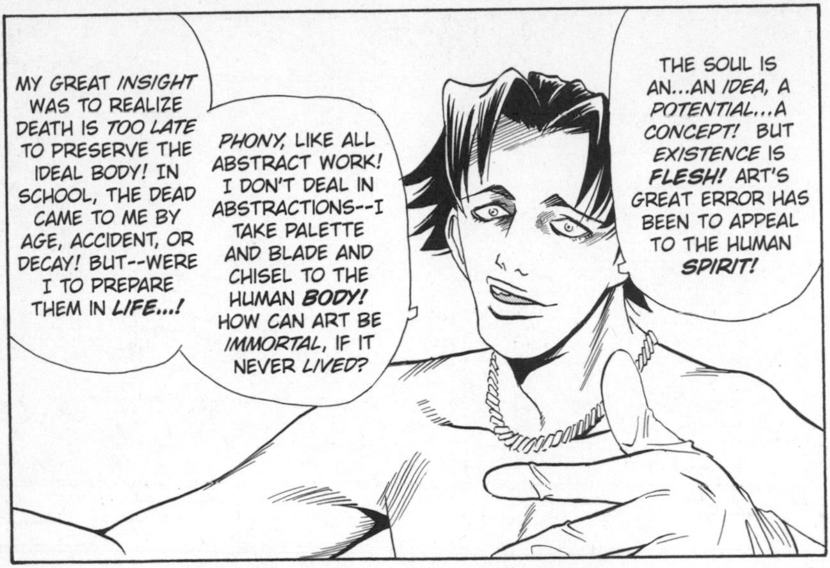
THE SOUL IS AN...AN *IDEA*, A *POTENTIAL*...A *CONCEPT!* BUT *EXISTENCE* IS ***FLESH!*** ART'S GREAT ERROR HAS BEEN TO APPEAL TO THE HUMAN ***SPIRIT!***
PHONY, LIKE ALL ABSTRACT WORK! I DON'T DEAL IN ABSTRACTIONS--I TAKE PALETTE AND BLADE AND CHISEL TO THE HUMAN ***BODY!*** HOW CAN ART BE *IMMORTAL*, IF IT NEVER *LIVED?*
MY GREAT *INSIGHT* WAS TO REALIZE DEATH IS *TOO LATE* TO PRESERVE THE IDEAL BODY! IN SCHOOL, THE DEAD CAME TO ME BY AGE, ACCIDENT, OR DECAY! BUT--WERE I TO PREPARE THEM IN ***LIFE...!***
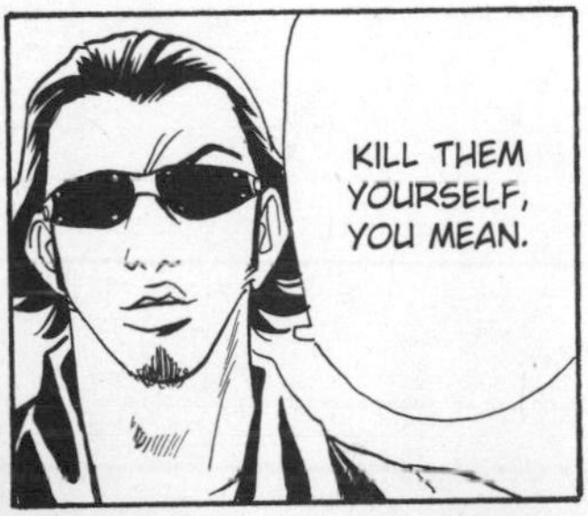
KILL THEM YOURSELF, YOU MEAN.
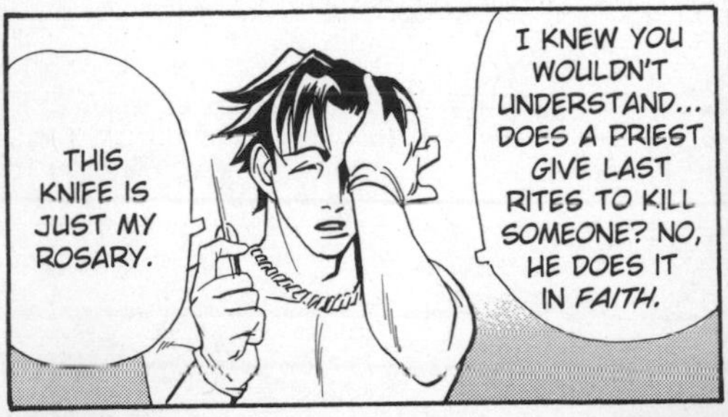
I KNEW YOU WOULDN'T UNDERSTAND... DOES A PRIEST GIVE LAST RITES TO KILL SOMEONE? NO, HE DOES IT IN *FAITH*.
THIS KNIFE IS JUST MY ROSARY.
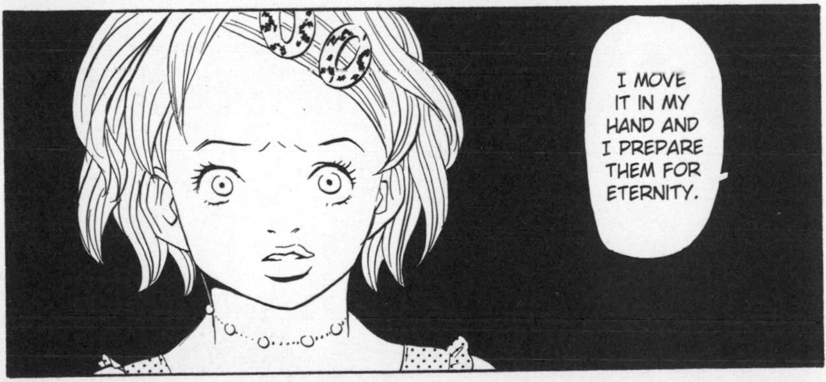
I MOVE IT IN MY HAND AND I PREPARE THEM FOR ETERNITY.

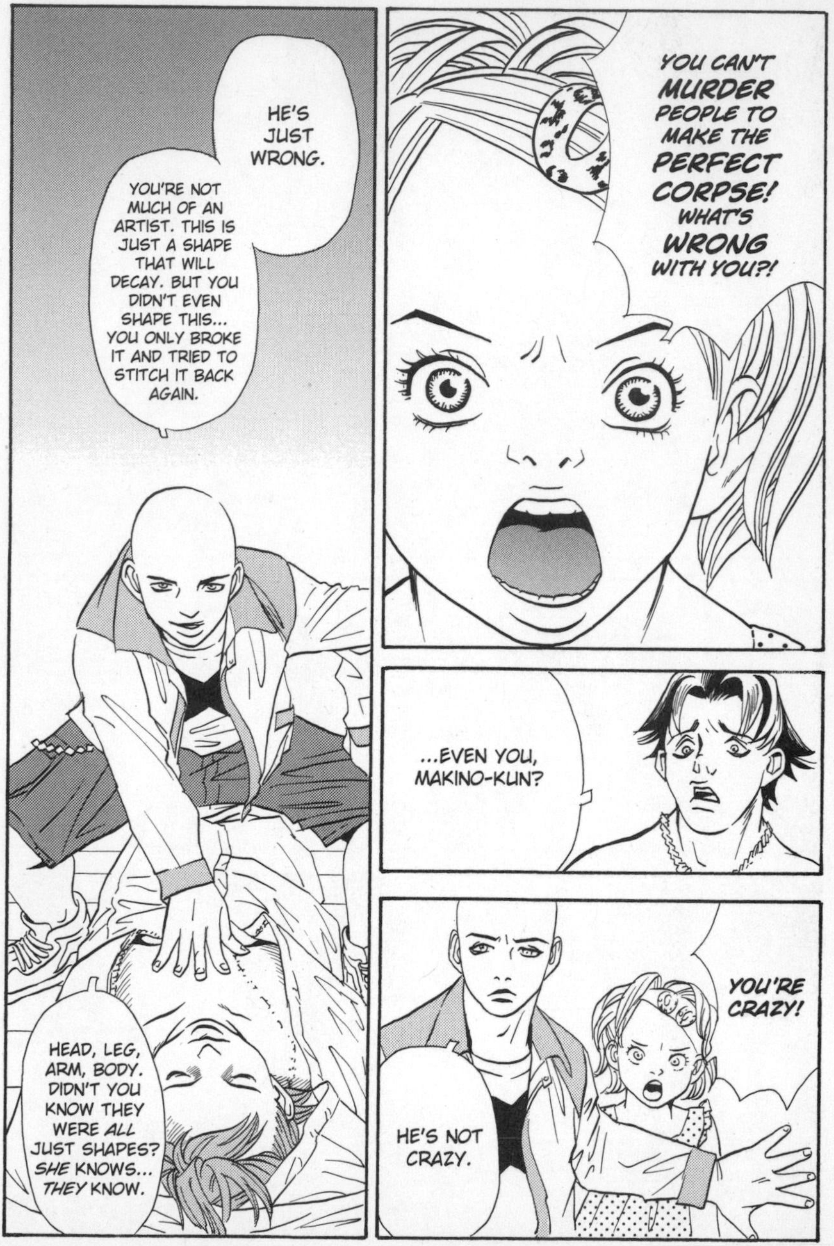
YOU CAN'T MURDER PEOPLE TO MAKE THE PERFECT CORPSE! WHAT'S WRONG WITH YOU?!
...EVEN YOU, MAKINO-KUN?
YOU'RE CRAZY!
HE'S NOT CRAZY.
HE'S JUST WRONG.
YOU'RE NOT MUCH OF AN ARTIST. THIS IS JUST A SHAPE THAT WILL DECAY. BUT YOU DIDN'T EVEN SHAPE THIS... YOU ONLY BROKE IT AND TRIED TO STITCH IT BACK AGAIN.
HEAD, LEG, ARM, BODY. DIDN'T YOU KNOW THEY WERE *ALL* JUST SHAPES? *SHE* KNOWS... *THEY* KNOW.

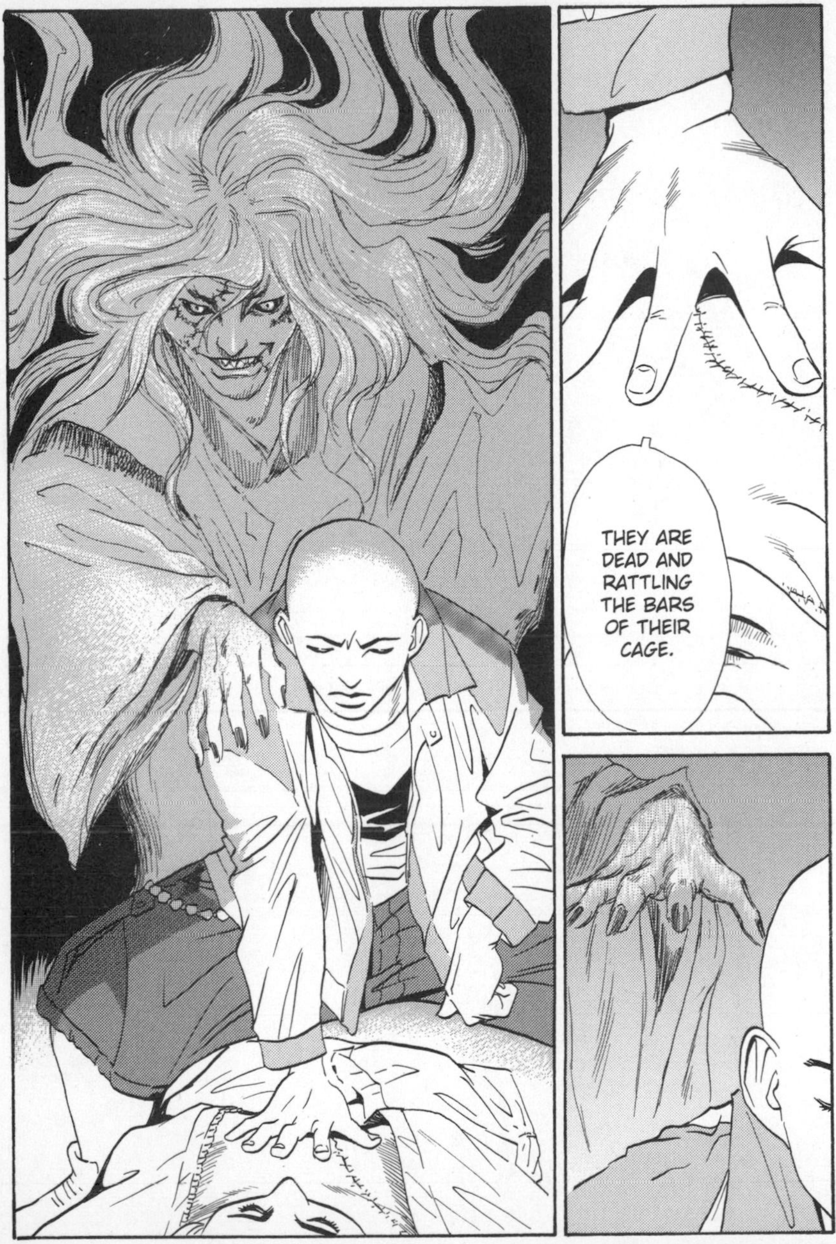
THEY ARE DEAD AND RATTLING THE BARS OF THEIR CAGE.

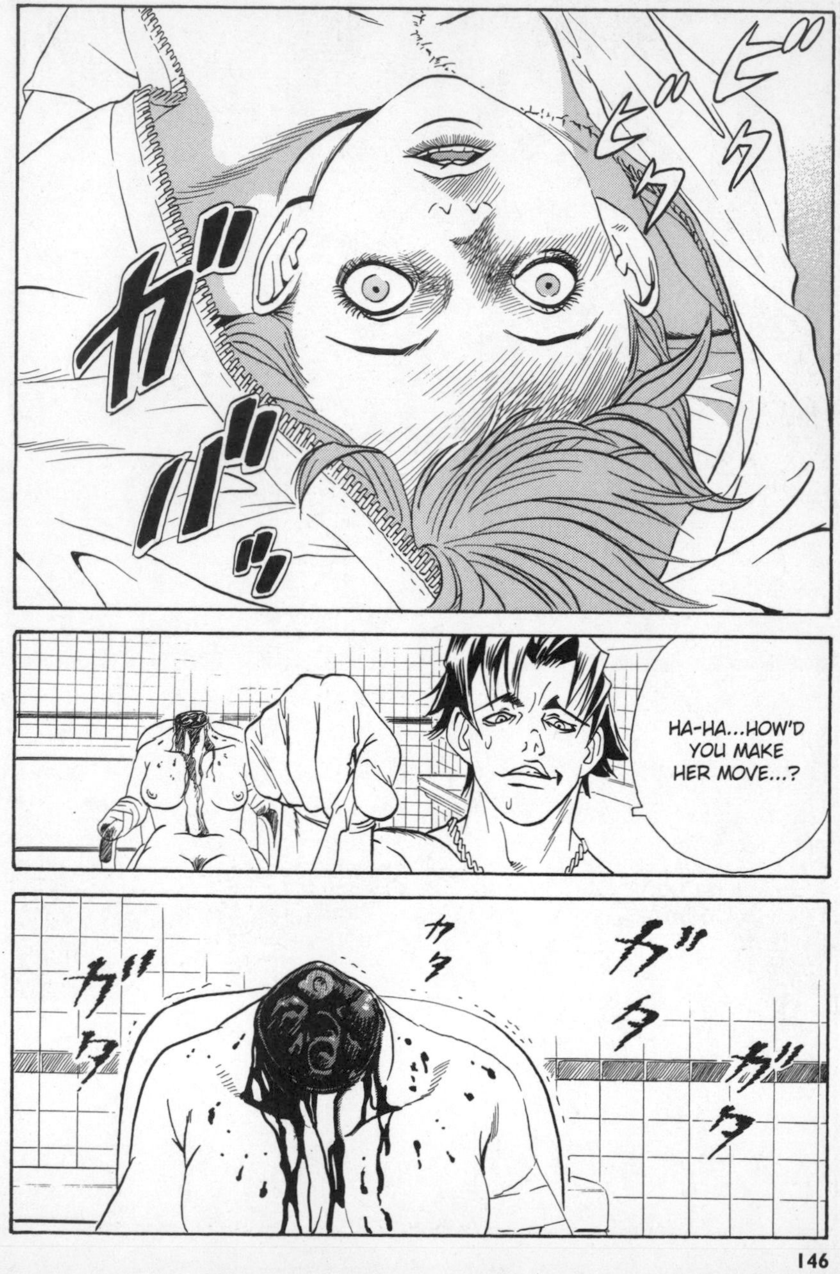
ビクビク
ガバッ
HA-HA...HOW'D YOU MAKE HER MOVE...?
ガタ
ガタ
カタ
ガタ

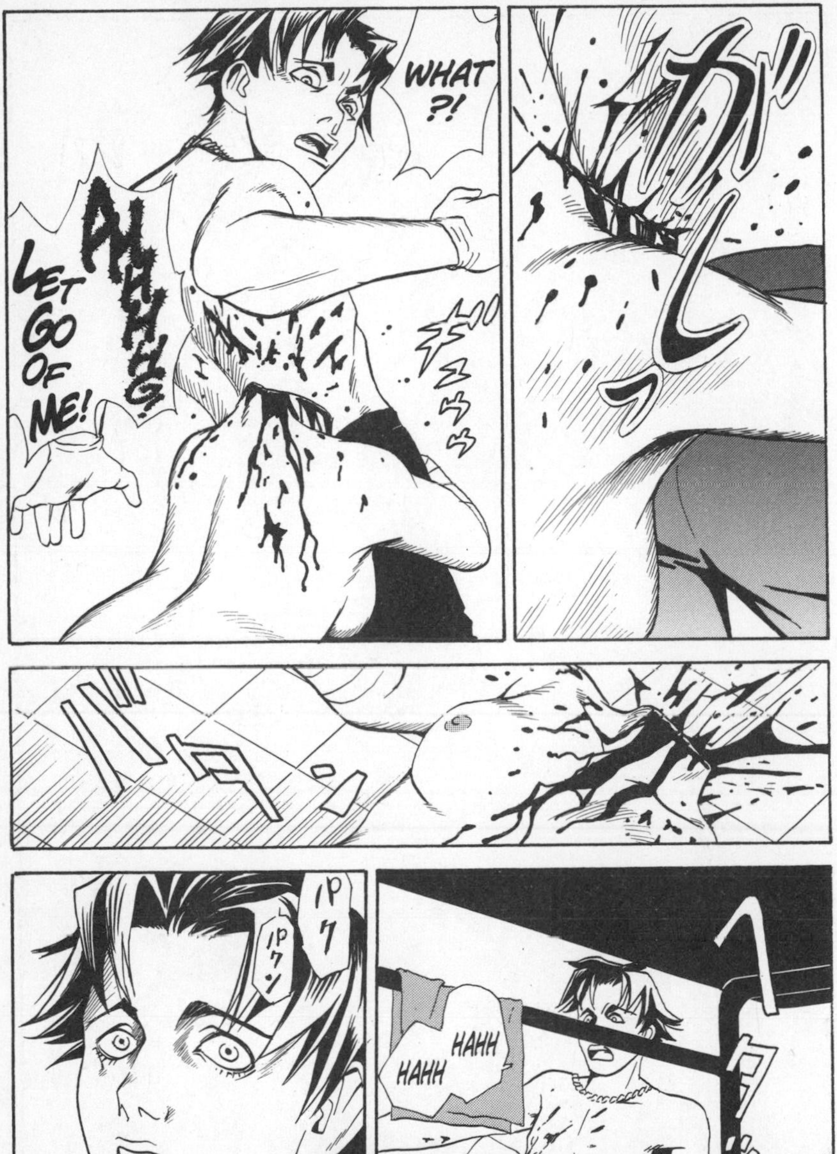
がしっ
WHAT ?!
AHHHHG!
LET GO OF ME!
ギュウウ
HAHH HAHH
HAHH
パク
パクン

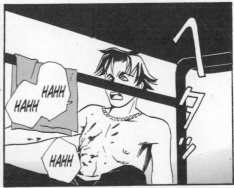

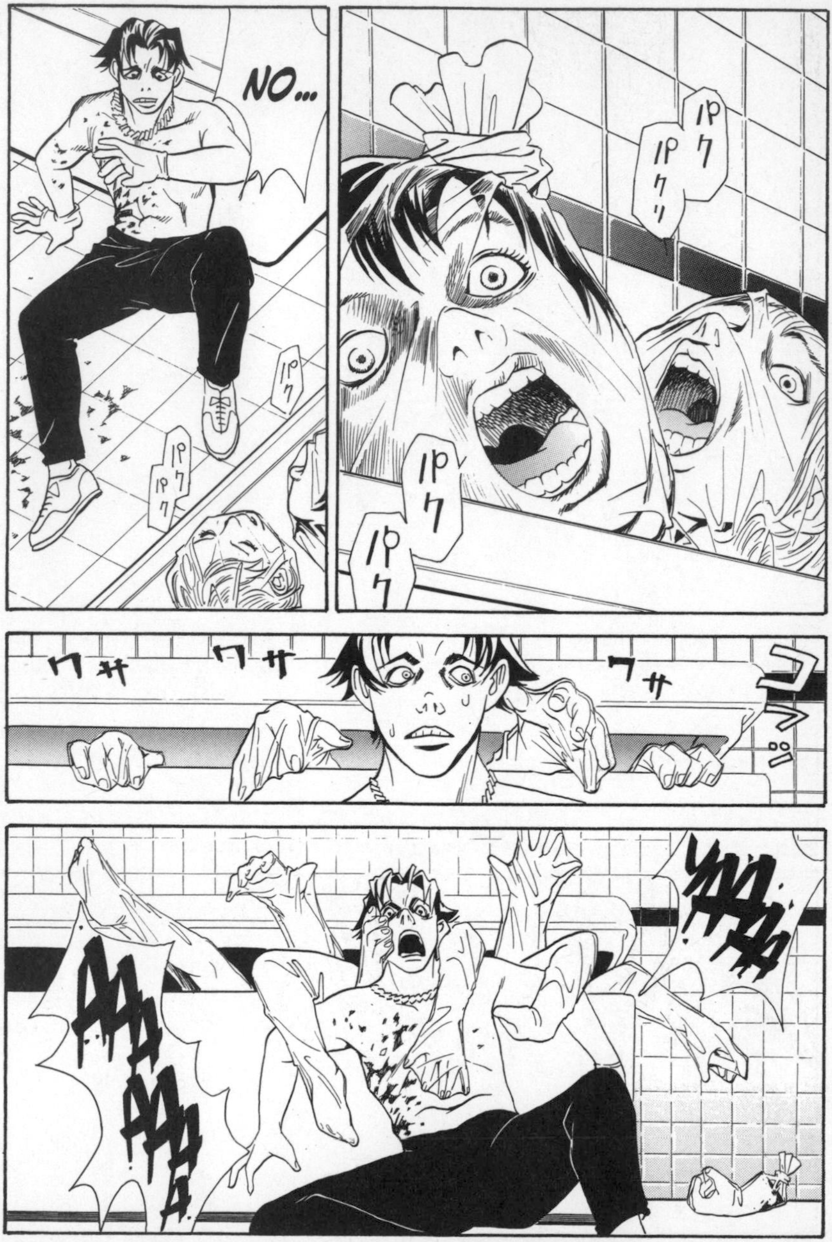
パク
パクッ
パク
パク
NO...
パク
パクパク
パク
コソッ
ワサ
ワサ
ワサ

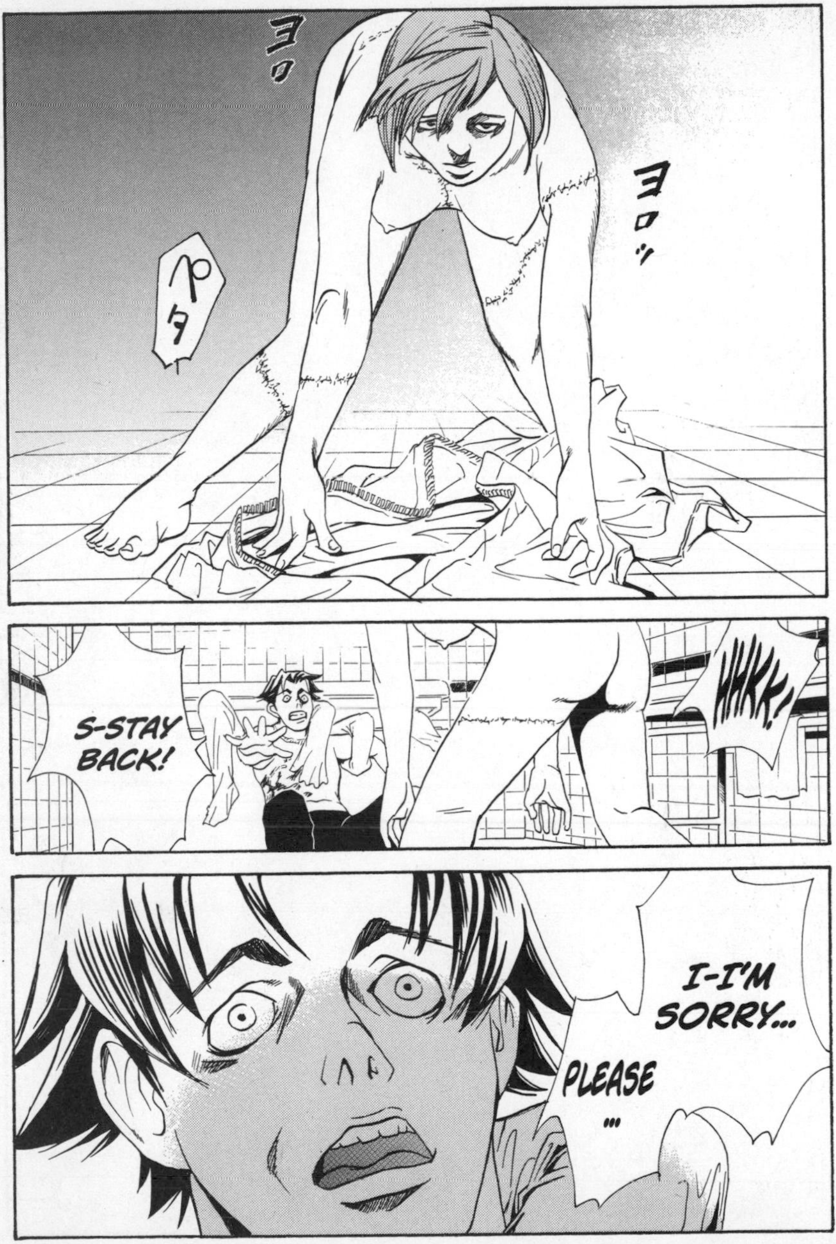
ヨロ
ヨロッ
ペタ
HKK!
S-STAY BACK!
I-I'M SORRY...
PLEASE ...

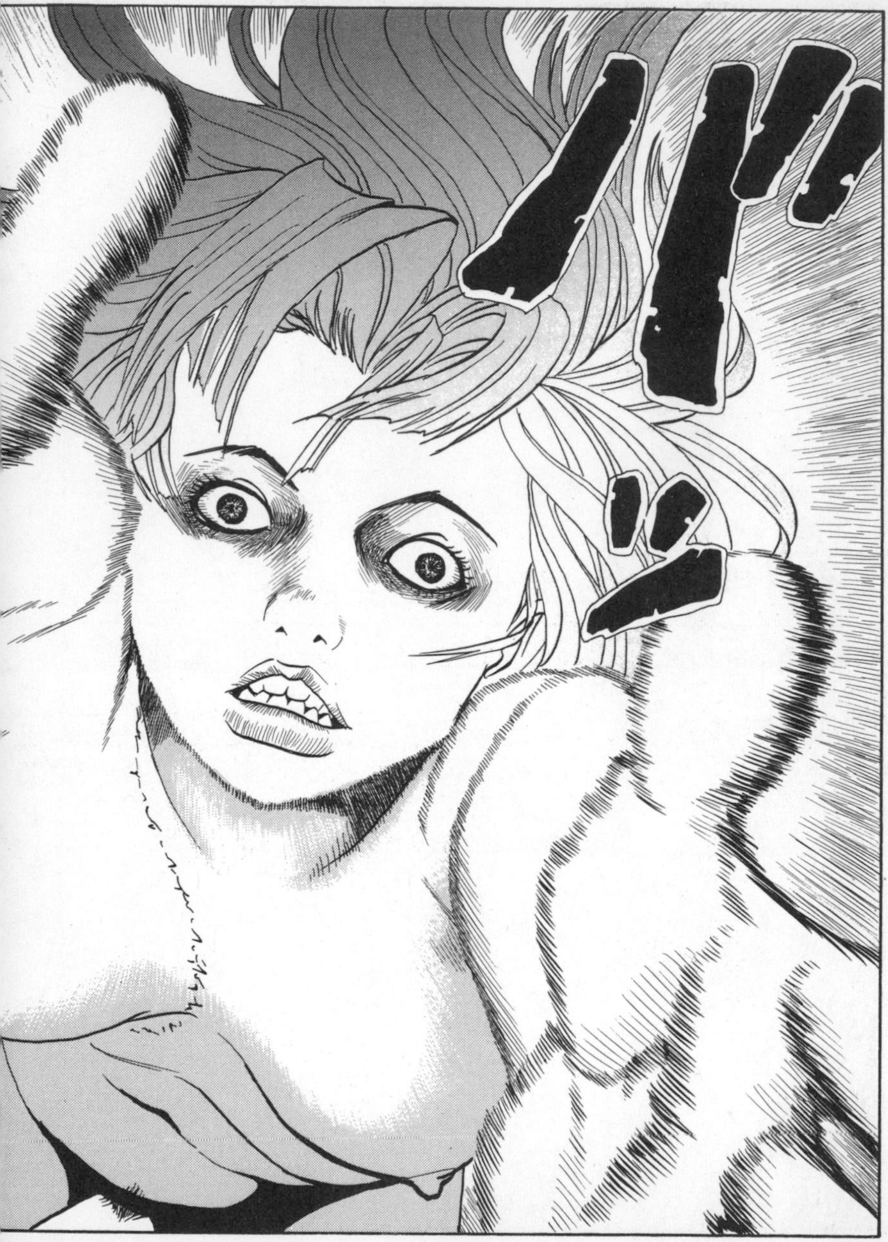

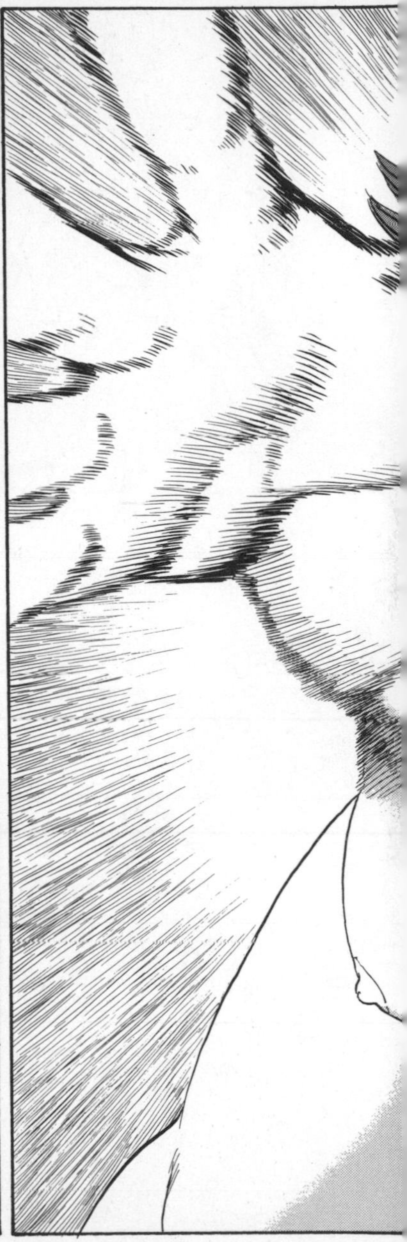

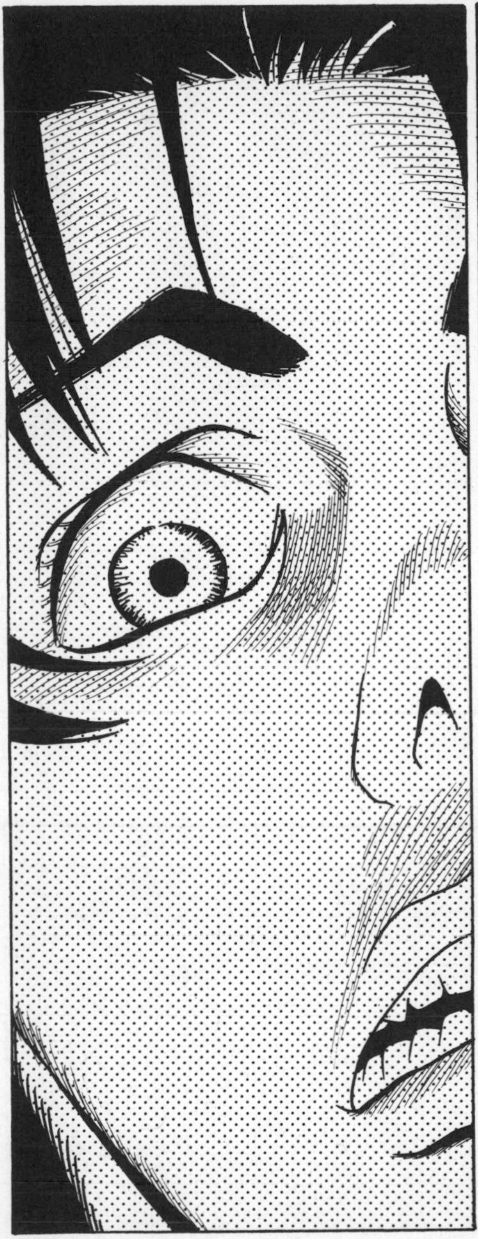

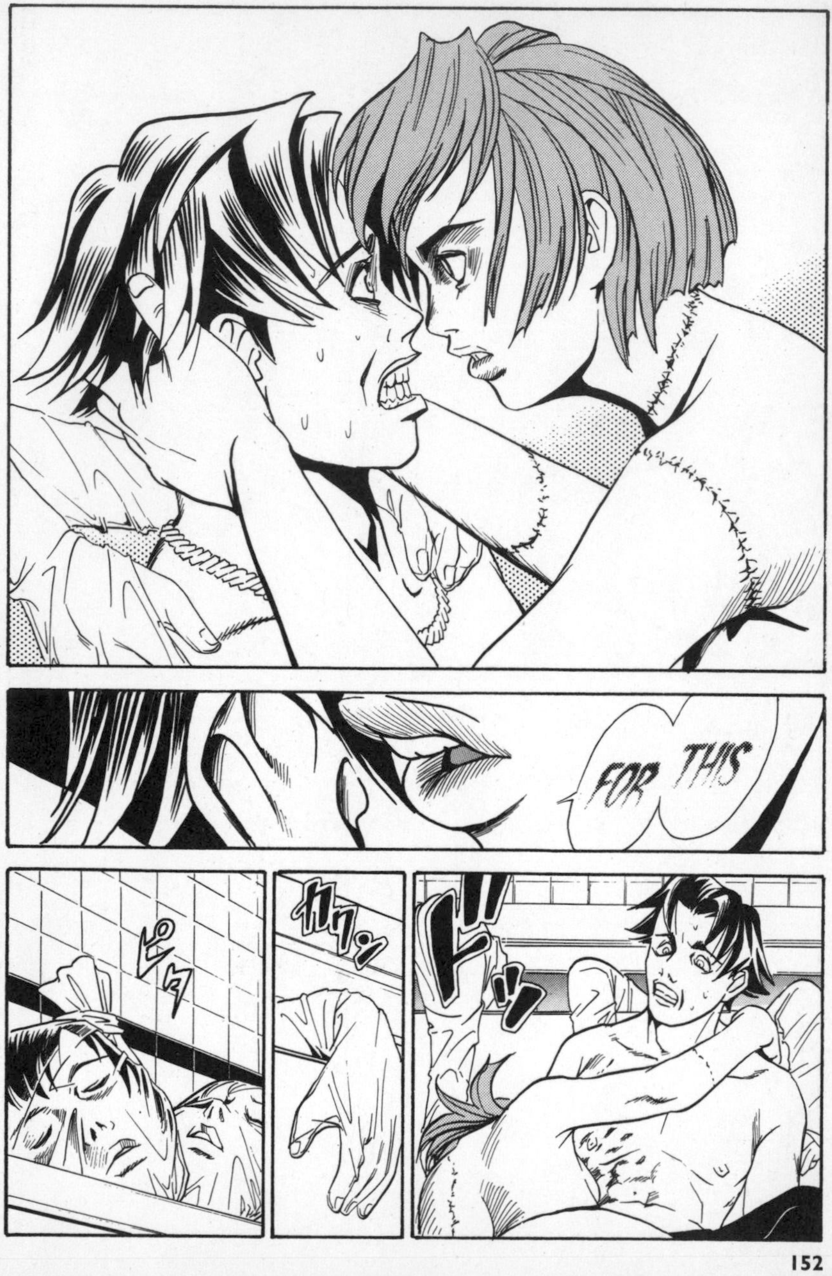
FOR THIS
ドッ
カクッ
ピク

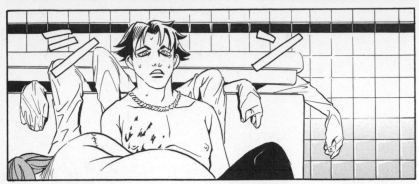

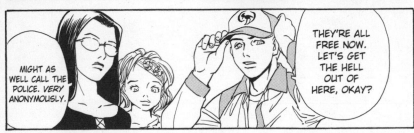

THEY'RE ALL FREE NOW. LET'S GET THE HELL OUT OF HERE, OKAY?
MIGHT AS WELL CALL THE POLICE. *VERY* ANONYMOUSLY.
NOT THAT I THINK THEY'LL GET A CONFESSION OUT OF HIM...OR ANYTHING MUCH ELSE.
THIS ...
ISN'T ...
HA HA HA ...

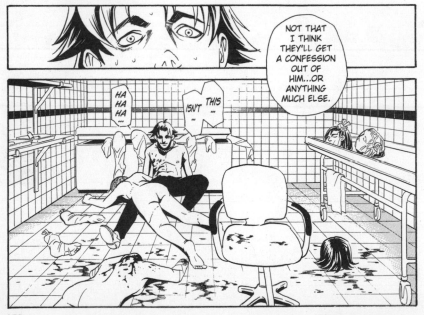

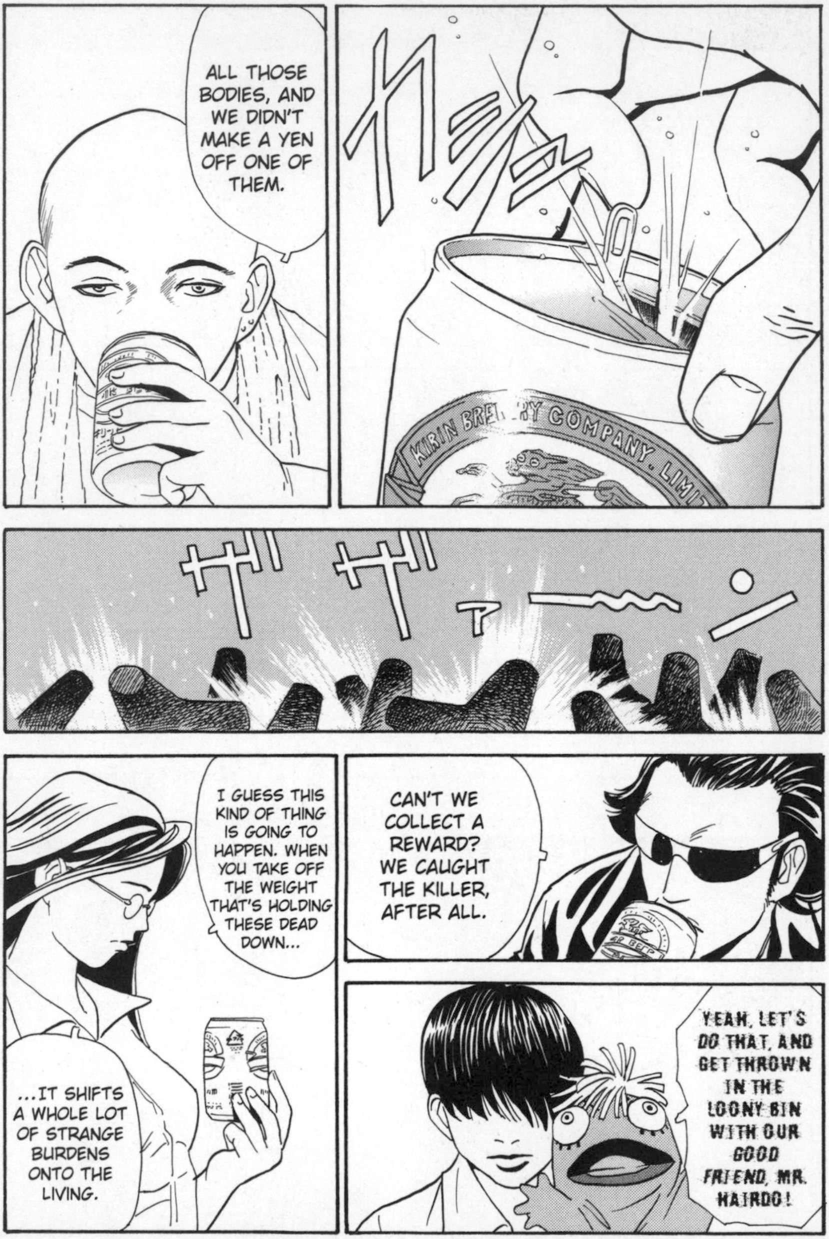
ALL THOSE BODIES, AND WE DIDN'T MAKE A YEN OFF ONE OF THEM.
KIRIN BREWERY COMPANY, LIMITED
CAN'T WE COLLECT A REWARD? WE CAUGHT THE KILLER, AFTER ALL.
YEAH, LET'S *DO* THAT, AND GET THROWN IN THE LOONY BIN WITH OUR *GOOD FRIEND*, MR. HAIRDO!
I GUESS THIS KIND OF THING IS GOING TO HAPPEN. WHEN YOU TAKE OFF THE WEIGHT THAT'S HOLDING THESE DEAD DOWN...
...IT SHIFTS A WHOLE LOT OF STRANGE BURDENS ONTO THE LIVING.

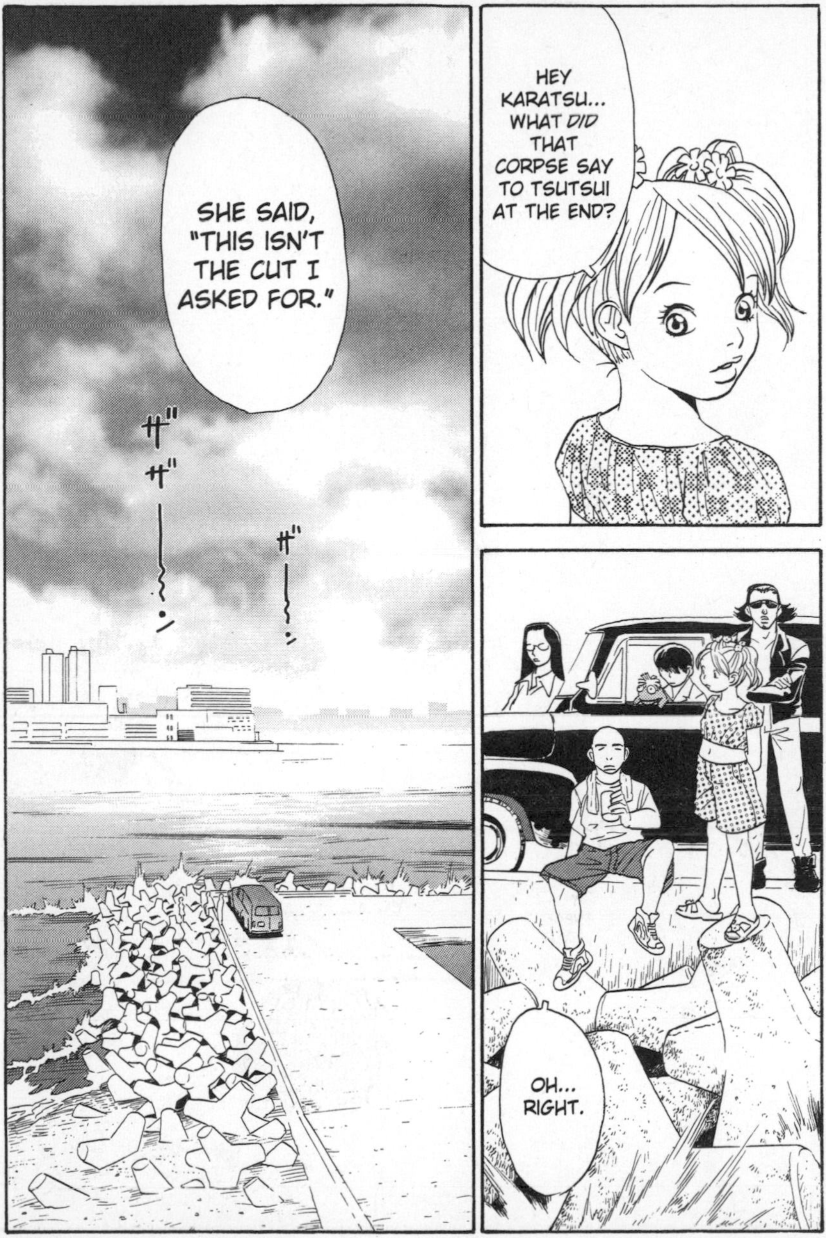
HEY KARATSU... WHAT *DID* THAT CORPSE SAY TO TSUTSUI AT THE END?
OH... RIGHT.
SHE SAID, "THIS ISN'T THE CUT I ASKED FOR."
ザザー～ッ
ザー～ッ

3rd delivery: magician of lost love—the end

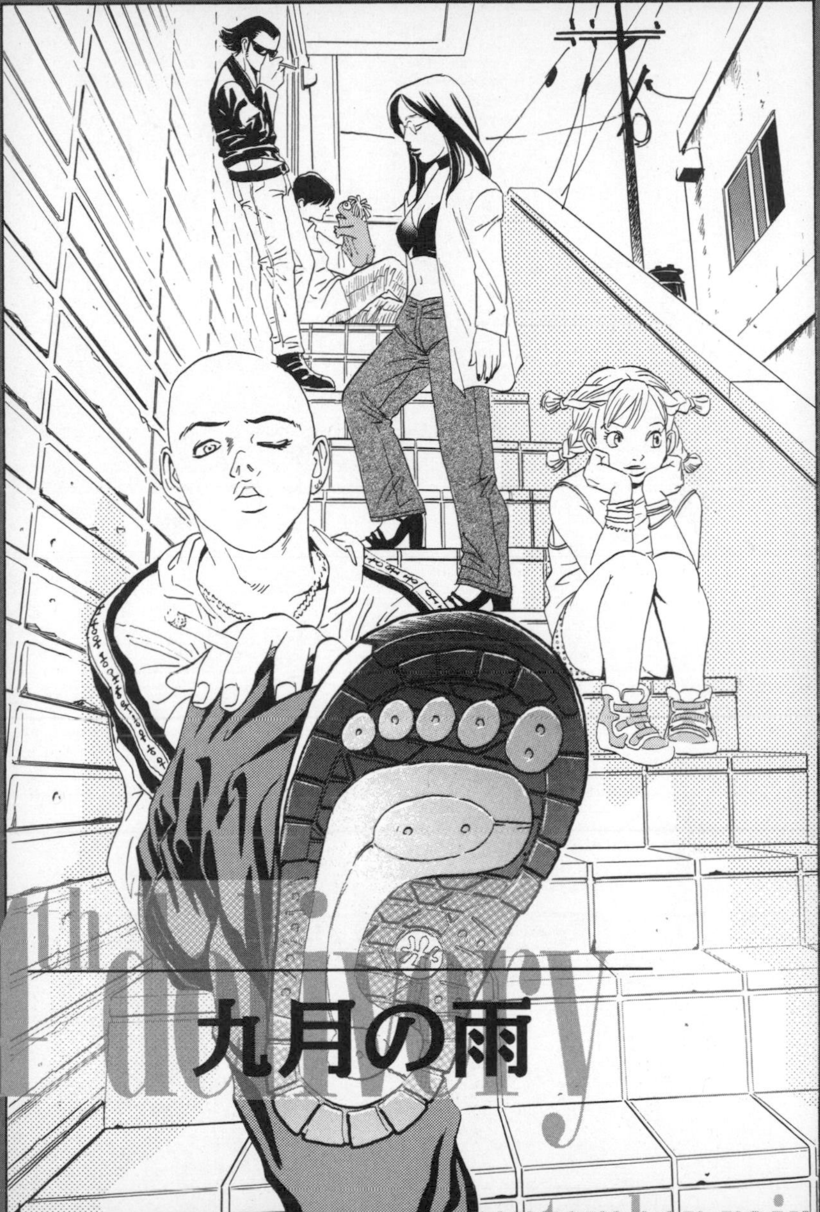

4th delivery 九月の雨

september rain

...FOR DAYS.

I FEEL LIKE WE'VE BEEN EATING THE SAME BRAND OF INSTANT NOODLES...

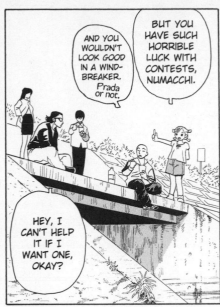

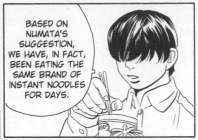

BASED ON NUMATA'S SUGGESTION, WE HAVE, IN FACT, BEEN EATING THE SAME BRAND OF INSTANT NOODLES FOR DAYS.
WITH EVERY STICKER FROM BENEATH THE LID, YOU GET THE CHANCE TO WIN A *FREE* PRADA SPORTS WIND-BREAKER!
AND *LOOK* AT ALL THESE WE'VE GOT NOW!
BUT YOU HAVE SUCH HORRIBLE LUCK WITH CONTESTS, NUMACCHI.
AND YOU WOULDN'T LOOK GOOD IN A WIND-BREAKER.
Prada or not.
HEY, I CAN'T HELP IT IF I WANT ONE, OKAY?
I THINK THE COAST IS CLEAR.
スクッ
GREAT. LET'S GET STARTED.
コキ コキ

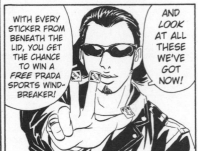

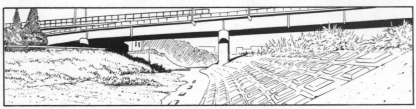

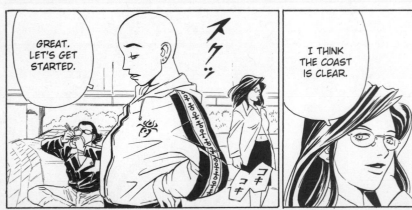

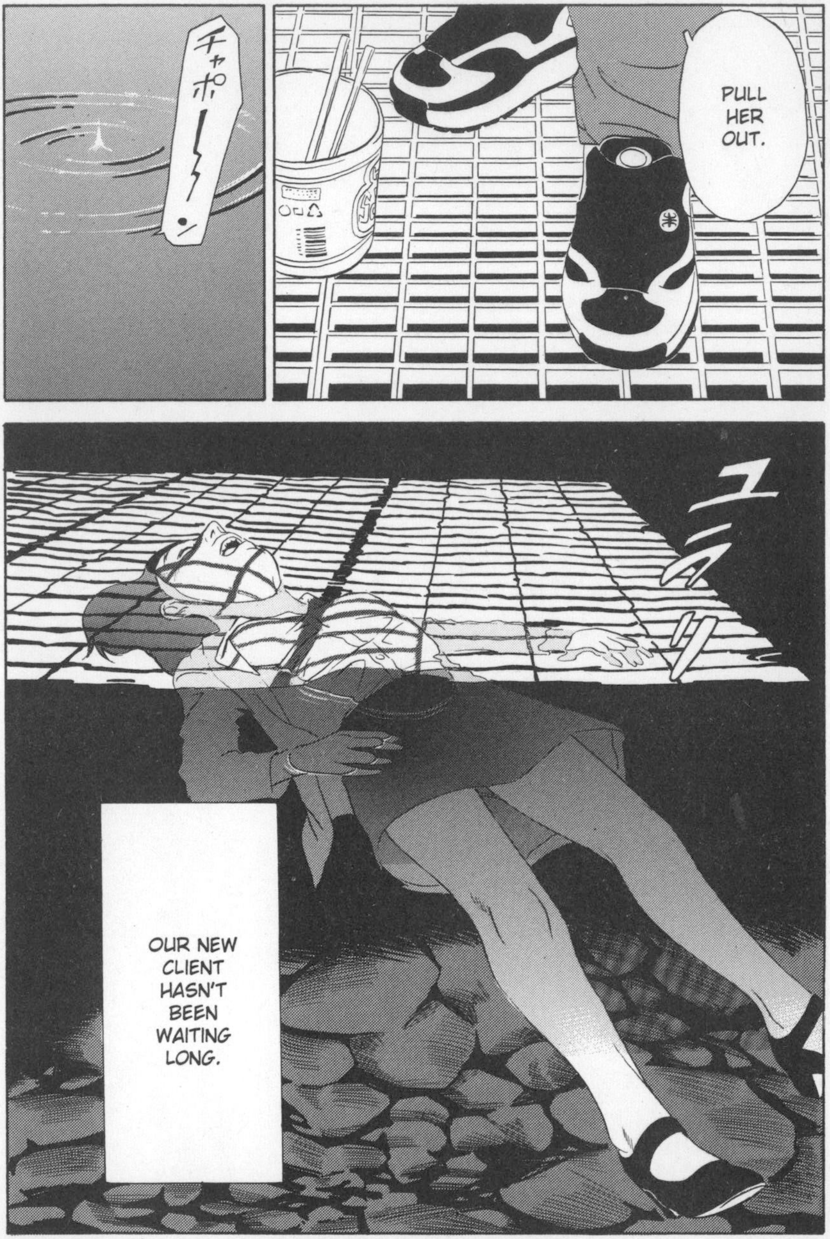
PULL HER OUT.
チャポーン
OUR NEW CLIENT HASN'T BEEN WAITING LONG.

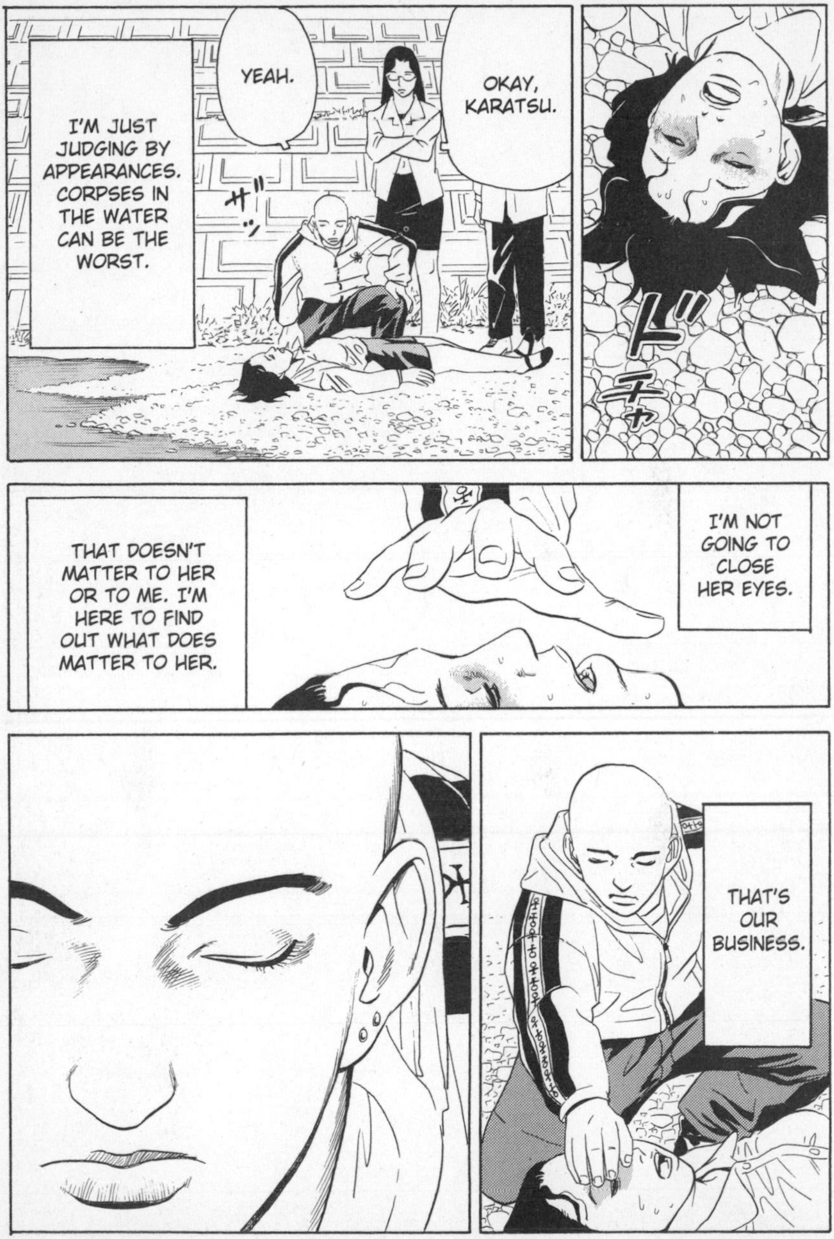
ドチャ
OKAY, KARATSU.
YEAH.
ザッ
I'M JUST JUDGING BY APPEARANCES. CORPSES IN THE WATER CAN BE THE WORST.
I'M NOT GOING TO CLOSE HER EYES.
THAT DOESN'T MATTER TO HER OR TO ME. I'M HERE TO FIND OUT WHAT DOES MATTER TO HER.
THAT'S OUR BUSINESS.

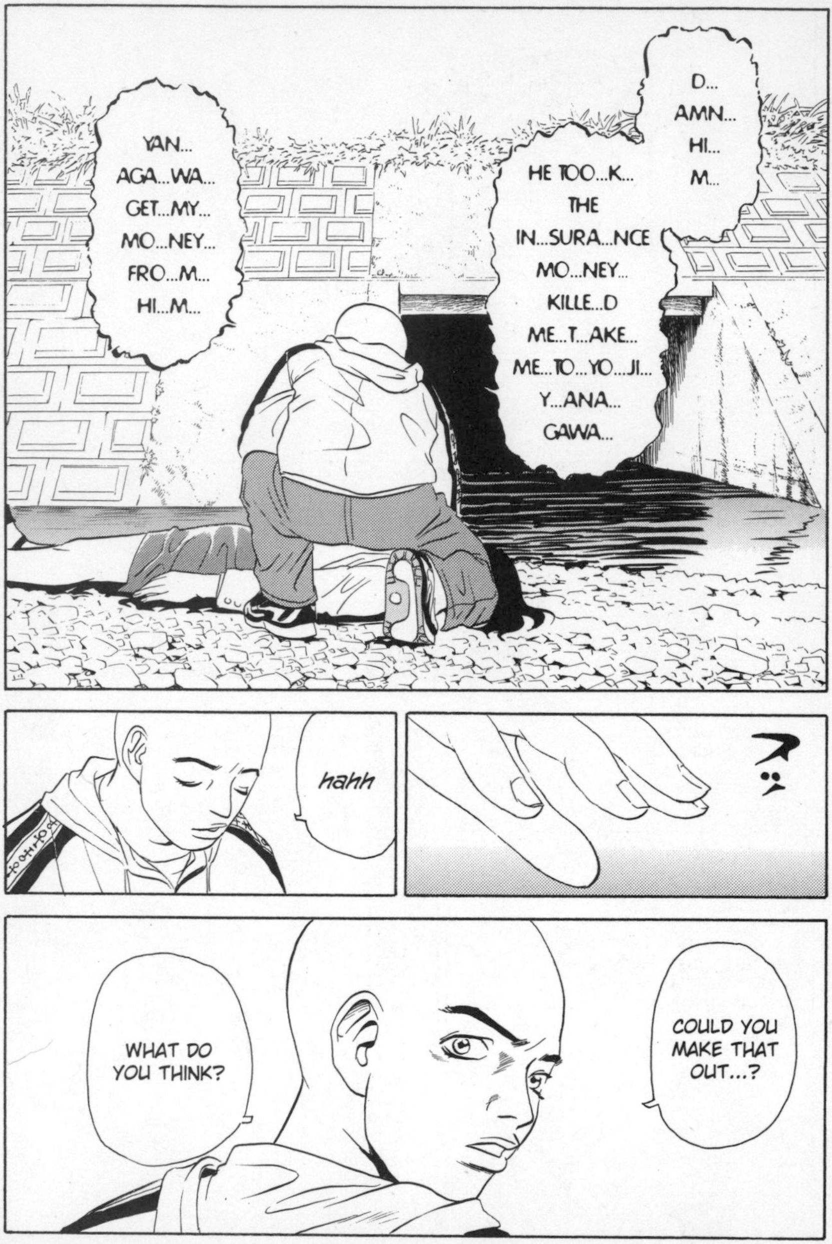
D... AMN... HI... M...
HE TOO...K... THE IN...SURA...NCE MO...NEY... KILLE...D ME...T...AKE... ME...TO...YO...JI... Y...ANA... GAWA...
YAN... AGA...WA... GET...MY... MO...NEY... FRO...M... HI...M...
スッ
hahh
COULD YOU MAKE THAT OUT...?
WHAT DO YOU THINK?

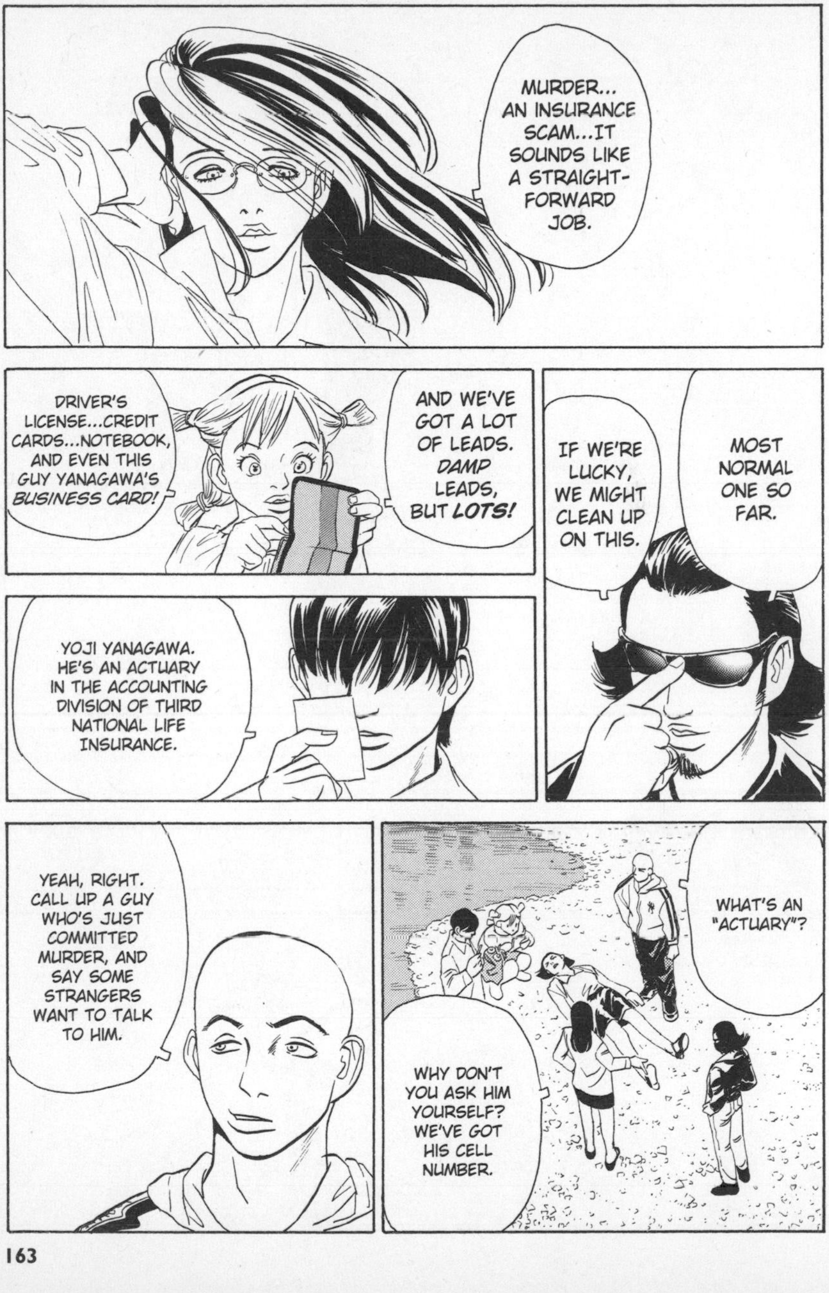
MURDER... AN INSURANCE SCAM...IT SOUNDS LIKE A STRAIGHT-FORWARD JOB.
MOST NORMAL ONE SO FAR.
IF WE'RE LUCKY, WE MIGHT CLEAN UP ON THIS.
DRIVER'S LICENSE...CREDIT CARDS...NOTEBOOK, AND EVEN THIS GUY YANAGAWA'S *BUSINESS CARD!*
AND WE'VE GOT A LOT OF LEADS. *DAMP* LEADS, BUT ***LOTS!***
YOJI YANAGAWA. HE'S AN ACTUARY IN THE ACCOUNTING DIVISION OF THIRD NATIONAL LIFE INSURANCE.
WHAT'S AN "ACTUARY"?
WHY DON'T YOU ASK HIM YOURSELF? WE'VE GOT HIS CELL NUMBER.
YEAH, RIGHT. CALL UP A GUY WHO'S JUST COMMITTED MURDER, AND SAY SOME STRANGERS WANT TO TALK TO HIM.

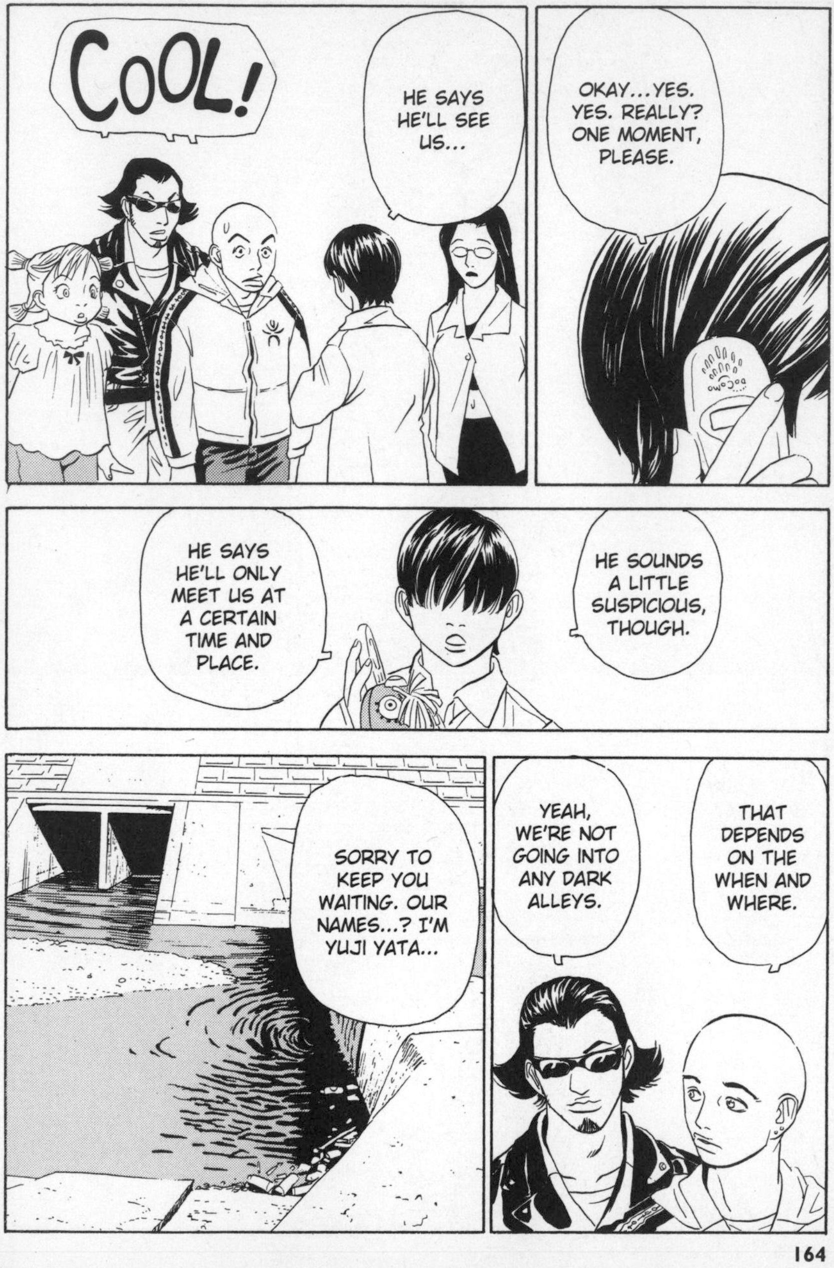
OKAY...YES. YES. REALLY? ONE MOMENT, PLEASE.
HE SAYS HE'LL SEE US...
COOL!
HE SOUNDS A LITTLE SUSPICIOUS, THOUGH.
HE SAYS HE'LL ONLY MEET US AT A CERTAIN TIME AND PLACE.
THAT DEPENDS ON THE WHEN AND WHERE.
YEAH, WE'RE NOT GOING INTO ANY DARK ALLEYS.
SORRY TO KEEP YOU WAITING. OUR NAMES...? I'M YUJI YATA...

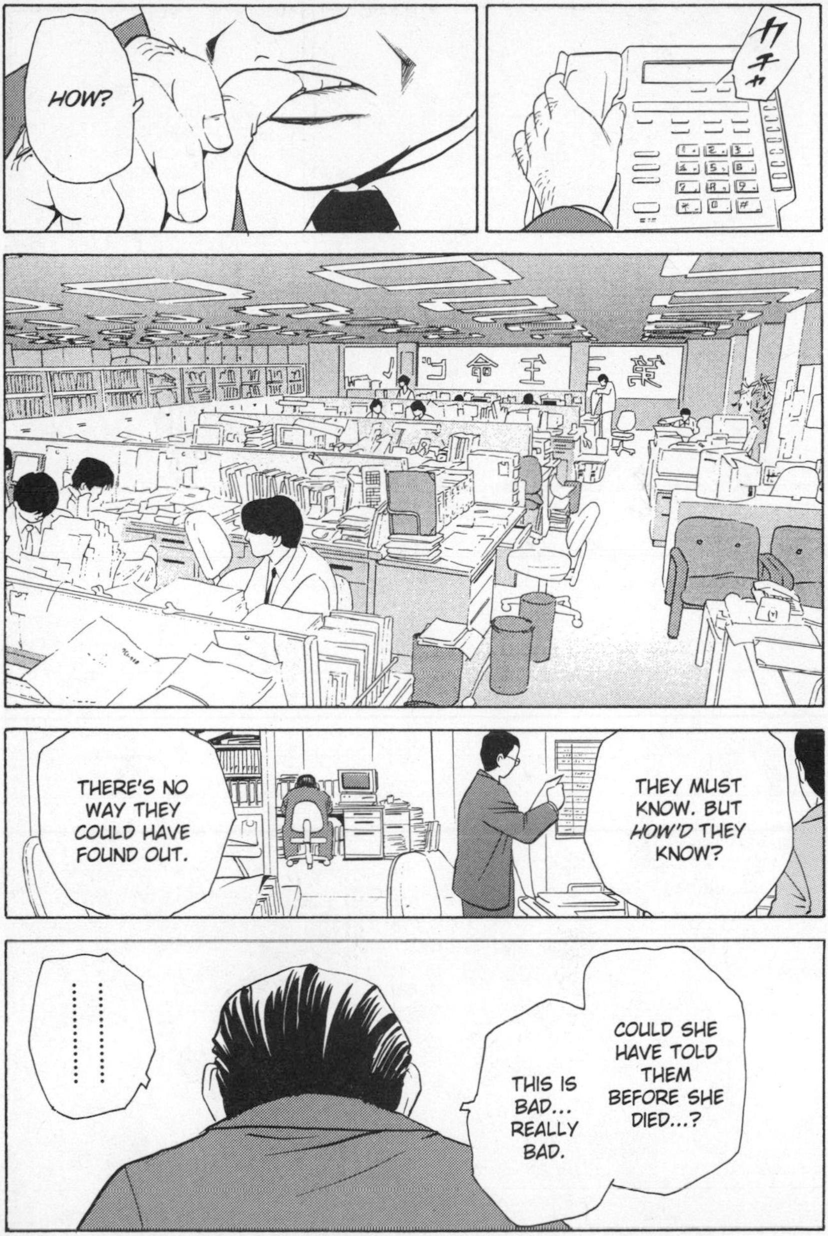
カチャ
HOW?
THEY MUST KNOW. BUT HOW'D THEY KNOW?
THERE'S NO WAY THEY COULD HAVE FOUND OUT.
COULD SHE HAVE TOLD THEM BEFORE SHE DIED...?
THIS IS BAD... REALLY BAD.
......

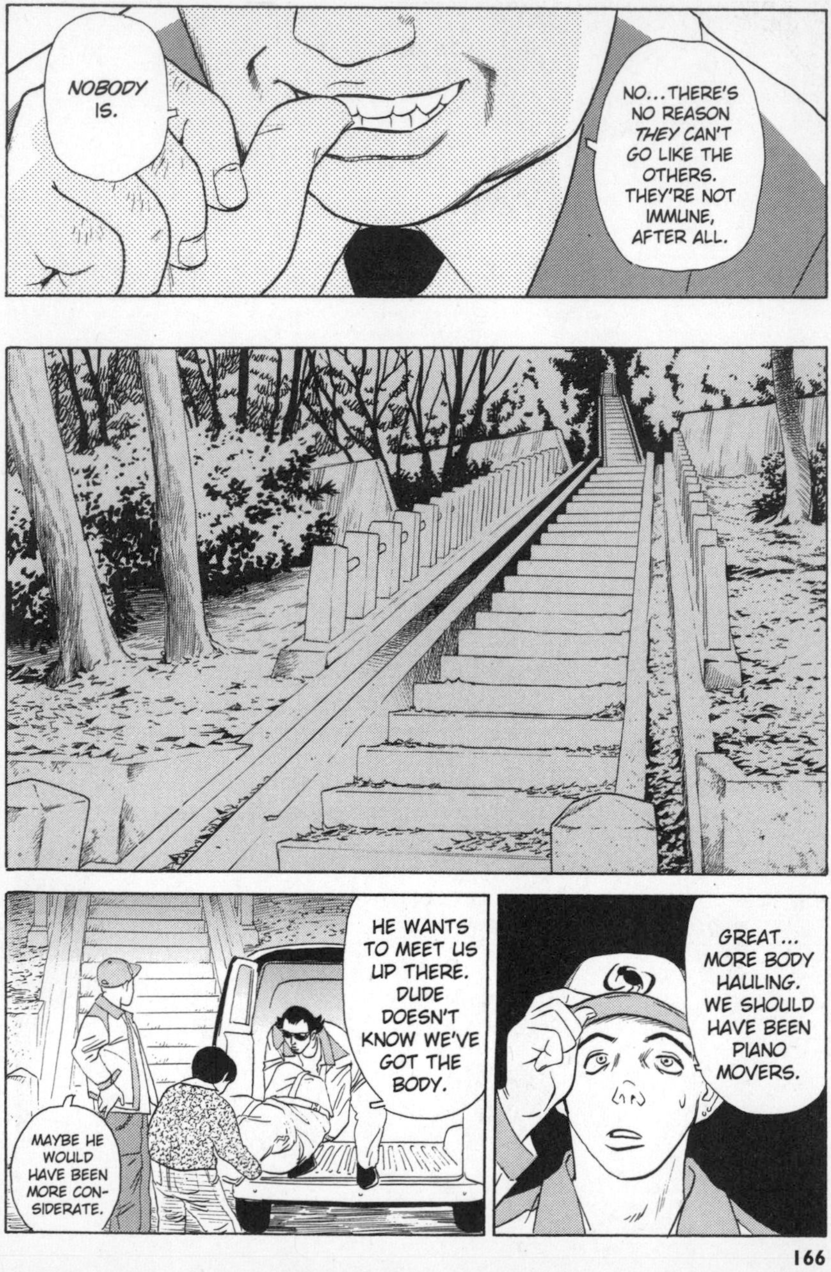
NO... THERE'S NO REASON *THEY* CAN'T GO LIKE THE OTHERS. THEY'RE NOT IMMUNE, AFTER ALL.
NOBODY IS.
GREAT... MORE BODY HAULING. WE SHOULD HAVE BEEN PIANO MOVERS.
HE WANTS TO MEET US UP THERE. DUDE DOESN'T KNOW WE'VE GOT THE BODY.
MAYBE HE WOULD HAVE BEEN MORE CONSIDERATE.

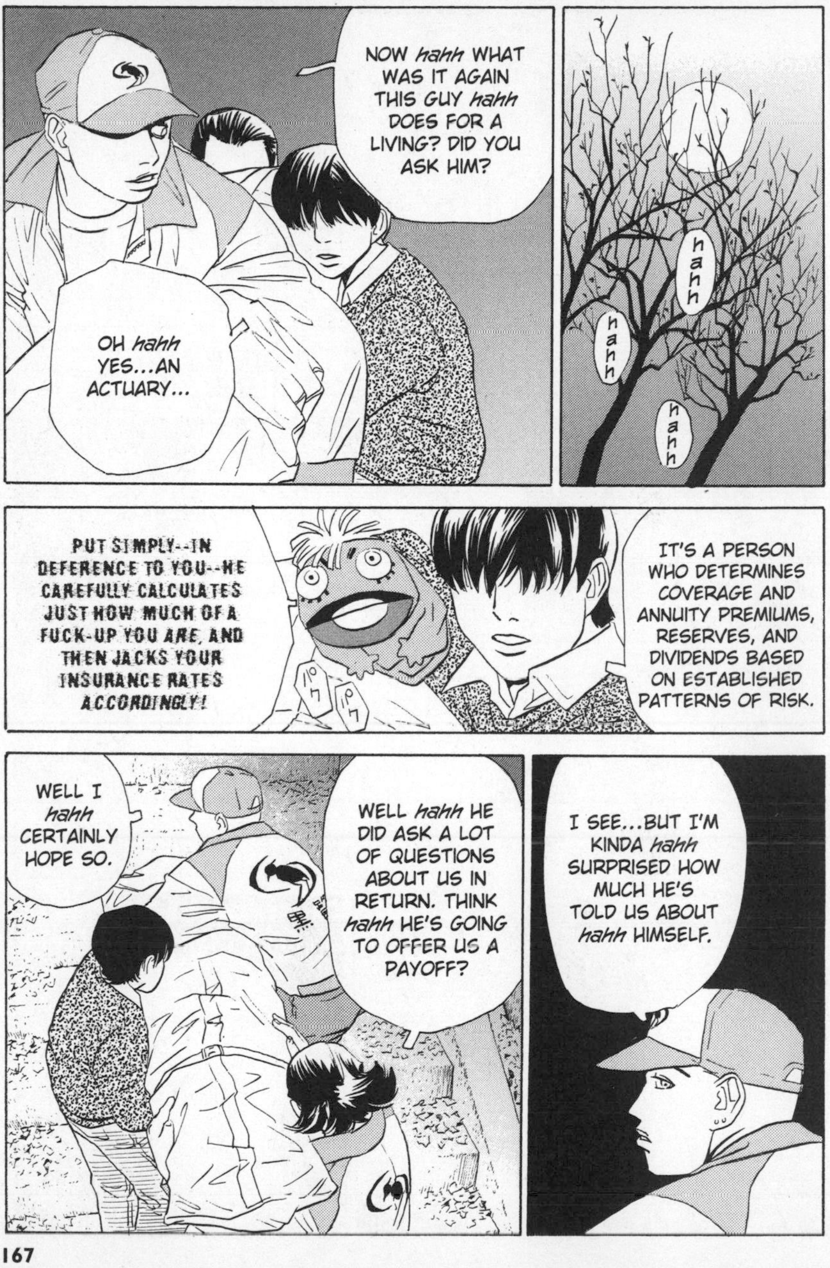
hahh
hahh
hahh
NOW hahh WHAT WAS IT AGAIN THIS GUY hahh DOES FOR A LIVING? DID YOU ASK HIM?
OH hahh YES...AN ACTUARY...
IT'S A PERSON WHO DETERMINES COVERAGE AND ANNUITY PREMIUMS, RESERVES, AND DIVIDENDS BASED ON ESTABLISHED PATTERNS OF RISK.
PUT SIMPLY--IN DEFERENCE TO YOU--HE CAREFULLY CALCULATES JUST HOW MUCH OF A FUCK-UP YOU ARE, AND THEN JACKS YOUR INSURANCE RATES ACCORDINGLY!
I SEE...BUT I'M KINDA hahh SURPRISED HOW MUCH HE'S TOLD US ABOUT hahh HIMSELF.
WELL hahh HE DID ASK A LOT OF QUESTIONS ABOUT US IN RETURN. THINK hahh HE'S GOING TO OFFER US A PAYOFF?
WELL I hahh CERTAINLY HOPE SO.

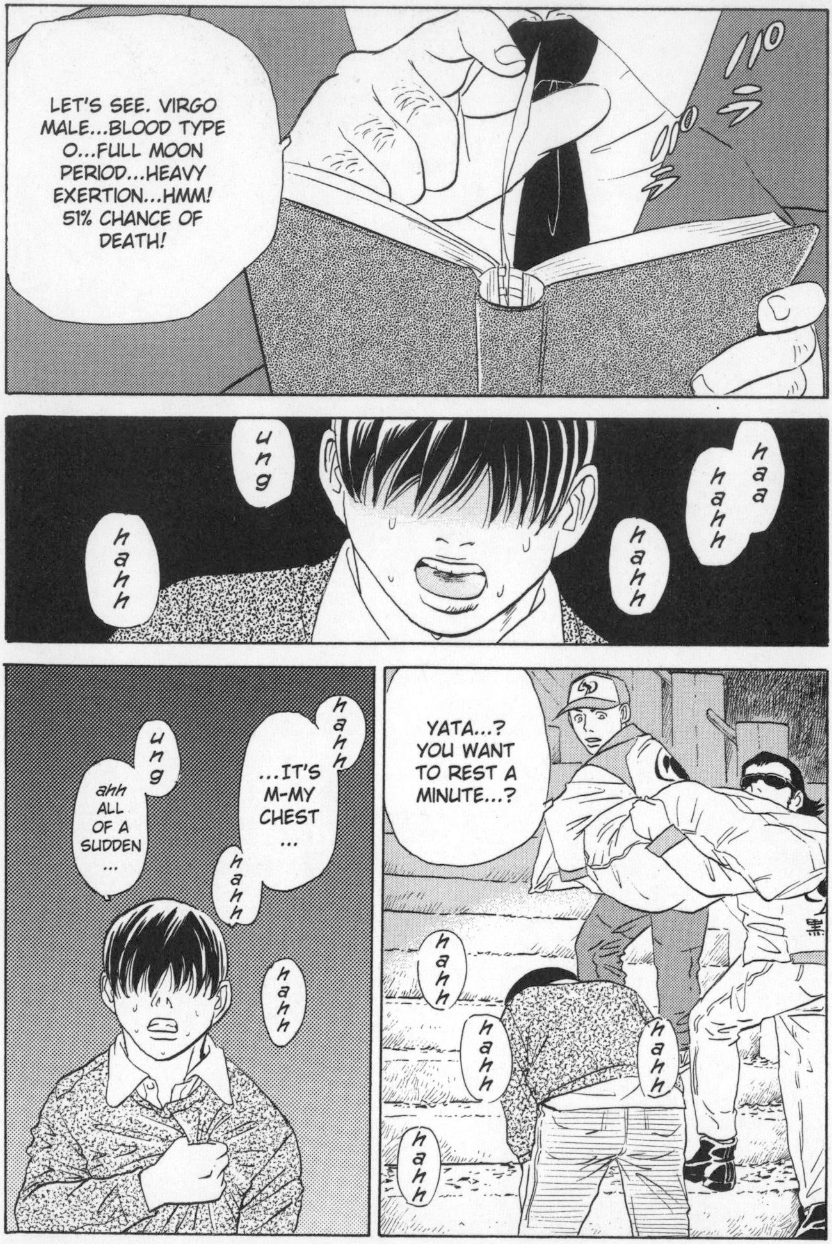
パラ
パラ
LET'S SEE. VIRGO MALE...BLOOD TYPE O...FULL MOON PERIOD...HEAVY EXERTION...HMM! 51% CHANCE OF DEATH!
haa hahh
hahh
ung
hahh
YATA...? YOU WANT TO REST A MINUTE...?
hahh
hahh
hahh
hahh
hahh
...IT'S M-MY CHEST ...
ung
ahh ALL OF A SUDDEN ...
hahh
hahh

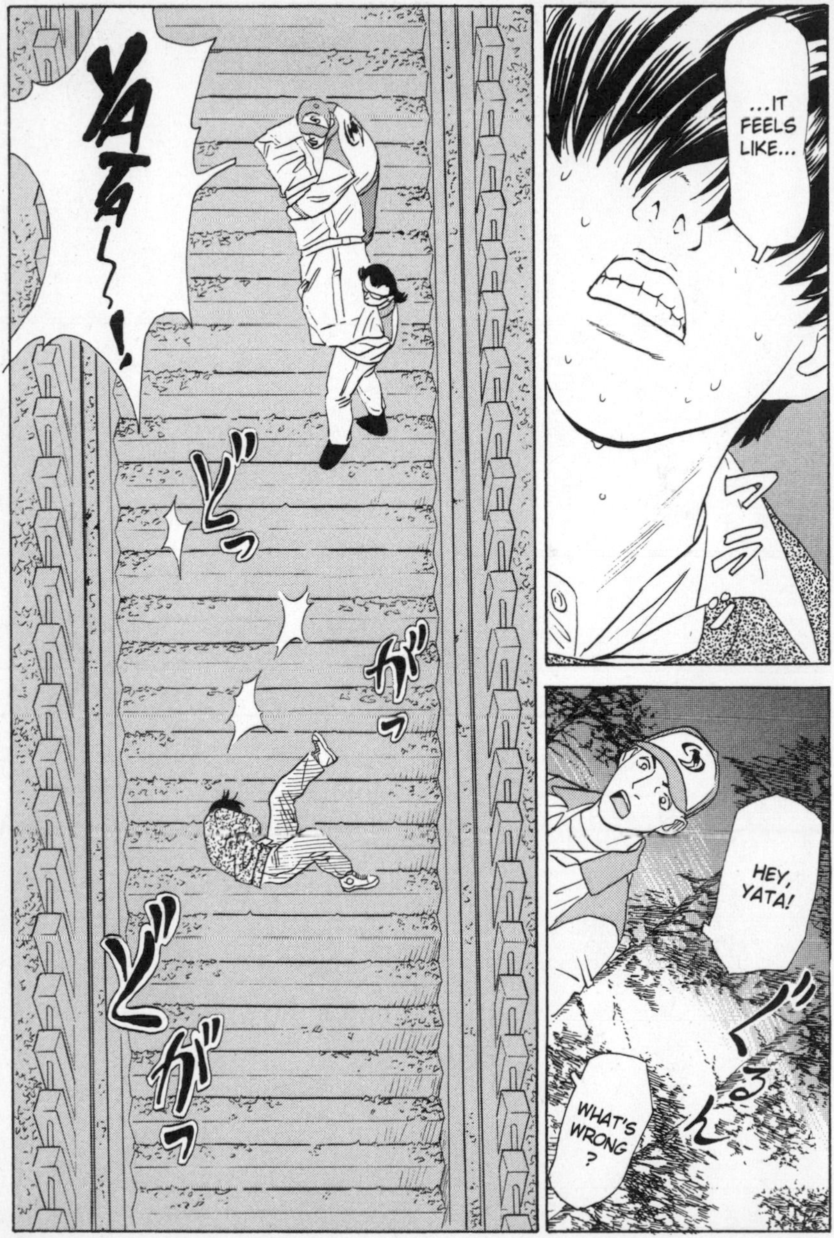
...IT FEELS LIKE...
HEY, YATA!
ぐるん
WHAT'S WRONG?
YATA~~!
どっ
がっ
どがっ

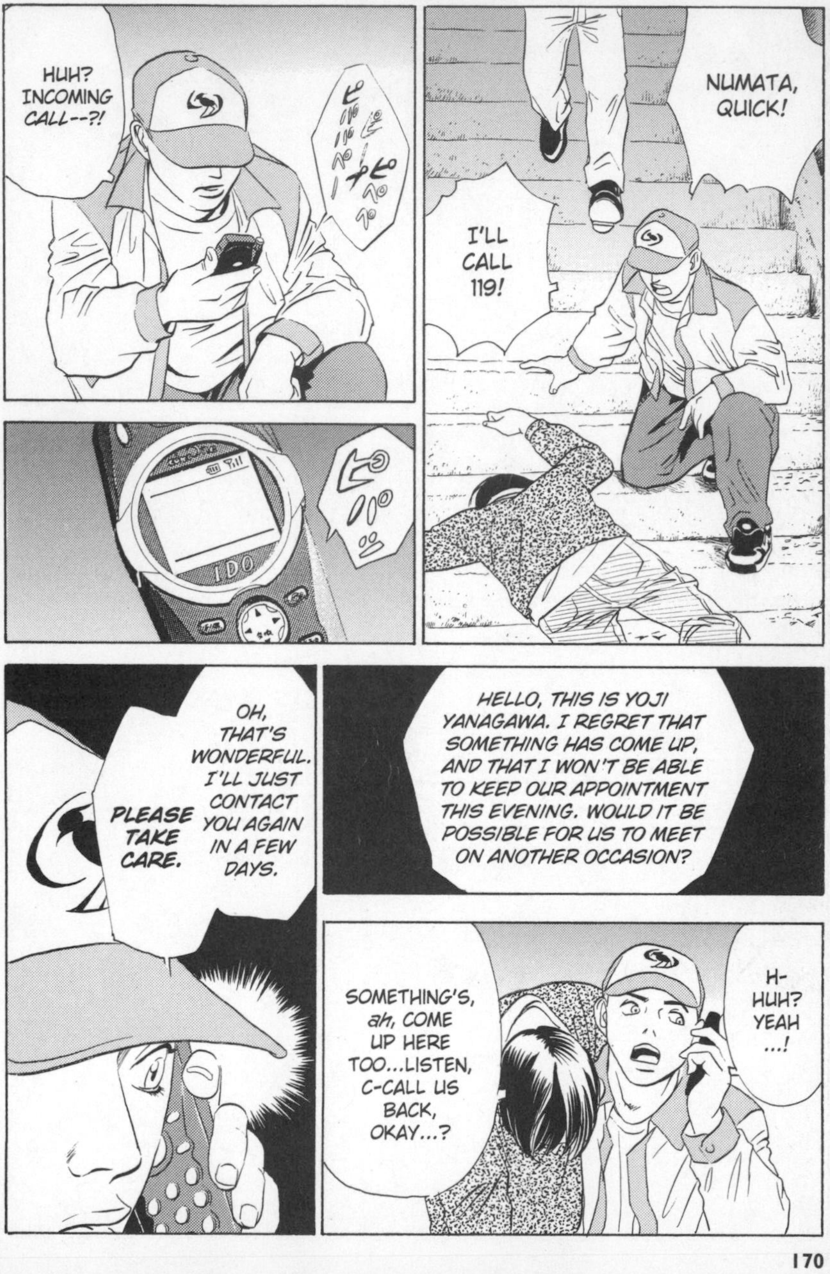
NUMATA, QUICK!
I'LL CALL 119!
HUH? INCOMING CALL--?!
HELLO, THIS IS YOJI YANAGAWA. I REGRET THAT SOMETHING HAS COME UP, AND THAT I WON'T BE ABLE TO KEEP OUR APPOINTMENT THIS EVENING. WOULD IT BE POSSIBLE FOR US TO MEET ON ANOTHER OCCASION?
H-HUH? YEAH ...!
SOMETHING'S, *ah*, COME UP HERE TOO...LISTEN, C-CALL US BACK, OKAY...?
OH, THAT'S WONDERFUL. I'LL JUST CONTACT YOU AGAIN IN A FEW DAYS.
PLEASE TAKE CARE.

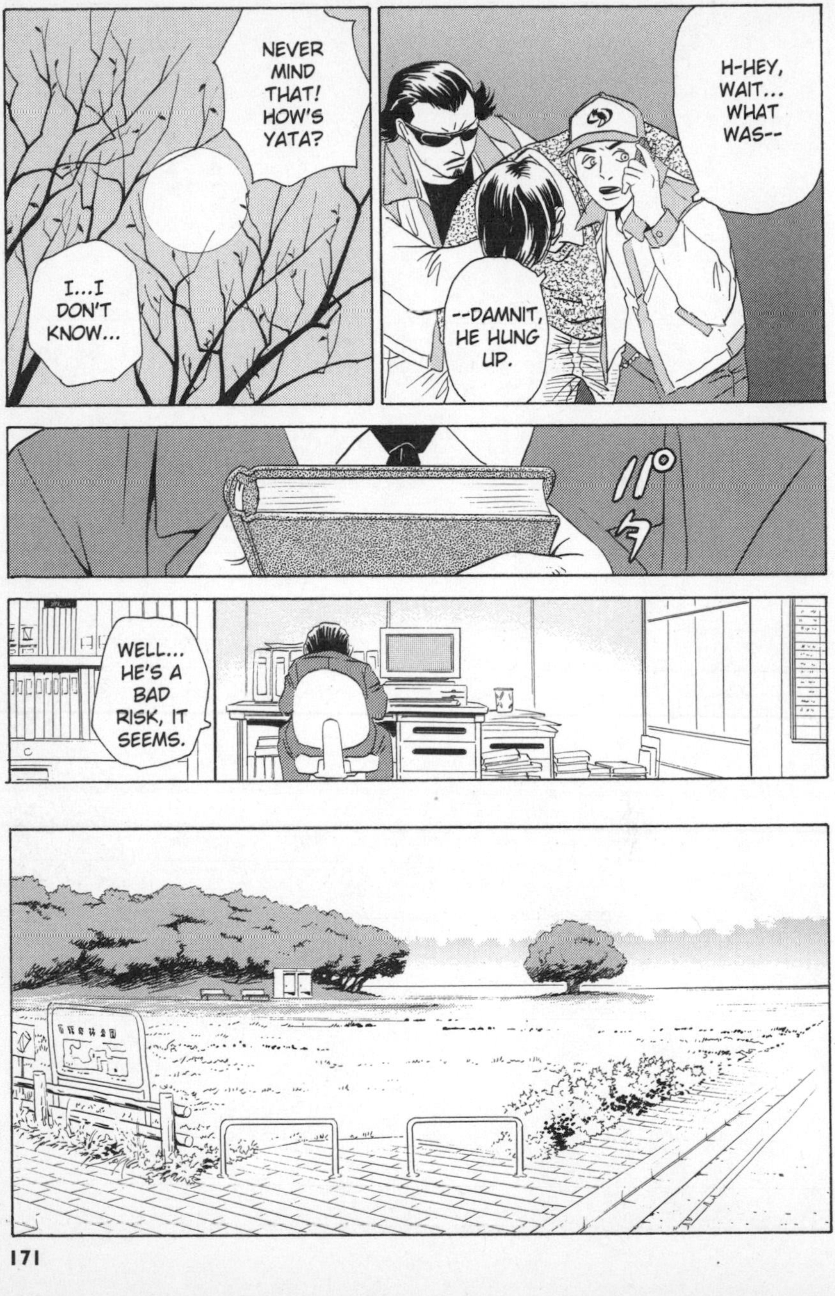
H-HEY, WAIT... WHAT WAS--
--DAMNIT, HE HUNG UP.
NEVER MIND THAT! HOW'S YATA?
I...I DON'T KNOW...
パタ
WELL... HE'S A BAD RISK, IT SEEMS.

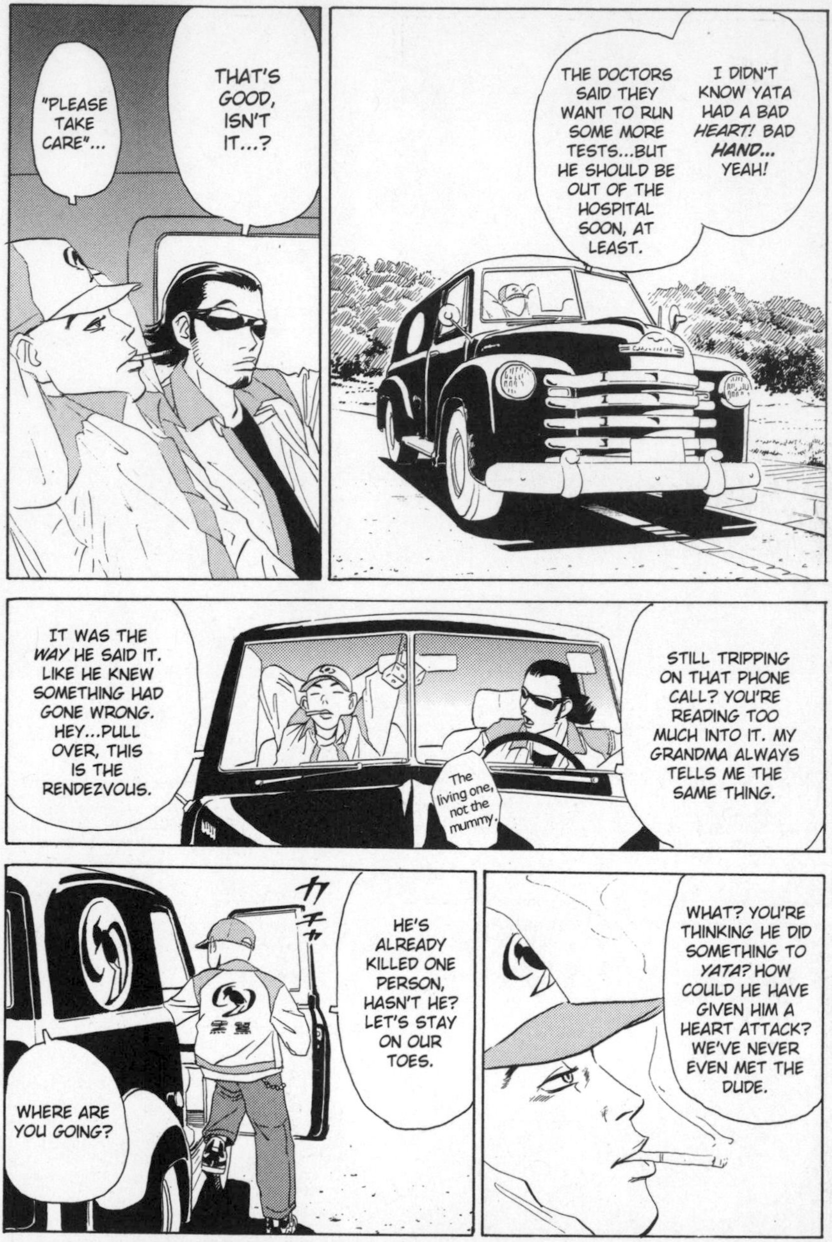
I DIDN'T KNOW YATA HAD A BAD *HEART!* BAD ***HAND...*** YEAH!
THE DOCTORS SAID THEY WANT TO RUN SOME MORE TESTS...BUT HE SHOULD BE OUT OF THE HOSPITAL SOON, AT LEAST.
THAT'S GOOD, ISN'T IT...?
"PLEASE TAKE CARE"...
STILL TRIPPING ON THAT PHONE CALL? YOU'RE READING TOO MUCH INTO IT. MY GRANDMA ALWAYS TELLS ME THE SAME THING.
The living one, not the mummy.
IT WAS THE *WAY* HE SAID IT. LIKE HE KNEW SOMETHING HAD GONE WRONG. HEY...PULL OVER, THIS IS THE RENDEZVOUS.
WHAT? YOU'RE THINKING HE DID SOMETHING TO *YATA?* HOW COULD HE HAVE GIVEN HIM A HEART ATTACK? WE'VE NEVER EVEN MET THE DUDE.
カチャ
HE'S ALREADY KILLED ONE PERSON, HASN'T HE? LET'S STAY ON OUR TOES.
WHERE ARE YOU GOING?

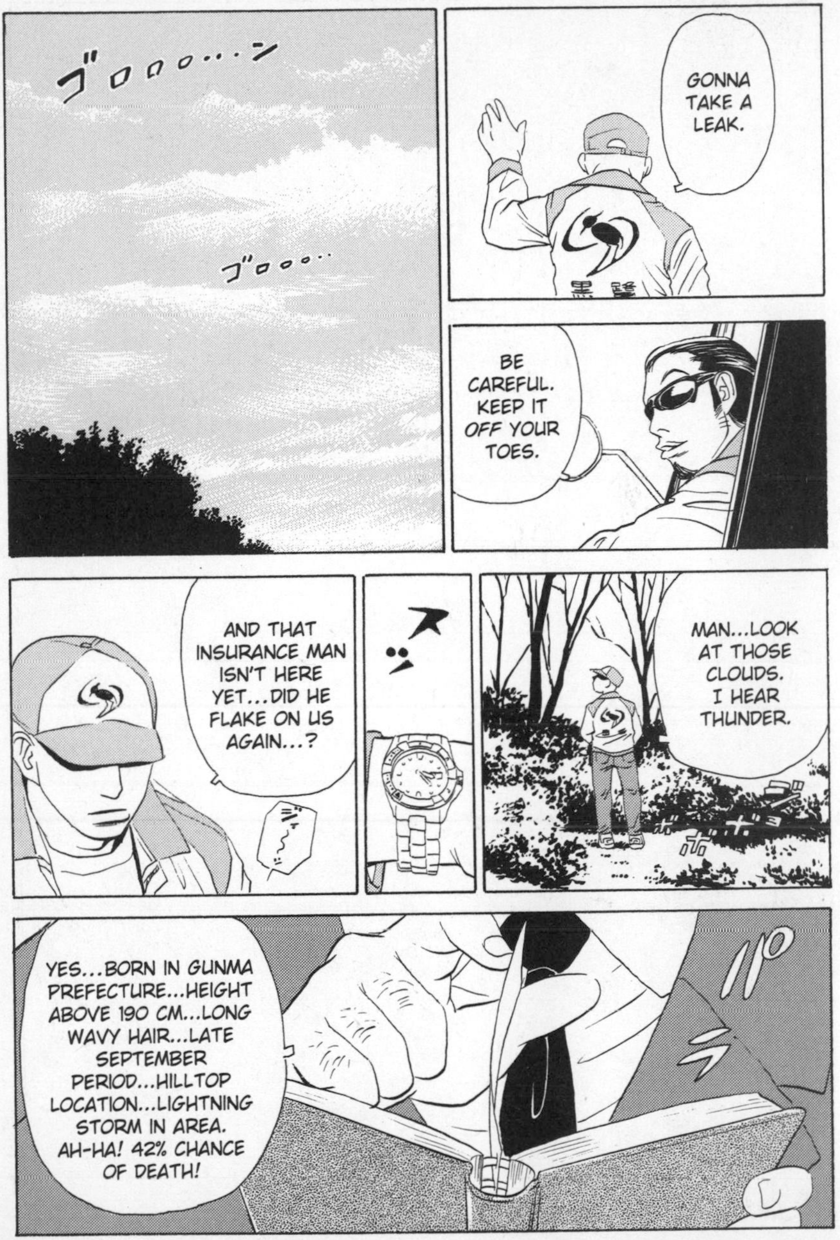
GONNA TAKE A LEAK.
BE CAREFUL. KEEP IT OFF YOUR TOES.
ゴロロロ…ン
ゴロロロ…
MAN...LOOK AT THOSE CLOUDS. I HEAR THUNDER.
AND THAT INSURANCE MAN ISN'T HERE YET...DID HE FLAKE ON US AGAIN...?
YES...BORN IN GUNMA PREFECTURE...HEIGHT ABOVE 190 CM...LONG WAVY HAIR...LATE SEPTEMBER PERIOD...HILLTOP LOCATION...LIGHTNING STORM IN AREA. AH-HA! 42% CHANCE OF DEATH!
パラ

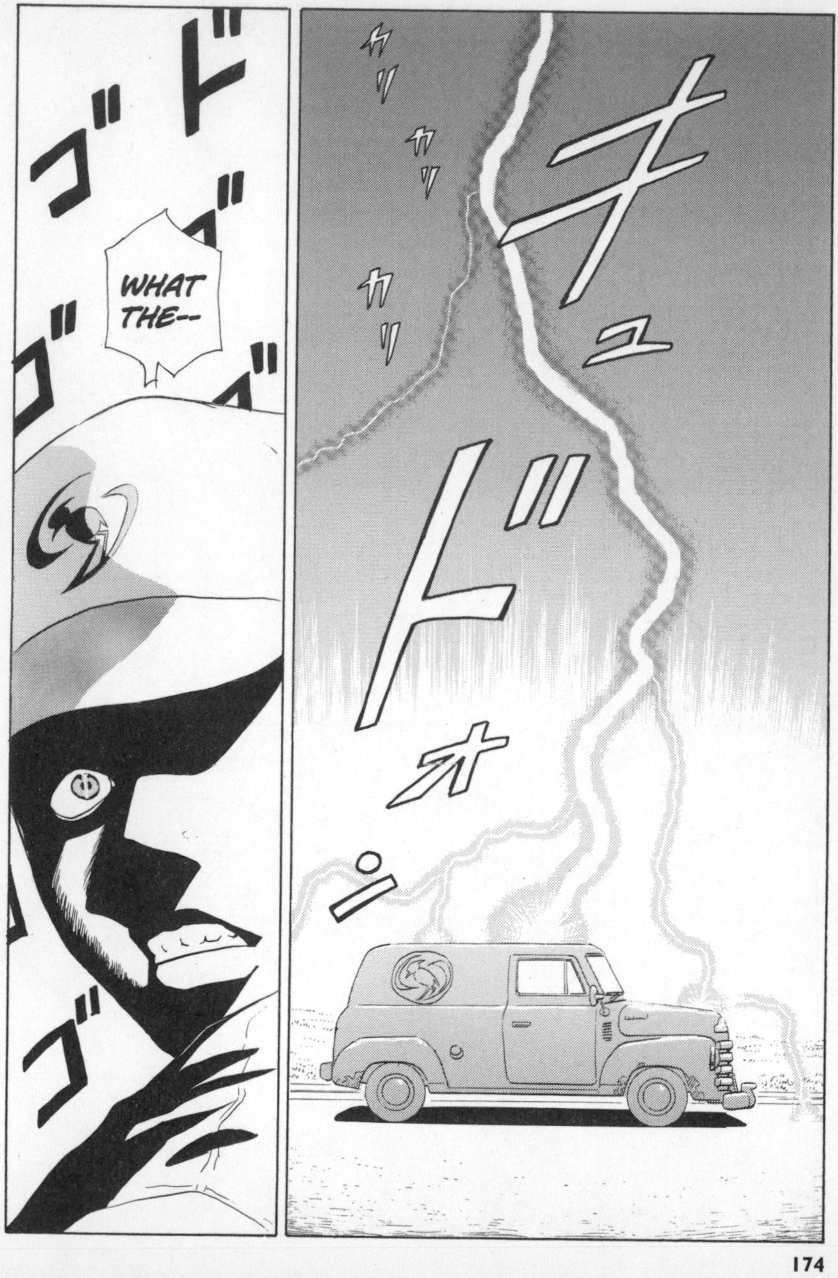
カッ カッ カッ
チュドォン
WHAT THE--
ドドド
ゴゴゴ

NUMATA! ARE YOU ALL RIGHT?

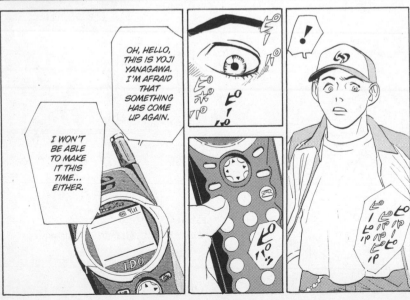

OH, HELLO, THIS IS YOJI YANAGAWA. I'M AFRAID THAT SOMETHING HAS COME UP AGAIN.

I WON'T BE ABLE TO MAKE IT THIS TIME... EITHER.

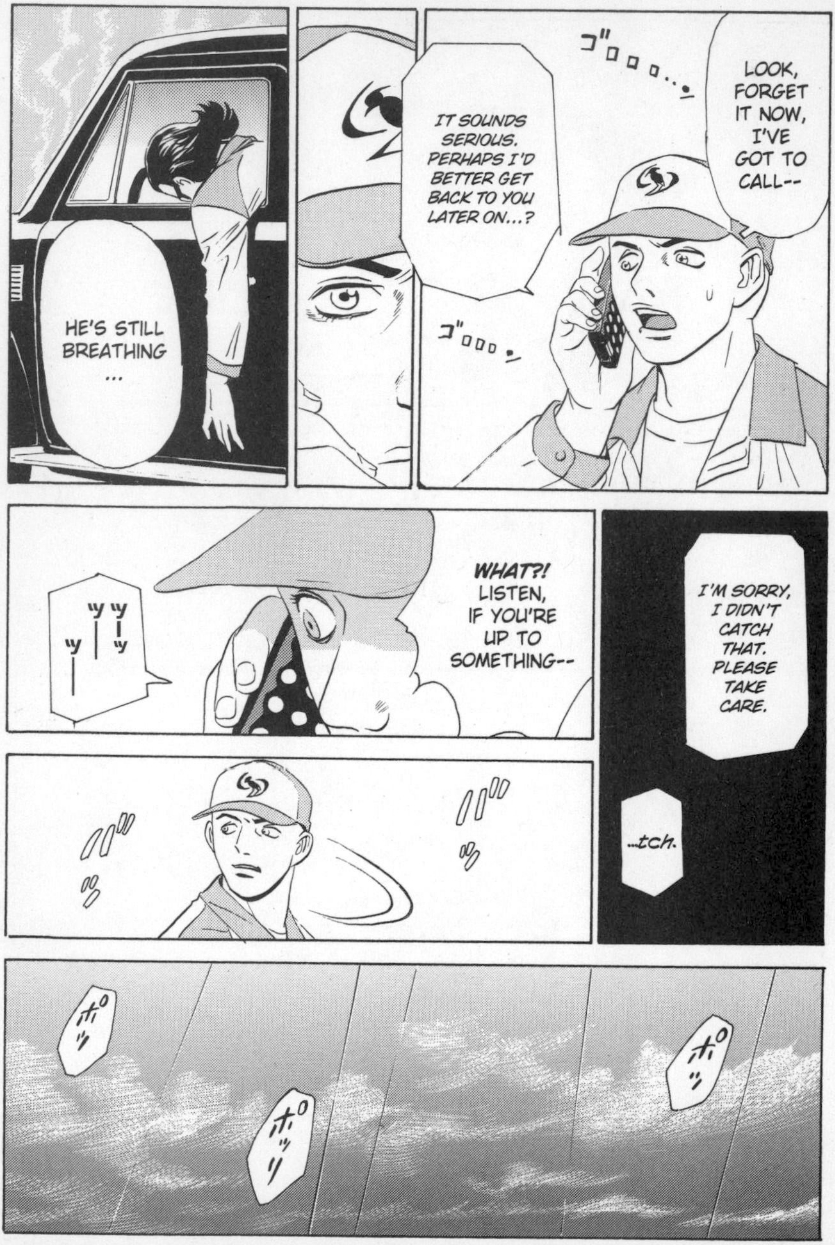
ゴロロロ…ッ
LOOK, FORGET IT NOW, I'VE GOT TO CALL--
ゴロロロッ
IT SOUNDS SERIOUS. PERHAPS I'D BETTER GET BACK TO YOU LATER ON...?
HE'S STILL BREATHING ...
I'M SORRY, I DIDN'T CATCH THAT. PLEASE TAKE CARE.
...tch.
WHAT?! LISTEN, IF YOU'RE UP TO SOMETHING--
ツーツーツー
ポツ
ポツ
ポツリ

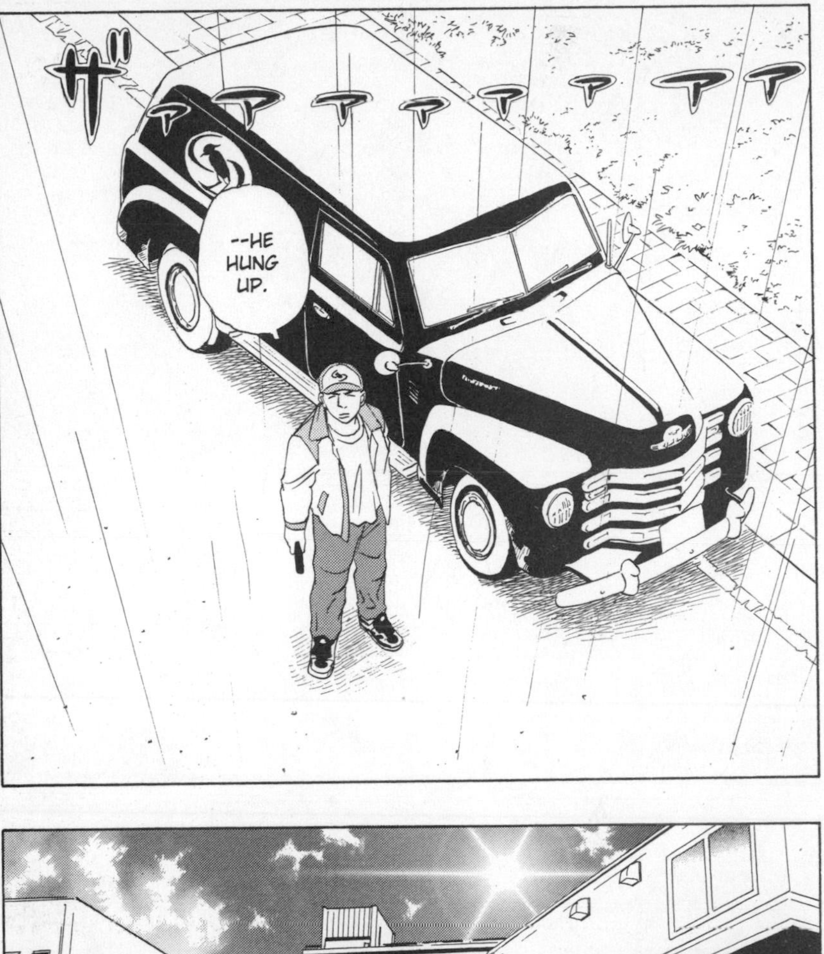
ザアアアアアアアア
--HE HUNG UP.

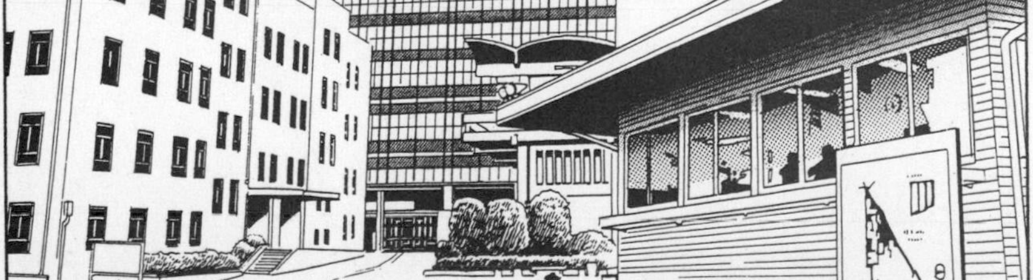

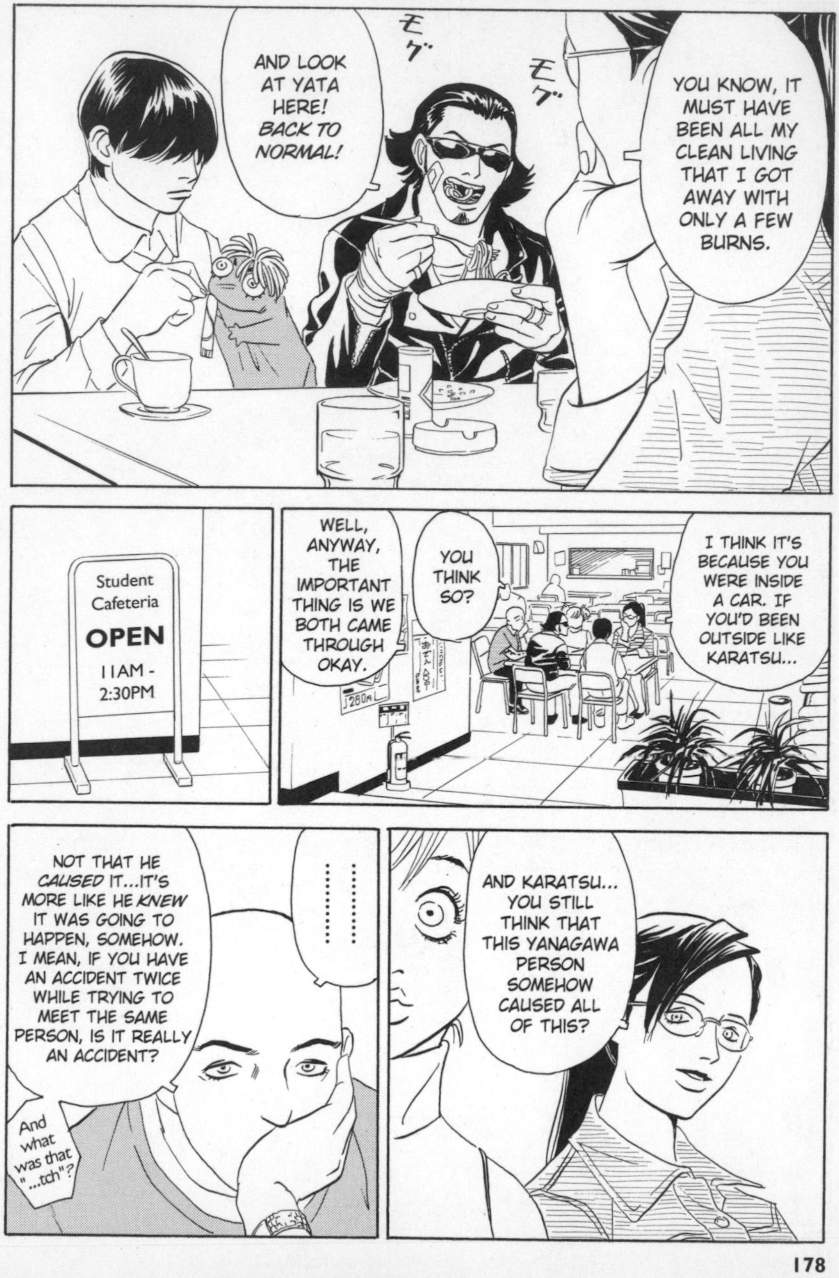
YOU KNOW, IT MUST HAVE BEEN ALL MY CLEAN LIVING THAT I GOT AWAY WITH ONLY A FEW BURNS.
モグ
モグ
AND LOOK AT YATA HERE! *BACK TO NORMAL!*
I THINK IT'S BECAUSE YOU WERE INSIDE A CAR. IF YOU'D BEEN OUTSIDE LIKE KARATSU...
YOU THINK SO?
WELL, ANYWAY, THE IMPORTANT THING IS WE BOTH CAME THROUGH OKAY.
Student Cafeteria
OPEN
11AM - 2:30PM
AND KARATSU... YOU STILL THINK THAT THIS YANAGAWA PERSON SOMEHOW CAUSED ALL OF THIS?
......
NOT THAT HE *CAUSED* IT...IT'S MORE LIKE HE *KNEW* IT WAS GOING TO HAPPEN, SOMEHOW. I MEAN, IF YOU HAVE AN ACCIDENT TWICE WHILE TRYING TO MEET THE SAME PERSON, IS IT REALLY AN ACCIDENT?
And what was that "...tch"?

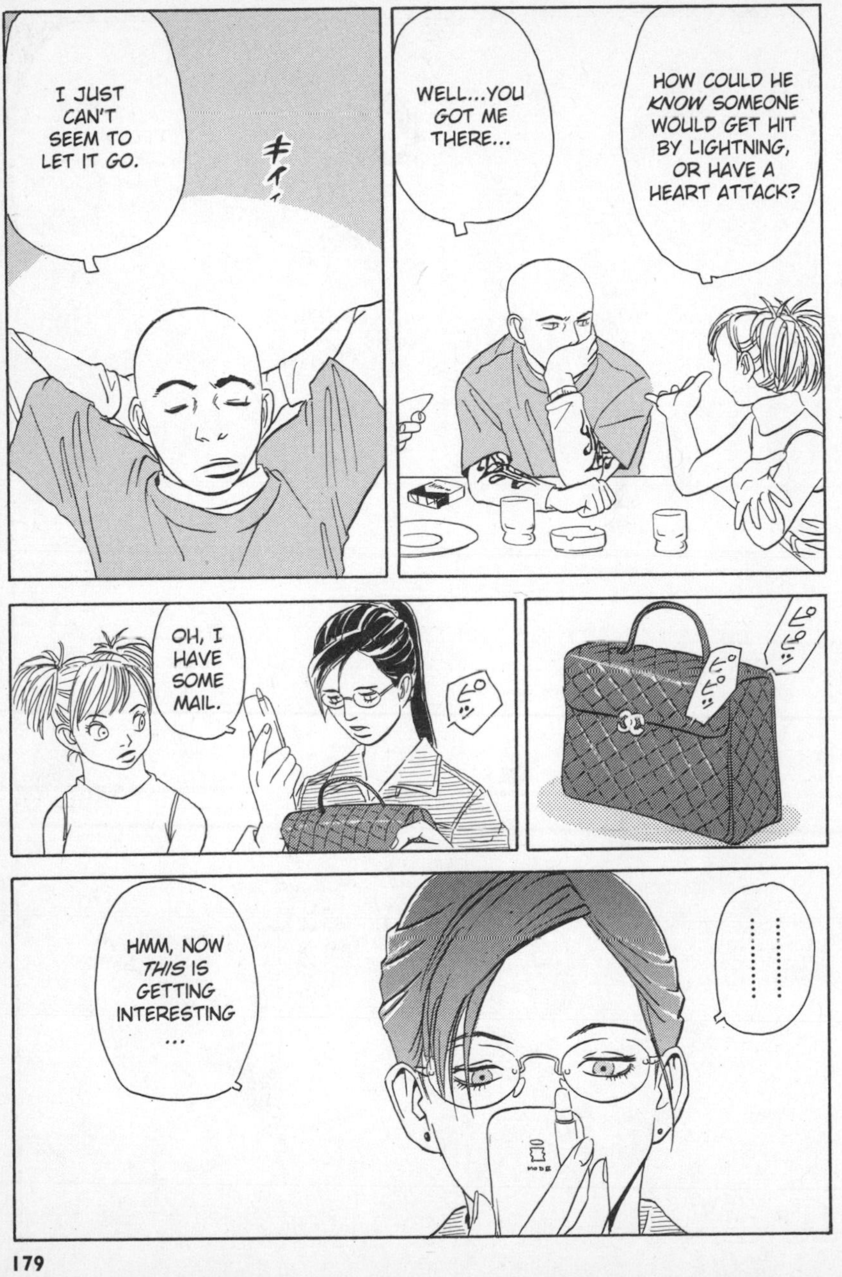
HOW COULD HE KNOW SOMEONE WOULD GET HIT BY LIGHTNING, OR HAVE A HEART ATTACK?
WELL...YOU GOT ME THERE...
I JUST CAN'T SEEM TO LET IT GO.
OH, I HAVE SOME MAIL.
......
HMM, NOW THIS IS GETTING INTERESTING ...

SOMEONE ON *CORPSE CHAT* HAS A FRIEND IN THE INSURANCE INDUSTRY... APPARENTLY YANAGAWA HAS QUITE A REPUTATION.

I'VE BEEN ASKING AROUND ON MY HOMEPAGE ABOUT THAT BODY AND YANAGAWA, BUT...

WHAT'S UP?

...HM? A FILE?

WHAT'S THIS?

4	Oichiro Hara	34	Japan Fire	¥25,000,000	
	Katahiko Sugimoto	24	Fuji Fire	¥20,000,000	
	Yoshiyuki Sato	44	Yasuda Fire	¥45,000,000	
	Takashi Morishita	35	Sendai Fire	¥30,000,000	
	Tomoko Miyamura	27	Yasuda Fire	¥25,000,000	
	Seiko Tanaka	40	Dowa Fire	¥50,000,000	
10	Shiho Nishio	33	Mitsui Sea	¥120,000,000	
11	Masayuki Yoshida	22	Mitsui Sea	¥15,000,000	

THIS WAS THE "INSURANCE MONEY" SHE WAS TALKING ABOUT?

SHE AND YANAGAWA WERE SUSPECTED OF RUNNING AN INSURANCE FRAUD RING TO HELP PEOPLE COLLECT ON PHONY ACCIDENTS...EXCEPT THE ACCIDENTS WERE REAL--AND FATAL.

THIS ATTACHMENT SHOWS PAYOUTS THAT WERE MADE IN THE PAST FEW YEARS...ALL TO OUR DEAD CLIENT.

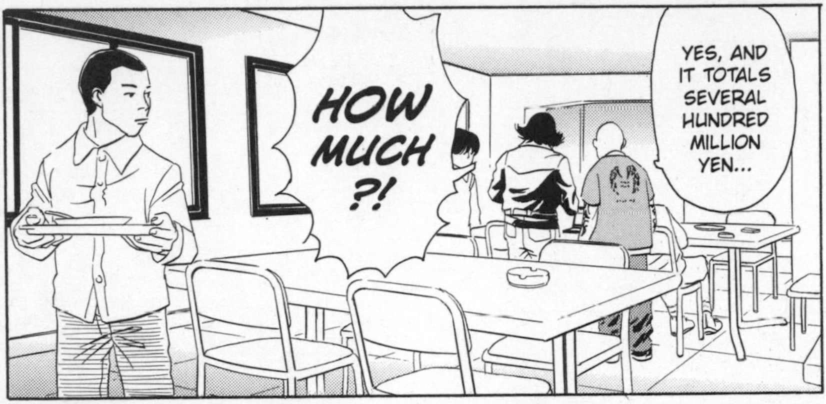
YES, AND IT TOTALS SEVERAL HUNDRED MILLION YEN...
HOW MUCH ?!

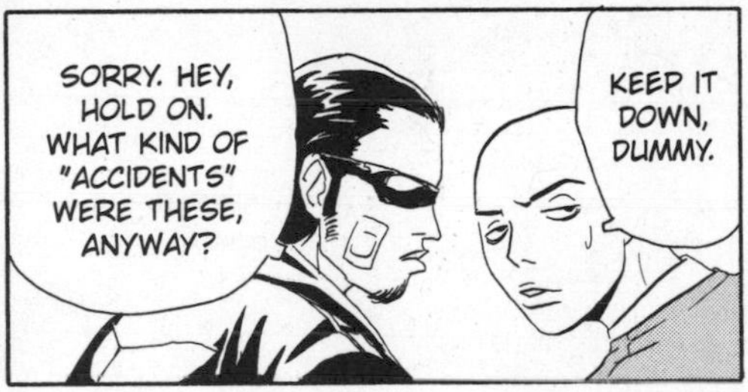
KEEP IT DOWN, DUMMY.
SORRY. HEY, HOLD ON. WHAT KIND OF "ACCIDENTS" WERE THESE, ANYWAY?

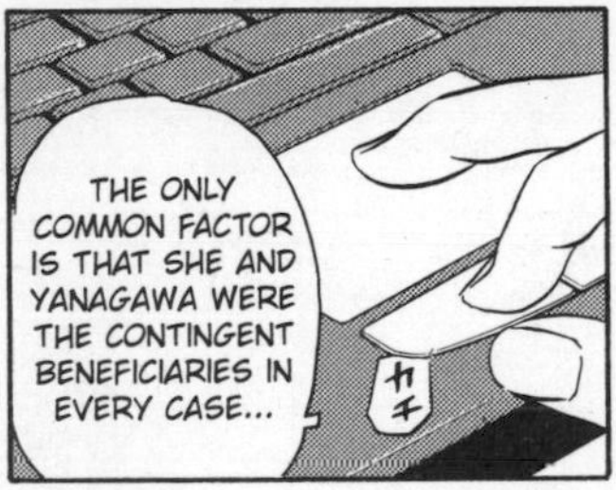
THE ONLY COMMON FACTOR IS THAT SHE AND YANAGAWA WERE THE CONTINGENT BENEFICIARIES IN EVERY CASE...
カチ

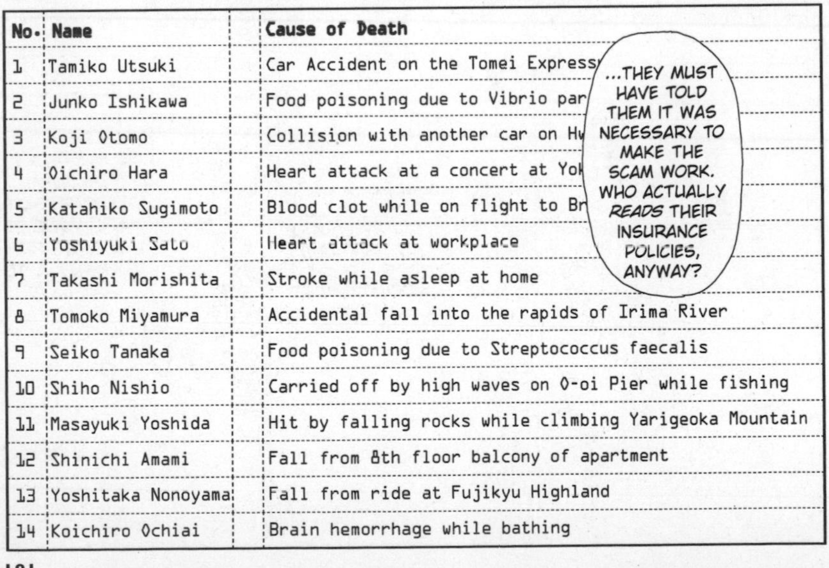

No.	Name	Cause of Death
1	Tamiko Utsuki	Car Accident on the Tomei Express
2	Junko Ishikawa	Food poisoning due to Vibrio par
3	Koji Otomo	Collision with another car on Hw
4	Oichiro Hara	Heart attack at a concert at Yok
5	Katahiko Sugimoto	Blood clot while on flight to Br
6	Yoshiyuki Sato	Heart attack at workplace
7	Takashi Morishita	Stroke while asleep at home
8	Tomoko Miyamura	Accidental fall into the rapids of Irima River
9	Seiko Tanaka	Food poisoning due to Streptococcus faecalis
10	Shiho Nishio	Carried off by high waves on O-oi Pier while fishing
11	Masayuki Yoshida	Hit by falling rocks while climbing Yarigeoka Mountain
12	Shinichi Amami	Fall from 8th floor balcony of apartment
13	Yoshitaka Nonoyama	Fall from ride at Fujikyu Highland
14	Koichiro Ochiai	Brain hemorrhage while bathing

...THEY MUST HAVE TOLD THEM IT WAS NECESSARY TO MAKE THE SCAM WORK. WHO ACTUALLY *READS* THEIR INSURANCE POLICIES, ANYWAY?

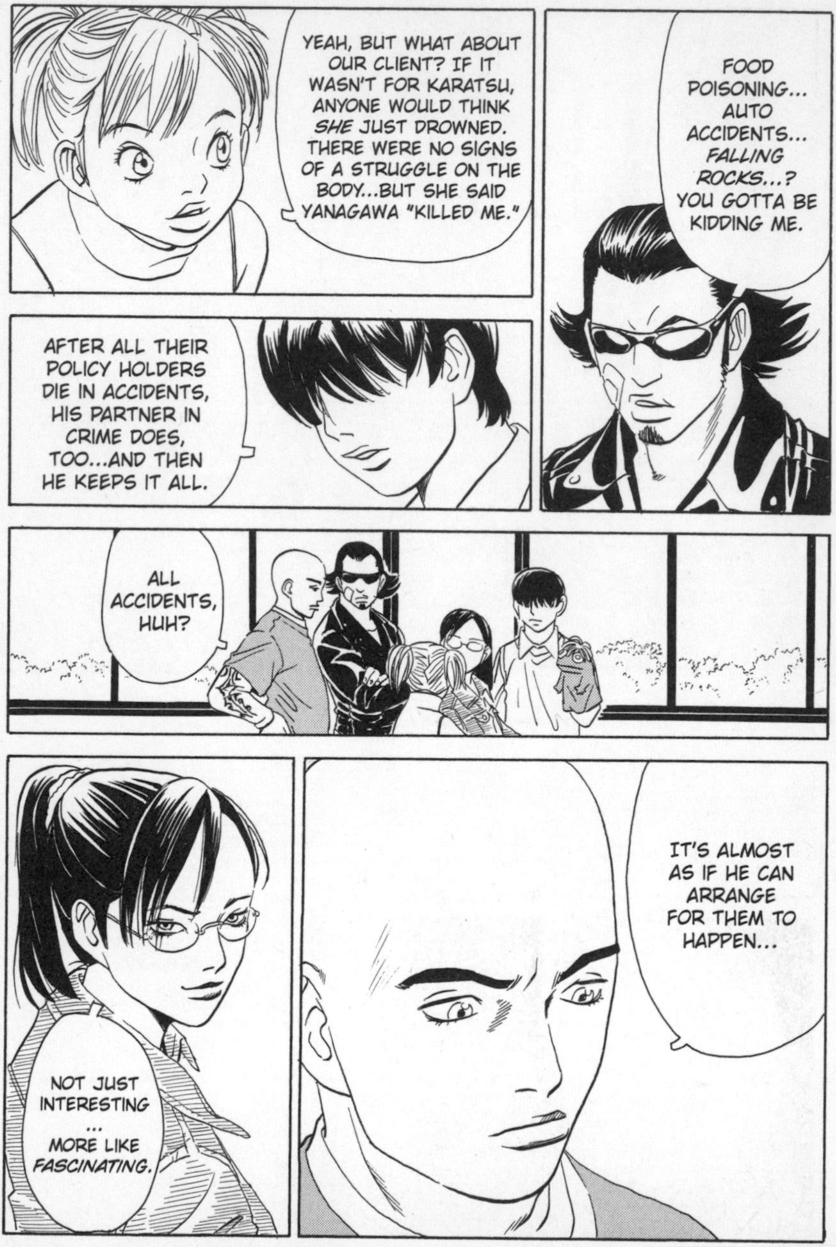
FOOD POISONING... AUTO ACCIDENTS... *FALLING ROCKS...?* YOU GOTTA BE KIDDING ME.
YEAH, BUT WHAT ABOUT OUR CLIENT? IF IT WASN'T FOR KARATSU, ANYONE WOULD THINK *SHE* JUST DROWNED. THERE WERE NO SIGNS OF A STRUGGLE ON THE BODY...BUT SHE SAID YANAGAWA "KILLED ME."
AFTER ALL THEIR POLICY HOLDERS DIE IN ACCIDENTS, HIS PARTNER IN CRIME DOES, TOO...AND THEN HE KEEPS IT ALL.
ALL ACCIDENTS, HUH?
IT'S ALMOST AS IF HE CAN ARRANGE FOR THEM TO HAPPEN...
NOT JUST INTERESTING ... MORE LIKE *FASCINATING.*

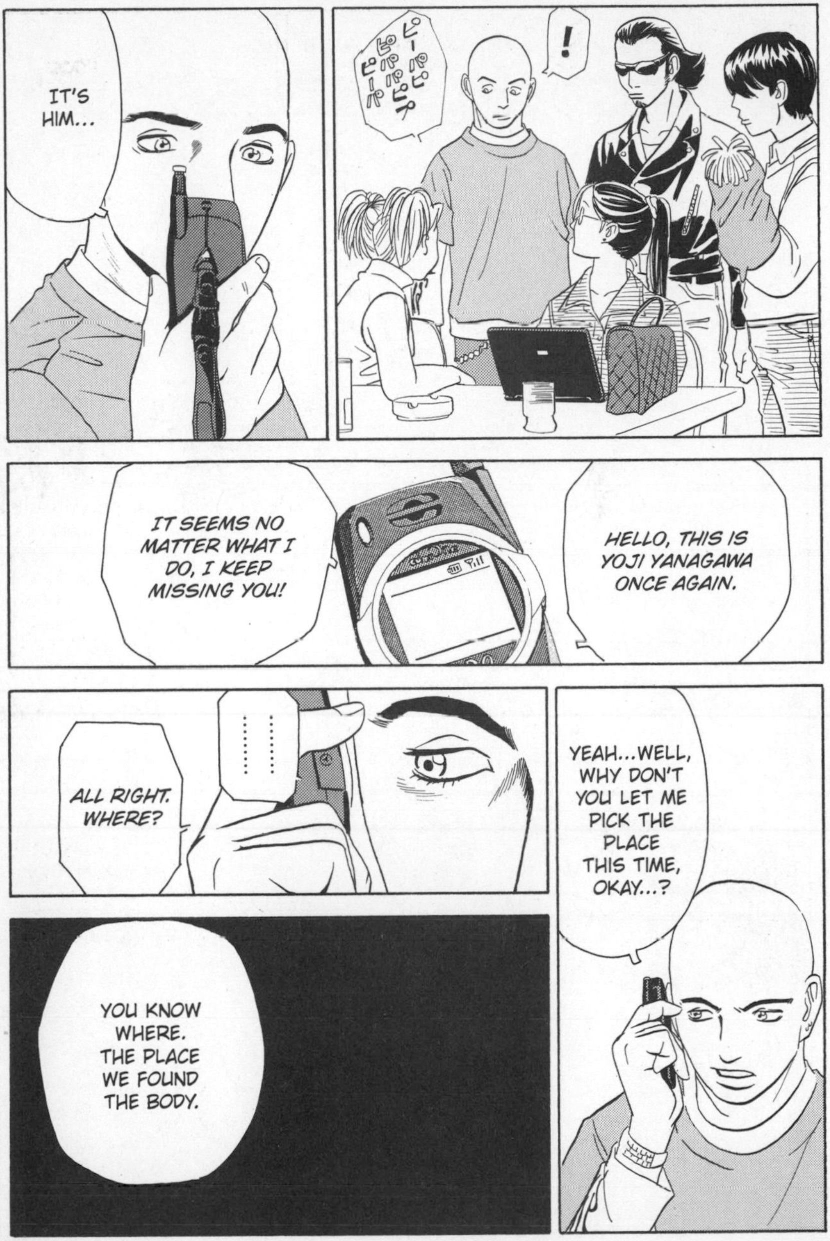
ピーパピ
ピパパピプ
ピーパ
!
IT'S HIM...
HELLO, THIS IS YOJI YANAGAWA ONCE AGAIN.
IT SEEMS NO MATTER WHAT I DO, I KEEP MISSING YOU!
YEAH...WELL, WHY DON'T YOU LET ME PICK THE PLACE THIS TIME, OKAY...?
......
ALL RIGHT. WHERE?
YOU KNOW WHERE. THE PLACE WE FOUND THE BODY.

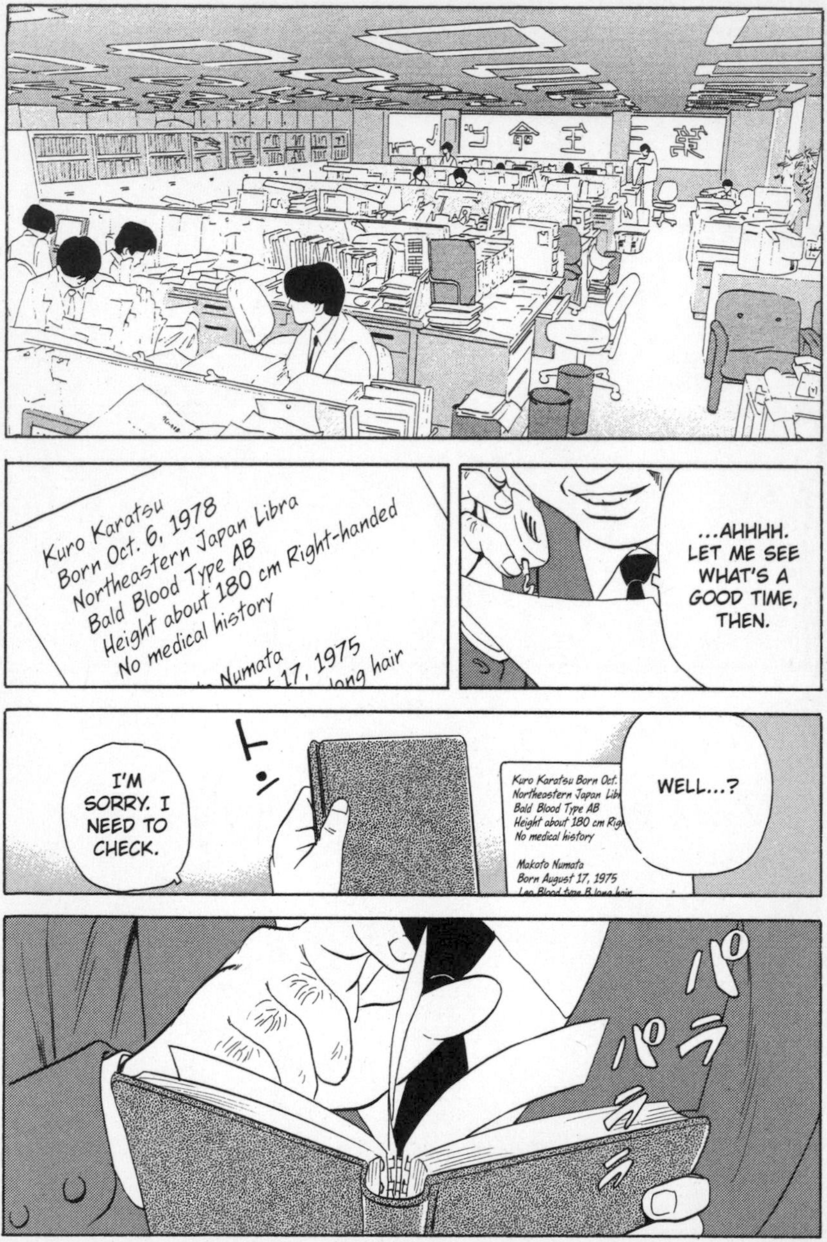
...AHHHH. LET ME SEE WHAT'S A GOOD TIME, THEN.
Kuro Karatsu
Born Oct. 6, 1978
Northeastern Japan Libra
Bald Blood Type AB
Height about 180 cm Right-handed
No medical history
WELL...?
Kuro Karatsu Born Oct.
Northeastern Japan Lib
Bald Blood Type AB
Height about 180 cm Rig
No medical history
Makoto Numata
Born August 17, 1975
トッ
I'M SORRY. I NEED TO CHECK.
パ
パラ
ラ

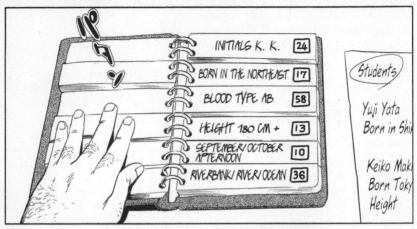

Students

Yuji Yata
Born in Shin

Keiko Maki
Born Toky
Height

HEY, I'M WAITING.

Searching...
This may take
a moment.

LET'S SEE...

24	17	58	13	10	36

(Between 4-6PM)

Chance of death is | 96% |

YOU DO MEAN AFTERNOON, RIGHT? ANOTHER EARLY MORNING'S GOING TO KILL ME.

YES, THANKS FOR YOUR PATIENCE. HOW ABOUT TOMORROW AT FIVE?

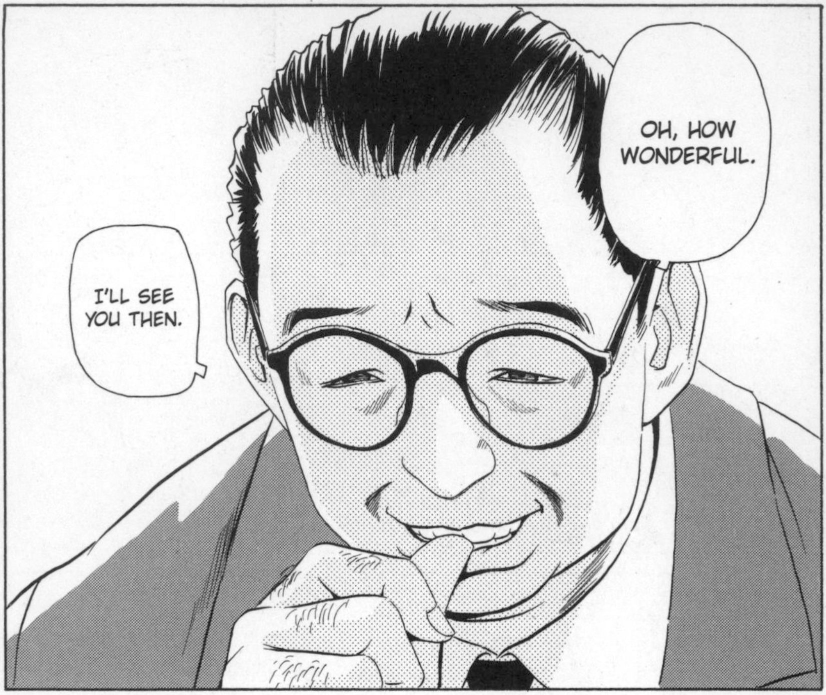
OH, HOW WONDERFUL.
I'LL SEE YOU THEN.

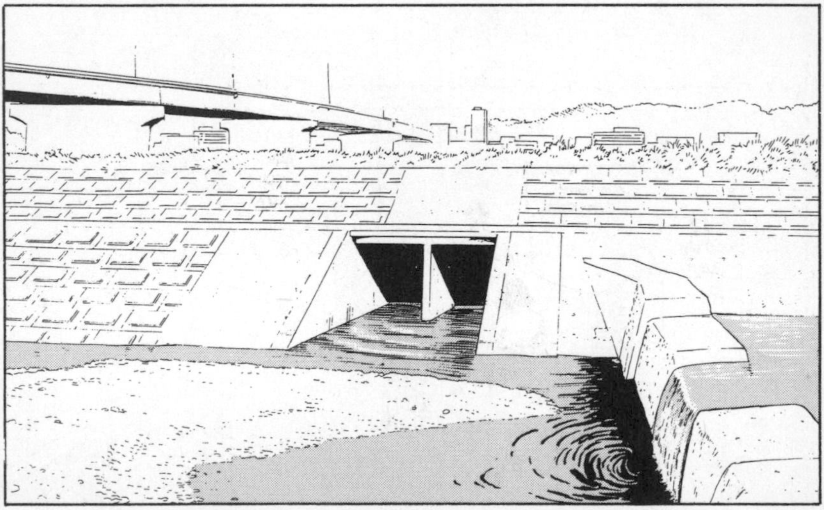

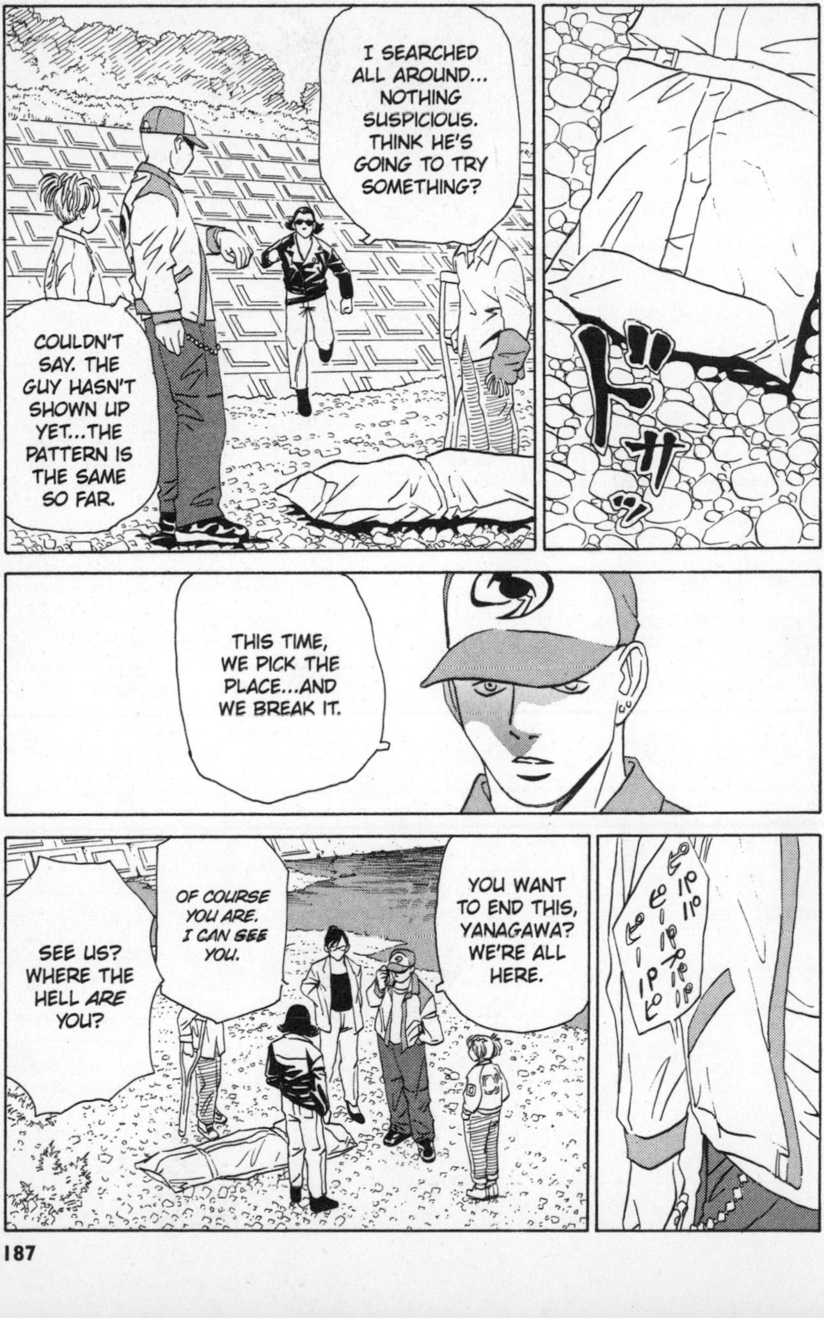
ドサッ
I SEARCHED ALL AROUND... NOTHING SUSPICIOUS. THINK HE'S GOING TO TRY SOMETHING?
COULDN'T SAY. THE GUY HASN'T SHOWN UP YET...THE PATTERN IS THE SAME SO FAR.
THIS TIME, WE PICK THE PLACE...AND WE BREAK IT.
ピピピ
YOU WANT TO END THIS, YANAGAWA? WE'RE ALL HERE.
OF COURSE YOU ARE. I CAN SEE YOU.
SEE US? WHERE THE HELL *ARE* YOU?

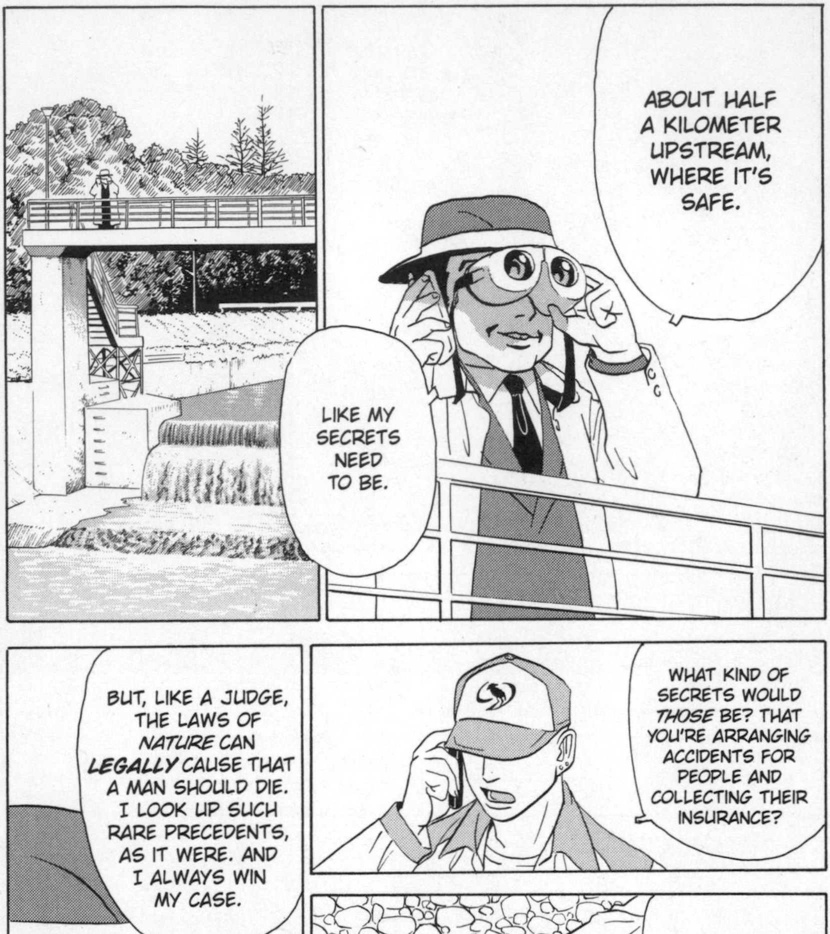
ABOUT HALF A KILOMETER UPSTREAM, WHERE IT'S SAFE.
LIKE MY SECRETS NEED TO BE.
WHAT KIND OF SECRETS WOULD *THOSE* BE? THAT YOU'RE ARRANGING ACCIDENTS FOR PEOPLE AND COLLECTING THEIR INSURANCE?
ARRANGING....? I DON'T KNOW WHAT THE WOMAN TOLD YOU, BUT YOU'RE QUITE MISTAKEN.
I DON'T ARRANGE ANYTHING. THAT WOULD BE A CRIME.
BUT, LIKE A JUDGE, THE LAWS OF *NATURE* CAN ***LEGALLY*** CAUSE THAT A MAN SHOULD DIE. I LOOK UP SUCH RARE PRECEDENTS, AS IT WERE. AND I ALWAYS WIN MY CASE.

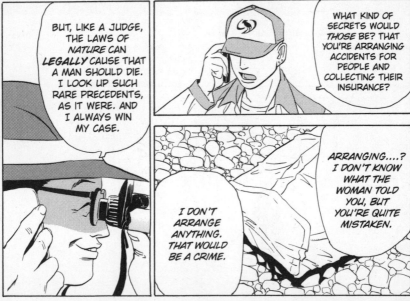

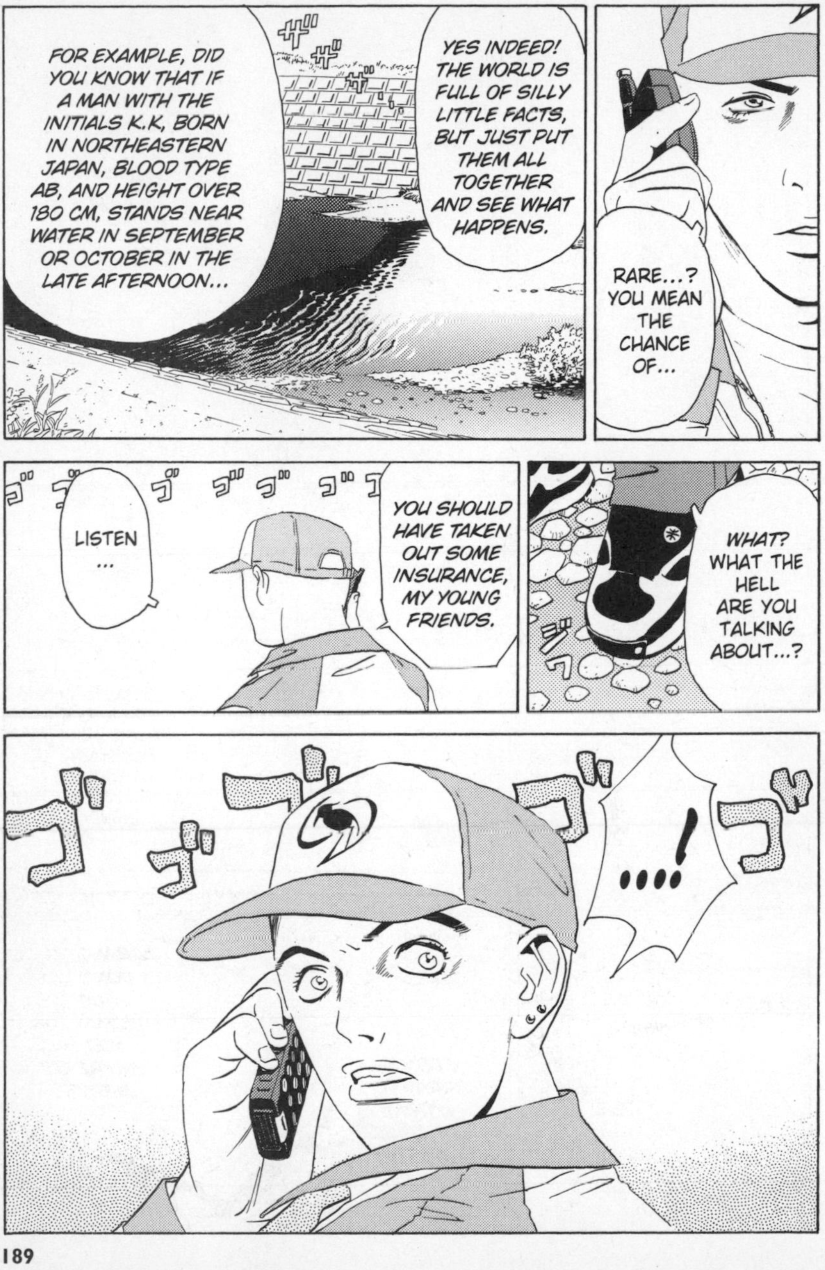
RARE...? YOU MEAN THE CHANCE OF...
YES INDEED! THE WORLD IS FULL OF SILLY LITTLE FACTS, BUT JUST PUT THEM ALL TOGETHER AND SEE WHAT HAPPENS.
ザ ザ ザ
FOR EXAMPLE, DID YOU KNOW THAT IF A MAN WITH THE INITIALS K.K, BORN IN NORTHEASTERN JAPAN, BLOOD TYPE AB, AND HEIGHT OVER 180 CM, STANDS NEAR WATER IN SEPTEMBER OR OCTOBER IN THE LATE AFTERNOON...
WHAT? WHAT THE HELL ARE YOU TALKING ABOUT...?
YOU SHOULD HAVE TAKEN OUT SOME INSURANCE, MY YOUNG FRIENDS.
LISTEN ...
ゴ ゴ ゴ ゴ ゴ ゴ
....!
ゴ ゴ ゴ ゴ ゴ ゴ

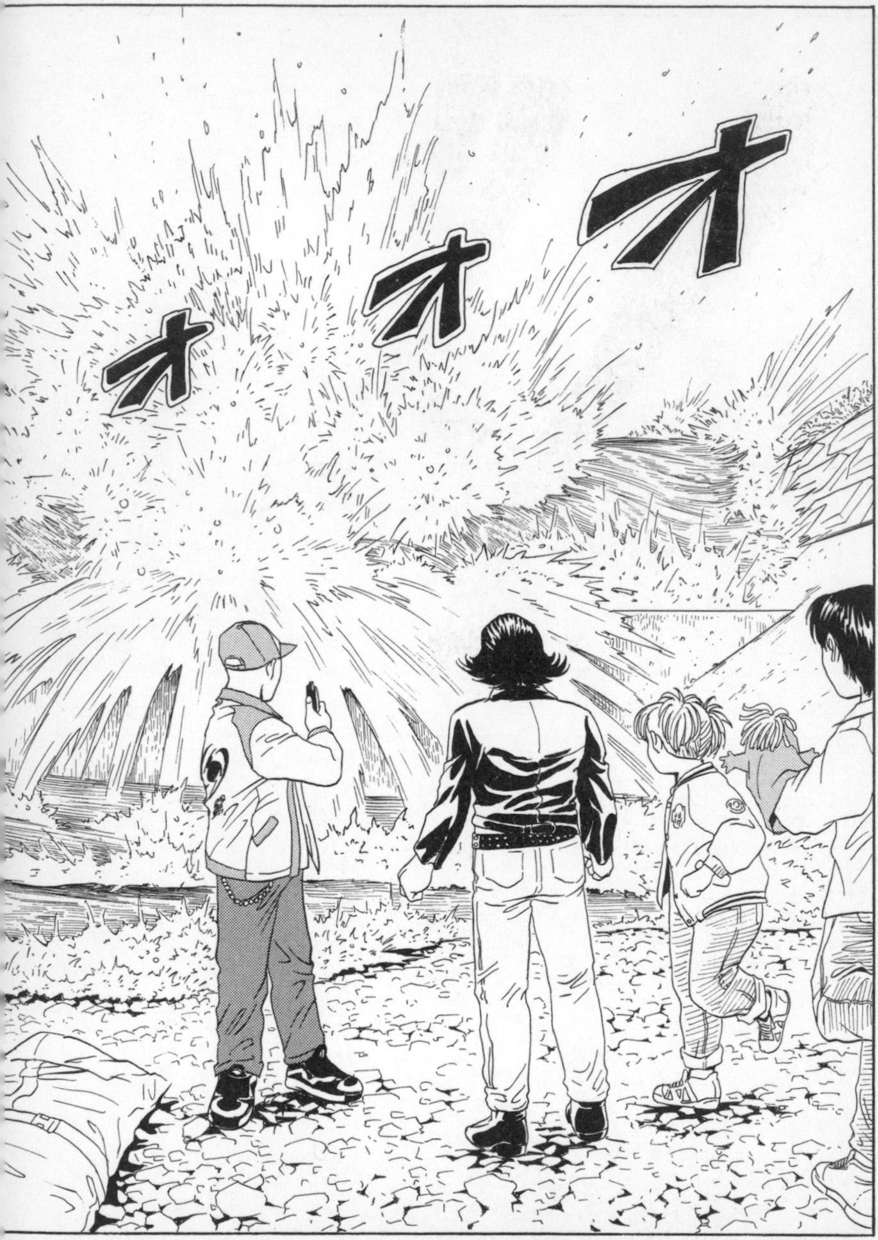
オオオ

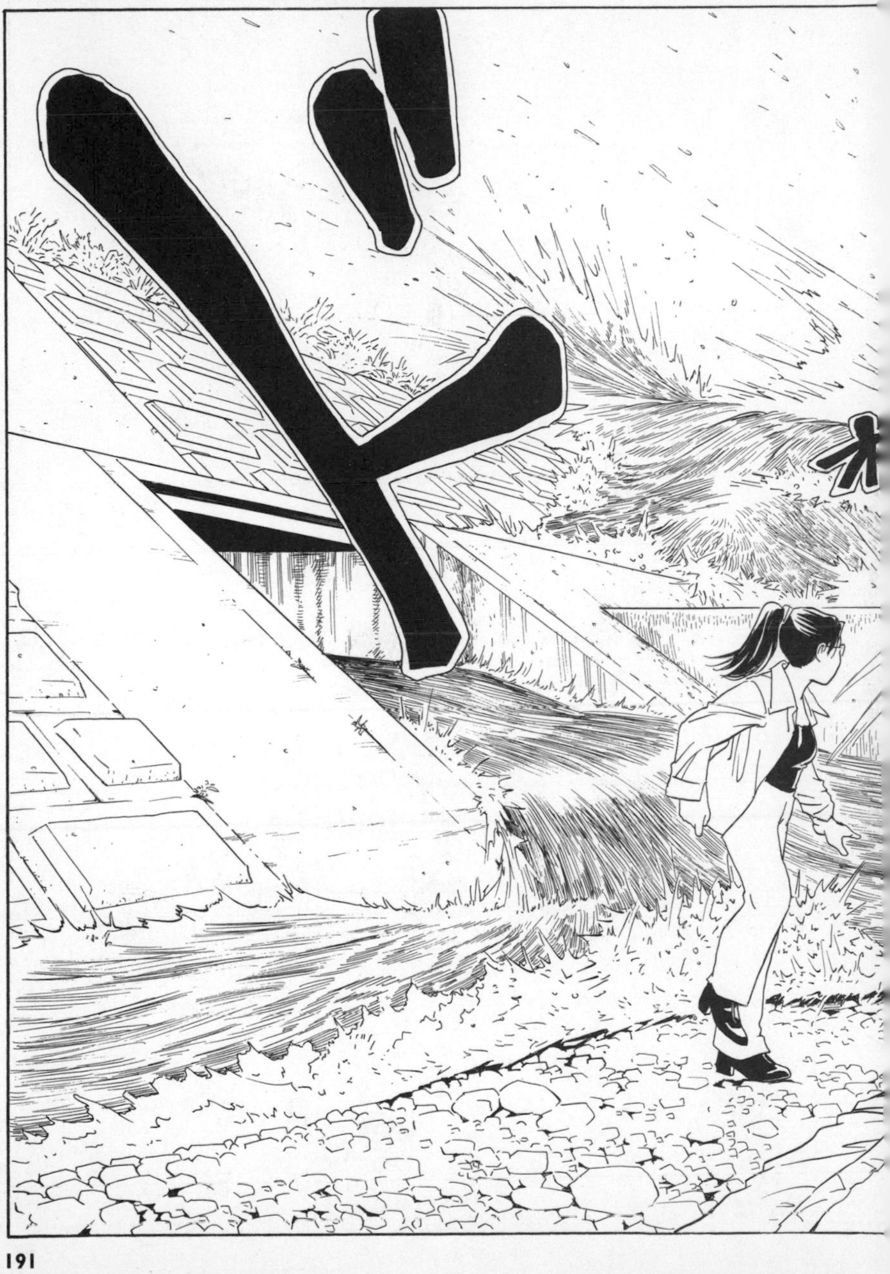
ド
オ

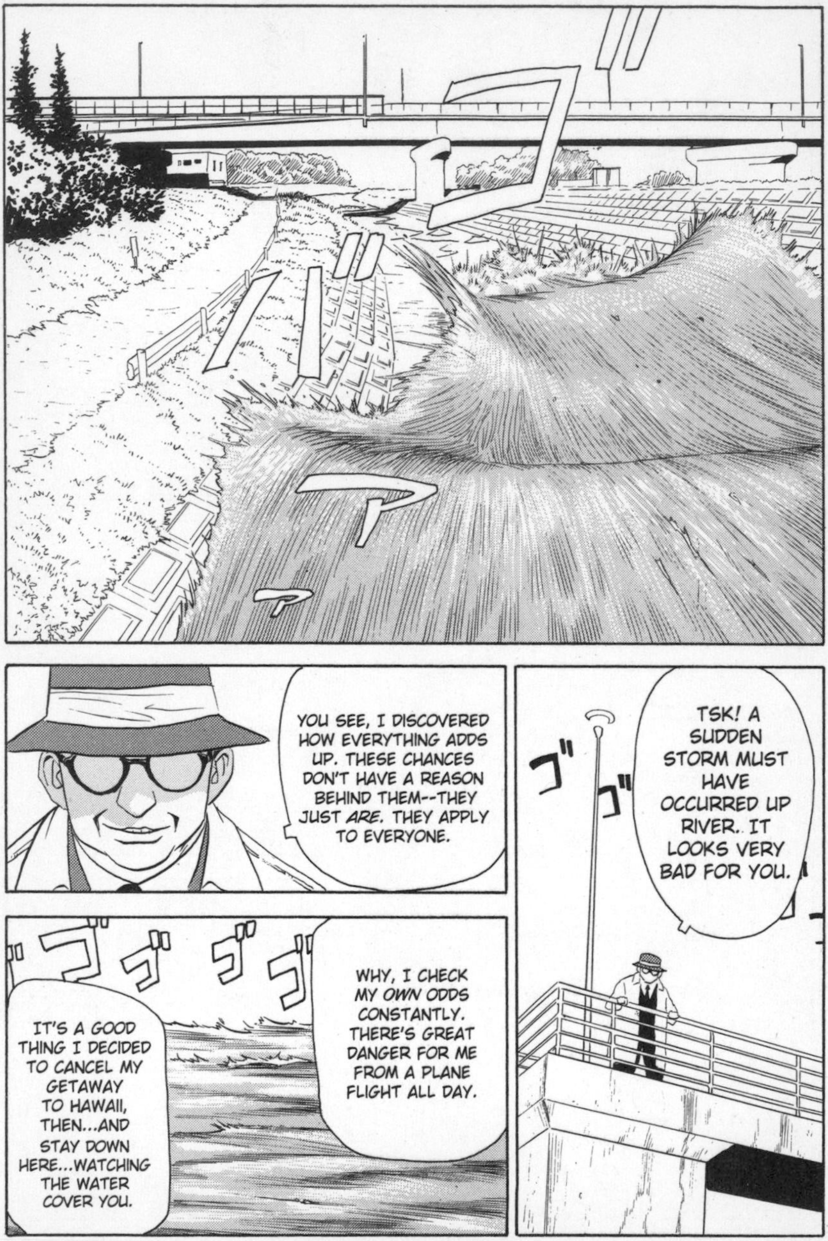
TSK! A SUDDEN STORM MUST HAVE OCCURRED UP RIVER.. IT LOOKS VERY BAD FOR YOU.
YOU SEE, I DISCOVERED HOW EVERYTHING ADDS UP. THESE CHANCES DON'T HAVE A REASON BEHIND THEM--THEY JUST *ARE*. THEY APPLY TO EVERYONE.
WHY, I CHECK MY *OWN* ODDS CONSTANTLY. THERE'S GREAT DANGER FOR ME FROM A PLANE FLIGHT ALL DAY.
IT'S A GOOD THING I DECIDED TO CANCEL MY GETAWAY TO HAWAII, THEN...AND STAY DOWN HERE...WATCHING THE WATER COVER YOU.

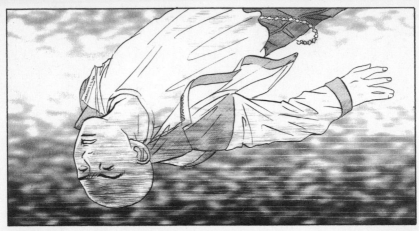

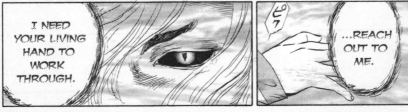

KURO...
ピク
...REACH OUT TO ME.
I NEED YOUR LIVING HAND TO WORK THROUGH.
REACH OUT, AND YOU SHALL NOT DIE TODAY.
ゴゴゴゴゴ

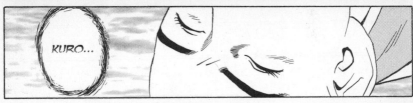

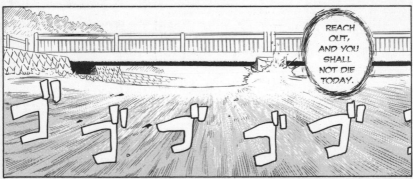

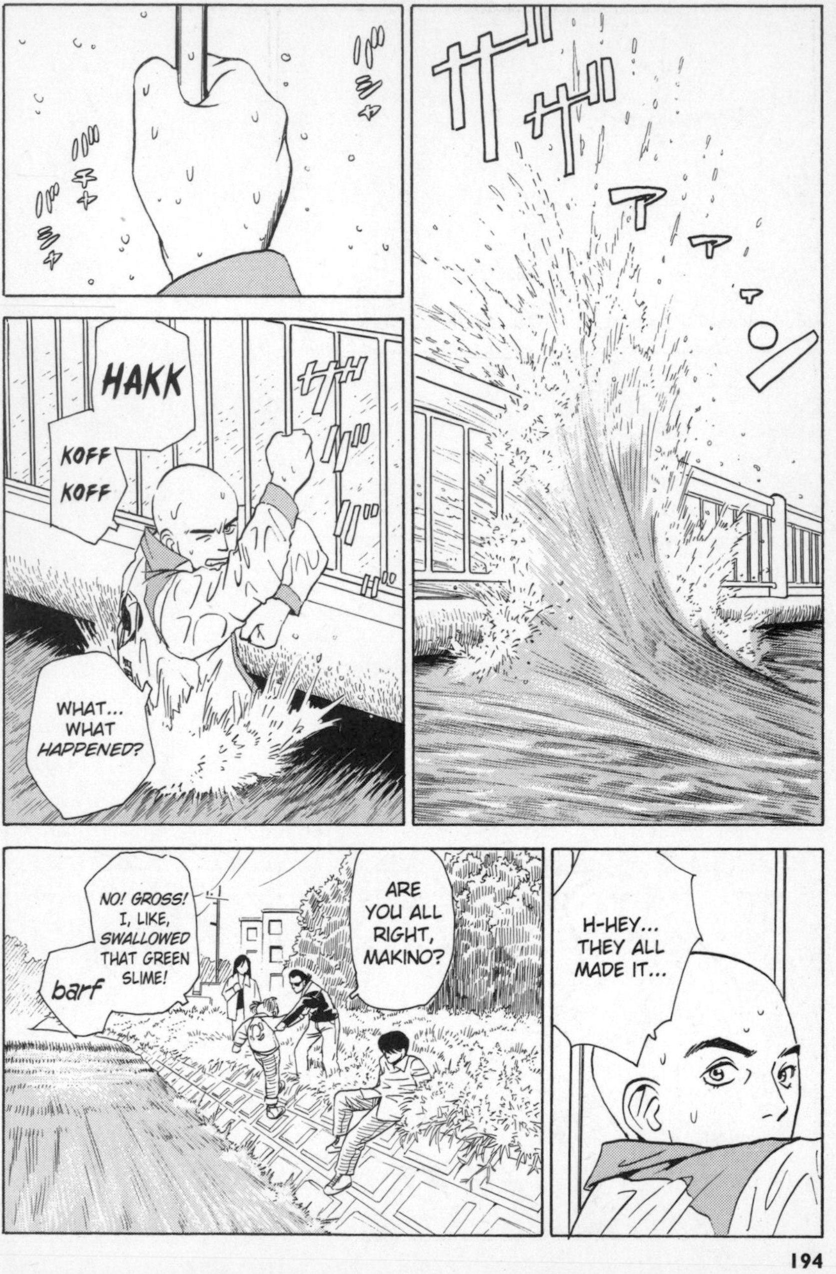
HAKK
KOFF KOFF
WHAT... WHAT HAPPENED?
H-HEY... THEY ALL MADE IT...
ARE YOU ALL RIGHT, MAKINO?
NO! GROSS! I, LIKE, SWALLOWED THAT GREEN SLIME!
barf

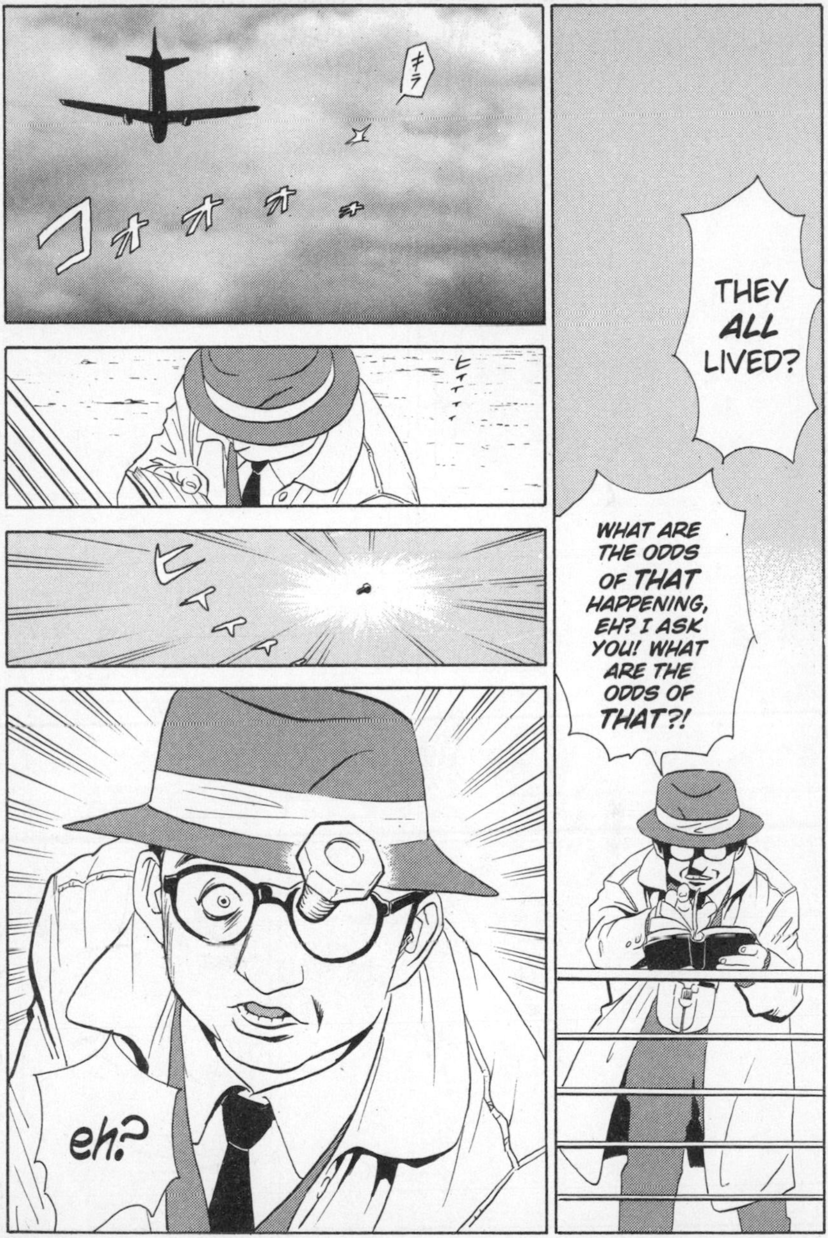

THEY ALL LIVED?
WHAT ARE THE ODDS OF THAT HAPPENING, EH? I ASK YOU! WHAT ARE THE ODDS OF THAT?!
キラ
コォオオォ
ヒィイイイ
eh?

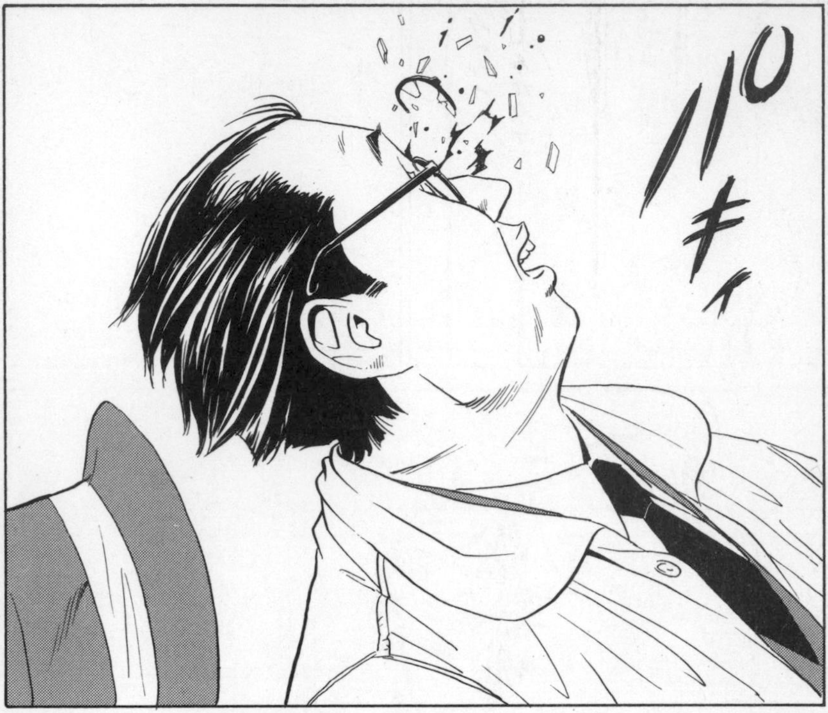
パキィ
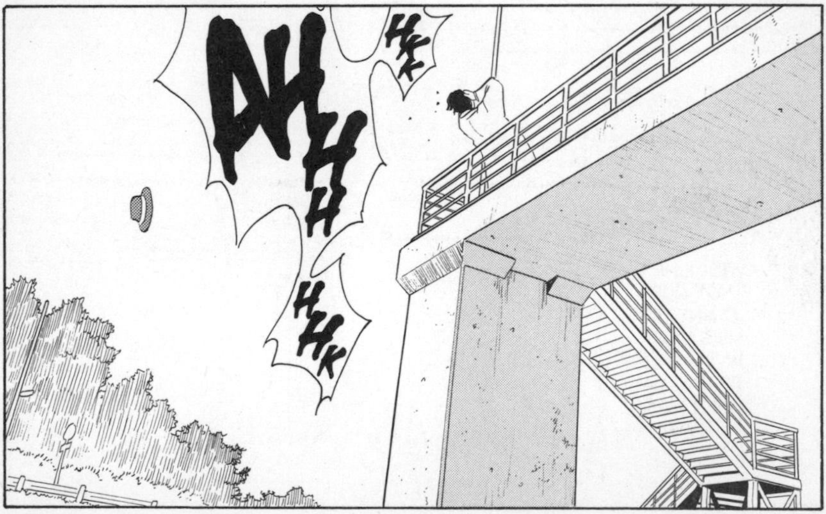
HKK
AHHH
HHHK

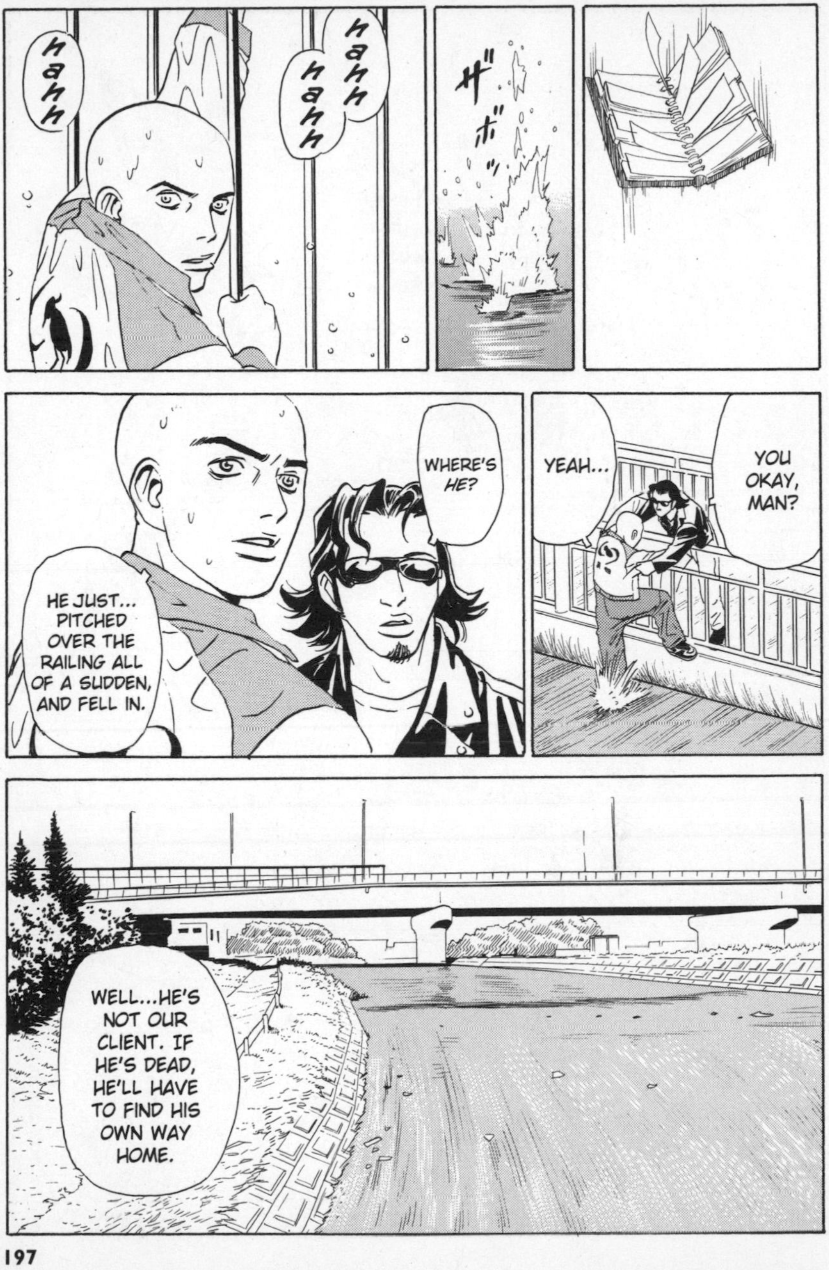
ザボッ
hahh
hahh
hahh
YOU OKAY, MAN?
YEAH...
WHERE'S HE?
HE JUST... PITCHED OVER THE RAILING ALL OF A SUDDEN, AND FELL IN.
WELL...HE'S NOT OUR CLIENT. IF HE'S DEAD, HE'LL HAVE TO FIND HIS OWN WAY HOME.

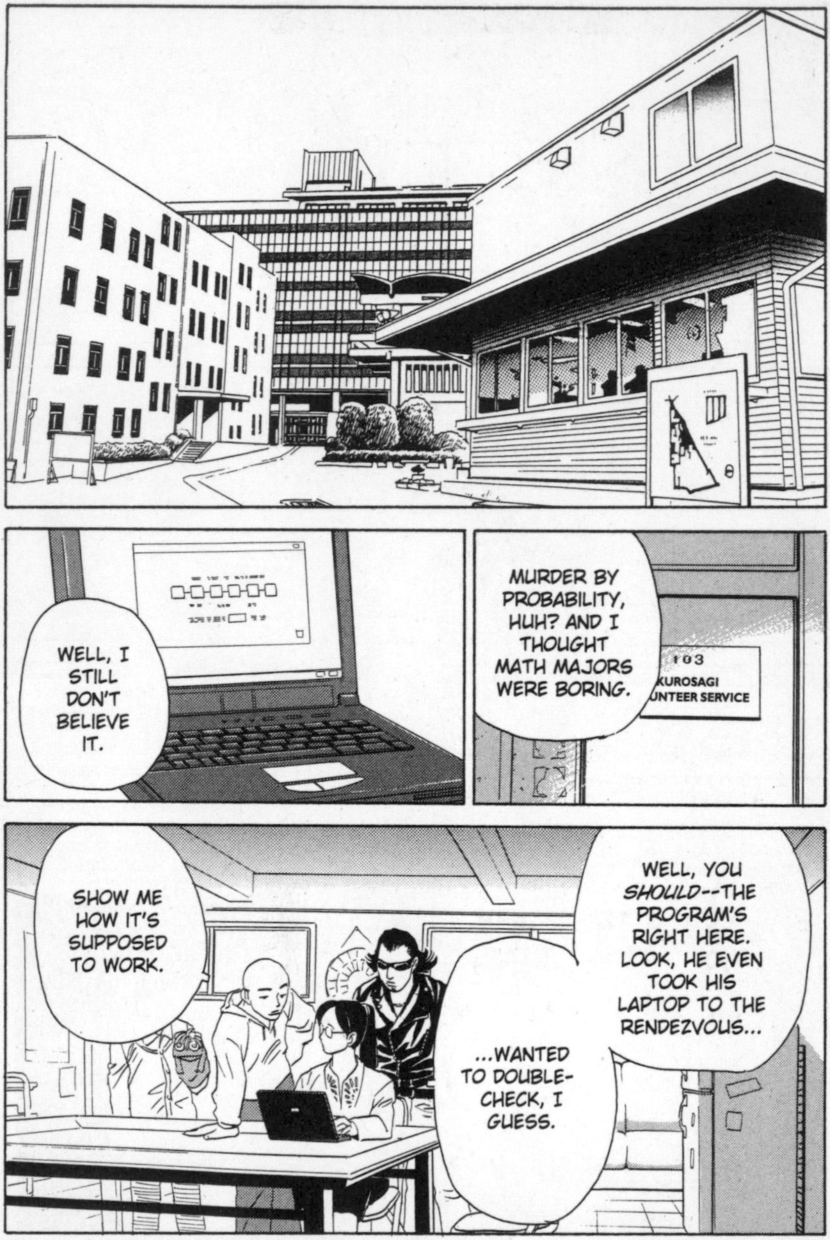
MURDER BY PROBABILITY, HUH? AND I THOUGHT MATH MAJORS WERE BORING.
103
KUROSAGI
UNTEER SERVICE
WELL, I STILL DON'T BELIEVE IT.
WELL, YOU *SHOULD*--THE PROGRAM'S RIGHT HERE. LOOK, HE EVEN TOOK HIS LAPTOP TO THE RENDEZVOUS...
...WANTED TO DOUBLE-CHECK, I GUESS.
SHOW ME HOW IT'S SUPPOSED TO WORK.

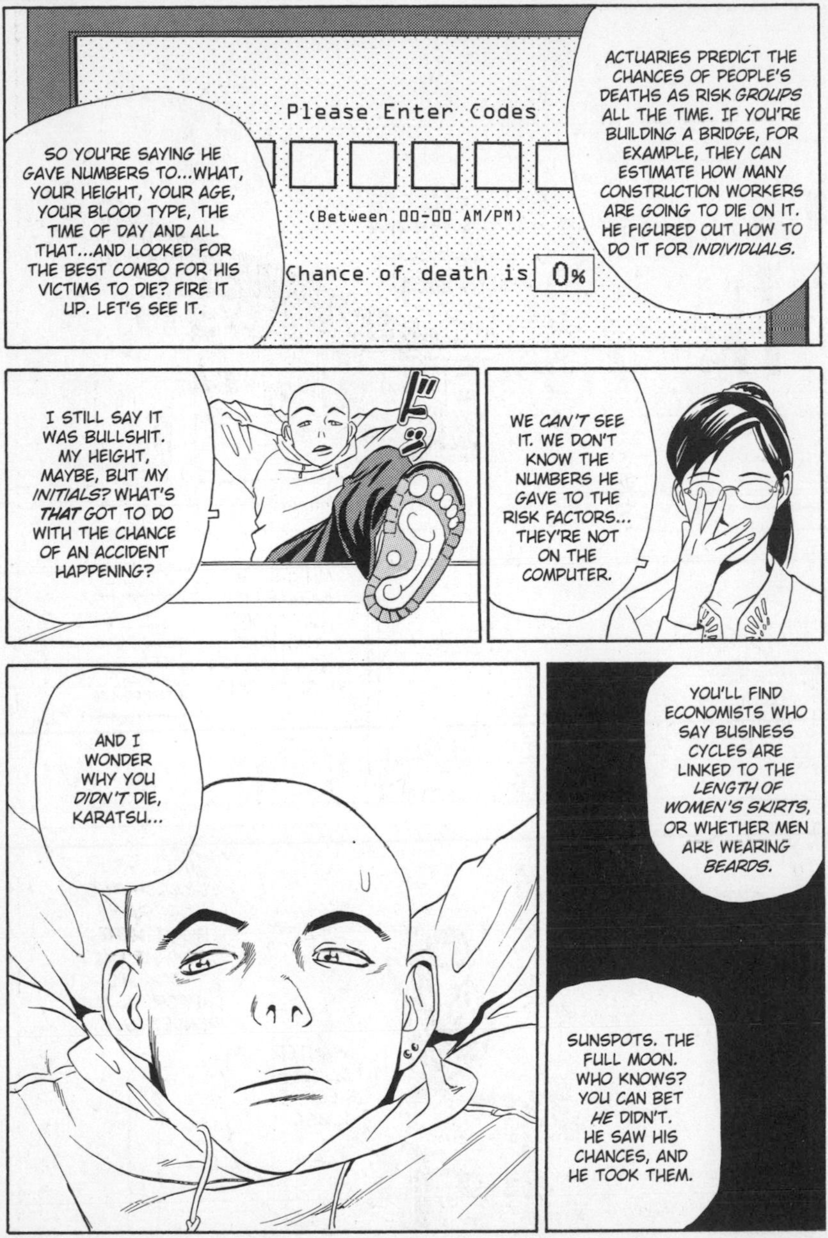
ACTUARIES PREDICT THE CHANCES OF PEOPLE'S DEATHS AS RISK *GROUPS* ALL THE TIME. IF YOU'RE BUILDING A BRIDGE, FOR EXAMPLE, THEY CAN ESTIMATE HOW MANY CONSTRUCTION WORKERS ARE GOING TO DIE ON IT. HE FIGURED OUT HOW TO DO IT FOR *INDIVIDUALS*.
Please Enter Codes
(Between 00-00 AM/PM)
Chance of death is 0%
SO YOU'RE SAYING HE GAVE NUMBERS TO...WHAT, YOUR HEIGHT, YOUR AGE, YOUR BLOOD TYPE, THE TIME OF DAY AND ALL THAT...AND LOOKED FOR THE BEST *COMBO* FOR HIS VICTIMS TO DIE? FIRE IT UP. LET'S SEE IT.
WE *CAN'T* SEE IT. WE DON'T KNOW THE NUMBERS HE GAVE TO THE RISK FACTORS... THEY'RE NOT ON THE COMPUTER.
I STILL SAY IT WAS BULLSHIT. MY HEIGHT, MAYBE, BUT MY *INITIALS?* WHAT'S *THAT* GOT TO DO WITH THE CHANCE OF AN ACCIDENT HAPPENING?
YOU'LL FIND ECONOMISTS WHO SAY BUSINESS CYCLES ARE LINKED TO THE *LENGTH OF WOMEN'S SKIRTS*, OR WHETHER MEN ARE WEARING *BEARDS*.
SUNSPOTS. THE FULL MOON. WHO KNOWS? YOU CAN BET *HE* DIDN'T. HE SAW HIS CHANCES, AND HE TOOK THEM.
AND I WONDER WHY YOU *DIDN'T* DIE, KARATSU...

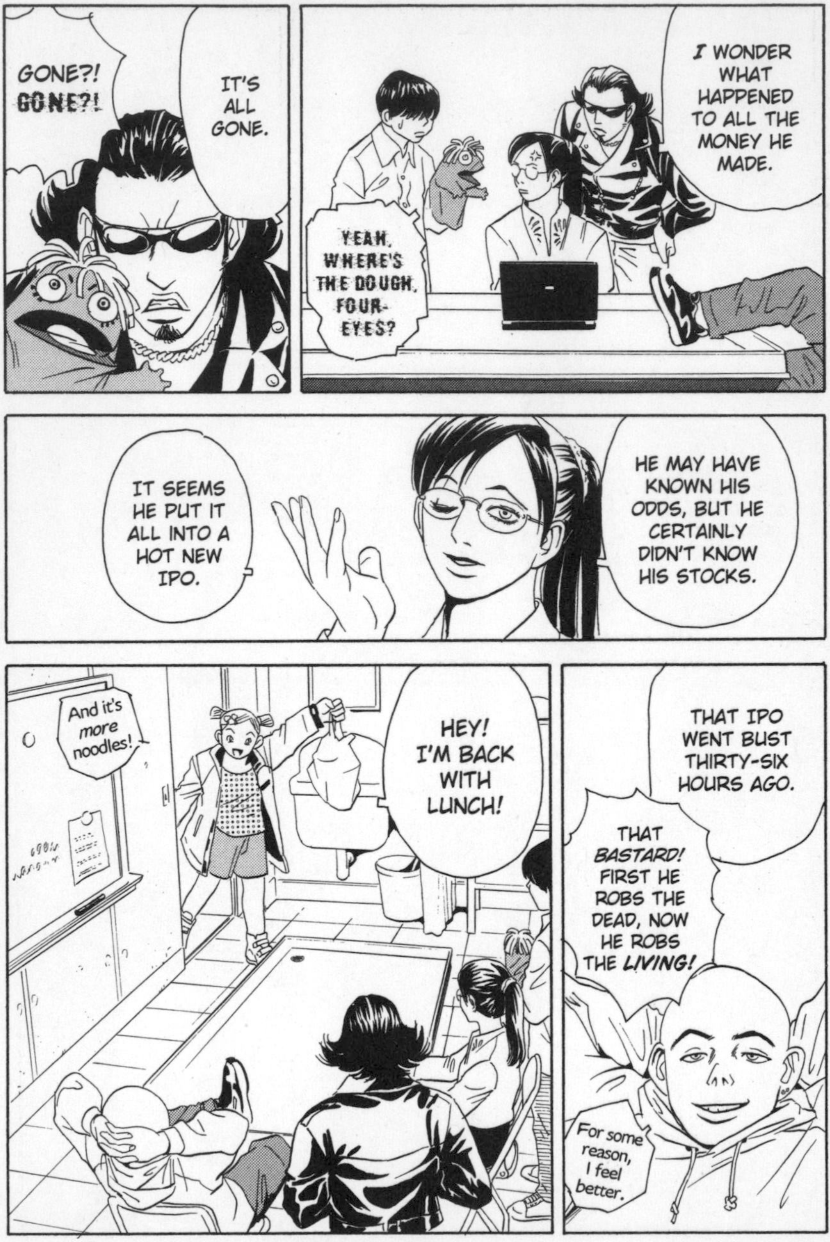
I WONDER WHAT HAPPENED TO ALL THE MONEY HE MADE.
YEAH, WHERE'S THE DOUGH, FOUR-EYES?
IT'S ALL GONE.
GONE?! GONE?!
HE MAY HAVE KNOWN HIS ODDS, BUT HE CERTAINLY DIDN'T KNOW HIS STOCKS.
IT SEEMS HE PUT IT ALL INTO A HOT NEW IPO.
THAT IPO WENT BUST THIRTY-SIX HOURS AGO.
THAT *BASTARD!* FIRST HE ROBS THE DEAD, NOW HE ROBS THE *LIVING!*
For some reason, I feel better.
HEY! I'M BACK WITH LUNCH!
And it's *more* noodles!

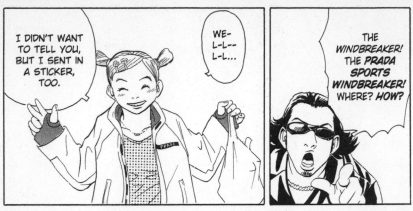

THE WINDBREAKER! THE PRADA SPORTS WINDBREAKER! WHERE? HOW?
WE-L-L--L-L...
I DIDN'T WANT TO TELL YOU, BUT I SENT IN A STICKER, TOO.
A STICKER? I SENT IN TWENTY STICKERS!
SHE SAID YOU HAD NO LUCK WITH CONTESTS.
AND THAT YOU WOULDN'T LOOK GOOD IN ONE.
I ATE TWENTY BOWLS OF THAT SHIT!
YEAH, WELL...SOME THINGS JUST AREN'T MEANT TO BE, NUMATA.

4th delivery: september rain—the end
continued in *the kurosagi corpse delivery service* vol. 2

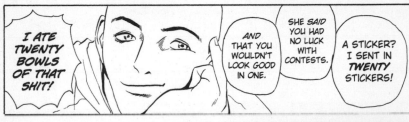

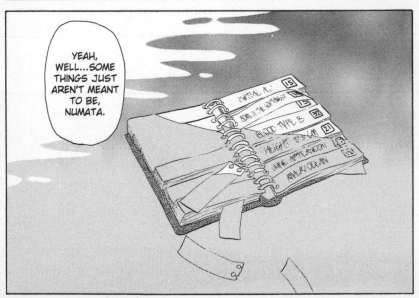

the KUROSAGI corpse delivery service

黒鷺死体宅配便

eiji otsuka 大塚英志 housui yamazaki 山崎峰水

designer **HEIDI FAINZA**
editorial assistant **RACHEL MILLER**
art director **LIA RIBACCHI**
publisher **MIKE RICHARDSON**

English-language version
produced by Dark Horse Comics

Published by
Dark Horse Manga
A division of Dark Horse Comics, Inc.
10956 SE Main Street
Milwaukie, OR 97222
www.darkhorse.com

To find a comics shop in your area,
call the Comic Shop Locator Service
toll-free at 1-888-266-4226

First edition: July 2006
ISBN-10: 1-59307-555-3
ISBN-13: 978-1-59307-555-2

3 5 7 9 10 8 6 4

PRINTED IN CANADA

DISJECTA MEMBRA

SOUND FX GLOSSARY AND NOTES ON KUROSAGI VOL. 1 BY TOSHIFUMI YOSHIDA
introduction and additional comments by the editor

TO INCREASE YOUR ENJOYMENT of the distinctive Japanese visual style of this manga, we've included a guide to the sound effects (or "FX") used in this manga adaptation of the anime film. It is suggested the reader not constantly consult this glossary as they read through, but regard it as supplemental information, in the manner of footnotes. If you want to imagine it being read aloud by Osaka, after the manner of her lecture to Sakaki on hemorrhoids in episode five, please go right ahead. In either Yuki Matsuoka or Kira Vincent-Davis's voice—I like them both.

Japanese, like English, did not independently invent its own writing system, but instead borrowed and modified the system used by the then-dominant cultural power in their part of the world. We still call the letters we use to write English today the "Roman" alphabet, for the simple reason that about 1600 years ago the earliest English speakers, living on the frontier of the Roman Empire, began to use the same letters the Romans used to write their Latin language, to write out English.

Around that very same time, on the other side of the planet, Japan, like England, was another example of an island civilization lying across the sea from a great empire, in this case, that of China. Likewise, the Japanese borrowed from the Chinese writing system, which then as now consists of thousands of complex symbols—today in China officially referred to in the Roman alphabet as *hanzi*, but which the Japanese pronounce as *kanji*. For example, all the Japanese characters you see on the front cover of *The Kurosagi Corpse Delivery Service*—the seven which make up the original title and the four each which make up the creators' names—are examples of kanji. Of course, all of them were hanzi first; although the Japanese did later invent some original kanji of their own, just as new hanzi have been created over the centuries as Chinese evolved.

(Note that whereas both *kanji* and *hanzi* are methods of writing foreign words in Roman letters, "kanji" gives English speakers a fairly good idea of how the Japanese word is really pronounced—*khan-gee*—whereas "hanzi" does not—in Mandarin Chinese it sounds something like *n-tsuh*). The reason is fairly simple: whereas the most commonly used method of writing Japanese in Roman letters, called the Hepburn system, was developed by a native English speaker, the most commonly used method of writing Chinese in Roman letters, called the Pinyin system, was developed by native Mandarin speakers. In fact Pinyin was developed to help teach Mandarin pronunciation to speakers of other Chinese dialects; unlike Hepburn, it was not intended as a learning tool for English speakers *per se*, and hence has no particular obligation to "make sense" to English speakers or, indeed, users of other languages spelled with the Roman alphabet).

Whereas the various dialects of Chinese are written entirely in hanzi, it is impractical to render the Japanese language entirely in them. To compare once more, English is a notoriously difficult language in which to spell properly, and this is in part because it uses an alphabet designed for another language, Latin, whose sounds are different. The challenges the Japanese faced in using the Chinese writing system for their own language were even greater, for whereas spoken English and Latin are at least from a common language family, spoken Japanese is unrelated to any of the various dialects of spoken Chinese. The complicated writing system Japanese evolved represents an adjustment to these differences.

When the Japanese borrowed hanzi to become kanji, what they were getting was a way to write out (remember, they already had ways to *say*) their vocabulary. Nouns, verbs, many adjectives, the names of places and people—that's what kanji are used for, the fundamental data of the written language. The practical use and processing of that "data"—its grammar and pronunciation—is another matter entirely. Because spoken Japanese neither sounds nor functions like Chinese, the first work-around tried was a system called *manyogana*, where individual kanji were picked to represent certain syllables in Japanese (a similar method is still used in Chinese today to spell out foreign names).

The commentary in *Katsuya Terada's The Monkey King* (also available from Dark Horse, and also translated by To-shifumi Yoshida) notes the importance that not only Chinese, but Indian culture had on Japan at this time in history—particularly, Buddhism. It is believed the Northeast Indian *Siddham* script studied by Kukai (died 835 AD), founder of the Shingon sect of Japanese Buddhism, inspired him to create the solution for writing Japanese still used today. Kukai is credited with the idea of taking the manyogana and making the shorthand versions of them now known simply as *kana*. The improvement in efficiency was dramatic—a kanji, used previously to represent a sound, that might have taken a dozen strokes to draw, was now reduced to three or four.

Unlike the original kanji it was based on, the new kana had *only* a sound meaning. And unlike the thousands of kanji, there are only 46 kana, which can be used to spell out any word in the Japanese language, including the many ordinarily written with kanji (Japanese keyboards work on this principle). The same set of 46 kana is written two different ways depending on their intended use; cursive style, *hiragana*, and block style, *katakana*. Naturally, sound FX in manga are almost always written out using kana.

Kana works somewhat differently than the Roman alphabet. For example, while there are separate kana for each of the five vowels (the Japanese order is not A-E-I-O-U as in English, but A-I-U-E-O), there are, except for "n," no separate kana for consonants (the middle "n" in the word ninja illustrates this exception). Instead, kana work by grouping together consonants with vowels: for example, there are five kana for sounds starting with "k," depending on which vowel follows it—in Japanese vowel order, they go KA, KI, KU, KE, KO. The next set of kana begins with "s" sounds, so SA, SHI, SU, SE, SO, and so on. You will observe this kind of consonant-vowel pattern in the FX listings for *Kurosagi* Vol. 1 below.

Katakana are almost always used for manga sound FX, but on occasion (often when the sound is one made by a person) hiragana are used instead. In *Kurosagi* Vol. 1 you can see one of several examples on page 21, panel 3, when Karatsu smacks the back of his head with a "PACHIN" sound, which in hiragana style is written ぱちん. Note its more cursive appearance compared to the other FX. If it had been written in katakana style, it would look like パチン.

To see how to use this glossary, take an example from page 3: "3.1 FX: BAKO BAKO BAKO—sound of a distant helicopter." 3.1 means the FX is the one on page 3, in panel 1 (in this case, of course, the only panel on the page). BAKO BAKO BAKO are the sounds these kana—バコバコバコ—literally stand for. After the dash comes an explanation of what the sound represents (in some cases, such as this one, it will be less obvious than others). Note that in cases where there are two or more different sounds in a single panel, an extra number is used to differentiate them from right to left (for example, 7.3.1 and 7.3.2); or, in cases where right and left are less clear (for example, 18.7.1 and 18.7.2) in clockwise order.

The use of kana in these FX also illustrates another aspect of written Japanese—its flexible reading order. For example, the way you're reading the pages and panels of this book in general: going from right-to-left, and from top to bottom—is the order in which Japanese is also written in most forms of print: books, magazines, and newspapers. However, if you look closely those kana examples given above, you'll notice something interesting. They read "Western" style—left-to-right! In fact, many of the FX in *Kurosagi* (and manga in general) read left-to-right. On page 141 you can even find them going in both directions—141.1 is going right-to-left, but 141.5 is going left-to-right. This kind of flexibility is also to be found on Japanese web pages, which themselves usually read left-to-right. In other words, Japanese doesn't simply read "the other way" from English; the Japanese themselves are used to reading it in several different directions.

As might be expected, some FX "sound" short, and others "sound" long. Manga represent this in different ways. One of many examples of "short sounds" in *Kurosagi* Vol. 1 is to be found in 7.3, with its BUCHI and DOSA. Note the small ツ mark at the end of each. This is ordinarily the katakana for the sound "tsu," but its half-size use at the end of FX like this means the sound is the kind which stops or cuts off suddenly; that's why these sounds are written as BUCHI and DOSA and not BUCHITSU and DOSATSU—you don't "pronounce" the TSU in such cases.

Note the small "tsu" has another occasional use *inside*, rather than at the end, of a particular FX, as seen in 7.6's NCCHI ZUN CHAKA NCCHI ZUZUCHAKA—here it's at work between the "N" ン and the "CHI" チ to indicate a doubling of the consonant sound that follows it.

There are three different ways you may see "long sounds"—where a vowel sound is extended—written out as FX. One is with an ellipsis, as in 19.3's VUUUUN. Another is with an extended line, as in 70.1's MIIIIIN MIN MIN. Still another is by simply repeating a vowel several times, as in 141.1's KIIII. As a visual element in manga, FX are an art rather than a science, and are used in a less rigorous fashion than kana are in standard written Japanese.

The explanation of what the sound represents may sometimes be surprising; but every culture "hears" sounds differently. Note that manga FX do not even necessarily represent literal sounds; for example 153.1 FX: SHIN—in manga this is the figurative "sound" of silence. 14.1 FX: BIKU, representing a shudder, is another one of this type. Such "mimetic" words, which represent an imagined sound, or even a state of mind, are called *gitaigo* in Japanese. Like the onomatopoeic *giseigo* (the words used to represent literal sounds—i.e., most FX in this glossary are classed as giseigo), they are also used in colloquial speech and writing. A Japanese, for example, might say that something bounced by saying PURIN, or talk about eating by saying MUGU MUGU. It's something like describing chatter in English by saying "yadda yadda yadda" instead.

One important last note: all these spelled-out kana vowels should be pronounced as they are in Japanese: "A" as *ah*, "I" as *eee*, "U" as *ooh*, "E" as *eh*, and "O" as *oh*.

2.1 Note that all four chapter titles in this volume are the names of songs by Hiromi Ota, a J-pop singer who had a popular debut in the 1970s.

3.1 **FX: BAKO BAKO BAKO**— sound of a distant helicopter

6.1 **FX: BUN BUN BUBUN**—sound of buzzing flies

7.1 **FX/balloon: PIKUN**—twitch

7.2 **FX: BIKU BIKUN BIKUN**— sound of body convulsing

7.3.1 **FX/white: BUCHI**—sound of rope snapping

7.3.2 **FX/balloon: DOSA**—sound of body thudding on ground

7.5 **FX: ZU ZURU**—sound of body dragging itself on the ground

7.6 **FX: NCCHI ZUN CHAKA NCCHI ZUZUCHAKA**—sound of music being overheard on someone's headphones

10.1 **FX: TSUU TSUKU TSUU CHA ZUNCHAKA ZUTCHA TSUU TSUKU ZUN**—sound of music being overheard on someone's headphones

10.2 Aokigahara Forest is a real place, and it really is famous for suicides. Japan, incidentally, has about twice the suicide rate of the U.S. Translator Toshifumi Yoshida notes that the location first gained notoriety when novelist Seicho Matsumoto wrote his book *Tower of the Sea*, where a character commits suicide in Aokigahara. When the novel was made into a TV movie in 1973, Aokigahara became synonymous with suicide.

10.3 FX: BAKO BAKO BAKO—
sound of a helicopter

10.4 These boxes also exist, and are located at various points along the forest paths. Yoshida notes their messages tend to be blunt; rather than reassuring people life isn't so hopeless, the flyers ask potential suicides to consider: "You may think you will leave a beautiful corpse, but your body will be ravaged by wildlife before rotting and eventually leaving only your bones." The translator points interested readers to http://www.tanteifile.com/baka/ 2002/ 09/22_01_shinrei2_04/ which documents a group of reporters going into Aokigahara. They claim that their compasses became useless, and to have eventually stumbled across someone's personal effects, including a copy of a notorious "Perfect Suicide" how-to manual with blood on the pages. Note the "Suicide Preven- tion Message Box" is just like the one seen here (except in this version, its sign has been translated into English).

11.3 FX: PURAN—sound of an arm falling out of the stretcher

13.6.1 FX: NU—hand reaching for shoulder

14.1 FX: BIKU—scared shudder

14.5 FX: PA PA—sound of a camera flash

17.1 FX: PAKU PAKU—sound of the puppet's mouth flapping. Note the game *Pac-Man* was named for this FX. I asked Japanese Licensing Manager (and translator of DH's *Reiko the Zombie Shop*) Michael

Gombos why, if that was the case, Pac-Man doesn't go "paku paku"— I always heard the sound he makes as "waku waku." Mr. Gombos replied that *is* "paku paku"—a case that only demonstrates the point made above about different cultures hearing things differently.

17.4 FX: PAN PAN—brushing dirt off pants

18.7.1 FX: BUUUN—buzzing fly

18.7.2 FX/balloon: PITA—sound of fly landing on eye

19.1 FX: BUUUN BUBUUUN— buzzing flies

19.2 FX: BUBUN—sound of flies

19.3 FX: BUUUUN—buzzing flies

19.5 FX: BA—sound of Karatsu turning around quickly

20.1.1 FX: BUBUN—sound of flies

20.1.2 FX: BUUUUN—buzzing flies

20.1.3 FX: BUUUUN—more buzzing flies

20.2 FX: BUUUUN—buzzing flies

21.3 FX: PACHIN—slapping own head

21.4 FX: KOKI—cracking neck

21.5 FX: GA—footstep

21.6 FX: ZA—kneeling into leaves

22.5 FX: PITA—sound of hand placed on body

22.6 Until fairly recent decades, an ancient tradition was to be found in Japan (and particularly in north- eastern Honshu, where Kuro Karatsu is from) where young blind girls would be chosen to undergo a harsh religious initiation involving starvation, exposure to cold, and the memorization of *sutras*, Buddhist prayers (see 11.4). At the end they were considered *Itako*, spiritualists who could now contact the dead. It is said that elderly itako still practice their calling, but in contemporary popular culture the concept has been expanded—for example, Anna in Hiroyuki Takei's manga *Shaman King* is an itako, even though she is sighted. Of course, Karatsu is neither blind nor female, but see the translator's comments for 44.1 below.

26.3 FX: SHUBO—lighter being lit

26.4 FX/balloon: FUUU—exhaling smoke

27.4 FX: GUSHI—putting out cigarette

27.6 FX: GOGOGOGO—sound of the furnace burning

28.2 FX: GORORORO—sound of the table being rolled out of the furnace

32.1 FX: BAN—placing hand on body

34.2 FX/balloon: HIRA—sound of lottery ticket sliding out of notebook

35.4 FX/balloon: KATA KATATA—typing sound

36.1-4 If you want to grow up to be an editor and get good car insurance rates (see 167.3 below) it is especially important to practice good spelling online, as that is where people do most of their writing these days. I personally think teachers should practice this with students if they've got computers in class. Never mind the porn filters, we need bad grammar filters to protect our children.

37.1.1 FX/black: GAYA GAYA—crowd noise

37.1.2 FX/white: WAI WAI—more crowd noise

38.1 FX: PII PAA PII POPOPOP PII PO—cell ringing

38.5 FX: PUWAAAAN—sound of train

39.1 FX: GATAN GOTON GATAN GOTOTON—sound of train on the tracks

40.4 FX: ZEI ZEI—panting

40.5 FX: DOSA—putting body down

41.1 FX: SHUGOGOGO—sound of a propane stove

41.2 "Numacchi," as you might guess, is a cute way of saying "Numata."

42.2 FX: MOZO—body bag moving

42.3 FX/balloon: JI—zipper starting to open

42.4 FX: JIIIII—zipper unzipping

43.1 FX/Balloons: ZU ZURI—dragging sound

44.1 The translator theorizes that the mysterious spirit that accompanies Karatsu may be a traditional itako who was an ancestor of his. Judging by the events of this volume, Karatsu himself is not necessarily aware of her (if it indeed is a "her") presence, and no one else can see her either. The identity of this spirit is one of the as-yet unresolved mysteries of the story.

44.4 FX: GABA—getting up suddenly

45.1 FX/balloon: KII—sound of cab braking.

45.2 FX: GACHA—car door opening

45.3 FX/balloon: BURORORO—cab driving away

46.4 FX: GURI—putting his dowsing ring on

46.6 FX: CHARIIIN—the dowsing pendulum making a ringing sound

47.2 FX/balloon: KASA—rustling leaves

47.3 FX/balloons: KARI GARIRI—sound of nails scratching then digging into outside wall

48.1 FX: BAN—hand slamming into window

48.2 FX: BAN BAN BAN BAN—palm hammering on window

49.1 FX: BAN BAN BAN BAN BAN—more hammering

49.2 FX: BASHAAAN—sound of breaking glass

49.3 FX: BA—hand grabbing ledge

49.4 FX: ZURI—body lifting up

49.5 FX: ZUZUZU—body slowly climbing in

50.1 FX: DOSA—sound of body landing in room

50.2 FX: ZUZU—body dragging itself on floor

50.3 FX: DO—back bumping into wall

51.1 FX: DAAAAAN—sound of a shotgun firing

51.3 Aosagi's remark is so bizarre by American standards it might almost seem a mistake—but that's what she said. Very few Japanese own actual firearms (if they do, it would be a shotgun or rifle for hunting, as portrayed here—private ownership of handguns is, practically speaking, forbidden) and even if they did, they would be unlikely to think of

them as home-defense weapons. Very roughly, Japan has one one-hundredth the gun death rate of the U.S.; should certain crimes portrayed in this manga seem shocking, it is worth bearing in mind that Japan in real life is a considerably less violent and more law-abiding society than our own.

51.5 FX: KIII—door creaking

54.1 FX: PA PA—lights coming on

56.1 FX: SU—Karatsu stepping forward

58.1.1 FX/white: BIKUN BIKUN—body starting to twitch

58.1.2 FX/black: GUGU—body starting to rise

58.2 FX: ZU ZU—body starting to stand

59.2 FX: BAKOON—blam

59.3 FX: GIRO—glare

59.4.1 FX/white: BETA BETA—sound of bare feet walking

59.4.2 FX/black: GASHA—reloading sound

60-61.1 FX: BA—sound of Yuki's corpse grabbing her father

62.2 FX: HA—coming out of trance

62.4.1 FX/small: PORO—parts falling off of face

62.4.2 FX: GEBOBOBO—vomiting blood

62.5 FX: BACHA BETA—body falling onto Yamakawa's face

62.6.1 FX/white: BECHA—loud bloody splash

62.6.2 FX/black: DO—an organ hitting floor

63.1 FX: DOCHA—body falling in a wet thud

63.2 FX/balloons: GEHO GEHO—coughing

64.4 FX/balloon: GOHO GEHO—coughing up smoke

65.1 FX: PAKU PAKU—puppet's mouth moving

65.2 FX: PURU PURU—small trembling

65.6 FX: ZU—picking up ticket

66.3 FX: GATA GOTO GATAN—sound of a older car's suspension

66.4.1 FX/white: PASUN PUSUN PAN—sound of an old car's engine

66.4.2 FX/black: GATA GOTO KISHI—more old suspension noise

67.1 FX: GATA GATAN GOTO GAKON—old car sounds

67.2 FX: GOTO GOTON GATAN—more old car sounds

66.3 FX: GOTO GATA—still some more

68.1 FX: GAKO GAKO—old car noises

68.2 FX/balloon: KIKII—sound of brakes

68.3 FX: PINPOOON—doorbell sound

69. 1 *Tono Monogatari*, or "Tales of Tono" (the first "o" in "Tono" is pronounced long, and you will thus sometimes see it spelled in English as *Touno* or *Tohno*) is a classic collection of Japanese folklore, first published in 1910 or 1912 (reports vary). Kunio Yanagita, touring Japan as a government agricultural and trade inspector, became interested in the traditional stories he would hear while visiting various localities.

Aozasa Village is associated with the modern city of Tono in Iwate Prefecture, and, like the Aokigahara Forest featured in "Less Than Happy," is a real place. You can see images of the Dendera Field where this chapter opens at: http://www.sukima.com/12_touhoku00_04/02dendera.htm Note that the original version of the quote on this page goes into much greater detail; for example, Yanagita remarked that Aozasa Village's Dendera Field was also used by the neighboring locales Kamisato, Ashiraga, and Ishida.

69.2 FX: PATAMU—sound of a book closing.

69.3 The mountain story to which he refers is that of *Uba Sute Yama*, literally "Elder Cast Off Mountain." There is a similar story in Japanese folklore called *The Ballad of Narayama*, which would seem to refer to a different mountain.

70.1 FX: MIIIIIN MIN MIN MIIIIIN MIN MIN—sound of cicadas.

70.4 FX: DOSUN—thud

74.2 FX: KUN KUKUN—sound of the pendulum tugging

74.3 He literally did say "Bingo!" in the original Japanese. Do they play it there, or just use the expression? When was the last time you saw someone play bingo in a manga?

75.3 Such an altar would ordinarily contain ritual objects used in daily Buddhist worship, including a symbolic offering of food—hence Makino's theory about the rat. An excellent image of how a home altar such as this might be arranged ordinarily in the *Jodo Shinshu* sect (there are many) of Buddhism can be seen at: http://shinmission_sg.tripod.com/id36.html

76.1 **FX: GAKON**—altar door forced open

77.6 **FX: PITA**—sound of fingertips touching corpse

79.4 **FX: GACHA**—sound of door opening

81.4 Originally Karatsu compared it to a Japanese TV show called *Otakara Kanteidan*, "Treasure Appraisers," but its premise is very similar to PBS's *Antiques Roadshow*, so the editor just plugged that in.

83.6 **FX: GUI**—putting on ring

83.7 **FX: CHARIIIN**—the pendulum chain ringing as he drops the weighted end

85.1 **FX: HYUUUU**—sound of wind

85.5 **FX: PECHI PECHI**—tapping the sign

86.5 **FX/balloon: GIKU**—gulp sound effect

86.6 **FX/balloon: KUI KUI**—sounds of fingers pointing down

87.1 **FX: GATA GATA GATA**—sound of the car rattling

87.2 **FX: GOGOGOGOGOGO**—sound of the car on the highway

88.4 **FX: GARARAN**—sound of trash being moved around

89.3 **FX: KUN**—arm suddenly swinging over to point

89.4 **FX/small: GASA DOSA**—sound of rustling bushes followed by a thud

90.1 **FX: DODO**—running sound

90.2 **FX: BURORORO**—truck starting to drive off

90.3 **FX/balloon: ZA**—stepping onto the road

91.1 **FX: BAN**—sound of fist hitting windshield

91.2 **FX: PARA PARA**—sound of glass shards falling

92.1 **FX: GWOOO**—speeding down highway

93.1 **FX: KOAAAA**—sound of a crow

93.2 **FX/balloon: KOAAA**—more cawing

94.2-3 8000 yen a month *is* dirt cheap, even for such basic accommodations, but oddly enough a sixty-year-old apartment building might be more easily thought "ancient" in Tokyo than in many younger American cities. By contrast, in the editor's neighborhood in Portland (the oh-so-trendy NW 23rd) there are a dozen or more apartment buildings dating from the 1920s and 1930s—including the Irving, where Gus Van Sant shot *Drugstore Cowboy*, as the plaque outside will be glad to tell you. Makino's mention that the place is sixty years old implies the apartment was built during the Second World War (this story first appeared in the Japanese magazine *Psycho Ace*—a spinoff of *Shonen Ace* named, naturally, for its hit manga *MPD Psycho*—in late 2000) and was therefore one of the relatively few to survive that era. However, in Tokyo, even a thirty-year-old building might be thought ripe for redevelopment. Japan's construction sector is much larger than America's relative to the country's size, with political clout that often leads both to things getting built for which there is no need (shorelines filled with those caltrop-like breakwaters you see in anime, highways to nowhere) and to things getting torn down without good reason (i.e., "old" buildings). It's only the editor's opinion, but this may be one of the reasons why Tokyo, surely one of the greatest cities of the world, is generally lacking in great or even attractive architecture. Why bother, when it's just going to get bulldozed in another generation? Mamoru Oshii touched on this theme in his films *Patlabor 1* and *Jin-Roh*.

95.3 The sign says "Quiet in the hallway!"

96.4 **FX: PITA**—fingertips touching body

98.3 **FX: KIII**—creaking door

98.6 **FX: GACHARI**—sound of altar door being locked

100.1 **FX: NUKU**—standing up

101.1 **FX: MYAA MYAA**—sound of gulls

101.2 Note the bag marked "Kadokawa"— the original publishers of *The Kurosagi Corpse Delivery Service*.

103.3 **FX/balloon: ZA**—sound of sandals in gravel

104.2 **FX: ATA FUTA**—panicked sound

105.4 **FX: KUN KUN**—sound of pendulum tugging

105.7 **FX: ZA**—footstep

113.4 **FX: SHAKIN**—sound of scissors closing

116.1 **FX/balloons: GAKI GAKI BAKI**—pry bar hitting car trunk

117.2 **FX: BAKAN**—trunk breaking open

120.2 **FX: MUGYU**—sound of the others squeezing in close

120.4 Saburo is a character from Machiko Hasegawa's manga of everyday life, *Sazae-San*, which ran from 1946 to 1974, and has been a regular anime show since 1969. It's one of the few manga of which it can probably be said that *every* Japanese person has heard of it— everyone, that is, except Makino.

121.1 **FX: GIKU**—gulp

121.2 **FX: BATAN**—quickly closed trunk

124.2 **FX: SUU**—sound of gauze pressed on body

124.4 **FX: GACHA**—door opening

125.5 **FX/balloon: KACHA**—camera shutter

127.1 **FX/small: KOKI**—neck crack

129.1 **FX: GACHA**—opening door

129.3 **FX: BATAM**—closing door

130.4 **FX: GATA**—starting to get up out of chair

132.3 **FX: PAN PAN**—hitting sheet of paper

132.4 **FX: PORI PORI**—scratching head

135.5 **FX/balloon: PAPAAN**—honking horn

138.3 **FX: BAKAN**—striking locker door

139.1 **FX/balloon: KACHA**—door opening

139.2 **FX: GO**—foot bumping severed head

140.1 **FX: GAPA**—sound of a freezer being opened

140.3 **FX/balloons: GAKI GAN GAKIN**—sound of something hitting doorknob

140.4 **FX/balloon: KACHARI**—sound of door unlatching

141.1 **FX: KIIII**—door creaking open

141.5 **FX: JIIII**—sound of opening zipper

146.1.1 **FX/white: BIKU BIKU**—body starting to convulse

146.1.2 **FX/black: GABA**—eyes popping open

146.3 **FX: GATA GATA KATA GATA**—headless body starting to shake

147.1 **FX: GASHI**—headless body grabbing Tsutsui

147.2 **FX: GYUUU**—arms squeezing Tsutsui

147.3 **FX: BATAN**—headless body falling and hitting ground

147.4 **FX: HETA**—Tsutsui slumping down to the ground

147.5 **FX/balloons: PAKU PAKU**—sound of flapping mouths

148.1.1 **FX/balloon: PAKU PAKURI**—sound of flapping mouths

148.1.2 **FX/balloon: PAKU PAKU**—sound of flapping mouths

148.2.1 **FX/balloon: PAKU**—sound of flapping mouths

148.2.2 **FX/balloon: PAKU PAKU**—sound of flapping mouths

148.3.1 **FX/white: KPFU**—sound of a refrigerator door popping open

148.3.2 **FX/Black: WASA WASA WASA**—arms inside plastic backs reaching out

149.1.1 **FX/black: YORO**—stagger

149.1.2 **FX/white: PATA**—sound of a footstep on bare tile

150-151.1 **FX: BA**—corpse suddenly lashing out.

152.3 **FX: DO**—body crumpling into Tsutsui's lap

152.4 **FX: KAKUN**—hand suddenly stopping movement

152.5 **FX: PITA**—flapping mouth suddenly going silent

153.1 **FX: SHIN**—sound of silence

154.1 **FX: KASHU**—sound of beer can opening

154.3 **FX: ZAZAAAAN**—crashing waves

155.3 **FX: ZAAAN ZAZAAAN**—sound of distant waves

158.2 **FX: ZU ZUU**—noodle-slurping noises

159.6.1 **FX: SUKU**—Karatsu standing up

159.6.2 **FX/balloons: KOKI KOKI**—cracking back

160.2 **FX: CHAPOON**—splash of a pebble hitting water

160.3 **FX: YURAI**—sound of a body floating in water

161.1 **FX: DOCHA**—wet thud

161.2 **FX: ZA**—sound of Karatsu kneeling in gravel

162.2 **FX: SU**—taking hands off body

165.1 **FX/balloon: KACHA**—hanging up phone

167.1 FX/balloons: HAA HAA HAA— panting

167.3 FX/balloons: PAKU PAKU— sound of flapping mouth. Somewhat suspiciously, perhaps, neither Yata nor the puppet are seen to be breathing hard in this panel. Recently, when the editor was getting a new car insurance policy, he got to the point in the interview with the agent where they ask for your profession. When he said, "editor," the agent noted cheerfully that this seemed to drop my premium considerably. It's a good thing I didn't mention the "manga" part.

168.1 FX: PARA PARA— flipping through book

168.1 The editor is himself a Virgo male with blood type O, so he will certainly take this under advisement.

169.2 FX: GURUN— sound of world spinning

169.3 FX: DO GA DOGA— sound of Yata falling down steps

170.1 119, rather than 911, is the emergency number for fire and ambulance in Japan, as well as Taiwan and South Korea (although unlike the U.S., Japan has a separate number for emergency calls to the police—namely, 110).

170.2 FX/balloon: PIPEPE PEEPU PIPAPAPA— cell ringing

170.3 FX/balloon: PIPA— answering phone

171.3 FX: PATA— sound of a book closing

172.5 FX: KACHA— opening car door

173.3 FX: GORORON GORORO— sky rumbling

173.5 FX: SU— raising arm

173.6 FX/balloon: JIII— zipper closing

173.7 FX: PARA— flipping though book

174.1 FX: KARI KARI KARI KYUD-WOOOON— air crackling then a loud lightning strike

174.2 FX: DOGOGOGOGOGO— loud rumbling sound

175.3 FX/balloon: PIPAAPI PIPA-PAPIPA PIIPIPA— cell ringing

175.4 FX: PII PA PII PA PI PIPOPA— cell continuing to ring

175.5 FX/balloon: PIPA— answering cell

176.5 FX/balloon: TSUU TSUU TSUU— disconnect tone

176.6 FX: BA BA— looking around quickly

176.7 FX/balloons: POTSU POTSU POTSU— raindrops

177.1 FX: ZAAAAA— pouring rain

178.1 FX: MOGU MOGU— eating sounds

179.3 FX/balloons: PIPI PIPI— an e-mail notice beep from cell

179.4 FX/balloon: PI— button press sound

180.2 FX/balloon: KACHI— putting cable into cell

180.3 FX: PA PA— file opening on computer

181.3 FX/balloon: KACHI— mouse click

183.1 FX: PEE PAPI PIPAPAPIPU PIPA— cell ringing

184.4 FX: TON—putting book down

184.5 FX: PARA PARA—flipping though pages

185.1.1 FX: PATAN—flipping page

185.1.2 FX: PATAN—page sections being flipped over

185.4 FX/balloon: KATA KATATA—clicking way on keyboard

187.1 FX: DOSA—dropping body bag

187.4 FX/balloon: PIPAPA PIPAPU-PAPA PIPAPI—cell ringing

189.3 FX: JIWA—water level rising

189.4 FX: GOGOGOGOGO—distant rumbling of rushing water

189.5 FX: GOGOGOGOGO—getting louder

190-191.1 FX: DWOOOOO—rushing wall of water

192.1 FX: GOBAAAAA—water rushing by

192.2 FX: GOGOGO—rushing water sound

192.4 FX: GOGOGOGOGO—rushing water

193.3 FX/balloon: PIKU—hand twitching

193.5 FX: GOGOGOGO—rushing water

194.1 FX: ZAZAAAN—rushing rlver water being kicked up

194.2 FX: BASHA BASHA BASHA—sound of splashing

194.3 FX: ZABABABA—sound of Karatsu pulling his body out of the water

195.2.1 FX: KWOOOO—sound of a plane flying overhead

195.2.2 FX/balloon: KIRA—glint of light in the air

195.3 FX: HIIIIII—sound of something falling

195.4 FX: HEEEEEEE—getting louder

196.1 FX: PAKIII—sound of a bolt falling through glasses at terminal velocity into eye socket

197.2 FX: ZABO—book falling into water

STOP!

THIS IS THE BACK OF THE BOOK!

This manga collection is translated into English, but arranged in right-to-left reading format to maintain the artwork's visual orientation as originally drawn and published in Japan. If you've never read comics this way before, take a look at the diagram below to give yourself an idea of how to go about it. Basically, you'll be starting in the upper right-hand corner, and will read each word balloon and panel moving right-to-left. It may take a little getting used to, but you should get the hang of it very quickly. Have fun! If this is the millionth manga you've read this way, never mind. ^_^

1
...
2
THEY TALK TO YOU BECAUSE YOU'RE THE KIND OF GUY WHO CAN'T SAY NO.
3
...YES.
4
RIGHT. SO LET'S TAKE THIS HORRIBLE, STINKING, ROTTING THING BACK TO CAMPUS. QUICK, BEFORE THE COPS NOTICE.
5
BACK TO CAMPUS?!
6
KARATSU, THERE'S NOTHING IN THE HANDBOOK THAT SAYS STUDENTS CAN'T POSSESS CORPSES--OR, IN YOUR CASE, VICE-VERSA.

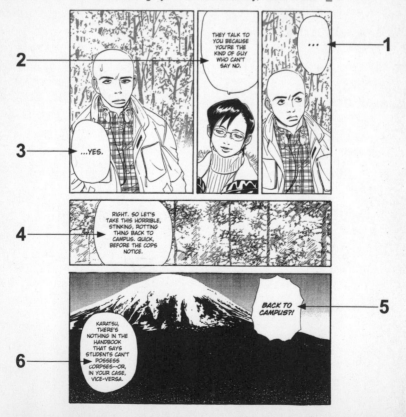